The Convergence of Theology

A Festschrift Honoring Gerald O'Collins, S.J.

GERALD O'COLLINS, S.J.
Priest, Professor, Author

The Convergence of Theology

A Festschrift Honoring Gerald O'Collins, S.J.

Edited by
Daniel Kendall, S.J., and Stephen T. Davis

Foreword by
The Most Reverend George Carey,
Archbishop of Canterbury

PAULIST PRESS
New York/Mahwah, N.J.

Unless otherwise noted, scripture citations are the author's own translation.

Book design by Theresa M. Sparacio

Cover design by Lynn Else

Library of Congress Cataloging-in-Publication Data

The convergence of theology : a festschrift honoring Gerald O'Collins, S.J. / edited by Daniel Kendall and Stephen T. Davis ; foreword by George Carey.
    p. cm.
Includes bibliographical references and index.
ISBN 0-8091-4015-2
    1. Theology, Doctrinal. 2. Catholic Church—Doctrines. I. O'Collins, Gerald.
II. Kendall, Daniel. III. Davis, Stephen T., 1940-

BX1751.2.C646 2001
230′2—dc21
                                       00-053740

Distributed in Australia by
Rainbow Book Agencies Pty.Ltd/
Word of Life Distributors
303 Arthur Street
Fairfield, VIC 3078

Published by Paulist Press
997 Macarthur Boulevard
Mahwah, New Jersey 07430

www.paulistpress.com

Printed and bound in the
United States of America

Contents

with appreciation of your support, Mike

v

Foreword

✠ *The Most Reverend George Carey,*
Archbishop of Canterbury

I feel very honoured to be asked to write the Foreword for this Festschrift, because Fr. Gerald O'Collins has become over the years a dear friend and colleague. We first met over twenty years ago when, as an Anglican priest in a parish in Durham, I was asked to represent the Church of England in an ecumenical gathering in Rome. Gerald was one of the guest speakers. To this day I can remember his lively and arresting lecturing style, the scholarship that underpinned it all, and his rocklike commitment to the Christian faith. That youthful enthusiasm combined with serious scholarship has made him the compelling teacher and theologian we know today.

He is, as Professor Stephen Davis comments, preeminently a theologian of the incarnation and the resurrection. His knowledge of the scriptures is deep and fertile, and his knowledge of academic studies no less than that. It is from these sources that he has produced some of the most penetrating and convincing writings of our day. We must be cautious, however, lest it be assumed that his commitment to incarnation and resurrection means that he limits himself to these great areas of research. Far from it. Indeed, we might say, the centrality of these doctrines leads him to weave them into the entire corpus of theology presented to the general public in over thirty books, to say nothing of his contributions to academic journals.

I still recall reading *Fundamental Theology* for the first time and the sense of excitement as this Catholic scholar spoke to me and for me. As someone who came to a living faith through the Anglican evangelical tradition I was taught to regard all Catholics with suspicion. This did not last long as I encountered catholic spirituality in its profound

1

devotion to our Lord. Vatican II, occurring as it did just at the time of my theological studies, revealed to me the future of ecumenism. The council's renewed commitment to the primacy of scripture in revelation, its rediscovery of the pilgrim church, to say nothing of the *aggiornamento* of the church (and by implication of all denominations), gave me hope for the future of all churches. In the ups and downs of ecumenism since then, Fr. Gerald O'Collins has been for thousands a sound guide to the treasures of scripture and a wise and patient interpreter of the Roman Catholic Church's appropriation of the teaching of the council. But, as one of the great theologians of the Anglican Church, Bishop Kenneth Cragg, once said: "To be hospitable, one must have a home," and Gerry's home is undoubtedly his own beloved church. From the security this gives he is able to reaffirm other Christians—noting the many points of contact and the remaining differences to be explored and to be resolved—through going deeper into the faith received from the fathers and saints of the church.

It gave me great joy to ask Fr. O'Collins to write the Archbishop of Canterbury's Lent book for the year 2000 "Following the Way." As the first Lent book in that series written by a non-Anglican, it is a profound study of discipleship that will be a blessing to many. I was thrilled to write this Foreword and to offer a personal tribute to a scholar, teacher, and fellow disciple. This collection of essays, from some of the best living theologians, is a fitting testimony to the esteem in which Fr. O'Collins is held. As we celebrate his seventieth birthday we hail this youthful septuagenarian and long for yet more writings to pour from his pen.

Preface

Daniel Kendall, S.J., and Stephen T. Davis

It has been a joy for us to put together this Festschrift in honor of our esteemed colleague and friend Gerald O'Collins, S.J. The book is called *The Convergence of Theology* in recognition of the fact that Gerry's contributions to the world of late-twentieth-century Christian theology have been deep, multifaceted, and interdisciplinary. He has written influential essays and books in New Testament studies, fundamental theology, spirituality, and theology proper, with his writings in theology covering such topics as revelation, the use of scripture, Christology, and the resurrection of Jesus. Although he has not (or has not yet) written a systematic theology, we believe that there is a thematic unity in Gerry's writings, one that is reflected in the present volume of essays in his honor.

Daniel Kendall, a fellow Jesuit, first met Gerry in Rome in 1971, where Dan was a student. At that time Gerry was visiting and giving lectures while attached to the Jesuit Theological College in Melbourne. Two years later, when Gerry joined the faculty at the Gregorian University, Dan became his first doctoral student. Since completing his degree in 1975, Dan and Gerry have jointly published several books and articles. The contributors to this Festschrift single out for citation two of those articles (e.g., "The Faith of Jesus," and "Mary Magdalene as Major Witness to Jesus' Resurrection"). During the last five years, Stephen Davis has joined Dan and Gerry in collaboration and research.

Stephen T. Davis first heard from Gerry via letter in 1994. Steve's book *Risen Indeed: Making Sense of the Resurrection* (Eerdmans, 1993) had just appeared, and Gerry read it, reviewed it favorably, and wrote Steve an appreciative letter. Steve wrote back, indicating how much Gerry's own writings about the resurrection of Jesus had been an inspiration and help to him. Then Gerry shared with Steve his long-nurtured hope of holding an ecumenical "Resurrection Summit" with notable scripture scholars, theologians, and philosophers, all or virtually all of whom held that the resurrection was a real event that happened to Jesus. After a great deal of planning and help from the Dr. Eugene and Maureen McCarthy Foundation, and their first face-to-face meeting (when in 1995 Steve arranged for Gerry to deliver a paper in Claremont), the summit was held at St. Joseph's Seminary in Dunwoodie, Yonkers, New York, in 1996. The result was *The Resurrection: An Interdisciplinary Symposium on the Resurrection of Jesus* (Oxford University Press, 1997), edited by Davis, Kendall, and O'Collins.

In 1998 a second symposium was held at the same location, this one on the Trinity. The result was: *The Trinity: An Interdisciplinary Symposium on the Trinity* (Oxford University Press, 1999), also edited by Davis, Kendall, and O'Collins. Finally, in 2000, an "Incarnation Summit" was held, also at St. Joseph's Seminary, and our hope is that a book will emerge from that conference too. This may or may not be the last of our summits, but Davis feels strongly that involvement with Gerry in planning and executing the three summits constitutes a highlight of his academic career.

Gerald O'Collins is a world-renowned theologian. He is classically trained. His linguistic abilities are excellent, in both ancient and modern languages. He has written over thirty-five books and over one hundred articles. He has trained generations of Catholic theologians at the Gregorian, and his worldwide influence among both Catholic and Protestant thinkers is impressive. Gerry is a careful scholar, a clear and engaging writer, and a sensible thinker whose arguments and conclusions are marked by balance, evenhandedness, and cogency. At home in the technical worlds of Greek grammar and dogmatic theology, Gerry is also always concerned with the evangelistic, spiritual, and pastoral implications of what he writes.

But those accomplishments alone do not account for the outpouring of enthusiasm that followed our approaching various scholars about participating in this Festschrift. As we all know, Gerry is also an open-minded, energetic, witty, and congenial person whom it is a joy to know. He is instantly at home in almost any social setting—whether in the classroom or at a party—and he puts people at ease. As a teacher he is popular with his students. The various colleges in Rome take turns inviting him over to break bread together and to discuss various theological topics. Of course Gerry's doctoral and licentiate seminar students look forward to similar evenings when they meet, present and critique each other's research topics, and then adjourn to a Roman restaurant as a group. Gerry is deeply and genuinely concerned about the welfare of the people he knows. He is a loyal, true, and helpful friend. He is a man of the scriptures and of prayer. He is a Christian and a priest through and through.

So in placing this Festschrift before the public, we are honoring not only a great scholar but an extraordinary human being.

The Convergence of Theology is divided into four sections, and these parts correspond to various theological topics Gerry has addressed in his many writings. Part I, "New Testament Studies," indicates how Gerry, while primarily a theologian, has, throughout his career, kept his hand in the world of scripture studies. We sadly note that his untimely death prevented Father Raymond E. Brown from contributing to this section of the Festschrift for his friend Gerry. But two New Testament scholars have contributed fine articles.

In "Peter as Resurrection Witness in the Lucan Narrative," Brendan Byrne, S.J., argues against the tradition that Mary Magdalene and/or certain other women were the first resurrection witnesses. According to Luke—so Byrne claims—the apostle Peter was in fact first. Byrne argues that the striking similarities between Luke 5:1–11 and John 21:1–19 show that the former text is or draws upon a misplaced resurrection appearance story; that is, the unnarrated but reported (Luke 24:34) resurrection appearance to Peter is behind or is embedded in Luke's story of Peter's call. Byrne answers possible objections to this thesis and suggests reasons why Luke would place an appearance story so early in his Gospel.

James D. G. Dunn, amplifying previous work of his own, explores in "Jesus the Judge" the usually neglected Pauline notion of Jesus as eschatological judge. He discusses the Old Testament and intertestamental concepts that formed the background of Paul's notion, as well as Paul's own forensic, courtroom-like picture of justification. He then interestingly develops the christological and soteriological implications of the idea of Jesus as judge, especially in relation to Paul's two-stage ("already"/"not yet") scheme of salvation.

Part II of this volume is entitled "Vatican I, Vatican II, and Catholic Theology." It deals primarily with theological issues internal to the Roman Catholic tradition. In "Why We Still Need Theologians," Father Mike Heher offers a fascinating glimpse of the global village as it finds expression in a certain large, multicultural parish in Cypress, California. Written by a working pastor who studied at the North American College in Rome and had Gerry as a teacher, the essay answers the question implicitly asked by its title in terms of the pastoral and practical concerns of an in-the-trenches parish priest.

In his essay, Francis A. Sullivan, S.J., explores the question of what conciliar statements mean. He argues against the idea that there is some core, pristine "original meaning" of every dogmatic statement; he points out instead that there will always be ambiguity and plurality of meaning, even among the bishops who were present and voting at the council in question. The main illustration that Sullivan uses in "The Meaning of Conciliar Dogmas" is the pronouncement of papal infallibility at Vatican I. Sullivan emphasizes the role of John Henry Newman, who was not present at the council but whose "moderate" interpretation of the dogma has gained the status of consensus among Catholic theologians and was confirmed at Vatican II.

Carmen Aparicio's paper focuses on the important changes that occurred between Vatican I and Vatican II in the discipline Catholics call fundamental theology. In "Bishop Paul-Joseph Schmitt and Vatican II: Jesus Christ, the Fullness of Revelation," Aparicio is primarily interested in Vatican II's famous *Dei Verbum*. She traces the role that the progressive council member Bishop Schmitt played in the development of the document. Schmitt's basic emphasis on the centrality of Christ won the day and dominates Catholic theology today.

Jared Wicks, S.J., is also interested in *Dei Verbum*; he offers a fascinating internal history of the development of its final version. His hero is the Dutch Jesuit Father Pieter Smulders. In "*Dei Verbum* Developing: Vatican II's Revelation Doctrine 1963–1964," Wicks shows how and why the traditionalist original version was changed— in part due to Smulders's work—to become the groundbreaking and forward-looking document that we know, one whose christological emphasis has proved highly influential.

Karl H. Neufeld, S.J., in "Globalization: Discovery of Catholicity" reflects on the relationship of scripture to fundamental theology since Vatican II. Because of *Dei Verbum,* fundamental theology of necessity now looks at its tasks differently. Events such as the collapse of Communism, the recognition of the horrors and implications of the Holocaust, the rise of new nations with their unique cultures, and the worldwide process of globalization have all contributed to the need to discover diverse ways of presenting and responding to the gospel. All these approaches, however, have one and the same "access"—Jesus Christ, who is "the way, the truth, and the life."

The third section of *The Convergence of Theology* is called "Fundamental Theology and Spirituality." This reflects Gerry's many writings in these areas. Nicholas King, S.J., in "Society, Academy, and Church: Who Can Read the Bible?" notes that people from both the academy and the church read the Bible, and each group has its own agenda and assumptions. This is fine, except that various ways of reading the Bible are often confused. The academy does have some rights over the Bible and its interpretation. Still, King argues, the Bible is primarily the church's gift to itself, and it has proprietary rights over that gift. The church is the privileged site for reading the Bible. In the end, academy and church can enrich each other in their uses of the Bible.

In "'Knowing' Jesus: Do Theologians Have a Special Way?" William Reiser, S.J., examines the way academics study religion. Reiser believes that professional theologians must speak as committed members of particular faith communities if they are to speak meaningfully to the church. This involves the spiritual development of the individual theologian, as well as learning, which is a "self-transcending process." To know Jesus is ultimately to experience God's salvation. To be Jesus' disciple always involves risks. The context for knowing Jesus always involves the community (Jesus' people). Reiser balances historical knowledge about Jesus (the academic approach) with the need for other factors such as salvation and grace.

In "Spiritual Direction in Dialogue with Fundamental Theology," Dominic Maruca, S.J., explores the relationship between (1) Gerald O'Collins's theological work and the new way that fundamental theology is practiced in Roman Catholic circles (in part because of O'Collins's writings) and (2) the discipline of spiritual direction. This discipline has also changed radically in the past forty years, and Maruca's essay is doubly interesting because its author has trained hundreds of spiritual directors practicing throughout the world.

Donna Orsuto contributes a fascinating essay for the Festschrift, in which she explicitly compares the writings of Gerald O'Collins with those of Catherine of Siena. In "Docility to the Holy Spirit and the Call to Follow Jesus: Catherine of Siena 'In Dialogue' with Gerald O'Collins," she compares their views on the activity of the Holy Spirit in bringing about the inner transformation that enables one to follow Jesus. She argues convincingly that the writings of Catherine complement Gerry's writings at this point.

In "The Church as Easter Witness in the Thought of Gerald O'Collins, S.J.," William Henn, O.F.M. Cap., is interested in the location in theology of the doctrine of the church. At one time among Catholics it was discussed primarily in fundamental theology, and in a way that was oriented toward apologetics. While Gerry rarely explicitly discusses the church in his writings, Henn points out that he does clearly emphasize the place of the passion and resurrection of Jesus in the foundation of the church. The church is thus part of systematic theology proper rather than part of the preamble to faith. The church, Henn says, is God's universal sacrament of salvation and has a trinitarian framework. As O'Collins has argued, Easter is the center around which all else in theology, including ecclesiology, revolves.

John Fuellenbach, S.V.D, also writes about the church. In "The Church in the Context of the Kingdom of God," he tries to back away from any triumphalist and ecclesiocentric identification of the church with the kingdom of God. He argues against that identification and shows the value of refusing to identify them, especially in relation to Vatican II and subsequent church documents. In them, clear distinctions are made between the kingdom present in history now and its future eschatological fullness. Moreover—so Fuellenbach argues—the kingdom of God works at certain times and places quite outside the church, even in the context of other religious traditions.

Michael Paul Gallagher, S.J., in "Roads to God: An Australian Exploration in Fiction," discusses the work of Australian novelist Patrick White. Gallagher sees deep theological significance in the Nobel Prize winner's seven novels, especially in terms of the sense of mystery latent (and often neglected) in the unusual and the ugly, and even in the evil and suffering experienced by ordinary folk. White testifies to the difficulty of faith, but also to the possibility (albeit fragmentary and momentary) of experience of God. According to

Gallagher, White exposes the shallowness and superficiality of modern secularism and rationalism. Life can include religious mystery; grace can be mediated, even through flawed people; redemption is possible.

In "'What Can Be Known About God Is Plain to Them': A Meditation on Religious Unbelief," Stephen T. Davis wonders why so many people do not believe the Christian message, especially in the light of Paul's claim (quoted in the title of Davis's essay) in Romans 1:19. Davis argues that the problem is primarily spiritual rather than intellectual; it has to do with what the Bible calls "hardening of the heart." People come to see God in their lives through what the Reformed theological tradition calls "the inward testimony of the Holy Spirit." Natural theology can play a role, however, in providing warrant to Christian belief.

Part IV of our book is called "Resurrection and Christology." These are doubtless the two topics for which Gerald O'Collins is best known, especially in non-Catholic theological circles. The initial essay in this section is by Avery Dulles, S.J. In "Jesus and Faith," Dulles joins forces with O'Collins and Kendall (and against much of the theological tradition) in arguing that the earthly Jesus had faith. Dulles detects the danger of a kind of psychological monophysitism in the traditional view that Jesus, the Son of God, did not need or have faith because he knew. Dulles also sees the danger of a kind of psychological nestorianism in the views of Hans Urs von Balthasar (as if the divine personal subject had no influence on the functioning of his human faculties). The earthly Jesus learned, trusted in, and obeyed the Father, and knew some things by faith (in analogous ways to the way we know things by faith). Still, he was not a Christian believer; he was and is our object of faith.

Janet Martin Soskice, in "Blood and Defilement: Reflections on Jesus and the Symbolics of Sex," raises a frequently asked theological question: How should Christology be affected by the "women's issue"? But her insights are new and helpful. She discusses 1 Cor 11:7–10, as well as reasons given in Christian history why Christ could not have been born a woman. But Soskice is dissatisfied with the typical retelling of Christ's story by feminists. She raises the biblical symbols of blood and defilement, arguing that new symbolic meaning can be found in them that is useful to those who take more traditional approaches to Christology and who are attuned to the needs and concerns of women.

Sensitively discussing various biblical themes and texts, she concludes that both men and women can signify Christ.

In "John Hick and the Historical Jesus," Paul Eddy complements Gerald O'Collins's own engagement with Hick's work from a historic orthodox perspective. Eddy does this by tracing Hick's christological pilgrimage from the early 1940s. At that time Hick underwent a profound conversion to evangelical Christianity. By 1959, Hick had moved to using *agapē* as a way of stating the dogma of the incarnation of Jesus Christ. The 1960s found Hick raising the question of the uniqueness of Jesus. By the 1970s Hick argued that Jesus probably did not teach that he was God incarnate. During the 1980s Hick described the incarnation as "myth." N. T. Wright, on the other hand, offers an interpretation of the historical data that directly challenges Hick's assessment of the relationships among the historical Jesus, the early church, and traditional Christology. Eddy analyzes Wright's arguments and compares them to Hick's.

Jacques Dupuis, S.J., in his "Universality of the Word and Particularity of Jesus Christ," wants to retain the constitutive value of Jesus Christ for the salvation of humankind and yet recognize the salvific significance of other religious paths. His stimulating paper argues for the universal operative presence of the Word of God in the world. He does not want to separate the Word and Jesus; he wants interrelatedness and complementarity between the two. His is a trinitarian model of Christology.

John O'Donnell, S.J., discusses Gerry's christological work in "The Person of Christ." O'Donnell wants to affirm that Jesus is a person, indeed a divine person, but to deny that Jesus is a human person. That is, there is no human subject of identity in Jesus Christ. O'Donnell strives to answer possible objections to this view, especially the criticism that it denies Jesus' full humanity. Jesus' personhood was essentially that of self-giving and did not necessarily involve self-consciousness. O'Donnell interestingly discusses how Jesus came to know his eternal personhood. Jesus, he says, is the eternal Person of the Son.

Finally, Paul Gwynne, O.M.I., in "Why Some Still Doubt That Jesus' Body Was Raised," touches on an issue that has been debated for centuries. Those who deny the empty tomb today usually begin with the claim that accounts of it in the Gospels are legendary. While

Gwynne believes the weight of evidence lies in favor of a historical empty tomb, he admits the considerable difference of opinion in the academic community on the matter. Ultimately each author examines this subject with deep philosophical and theological presuppositions. Gwynne concludes that these ultimately determine the author's own stance on the matter, rather than an impartial reading of the historical-exegetical arguments.

We place this book before the scholarly world with great enthusiasm. Not only are we pleased to honor our mutual friend Gerald O'Collins; we are convinced that *The Convergence of Theology* itself constitutes a significant contribution to the discipline of theology. We hope readers enjoy and learn from working through these important essays as much as we have.

Abbreviations

AAS	*Acta Apostolicae Sedis*
AB	Anchor Bible Series
ABD	*Anchor Bible Dictionary,* edited by David Noel Freedman (New York: Doubleday, 1992)
AD	*Acta et Documenta Concilio Oecumenico Vaticano II apparando*
AG	*Ad Gentes* (Decree on the Church's Missionary Activity)
AOT	*The Apocryphal Old Testament,* edited by H. F. D. Sparks (Oxford: Clarendon, 1984)
AS	*Acta Synodalia Sacrosancti Concilii Oecumenici Vaticani II*
BAGD	W. Bauer, W. F. Arndt, F. W. Gingrich, and F. W. Danker, *Greek-English Lexicon of the New Testament.* 2nd edition (Chicago: University of Chicago Press, 1979)
BWANT	Beiträge zur Wissenschaft vom Alten und Neuen Testament
C.E.	Common Era
CG	General Congregation (Session)
DRC	Dutch Reformed Church
DS	H. Denzinger and A. Schönmetzer, *Enchiridion Symbolorum,* 35th edition (Barcelona: Herder, 1973)

DV	*Dei Verbum* (Dogmatic Constitution on Revelation)
ÉGM	*Église de Metz*
ES	*Eye of the Storm,* by Patrick White (Harmondsworth: Penguin, 1973)
FL	*A Fringe of Leaves,* by Patrick White (Harmondsworth: Penguin, 1977)
GS	*Gaudium et Spes* (Constitution on the Church in the Modern World)
IDBS	*Interpreter's Dictionary of the Bible Supplementary Volume,* edited by K. Crim (Nashville: Abingdon, 1976)
JSOT	*Journal for the Study of the Old Testament*
JTS	*Journal of Theological Studies*
JVG	*Jesus and the Victory of God,* by N. T. Wright (Minneapolis: Fortress, 1996)
LG	*Lumen Gentium* (Dogmatic Constitution on the Church)
LXX	Septuagint
NRT	*La nouvelle revue théologique*
NT	New Testament
NTPG	N. T. Wright, *The New Testament and the People of God* (Minneapolis: Fortress, 1982)
NTS	*New Testament Studies*
OT	Old Testament
OTP	R. H. Charles (ed.), *The Old Testament Pseudepigrapha* (London: Darton, Longman & Todd, 1983)
PG	*Patrologia Graeca* (J.-P. Migne)

RC   *Riders in the Chariot,* by Patrick White
(Harmondsworth: Penguin, 1964)

RSR   *Recherches de science religieuse*

SC   *Sacrosanctum Concilium* (Constitution on the Sacred
Liturgy)

SM   *The Solid Mandela,* by Patrick White (Harmondsworth:
Penguin, 1969)

ST   *Summa Theologica*

TDNT   *Theological Dictionary of the New Testament,* edited
by G. Kittel and G. Friedrich, translated by G. W.
Bromiley, 10 vols. (Grand Rapids: Eerdmans, 1964–76)

TM   *Tree of Man,* by Patrick White (Harmondsworth:
Penguin, 1961)

TV   *The Vivisector,* by Patrick White (Harmondsworth:
Penguin, 1973)

UR   *Unitatis Redintegratio* (Decree on Ecumenism)

V   *Voss,* by Patrick White (Harmondsworth: Penguin,
1960)

WATSA   *What Are They Saying About . . .*

WUNT   Wissenschaftliche Untersuchungen zum Neuen
Testament

ZNW   *Zeitschrift für die neutestamentliche Wissenschaft*

I

New Testament Studies

1. Peter as Resurrection Witness in the Lucan Narrative

Brendan Byrne, S.J.

Over four decades Gerald O'Collins has played the leading role in mediating to the English-speaking world the renewal of interest in the resurrection, which became a feature of Christian theology after World War II. In a steady flow of books, articles, and lectures he has moved across the interface between theology and exegesis, paying particular attention to the origins of belief in the resurrection as recorded in the New Testament. Twenty years ago he sought to remind theologians of the strength and significance of the tradition of Peter as resurrection witness.[1] Later, in association with Daniel Kendall, he complemented this with a study drawing attention to the prominence of Mary Magdalene in the resurrection traditions reflected in the Gospels.[2]

Taken together, these two studies highlight the complexity of searching for the origins of Christian faith in the resurrection. In this tribute to one who has been in so many ways mentor, guide, and friend, I should like to pursue the quest a little further, paying particular attention to the Gospel of Luke. In this Gospel, I shall argue the tradition of Peter as prime resurrection witness finds its best, if obscure, reflection, and there I propose to seek it out. At the end, in this same connection, I shall offer some reflections on the tradition with respect to Mary Magdalene.

The New Testament associates two kinds of phenomena with the origins of belief that Jesus had been raised: the discovery of the empty tomb and appearances to select individuals and groups.[3] Following Joseph Fitzmyer, we can nominate six separate narratives in the gospel tradition describing these phenomena: Mark 16:1–8; Matt 23:1–20;

19

Luke 23:56b—24:53; John 20:1–29; 21:1–23 (the appendix to the Fourth Gospel); Mark 16:9–20 (the appendix to Mark).[4] Paul, however, provides the earliest account—in a creedal fragment prefacing a list of witnesses to the resurrection in 1 Cor 15:1–8:

> (3) "...that Christ died for our sins according to the scriptures,
> (4) and (that he) was buried and (that he) was raised on the
> third day according to the scriptures, (5) and (that he) appeared
> to Cephas, then to the Twelve,
> (6) then he appeared to more than five hundred of the brothers
> (and sisters) at once,
> ..., (7) then he appeared to James, then to all the apostles; (8)
> last of all, ..., he appeared to me...."

It is not clear in this statement where the actual creedal fragment ends and the supplementary list of witnesses provided by Paul himself takes over. Clearly, however, this traditional statement, which may well go back to within a decade or so of Jesus' death,[5] designates Peter (under his "rock" nickname "Cephas") as prime witness to the resurrection. "In this gospel," Paul reminds the Corinthians by way of introduction, "you stand firm and through it you are on the way to salvation" (vv. 1–2). The implication is that Christian faith is "firm" (cf. 15:58a) and salvific insofar as it rests upon Peter's "rocklike" witness.

The great puzzle, however, is to explain why the Pauline account and the various narratives contained in the Gospels pass like ships in the night, with so few points of contact. The one item on which all four Gospels agree and with which they all begin is that on the first day of the week women disciples found the tomb of Jesus empty; Mary Magdalene features in all four accounts and also in the summary contained in the Marcan appendix (16:9–11). Paul makes no mention of the empty tomb (though this motif may be implicit in the indication that Jesus was buried prior to being raised), nor does he accord any role specifically to women (though women witnesses are surely included among the "more than five hundred" to whom Jesus appeared at one time [1 Cor 15:6]). Most curious of all, granted the strength of the Pauline tradition in the matter, is the failure of the gospel tradition to provide a narrative of the primary appearance to Peter.[6] All we have is a promise in Mark (16:7) and a report in Luke (32:34), along with a narrative in the appendix to the Fourth Gospel that seems very much overlaid by other traditions (John 21:1–19).

PETER AS WITNESS TO THE RESURRECTION IN THE GOSPEL TRADITION

Let us review for a moment this scanty reference to Peter in the resurrection narratives of the Gospels. Setting aside the appendix (16:9–20), the Gospel of Mark contains no record of an appearance of the risen Jesus to anyone. But the young man in the white robe whom the women see at the empty tomb, after announcing that Jesus has been raised, instructs them to go and "tell the disciples and Peter, 'He is going ahead of you to Galilee; there you will see him'" (v. 7). We have then a promise of an appearance to Peter (and the others) in Galilee, a promise the eventual realization of which the Gospel surely presupposes (see 8:31; 9:31; 10:34; 14:28)—even if no such appearance occurs in its original version (1:1—16:8).

The Gospel of Matthew, despite the prominence it otherwise accords to Peter, is in its Easter narrative the most reticent of all in his regard. The instruction to the women ("Mary Magdalene and the other Mary") at the tomb concerning the disciples' going to Galilee (28:7) omits the specific mention of Peter that is found in Mark. As the women go off on their errand, the risen Jesus does suddenly appear. Calming their fear, he repeats the instruction to tell the "brothers" to go to Galilee, where they will see him (vv. 9–10). This promise finds fulfillment when Jesus appears to "the eleven disciples" on a mountain in Galilee and commissions them to go and make disciples of all nations (28:16–20). Peter is certainly included among the eleven but is in no way singled out. The abiding impression Matthew conveys is that the women, led by Mary Magdalene, are the prime witnesses and the bearers of instructions for the group of male disciples, who only subsequently—and not without hesitation on the part of some (v. 17)— see and recognize the risen Jesus.

The original ending of the Fourth Gospel (20:1–31) shows a similar pattern with respect to Peter. Mary of Magdala discovers the empty tomb (note, however, the plural "we" at the end of v. 2) and comes to tell Peter and the "other disciple" (v. 2). Peter, along with this disciple, runs to the tomb, enters it, sees the arrangement of the grave clothes but, unlike the other disciple, does not, it would appear, come to faith in the resurrection at this point. Subsequently, Jesus appears to Mary (vv. 11–18) and commissions her to bear the good news of his resurrection to his "brothers." Only in the evening of that same day does Jesus appear to them (without Thomas, vv. 19–23). But neither on the occasion of this appearance nor on its repetition eight days later (with Thomas, vv. 24–29) is Peter singled out in any way. The omission is not surprising granted the pattern in the closing chapters of this Gospel whereby Peter is constantly upstaged by the "disciple whom Jesus loved," the hero figure of the Johannine community.[7]

All has changed in this regard in the appendix to the Fourth Gospel (21:1–25). One function of the appendix seems to be that of bringing the Johannine community to acceptance of the primary pastoral role of Peter. It describes an appearance of the risen Lord to Peter and six other male disciples by the Sea of Tiberias in Galilee. At the urging of Peter, the disciples have gone back to fishing. After a night of fruitless labor, they follow the suggestion of a stranger on the shore to let down their nets for a catch. On doing so, they net a vast catch of fish, too large to haul into the boat. This leads "the disciple whom Jesus loved" to recognize the stranger on the shore as Jesus. Peter, on being told, impetuously leaps into the water to swim ashore. After a communal meal of bread and fish, Jesus submits Peter to a searching triple interrogation concerning his love, each time following Peter's response with a commission to take on his own pastoral role. Here, in some sense, we can recognize the appearance of the Lord to Peter in Galilee promised in Mark 16:7. But Peter's recognition of the Lord is mediated by the disciple whom Jesus loved. Influences of a tradition recording the appearance of Jesus to the disciples at a meal (Luke 24:36–43; cf. Acts 1:4) also seem to be present. A singular appearance to Peter such as 1 Cor 15:5 seems to imply is, then, enmeshed in a complex web of traditions.

The Gospel of Luke may seem to provide the exception to all this reticence, but even Luke tiptoes around the tradition of a personal appearance to Peter, failing to provide a full-blooded narrative. First of all, in line with his general tendency to play down failure on the part of the disciples, notably Peter, Luke prefaces Jesus' foretelling of Peter's denial at the Last Supper, with the encouraging words, "Simon, Simon, listen! Satan has demanded to sift all of you like wheat, but I have prayed for you [singular] that your own faith may not fail; and you, when once you have turned back, strengthen your brothers" (22:31–32). This vision of a future "strengthening" role for Peter's faith takes much of the sting out of his triple denial of Jesus (22:54–62). Subsequently, on the first day of the week, following the report of Mary Magdalene and the other women concerning the empty tomb and vision of angels, Peter, as in the Johannine narrative (20:4–10), goes to the empty tomb (Luke 24:12).[8] He does not see the risen Lord—only the abandoned grave clothes (cf. John 20:6–7)—and goes home "amazed at what had happened." This is not a statement of Easter faith.[9] Later, however, when the two disciples who have encountered the risen Jesus on the way to Emmaus (24:13–32) return to Jerusalem to report their good news, they are told by the eleven and their companions gathered together, "The Lord has risen indeed, and he has appeared to Simon" (v. 34). Luke then goes on to record an appearance of the Lord to this same group, a meeting that culminates with his ascension into heaven (24:36–53).

Luke's Gospel, then, is quite explicit about an appearance of the risen Lord to Peter, just as it has earlier indicated that Peter's faith will exercise a "strengthening" role in the community. The actual report in 24:34 indeed echoes the creedal fragment preserved in 1 Cor 15:5. But many questions remain. Why, first of all, a bare, retrospective report on the appearance? Why no narrative? If no narrative came to him in the tradition, Luke was surely capable of fleshing one out—as would seem to have been the case with respect to his masterpiece, the account of what took place on the road to Emmaus. Why no narrative, especially, in view of the notice about Peter's visit to tomb, which left him "amazed" (v. 12)? There is something unfinished and tantalizing about this detail. In narrative terms it would seem to require some form of closure beyond the bare report of an appearance given in v. 34. There is further narrative unevenness in that while it is "Peter" who goes to the tomb (v. 12), it is "Simon" to whom the Lord has appeared (v. 34).[10]

We can further ask why, granted the communal report about the appearance (in a kind of "Yes, we know all about it" sense), there is so much terror and hesitation when the Lord appears in their midst (vv. 37–38, 41). The witness of Peter, who must be numbered among the "eleven" (v. 33), has hardly had its "strengthening" effect. Clearly the narrative presupposes that at some time between his return from the empty tomb without having seen Jesus (cf. v. 24) and his presence with the rest later in evening, Simon/Peter had had an encounter with the risen Jesus. But Luke's record of this Petrine tradition, while definite, is clumsily and awkwardly inserted into the overall narrative, which in other respects (Emmaus) displays narrative ability at its peak. What is Luke up to in this regard?

JESUS, SIMON, AND AN ABUNDANT CATCH OF FISH
(LUKE 5:1–11 AND JOHN 21:1–19)

Many scholars have found elements of the "lost" appearance to Peter in Luke's account of the call of Simon early in the Gospel: 5:1–11.[11] Close inspection of the text reveals that Luke has drawn upon several traditions to build up the narrative. The overall setting—Jesus' teaching a large number of people from a boat just offshore—comes from Mark's setting for the parable discourse: Mark 4:1 (par. Matt 13:1–2). But in Luke's account it gradually becomes clear (v. 4: "let down your [plural] nets"; v. 5: "we have worked all night"; v. 6: "when they had done this, they…," etc.) that other fishermen besides Peter are involved; the call of Simon is also the call of James and John, sons of Zebedee (v. 10). This, together with the final statement (v. 11) about their leaving everything to follow him indicates that Mark's account of the call of the first four disciples (Mark 1:16–20 [par. Matt 4:18–22]) has also contributed to the Lucan narrative.

The Lucan account of the call outstrips the Marcan model in the sustained interaction between Jesus and Simon. The central point of this is the abundant catch of fish (vv. 6–7), followed by Simon's humble avowal of his unworthiness to be associated with Jesus ("Go away from me, Lord, for I am a sinful man!" [v. 8]) and Jesus' reassuring response to the effect that henceforth Simon would be catching people—not fish—alive (v. 10).

The striking similarities between this major element of the episode and the account in the Johannine appendix of the post-Easter appearance of Jesus in Galilee have long been noted:[12] the disciples have fished all night and caught nothing (Luke 5:5; John 21:3); at Jesus' command, they put out their nets and an extraordinarily plentiful catch ensues (Luke 5:6; John 21:6); Peter makes a strong response to the catch (Luke 5:8; John 21:7b); Jesus is called "Lord" (Luke 5:8 [previously, v. 4, "Master"]; John 21:7, 15, 16, 17); the remaining fishermen assist with the catch but are otherwise silent (Luke 5:7; John 21:8); the catch seems symbolic of a successful Christian mission (Luke 5:10b; cf. John 21:15–17 ["Feed my sheep,..."]); the theme of "following" (Jesus) is present (Luke 5:11; John 21:19, 22). Significantly, both accounts refer to Peter by the double name "Simon Peter" (Luke 5:8; John 21:2, 3, 7, 11, 15); indeed, this is the only time this double address occurs in Luke.

Furthermore, both episodes feature a call or commissioning of Peter in the face of a deep sense of unworthiness or sinfulness on his part. Jesus' triple interrogation of Peter about his love, at the end of which Peter is said to be deeply hurt (John 21:15–17), plausibly addresses and overcomes any lingering guilt or alienation created by his triple question. In Luke, following the amazing catch, Peter falls at Jesus' knees and exclaims, "Go away, Lord, for I am a sinful man" (5:8). This could simply reflect the reaction of a human being suddenly conscious of divine presence and power (cf. Isa 6:6).[13] On the other hand, it is somewhat odd, as up to this point the Lucan narrative has not indicated that Simon's life has been sinful in any notable way. The only thing we know about him is that Jesus has cured his mother-in-law of a fever (4:38–39).

It has not escaped scholarly notice that Peter's intense reaction makes a great deal of sense in a postresurrection setting.[14] Peter's denial of his master is a discrediting fact indelibly imprinted on the total passion tradition (Synoptics and John). Understandably a tradition describing an appearance of the risen Jesus to Peter would include some reference to this failure on the part of the leading male disciple—as seems in fact to be the case in the Johannine appendix. This, together with all the other features of similarity with that postresurrection scene (above all the wonderful catch), suggests that this central core of Luke's description of Peter's call draws upon a tradition of an appearance of the risen Lord to Peter in Galilee, a tradition also reflected (and more accurately located) in the Johannine appendix. Features common to both further suggest that the appearance occurred in a boat during a fishing episode and involved not only Peter's recognition of Jesus ("Lord!") but also, after the acknowledgment of his failure ("conversion"; cf. Luke 22:32), his rehabilitation and commissioning for the missionary (in John for the "pastoral") task.[15]

Two challenges to this hypothesis can be addressed briefly. The first suggests that behind the Gospel reports lie memories of two separate occasions upon which Jesus brought about an inexplicable abundance of fish (one during his ministry, one after the resurrection). This possibility, still maintained by a some conservative commentators,[16] is highly unlikely in view of the remarkable similarities between the two narratives.[17] More weighty is the view holding that the Lucan tradition rather than the Johannine has preserved the more original setting; that is, a tradition telling of a wonderful catch of fish during Jesus' historical ministry in Galilee has been relocated to the postresurrection era in the source tapped by the Johannine redactor.[18] Though some formidable names have held this view, the general nature of the Gospels makes the reverse movement much more likely: namely, that postresurrection features have left their imprint on the description of Jesus' earlier life, rather than vice versa.[19]

If this is correct, it seems reasonable to believe that embedded in the Lucan account of Peter's call (overblown in comparison with that in Mark/Matthew) is the basic kernel of the "lost" narrative of Jesus' postresurrection appearance to him, the episode to which Luke makes such tantalizing allusions in his account of the resurrection but which he never fully describes. Why Luke has preferred to retroject the narrative back in this way is something I shall take up shortly. Let us note, however, that by comparing this kernel with the account in John 21 we can construct with some plausibility the shape of a more original tradition that would fulfill the promise of Mark 16:7 (Peter and the other disciples would see Jesus in Galilee) and that would also correspond in some measure to the Pauline indication of Peter as prime resurrection witness. But first some remarks about the Johannine tradition.

In his discussion of the Johannine appendix, Raymond Brown has pointed out unevennesses in the narrative. The fish caught in such marvelous abundance play no part in the meal of bread and fish that Jesus provides for the disciples; he feeds them, it would appear, from the supply of bread and fish he has independently of the catch. Very plausibly Brown sees here a reflection of an appearance in Galilee to the Twelve at a meal of bread and fish.[20] It picks up the promise in Mark (16:7) that the other disciples, as well as Peter, would see Jesus in Galilee (cf. also Mark [appendix] 16:14). In Matthew it has retained its Galilean location but has undergone translation—typical for

Matthew—away from the lakeshore onto a high mountain, with all suggestion of a meal removed (Matt 28:16–20). Luke has preserved the meal context (bread and fish) but—again typically—relocated the appearance in Jerusalem. As Brown concedes, this is all very speculative. In the absence of more definite evidence, however, it is difficult to find a more plausible reconstruction than that which he suggests: that John 21 combines and to some extent intertwines traditional accounts of appearances of the risen Lord in Galilee, first to Peter while fishing, then to the Twelve at a meal. The two traditions correspond to the sequence ". . . and that he appeared to Cephas, then to the Twelve, . . ." of the Pauline creedal fragment (1 Cor 15:5).[21]

LUKE'S PROCEDURE AND AIMS

If this reconstruction is correct, then Luke or the tradition upon which he drew preserves the kernel of the prime resurrection appearance to Peter (Cephas) in the account of Peter's call (5:1–11). Granted that, of all the evangelists, Luke is the one most concerned to record the tradition of Peter as resurrection witness (esp. 24:34), what has led him to retroject the narrative back to an early part of the Gospel? The most obvious answer, of course, is that Luke's "geographical" schema required that all saving events occur in Jerusalem or its immediate vicinity (Emmaus). Since the beginning of Jesus' journey to Jerusalem (9:51), culminating in his entry into the city (19:28–44), the action of salvation has moved on from Galilee, never to return; Jerusalem will be the center from which the witness will fan out to "the ends of the earth" (Acts 1:8b).[22] There is no place, then, for an appearance to Peter located in Galilee.

But why, we might ask, could not Luke have shorn such a narrative of its Galilean location and placed it in a Jerusalem setting? This is precisely what he—or the tradition behind him—appears to have done with the second appearance, that to "the Twelve (Eleven)" at a meal involving bread and fish: Luke 24:36–43 (cf. 1 Cor 15:5 ["... and then to the Twelve"]; John 21:9–14). That he did not do so but chose to remain content with the bare report (24:34) was presumably due to the fact that the narrative of the appearance was so intricately tied to fishing and the lake as to be untranslatable to the urban context of Jerusalem; it had to retain a Galilean location. The only thing to do, then, was to find a suitable place for it in Jesus' Galilean ministry, and Luke's choice fell upon the moment of Peter's call.[23] At the same time the evangelist carefully preserved the tradition of Peter as prime resurrection witness in the appropriate place—the resurrection narrative— through the report in 24:34, itself foreshadowed by the assurance at the supper (22:32) and the visit of Peter to the tomb (24:12).[24]

Omitting the narrative of an appearance to Peter may also have had advantages for Luke. For one thing, it allowed him to give central place to the Emmaus story, with its sustained catechesis of the scriptural foretelling of the sufferings of the Messiah (vv. 25–27). To grasp the connection between the events that had occurred (Jesus' sufferings at the hands of the authorities) and the scriptural words about the Christ is, in Luke's analysis, an essential element of resurrection faith. The angels at the tomb urge the women to remember Jesus' own prophetic words to this effect (vv. 6–7) and Jesus repeats the entire catechesis when he appears later to the disciples (vv. 44–48). It thus features in some way in each of the three major elements of the Lucan story of the resurrection. To have included catechesis of this kind in a narrative recounting an appearance to Peter in a boat may have presented difficulties for Luke, difficulties that he managed to avoid by relocating the episode to the earlier Galilean ministry and making do with the simple report of 24:34.

We must also reckon with Luke's clear aim to portray Peter in as positive a light as possible. He could not fail to record the triple denial; it was so fixed an element in the passion tradition. But he could soften its impact by prefacing it with a prophecy of Jesus that affirmed that, though there would be a denial (manifesting Satan's temporary ascendency over the disciples), the lapse would be encompassed within Jesus' all-powerful prayer (22:31–34). Peter would emerge converted and able to function as " of the rest. When he goes out and weeps bitterly after the Lord has turned and looked at him in the courtyard of the high priest (22:61–62), one has the impression that healing and restoration have already begun. Why, then, Luke may have asked himself, go and bring it all up again by locating in the resurrection narrative a reminder of Peter's lapse and need for reconciliation?

At the other pole of the relocation—the narrative of the call in 5:1–11—adding elements of the appearance story to the bald Marcan narrative (Mark 1:16–20) also serves Luke's purpose. On the one hand, it anchors Peter's authority and commissioning in the historical life of Jesus, something that Luke may have regarded as a more secure foundation than a vision (cf. Acts 1:21–22).[25] On the other hand, Luke likes formal beginnings proleptic of significant developments to come. Contrary to his usual practice of preserving the Marcan order, he transfers the account of Jesus' visit to Nazareth (Mark 6:1–6) to an earlier location (Luke 4:16–30). There it serves as a formal inauguration of Jesus' ministry, the violent handling he receives from his townsfolk (vv. 23–30) anticipating the fate he would suffer from the leaders of his people in Jerusalem. Only after Jesus' ministry has been under way for sufficient time to establish a pattern and model (4:31–44) does Luke describe the calling of associates who will leave all and devote themselves exclusively to fishing for people (5:10). The call of the disciples, then, with the promise inherent in the symbolic catch and with the expanded focus on Peter—his hesitation, his conversion, his confession ("Lord"), his commission to "catch people alive"—inaugurates proleptically the mission of the church, which in Luke's view rests firmly on the faith and leadership of Peter.

An author aiming at a more strictly biographical narrative might have retained the account of the appearance in its "proper" (and original) location, that is, as part of the postresurrection story. Only the Johannine redactor has preserved it there—and done so, it would seem, in a way that rather mixed it up with the appearance to the wider group of the Twelve. But the Gospels are not primarily biographies. From beginning to end they are replete with the deeper awareness of Jesus' identity, status, and function that came to the disciples along with their faith in the resurrection. We never meet in the Gospels the purely "preresurrection" Jesus. The light of the resurrection shines through all; not even in Mark is it entirely dimmed (1:1; 1:10–11; 4:41; 6:45–52; 9:2–8; 12:35–37). Luke's retrojection, then, simply extends this process whereby it is always the risen Lord that one encounters in the Gospel.

MARY MAGDALENE AS WITNESS

What, then, of Mary Magdalene? If the primary appearances to the male disciples seem associated with Galilee, the total gospel tradition (including the Marcan appendix) associates the women, specifically Mary, with the discovery of the empty tomb in Jerusalem.[26] In

Mark the women are commissioned to tell the good news to the remaining disciples but fail to do so (v. 8); in Luke they are not specifically commissioned for this purpose but do in fact make a report, which is regarded as an "idle tale" and is met with disbelief (vv. 9–11; cf. vv. 22–23). While Mark and Luke divide in this comparatively minor way, Matthew and John (1–20) raise a whole new dimension. Beyond the mere discovery of the tomb, each recounts an *appearance* of the risen Lord to the women.[27] In Matthew (28:9–10) Jesus appears to Mary Magdalene and her companion ("the other Mary" [v. 1]) and repeats the commission given by the angel. The Fourth Gospel (1–20) makes Magdalene the prime witness of the risen Lord (20:11–17a), as well as messenger to the male disciples (v. 17b), a status confirmed by the Marcan appendix (16:6–10).

Mary's personal association with the total resurrection tradition is, then, very strong. The question remains, however, whether the tradition that goes beyond associating her with the empty tomb to nominate her prime resurrection witness (John, Marcan appendix, Matthew [along with the "other Mary"]) reflects the earliest strata or whether it represents a later development—along a trajectory that would grow from Matthew's inclusive reference, to the personalized drama of John, to the brief though emphatic ("...he appeared first...") notice in the Marcan appendix. A majority view of Gospel chronology holds the latter as the more likely development. The remarkable fact remains, however, that contrary to tendencies in a more androcentric direction—seen so clearly in the Deutero-Pauline and post-Pauline literature—the tradition of women's witness to the resurrection waxed rather than waned around the turn of the first Christian century.[28]

At first sight, Luke—of all the evangelists the most concerned with the physical reality of the resurrection of Jesus and with the establishment of witnesses (24:48; Acts 1:8, 22; 2:32; 3:16)—would seem the exception to all this. The Lucan narrative's location of appearances (to male disciples) in Jerusalem seems to have eclipsed the strong (and apparently growing) tradition allocating the primary witness in Jerusalem to women, specifically Mary Magdalene. Moreover, of all the evangelists, Luke seems most at pains to make clear that discovery of the empty tomb, even a vision of angels, is not sufficient to arouse belief in the resurrection (cf. Luke 24:9–12, 24); for that an appearance of the risen Lord is necessary.

Or necessary at least for the male disciples. With the women the case may be different. Prompted by the two men (angels) who addressed them at the tomb, they "remembered" the prophecy of Jesus concerning his death and resurrection (vv. 6–8). Whether this remembering implies faith in the resurrection is not entirely clear.[29] But in any case Luke in no way endorses the disciples' belittling of the women's report (24:11; cf. vv. 22–23); Jesus upbraids the Emmaus disciples for their "foolishness" and "slowness of heart to believe" (v. 25). The remembering—that is, coming to understand the terrible events that had happened in Jerusalem in the light of Jesus' own words and the scriptural prophecies—is, as noted above, central to resurrection faith for Luke. In a further instance of prolepsis (cf. 4:16–30 and 5:1–11), Luke has also moved the notice about the women who accompanied Jesus from Galilee and provided for him out of their resources from the account of the crucifixion (as in Mark [15:40–41] and Matthew [27:55–56]) to the narrative of his early ministry in Galilee (8:1–3). The ministry of women thus accompanies the total ministry of Jesus in Luke, from his early preaching, teaching, and healing up to his suffering, death, and resurrection. The "memory" of the women enfolds all these events, just as in the infancy narrative Mary the mother of Jesus "treasured all these words (things) and kept them in her heart" (2:19; 2:51b).

CONCLUSION

The Pauline tradition of Peter as prime witness to the resurrection (1 Cor 15:5) would seem to have its surest reflection in the Gospel of Luke. Not only do we find notice to this effect in 24:34 and hints in 22:32 and 24:12, but the earlier account of Peter's call (5:1–11), understood in the light of John 21:1–19, seems to contain the essential elements of an early narrative of that first appearance, retrojected back into the beginnings of Jesus' public ministry. On the analysis undertaken above, the tradition of an appearance to Mary Magdalene would seem to represent a later development. But, whatever be the case with respect to history (inevitably speculative in so many ways), she remains for readers of the Gospel a central vehicle of access to the risen Lord.

Notes

1. Gerald O'Collins, S.J., "Peter as Resurrection Witness," *Heythrop Journal* 22 (1981): 1–18.
2. Gerald O'Collins, S.J., "Mary Magdalene as Major Witness to Jesus' Resurrection," *Theological Studies* 48 (1987): 631–46.
3. Cf. O'Collins, "Peter as Resurrection Witness," 633.
4. Joseph A. Fitzmyer, S.J., *The Gospel according to Luke (X–XXIV)* (AB 28A; New York: Doubleday, 1985), 1535–37; also O'Collins, "Peter as Resurrection Witness," 633.
5. See R. H. Fuller, *The Formation of the Resurrection Narratives* (Philadelphia: Fortress, 1980), 10.
6. "(There is) scarcely another fact so unexpected and remarkable in the apostolic age as the notorious suppression of Peter as the first witness of the resurrection" (A. von Harnack; quoted in W. Dietrich, *Das Petrusbild der lukanischen Schriften* [BWANT 94; Stuttgart: Kohlhammer, 1972], 161, n. 277 [translation mine]); see also O. Cullmann, *Peter—Apostle, Disciple, Martyr,* 2nd ed. (Philadelphia: Westminster, 1962), 60.
7. See B. Byrne, "The Faith of the Beloved Disciple and the Community in John 20," *Journal for the Study of the New Testament* 23 (1985): 83–97.
8. The addition of P^{75} to the textual witness has virtually assured the authenticity of v. 12.
9. See R. C. Tannehill, *The Narrative Unity of Luke-Acts: A Literary Interpretation,* vol. 1, *The Gospel according to Luke* (Philadelphia: Fortress, 1986), 278–79.
10. See R. E. Brown, K. P. Donfried, and J. Reumann, eds., *Peter in the New Testament* (Minneapolis: Augsburg; New York: Paulist, 1973), 126.
11. See Joseph A. Fitzmyer, *Gospel according to Luke (I–IX)* (AB 28; New York: Doubleday, 1981), 560–62.
12. The classic comparison, to which this is much indebted, is that of Raymond Brown, *The Gospel according to John (XIII–XXI)* (AB 29A; New York: Doubleday, 1970), 1090; see further J. P. Meier, *A Marginal Jew: Rethinking the Historical Jesus,* vol. 2, *Mentor, Message and Miracle* (New York: Doubleday, 1994), 896–99.
13. See R. Pesch, *Der reiche Fischfang: Lk 5, 1–11/Jo 21,1–14: Wundergeschichte—Berufungserzählung—Erscheinungsbericht* (Düsseldorf: Patmos, 1969), 117–18.
14. See Fitzmyer, *Luke I–IX,* 561–62; Meier, *Marginal Jew,* 2:901.
15. See Brown, *John XIII–XXI,* 1092; Meier, *Marginal Jew,* 2:901–2.
16. E.g., I. H. Marshall, *The Gospel of Luke* (Exeter: Paternoster,

1978), 200; D. L. Bock, *Luke* (2 vols.; Grand Rapids: Baker, 1994, 1996), 1:449.

17. See esp. Brown, *John XIII–XXI,* 1090; Meier, *Marginal Jew,* 2:897–99.

18. So, e.g., Dietrich, *Das Petrusbild,* 54–56, 76; Fuller, *Formation of the Resurrection Narratives,* 151, 160–61.

19. See esp. the thorough discussion of Meier, *Marginal Jew*, 2:899–904.

20. Brown, *John XIII–XXI,* 1093–94.

21. See Fuller, *Formation of the Resurrection Narratives,* 114.

22. See Meier, *Marginal Jew*, 2:902.

23. The solemn blessing and commissioning of Peter, which Matthew adds to Peter's confession at Caesarea Philippi (16:17–19), may reflect a similar retrojection on the part of Matthew (see Brown, *John XIII–XXI,* 1088–89). However, traces of the appearance to Peter seem clearer in the episode of his walking on the water (Matt. 14:22–33, esp. vv. 28–31; cf. Mark 6:45–52).

24. See also John 21:3–9, where, though beaten in the "race" by the disciple whom Jesus loved, Peter enters first into the tomb.

25. Cf. R. Leaney, "Jesus and Peter: The Call and Post-resurrection Appearance (Lk v.1–11 and xxiv. 34)," *Expository Times* 65 (1953–54): 318–82, esp. 382, col. 2; Pesch, *Fischfang,* 142–43.

26. Kendall and O'Collins, "Mary Magdalene as Major Witness," 641.

27. My sense is that Kendall and O'Collins do not sufficiently advert to this distinction.

28. The high esteem accorded Mary Magdalene by major figures in the patristic era continued this trend; see Kendall and O'Collins, "Mary Magdalene as Major Witness," 632, 641–42.

29. Luke Timothy Johnson (*The Gospel of Luke* [Sacra Pagina 3; Collegeville, Minn.: Glazier, 1991], 391) has no doubt that the women come to belief at this point.

2. Jesus the Judge:
Further Thoughts of Paul's
Christology and Soteriology

James D. G. Dunn

"He shall come in glory to judge the living and the dead." So read the familiar words of the Nicene Creed, themselves a slight development of the Apostles' Creed: "from thence (God's right hand) he shall come to judge the living and the dead." The theme of Jesus as judge is thus familiar to Christian worshipers not only from countless repetitions of these creeds, but also from the rich iconography of Eastern Christianity and the more elaborate confessions of the West. And yet it is a subject that has attracted little close attention in recent christological studies.[1] Why this should be so is an interesting question in itself, but answering it adequately would involve too much speculation. At this point it may suffice simply to wonder whether the idea of Christ's (second) coming (*parousia*) has proved difficult enough to cope with without embracing the fuller picture of judgment by Christ, and whether the problem of reconciling Christ as justifier with Christ as judge has proved a little too confusing.

As a New Testament specialist, I am most interested in the NT teaching on the subject. And as one who recently attempted a comprehensive study of Paul's theology, but perhaps did not give enough attention to this aspect of that theology,[2] I take this opportunity, in expressing my appreciation to Gerry O'Collins for all his writings on matters christological, to extend my personal dialogue with him into this difficult area.

I

There is no difficulty in identifying how the idea of final divine judgment entered Christian thought. It was familiar in Greek thought, but particularly prominent in Jewish tradition,[3] and especially in the expectation of "the day of the Lord" as a day of vengeance and wrath.[4] Clearly, Paul simply took over this eschatological expectation, as the opening chapters of Romans sufficiently indicate: "we know that the judgment of God is in accordance with truth on those who practice such things" (2:2); "the day of wrath and of the revelation of the righteous judgment of God" (2:5); "the day when God is to judge" (2:16); "all the world become liable to God's judgment" (3:19).

What is striking, however, is the fact that Christ also appears in the judgment scene and even in the role of judge. In Pauline texts this feature figures most prominently in 2 Cor 5:10 ("All of us must appear before the judgment seat of Christ") and 2 Tim 4:1 ("Christ Jesus, who is to judge the living and the dead").[5] Equally striking is the fact that Paul can adapt the OT phrase to speak of "the day of Christ" (Phil 1:6, 10; 2:16), "the day of the Lord (Jesus)" (1 Cor 1:8; 5:5; 2 Cor 1:14; 1 Thess 5:2; 2 Thess 2:2).[6] The "day" in view is clearly the day of judgment (Rom 2:16; 1 Cor 3:13). Notable also are two other texts that envisage Christ's coming to exercise judgment: 1 Cor 4:5, "Do not pronounce judgment before the time, before the Lord comes, who will bring to light the things now hidden in darkness and will disclose the purposes of the heart"; 2 Thess 1:7, "when the Lord Jesus is revealed from heaven with his mighty angels in flaming fire, inflicting vengeance on those who do not know God and on those who do not obey the gospel of our Lord Jesus...."

Given this data, important questions naturally arise: From where did Paul derive this belief in Jesus as judge? And what is the significance of these data? To the first question there are two obvious answers.

II

Pre-Christian Jewish thought usually represents Yahweh as the one who will judge.[7] The idea that God *delegates* judgment or a share in judgment to another was already quite frequent in the thought of

Second Temple Judaism. Even the notion that God delegated judgment to his representatives on earth (e.g., Judg 2:16–18; 3:9–10; 2 Chr 19:6–8) and would call them to account (Ps 82) was already old. Similar delegation of judgment was anticipated for God's representatives in the age to come. For example, the Davidic messiah would judge (Isa 11:3), and the *Testament of Levi* looks to the Lord to "raise up a new priest to whom all the words of the Lord will be revealed. And he will execute true judgment on earth for many days" (18:2).

The extension of this line of thought to *final* judgment is not unexpected. Enoch's role in the judgment was the subject of some speculation. *Jubilees* presents him as the one established to keep a record of all the deeds of every generation till the day of judgment, who in particular bore witness against the Watchers (*Jub.* 4:17–24). Similarly, the first book of Enoch describes him as the "scribe of righteousness" who carried to the Watchers the heavenly sentence of condemnation (*1 Enoch* 12–16). In the *Testament of Abraham* (Recension B), however, Abraham is taken up to heaven and witnesses a judgment scene, where one judges and another brings the charges of sins. The archangel Michael tells Abraham that the judge is Abel. "And the one who produces (the evidence) is the teacher of heaven and earth and the scribe of righteousness, Enoch. "For the Lord sent them[8] here in order that they might record the sins and the righteous deeds of each person" (*T. Abr.* [B] 11:1–4). Particularly fascinating here is Michael's further comment: "It is not Enoch's business to give sentence; rather, the Lord is the one who gives sentence, and it is this one's [Enoch's] task only to write" (B 11:7).[9] It would appear that the *Testament of Abraham* attempts to correct or clarify some confusion on the point: some concluded that Enoch would have a share in the final judgment; in response, the *Testament of Abraham* makes it clear that Enoch's role would be more limited. Enoch's role as scribe is elaborated in *2 Enoch* (23:1–5; 40:13; 53:2; 64:5; 68:2).

The fact remains that the *Testament of Abraham* depicts Abel as "the judge" (*T. Abr.* [B] 10). Michael speaks: "Do you see the judge? This is Abel, who first bore witness, and God brought him here to judge" (B 11:2). Equally interesting is Recension A, where again Abel is depicted as sitting in judgment, as the angel Michael explains. The passage is intriguing and worth quoting at length (*T. Abr.* [A] 13:3–10):[10]

[Abel] sits here to judge every creature, examining both righteous and sinners, because God has said, "It is not I who judge you, but by man shall every man be judged." For this reason he has committed judgment to him, to judge the world until his own great and glorious coming [*parousia*]. And then, righteous Abraham, will follow the final judgment and retribution, eternal and unchangeable, which no one will be able to dispute. For all men have their origin from the first man; and so by his son they are first judged here. At the second coming [*deutera parousia*] they and every spirit and every creature will be judged by the twelve tribes of Israel. At the third stage they will be judged by the Sovereign God of all; and then at last will the whole process reach its end.

The date of the work remains unclear and may be later than Paul, but both recensions are certainly Jewish (rather than Christian) in character:[11] despite talk of "the second coming" here, there is no Christian input evident (Abel is not presented as a prototype of Jesus); the parousia is presumably that of God himself (cf. Mal 3:1–2).[12] Of particular interest at this point is the talk of *three* judgments: one by Abel; one by the twelve tribes of Israel; and a final, final judgment by the Sovereign God.

Certainly earlier than Paul is the fascinating Qumran document that focuses on the mysterious Melchizedek—11QMelch:

He [Melchizedek] will, by his strength, judge the holy ones of God [*El*], executing judgment as it is written concerning him in the Songs of David, who said "*Elohim* has taken his place in the divine council; in the midst of the gods [*Elohim*] he holds judgment" [Ps. 82:1]. And it was concerning him that he said, "El will judge the peoples" [Ps. 7:7–8]. As for that which he s[aid, "How long will you] judge unjustly and show partiality to the wicked? Selah" [Ps. 82:2], its interpretation concerns Belial and the spirits of his lot [who] rebelled by turning away from the precepts of God to…. And Melchizedek will avenge the vengeance of the judgments of God…. (11QMelch 9–13, trans. Vermes)

Whether Melchizedek is intended to be the equally mysterious figure of Gen 14:18–20 or possibly a heavenly figure ("King of righteousness") remains a matter of dispute.[13] Clearly, however, Psalm 82 is interpreted with reference to this Melchizedek: the (earthly) judges, themselves designated "god"' in the Psalm itself (82:6, "I say, 'You are gods [*Elohim*]…'"), are identified as Satan and the evil angels; and the initial figure ("God," *Elohim*) is identified as Melchizedek. The boldness of the Psalm's own speech ("You are gods"; cf. John 10:34–35) is surpassed by that of its interpretation at Qumran (Melchizedek is the first mentioned *Elohim*). However we interpret the figure Melchizedek, it seems clear enough that he has a role in heavenly judgment—though presumably the final line retains the thought that this role as heavenly judge is delegated by God.

Most stimulating for such reflection were the visions of Dan 7:9–14. The first vision spoke of "thrones" (plural)—it always being implied that the occupant of a "throne" exercised judgment. The indication of a second, empty throne was evidently sufficient to stimulate Rabbi Akiba's suggestion that the second throne was for the Messiah (*b. Hagigah* 14a; *b. Sanhedrin* 38b). According to the visions themselves, though, the most obvious candidate for the second throne was the manlike figure ("one like a son of man") who came with the clouds of heaven to the Ancient of Days and was given dominion and kingship (Dan 7:13–14). However, the implication was not actually taken up till the Similitudes of Enoch (*1 Enoch* 37–71), where the Elect One sits down on the throne of God's glory and judges "the secret things" and the rebellious angels (*1 Enoch* 49:4; 55:4; 61:8–9). The Elect One is evidently also the Son of Man (69:27), who is subsequently identified as Enoch (71:14). Again the awkward question of dating arises, but since Daniel's vision seems to have stimulated the writers of 4 Ezra and the Revelation of John in a similar way (4 Ezra 12:32–33; 13:10–11, 37–38; Rev 1:13–16; 14:14–16) in the aftermath of Jerusalem's destruction (70 C.E.), it is quite likely that the Similitudes come too late to have influenced Paul.[14] Curiously enough, the Synoptic tradition evidences a similar development in regard to talk of the Son of Man. That the Son of Man has a crucial role in the final judgment when he comes in glory is clear enough in its earliest written form (Mark 8:38; 13:26–27) (though what that role is is less clear) as is the fact that he sits at the right hand of God (Mark 14:62). But nowhere does the earliest written form of the Synoptic tradition speak of the Son of Man exercising judgment from the throne of glory. Only Matthew does so (Matt 19:28; 25:31–32; cf. 16:27 with Mark 8:38, par. Luke 9:26), and in language that raises the possibility that Matthew's redaction reflects the influence of the Similitudes.[15]

Paul does not show any clear evidence of making use of or being influenced by the Son of Man traditions within earliest Christianity,[16] but that particular possibility is neither here nor there. The idea of a divine agent, whether an exalted human or of heavenly origin, having part in God's final judgment seems to have been "in the air" around the time of Paul's writing. In addition, the use of Ps 110:1 in reference to Jesus was already well established before Paul: Jesus was the Lord to whom the Lord God had said, "Sit at my right hand until I make your enemies your footstool."[17] This conviction expressed in such imagery could hardly fail to suggest the corollary: that the risen and exalted Christ would have some share in that eschatological day of judgment.

In view of the *Testament of Abraham*'s conception of a second (stage of) judgment, to be exercised by the twelve tribes of Israel (*T. Abr.* [A] 13:6), we should also recall that this motif influenced earliest Christian thought. It presumably stemmed from Dan 7.22: in the LXX the text reads, "He gave judgment to the saints of the Most High." The idea developed into the thought of Israel being given to judge the Gentiles: "they [Israel] shall judge all the nations" (*Jub.* 32:19); "God will execute the judgment of the nations by the hand of his elect" (1QpHab 5:4); "they [the righteous] will judge [*krinousin*] [the] Gentiles" (Wis 3:8).[18] The Jesus tradition takes up the same motif, with an interesting twist, in what may be the final word in Q: "Truly I tell you, at the renewal of all things [*palingenesia*], when the Son of Man is seated on his throne of glory, you who have followed me will also sit on twelve thrones, judging the twelve tribes of Israel" (Matt 19:28, par. Luke 22:30). Paul transfers this same motif to the believers in Messiah Jesus (including Gentile believers) in 1 Cor 6:2: "Do you not know that the saints will judge the world?" If the thought of sharing in final judgment could be extended to include the saints, how much more natural and compelling would it be to envisage the exalted Jesus as having a determinative part or say in the final judgment.

What points of importance for our inquiry emerge from this brief survey? (a) The conception of others, including Israel, or the saints, and exalted heroes of Israel's history, sharing in the final judgment was quite commonly entertained. (b) Various roles were envisaged, including those of various courtroom officials: the usher who summons or gathers the participants to the place of judgment; the one who documents or brings the charges; the one who executes the judgment of the court; but also that of the judge himself. (c) All roles, including the last, were characteristically thought of as delegated by God, and so would not be thought to encroach upon the divine prerogative. (d) In at least some cases we probably have to speak of several judgments, and of judgments by saints and exalted ones as subordinate or preliminary (a lower court?) to the final judgment of God.

Against such a background it is easy to see how affirmation of the exalted lordship of the risen Christ would lead to or include already the implication that this exalted Christ would also have a part in the final judgment of all creation. Something along these lines undoubtedly lies behind Paul's talk of Jesus as judge.

III

The other source for Paul's theology of Jesus as judge is presumably his own conception of the process of salvation in terms of courtroom imagery—justification, acquittal. This has been a major subject of scholarly analysis and discussion for several centuries, and I have already written on it at length.[19] However, in focusing on the subject within a chapter entitled "The Beginning of Salvation" (in *The Theology of Paul the Apostle*), I may have distracted attention from the fact that the imagery has an essentially forensic character: it is derived from the courtroom, and not least from the thought of final judgment. When I returned to the subject in #18 of the same book, the focus had changed (to "the eschatological tension"), so that anyone concerned primarily with the theology of justification may have overlooked the comments on the future tense of justification.[20] I should rectify the misleading impression here.

The forensic character of the imagery of justification is sufficiently familiar and needs no further exposition.[21] What does need to be stressed, however, is that fundamental to Paul's concept of justification is its *future* orientation. "Not the hearers of the law are righteous before God, but the doers of the law shall be counted righteous [*dikaiōthēsontai*]" (Rom 2:13); the context shows clearly that final judgment is in view (2:5–13, 15–16). "By works of the law shall no flesh be justified/acquitted [*dikaiōthēsontai*] before him" (3:20), where again clearly final judgment is in view. "'God is one,' who will justify [*dikai/ō/sei*] circumcision from faith and uncircumcision through faith" (3:30); once again the universality of the claim looks to its implementation in universal (final) judgment.

The more frequent present tenses should probably be understood as describing the *character* of God who justifies rather than its *timing*. God is *ho dikaiōn*, "the one who justifies" (Rom 3:26; 4:5; 8:33); hence the present tenses also in 3:24 and 28. The thought is of a divine prerogative, which will be most fully demonstrated in the final judgment, as the sequence of argument in 3:4–6 and the context of 8:33 make plain. Likewise with Paul's occasional use of the noun *dikaiōsis* ("justification, vindication, acquittal"): in both cases the association of the term with resurrection (4:25, "he was raised because of our justification") and life (5:18, "through the righteous act of one to all men to righteousness of life"/"acquittal that brings life" [BAGD]) suggests that the thought is of the end of the process of salvation (cf. 6:5; 8:11; 11:15).

The mixture of tenses in Gal 2:16–17 similarly indicates that what may be a present pronouncement will (have to) be ratified by a final verdict of acquittal:

> We know that no human being is justified [*dikaioutai*—present] by works of the law but only through faith in Jesus Christ, and we have believed in Christ Jesus, in order that we might be justified [*dikaiōthōmen*—aorist] by faith in Christ and not by works of the law, because by works of the law shall no flesh be justified [*dikaiōthēsetai*—future; as in Rom 3:20]. But if in seeking to be justified [*dikaiōthēnai*—aorist] in Christ....

Similarly with Gal 3:8, 11, and 24; and in 5:4 the thought is of an aspiration to future justification: "you who are seeking to be justified [*dikaiousthē*] by the law." Hence the Christian alternative: "we (by contrast) by the Spirit, from faith, are awaiting eagerly the hope of righteousness" (5:5); that is, the hope is for "righteousness," the verdict of God's acquittal, as a still future good.

It is important therefore not to be misled by other aorist uses of the verb, which may seem to imply a verdict already passed, complete, and (by implication) irrevocable. Most notably the famous Rom 5:1: "Therefore, having been justified [*dikaiōthentes*] from faith..." (similarly Rom 4:2; 5:9; 1 Cor 6:11; Titus 3:7). Such texts may tempt us to limit the language of justification to the initial stage of the process of salvation, parallel to the washing and setting apart of 1 Cor 6:11, and with the language of "salvation" similarly limited to the end product of the process (as Rom 5:9–10).[22] In fact, however, Paul's usage shows that he does think of salvation as a process (as the present tenses of 1 Cor 1:18; 15:2; 2 Cor 2:15 confirm: "those who are being saved"), with "salvation" as the goal in view (Rom 5:9–10; 11:26; 13:11; Phil 1:19; 2:12; 1 Thess 5:8–9), but also with a present realization (Rom 8:24, "in terms of hope, we are saved [*esōthemen*]"). To that extent "justification" and "salvation" have a very similar soteriological function in Paul's theology: to indicate a process begun but not yet completed.[23]

So far as our present inquiry is concerned, the two-stage soteriology (beginning and end, justified already but not yet finally acquitted) is mirrored in the double role of Jesus in the process of justification: justified through faith in Christ, and Jesus the judge. Affirming Jesus as eschatological judge recognizes that justification is a process, that it is not complete in the moment faith is placed in Christ, and that Christ will also signal its completion, while at the same time giving reassurance that the judge is also the justifier. Something of this is indicated in a text already cited—Rom 4:25. Paul quotes a widely recognized variation on a well established early Christian formulation: "Jesus our Lord who was handed over because of our transgressions and was raised because of our justification"; the two stages of the crucial event (Jesus' death and resurrection) are mirrored in the two aspects/stages of the salvation process. Similarly Rom 5:10: "If when we were enemies we were reconciled to God through the death of his Son, how much more, having been reconciled, we shall be saved by his life." More explicit is Rom 8:33–34. The scene is the final judgment. Paul asks, in confident assurance: "Who will bring charges against the elect of God? It is God who justifies. Who is there to condemn? It is Christ (Jesus) who died, rather was raised, who also is at the right hand of God, who also intercedes on our behalf." Here the two aspects of 4:25 and 5:10 are held together: Jesus' death and resurrection together mean that he is able to plead with God the judge effectively on behalf of "the elect of God," and that no prosecutor will be able to overthrow that case.

In short, the conception of Jesus as judge may stem in part from a double conviction. (a) The whole of human history moves forward inexorably to a final judgment. (b) The saving event of Jesus (death and resurrection) does not eliminate the idea of final judgment or of the need for a final reckoning. Rather, the belief in justification by faith must be integrated into the prior belief in final judgment. That is most simply done by affirming the exalted Christ's role also in that judgment, and the most forceful statement to that effect is the affirmation of Jesus as judge. In so arguing, of course, I have no wish to suggest that the two "sources" of the Christian conception of Jesus as judge were alternatives or independent of each other. On the contrary, they likely interacted and reinforced each other more or less from the first. However, if there is anything in the above arguments, they have important corollaries for our understanding both of Paul's christology and of his soteriology.

IV

The christological corollaries should already be obvious. Two in particular merit further reflection. First, we need to note the different roles in judgment attributed to the exalted Jesus in the different texts. 2 Cor 5:10 and 2 Tim 4:1 (cited in section I above) do not hesitate to ascribe the role of judge as such to Jesus. Perhaps the same is implicit in the talk of "the day of Christ," "the day of the Lord (Jesus)" (also listed in section I above). Similarly, the depiction of the Lord (Jesus) as disclosing the purposes of the heart (1 Cor 4:5) clearly recalls the description of God as the one who searches the heart (Rom 8:27)[24] and suggests the picture of the discerning judge. On the other hand, the result of such disclosure is that "each one will receive commendation from God," God being, presumably, the higher authority. 1 Cor 3:10–15 somewhat confuses the picture by referring to Christ as the foundation (3:11, "that foundation is Jesus Christ") on which believers must build the superstructure that will be tested in that "day." More to the point, Rom 5:9–10 and 1 Thess 1:10 seem to envisage Jesus rather as the one who saves or rescues from God's (judicial) wrath, and Rom 8:33–34 (just cited) seems to envisage Jesus as the defense counsel pleading for the elect before God the judge. Whether 2 Thess 1:7 (also cited in section I above) refers to the one who carries out the judgment of the court or to the judge who enacts his own sentence, or indeed is formally independent of courtroom imagery (the avenging angel) remains unclear.

In all this Paul's usage reflects, to at least some degree, the variety of roles attributed to individuals such as Enoch, Melchizedek, Abel, the Elect One/Messiah, and even the saints. What does this tell us? At the very least that no clear and widely shared concept of final judgment and of those who were to share in that judgment had emerged in the Judaism of Paul's time. Within the fixed conviction of a final divine judgment, it seems to have been widely accepted that there was room enough to envisage others as having a share or being given a share in that judgment, even in the role of judge itself. In the light of this, Paul's own flexibility of imagery on the same subject, in relation to Jesus' own role as judge, should occasion no surprise.

As I tried to indicate in my *Theology of Paul,* such variety of imagery and role is wholly typical of Paul's Christology.[25] He envisages the exalted Christ in very personal terms as exalted Lord and soon to come (on clouds), but also as last Adam and divine Wisdom. Yet he can also speak of "Christ in me" and of Christ as a corporate entity, of believers "in Christ" and functioning as Christ's body. Jesus as judge obviously belongs with the first group of images, but given the variety of the imagery, we need to remember that it is *imagery* and not attempt to ascribe to it a literalness that would make it impossible to integrate the different roles indicated by the language used. As in other matters,[26] Paul was attempting to articulate convictions and hopes that went beyond the limitations of human speech. For us to attempt to order and integrate these images into a single coherent pattern would probably squeeze them into a mold of our own making— better to live with the confusion of the imagery in its richness and be content with the basic conviction that comes to expression in such rich diversity. That basic conviction seems to be that Jesus will have a determinative part in the final judgment of God, or even in still less precise terms, that the final judgment of God will be in accord with the gospel of Christ.

Second, elsewhere in the New Testament Jesus' role as judge is explicitly stated to have been appointed by God himself: Acts 10:42; 17:31, "he [Jesus] is the one ordained by God as judge of the living and the dead"; "he [God] has fixed a day on which he will have the world judged in righteousness by a man whom he has appointed, and of this he has given assurance to all by raising him from the dead"; John 5:22, 27, "the Father judges no one but has given all judgment to the Son";

"he [the Father] has given him authority to execute judgment, because he is the Son of Man." Paul's judgment texts are not so explicit, but the point may well be implicit anyway. This would all be the clearer if the role of Jesus as judge for Paul followed from his exaltation as Lord, since the influence of Ps 110:1 would likely carry over into the former role: it is in the role as Lord, appointed by God, at God's right hand, that the exalted Jesus exercises judgment. The importance of recognizing the delegated character of Christ's Lordship certainly comes to the fore in Paul's fullest statement on the point—1 Cor 15:24–28. Here Ps 110:1 is alluded to: "He [Christ] must reign until he has put all his enemies under his feet" (15:25). This is then glossed by citing Ps 8:7: "For he [God] has put all things in subjection under his feet" (15:27).[27] It would hardly strain the thought to include the role of judgment in the rule thus given to the exalted Christ. But Paul then goes on to make clear that the "all things" subjected to the Lord Christ do not, of course, include the one who put them in subjection to Christ (15:27). Rather, the end comes when Christ returns the royal authority delegated to him (15:24), and when Christ himself is subjected to God, "in order that God might be all in all" (15:28).

To restate the same point from another angle, there is no scope for the thought that Jesus as judge has replaced God, far less usurped God's role. On the contrary, God remains the judge, as passages such as Rom 2:2–11; 3:6; and 1 Cor 5:13 show clearly. In Rom 2:2–11, Paul makes a point of reasserting traditional Jewish emphases that God "will render to each according to his works" (2:6), and that "there is no partiality with God" (2:11), that is, in his judgment.[28] And in Rom 3:6 God's righteousness as judge provides the fundamental axiom from which Paul moves out and which he seeks to defend despite the corollaries that might be drawn from Israel's unfaithfulness (3:3–6). Most striking in this context is Rom 2:16, where Paul describes "the day when God is to judge the secrets of humankind in accordance with my gospel through Christ Jesus." As most commentators agree, the "through Jesus Christ" is to be taken with the verb "judge": in that final day God will judge "through Christ Jesus." Rom 8:31–39 maintains a similar balance. It is God who is "for us," demonstrated by the giving up of his Son (8:31–32). It is God who justifies and Christ who intercedes at God's right hand (8:33–34). The love from which nothing can separate us is "the love of God in Christ Jesus our Lord" (8:39).

It need hardly be said that the more explicit talk of Jesus as *judge* cannot, or should not, be taken independently of Paul's overall treatment of these themes. 2 Cor 5:10 ("the judgment seat of Christ") should not be regarded as contradictory to or inconsistent with Rom 14:10 ("the judgment seat of God"). Conceivably different judgments or, rather, different stages in the one (final) judgment are in view (if *T. Abr.* [A] 13 provides any sort of parallel). But even so, Paul would not want the judgment exercised by *Christ* to be conceived of as any other than the judgment of *God.* That judgment will be exercised by the exalted Jesus is a way of saying that the final judgment of God will be in accord with the character of God as revealed in Jesus. The later Pauline text, 2 Tim 4:1, makes the same point in its own way: the exhortation is made "in the presence of God and of Christ Jesus, who is to judge the living and the dead...," where, by implication, Christ Jesus speaks and acts for God.

There is no difficulty, then, in recognizing that Paul was well able to hold his Christology at this point within the monotheistic framework of his overall theology. God is the final judge, but he shares that judgment with Christ (as also with the saints); he judges through Christ; he judges with reference to and in accordance with the gospel of Christ's death and resurrection. This brings us to the soteriological corollary of this line of thought.

V

The soteriological consequences of any recognition of Jesus' role as judge also deserve some reflection. For, as noted at the beginning, there seems to be some tension between the thought of justification assured through faith in Christ and the thought of Jesus as judge also of those who believe. Alternatively expressed, how did Paul hold together the image of Jesus as savior and deliverer from divine wrath, or as counsel for the defense (Rom 5:9–10; 1 Thess 1:10; Rom 8:34), with the image of Jesus as judge?

Here again, we should note, the problem was not new. It was unavoidably bound up with the twin thoughts of God's election of Israel and of God's role as final judge. A too simple answer assumed that all Israel would be saved. This conviction provides the starting point for the famous Mishnah *Sanhedrin* 10—"All Israelites have a share in the world to come" (10:1)—although the developed tradition goes on to list the various exceptions. Others attempted to deal with the problem by declaring that only a "remnant" of Israel would be saved,[29] or by resorting to a sectarian definition of "the righteous" (e.g., *Psalms of Solomon, Qumran*). Others again acknowledged God's judgment on Israel, but distinguished that judgment, as the disciplining of a child by its father, from the punishment of condemnation that non-Israelites experienced.[30] But earlier, the classic prophets had repeatedly reminded Israel that Israel was *not* exempt from divine judgment for its sins.[31]

It is important to recognize how the same problem deeply troubled Paul. He highlights it in Rom 3:1–6, as an immediate consequence of his conviction that Israel stands under the same condemnation as all humankind (2:1—3:20): What does the acknowledgment of Israel's faith*less*ness to God say about God's faith*ful*ness to Israel (3:3–4) and about God's role as judge (3:5–6)? Paul's attempt to actually tackle this problem forms the climax of his theological exposition in Romans (Rom 9–11), where he tries to integrate the older ideas of God's judgment of wrath on Israel (9:22; 11:7–10, 25, 28, 31) and of Israel reduced to a remnant (9:27–29; 11:5) within an overall divine purpose of faithfulness to Israel and of mercy to all (11:28–32).

The problem of marrying the twofold thought of divine election of Israel with divine judgment on Israel can be focused in the soteriological pattern of Israel's religion. The pattern begins from the axiom of divine election, but it goes on from that to expect and require obedience to the law provided by the electing God. It holds out both promises of extended life to those who obey and warnings of fearful consequences for those who fail to obey. Deuteronomy is the archetypal statement of this soteriology.

This pattern was heavily criticized by generations of Christian scholarship as "legalistic" and more recently was reassessed by E. P. Sanders in terms of "covenantal nomism."[32] The former perspective can certainly be criticized for failing to appreciate the "covenantal presupposition" of all Israel's law keeping. Some would reply that the latter perspective should likewise receive criticism for an equivalent failure to appreciate the "conditionality" of the promise of life upon Israel's obedience.[33] A potential *rapprochement* between these two alternatives may be reached by describing the role of the law in Jewish understanding as "a way of life and a way to life."[34] If so, then a greater consensus can be expected on Israel's soteriological pattern as a two-stage soteriology: final salvation dependent *both* on the initial election of Israel *and* on Israel's consequent obedience to that law, to be demonstrated in the final judgment.

What needs to be brought out more clearly now is that this two-stage soteriology quite closely parallels Paul's two-stage soteriology outlined above (section III). The determinative effect of God's election in Israel's soteriology seems more or less precisely equivalent to the determinative effect of Christ's death for the one who believes (e.g., Rom 6:3–4; 7:4; 8:3) in Paul's soteriology. If so, then the question inevitably arises whether the second stage in Paul's soteriology is like-wise equivalent to the second stage in Israel's soteriology. In other words, is the role of Jesus executing judgment on believers within Paul's soteriology the same as the role of God executing judgment on Israel within Israel's soteriology?

Here the parallel between Rom 2:2–16 and 2 Cor 5:10 cannot be ignored. I would regard Rom 2:6–16 as a description of God's final judgment, which holds valid both before the gospel and under the gospel: the description of God's judgment as "through Jesus Christ" and "in accordance with my gospel" (2:16) is continuous with the description of future justification in 2:12–13.[35] The same judgment is in view when Paul speaks in terms of works good and bad (2:6–7, 9–10) as when he speaks of judgment according to the gospel (2:16). Others, however, would regard 2:12–13 as the old terms of final judgment, prior to the gospel, superseded by "But now apart from the law the righteousness of God has been revealed" of 3:21.[36] Yet the terms of 2 Cor 5:10 seem to echo those of Rom 2:6–13 to a significant extent: "all of us must appear before the judgment seat of Christ, in order that each may receive recompense for what has been done in the body, whether good or evil." Evidently, the gospel did not change Paul's belief that final judgment will be in reference to what one has done, one's deeds, good or bad. If, then, Jesus is not only counsel for the defense (Rom 8:34) but also judge (2 Cor 5:10), what does that say with regard to Paul's soteriology?

1 Cor 3:10–15 provides a possible answer: Christ is the inde-structible foundation; only the superstructure is tested (to destruction) by the fire of judgment; and even "if anyone's work is burned up...he himself will be saved, but so as by fire" (3:15). That, however, has

something of an echo of the special pleading evident in the earlier Jewish distinction between a suffering (of the righteous), which is disciplinary, and a suffering (of sinners), which is destructive. Here again Paul's two-stage soteriology faced the same sort of questions as Israel's two-stage soteriology.

My own attempt to clarify Paul's two-stage soteriology focused on the motif of "eschatological tension" and "already/not yet" familiar to students of Paul's theology,[37] already referred to above (section III). There again I was struck by the extent to which this Pauline pattern fitted his treatment of Israel in Rom 9–11: Israel as the chosen of God, but caught between the already and the not yet, between its own (temporary) disobedience and God's final purpose of mercy.[38] In both cases a process is begun (election, conversion/baptism), but not yet completed, whose completion is not yet evident and has yet to be secured.

Most striking in Paul's treatment are the frequent "ifs" in his exhortations to himself and his fellow believers. I cite only the most obvious. "If [*ei*] you [believers] live in accordance with the flesh, you will certainly die; but if [*ei*] by the Spirit you put to death the deeds of the body, you will live" (Rom 8:13; cf. Gal 6:8). "Heirs of God and heirs together with Christ, provided that [*eiper*] we suffer with him in order that we might also be glorified with him" (Rom 8:17).[39] "If God did not spare the natural branches, neither will he spare you…to you the goodness of God, if [*ean*] you continue in that goodness" (Rom 11:21–22). "The gospel…through which you are being saved, if [*ei*] you hold it firmly…unless [*ektos ei me*] you have believed in vain" (1 Cor 15:2). "[I want] to know him [Christ] and the power of his resurrection and the fellowship of his sufferings, being conformed to his death, if somehow [*ei pōs*] I may attain to the resurrection from the dead" (Phil 3:10–11).

In the face of such repeated reserve one can only ask whether the Pauline "if" is not equivalent to the Jewish "if you obey the law." "Conditionality" may not be the best word to describe this note of caution in Paul, but the "if" certainly should have a place in any attempts to restate his soteriology. And, linked to the eschatological tension, or eschatological reserve, it is hard to escape the conclusion that Paul both understood salvation to be in some degree dependent on continuing perseverance and allowed the possibility that the process of salvation would not be completed in some/many(?) cases.[40] Of course, the "if" needs to be held together with the confidence Paul elsewhere expresses in God completing what he has begun; but a text such as Phil 1:6 needs to be balanced with its parallel in Gal 3:3, where the confidence of the former is matched by the anxiety of the latter (cf. Gal 1:6; 5:4); and the assurance of the final scene in Rom 8:28–39 neither denies nor cancels out the earlier "ifs" (8:13, 17).

A theoretical solution might propose that those who do not persevere simply demonstrate that they never began.[41] However, that is the solution of the more black-and-white theologian who wrote 1 John (2:19) and does not reflect the much more nuanced and cautious theology of Paul; nor does it do any justice to the earnestness of Paul's exhortations to his readers on the need to live out their faith to the end. Alternatively, a solution is possible in terms of universalism and a theology of the cross that effects "the restoration of all things,"[42] though a similar universalistic argument in reference to Israel's two-stage soteriology could be mounted on Rom 11:28–32. Even so, it is hard to correlate such universal "universalism" with passages such as Rom 2:8–9 and 14:15; 1 Cor 9:27; and 2 Thess 1:7–9.

In short, it is difficult to avoid seeing Paul's two-stage soteriology as parallel to Israel's two-stage soteriology. This means recognizing a similar degree of assurance resting on God's election in both cases, both able to cry triumphantly in reference to the final judgment, "Who will bring charges against the elect of God?" (Rom 8:33), but also a similar note of reserve. The assurance should not become presumption, the fault for which Paul criticized his fellow Jews (Rom 2:17–29) and against which he warned his fellow believers (11:17–24). Rather, it should become the basis and source for living in accordance with the Spirit and thus fulfilling the requirement of the law (8:1–4). For Paul, of course, there were crucial differences between the two, in the effect of Christ's death and resurrection, and in the gift of the Spirit. But the fact that he envisaged Jesus also in the role of eschatological judge should be enough to remind us that a clear note of reserve remained part of his soteriology.

VI

To sum up, Jesus as judge is a too much neglected feature of earliest Christian theology, and particularly of Pauline theology. The importance of the motif needs, therefore, to be restated. First, in relation to Christology and to Paul's conception of God. For Paul, Christ absorbs all the key roles in final judgment attributed in Second Temple Judaism to other salvific figures, exalted human or heavenly. The role(s) attributed to Jesus in no way infringe on the absoluteness of God's prerogative as final judge as well as initial Creator. But they do express the early Christian conviction that the final judgment would be in accord with the saving event enacted in Jesus' death and resurrection, that the character of God's final judgment would be of a piece with his righteousness and love expressed in and through Jesus. Not only that, but if the language can be pressed, they express the assurance that Jesus himself would be involved in that final reckoning, as agent for and intercessor before God.

Second, the thought of Jesus as judge underlines the "not-yet"ness of Paul's soteriology, the "ifs" that seem integral to it. Whether the warning that Jesus will be judge is entirely equivalent to the warnings to Israel of old that the Israel chosen by God is itself liable to judgment for its disobedience is something requiring further study. Whether there is a degree of provisionality in Paul's understanding of the process of salvation equivalent to the provisionality in Israel's covenantal nomism is also something that needs further discussion. At the very least, however, no one should take lightly the moral seriousness of Paul's own call for "the obedience of faith."

Notes

1. Including the honoree's *Christology: A Biblical, Historical, and Systematic Study of Jesus* (Oxford: Oxford University Press, 1995). Even J. Moltmann (*The Coming of God: Christian Eschatology* [London: SCM, 1996]) raises the subject only in relation to his discussion of universalism.

2. J. D. G. Dunn, *The Theology of Paul the Apostle* (Grand Rapids: Eerdmans; Edinburgh: T & T Clark, 1998); I thus include myself with those referred to in n. 1.

3. See further TDNT 3:933–35; ABD 2:82–83.

4. E.g., Isa 13:9, 13; 34:8; Ezek 7:7–12; Joel 2:1–2; Zeph 1:7—2:3; 3:8; Mal 4:1, 5; *Jub.* 5:10–16; see also, e.g., Dan 7:9–11; *Jub.* 5:10–16; *1 Enoch* 90:20–27.

5. See Acts 10:42, Jesus "is the one ordained by God as judge of the living and the dead"; 17:31, God "has fixed a day on which he will have the world judged in righteousness by a man whom he has appointed." Rom 14:10, "We shall all stand before the judgment seat of God" (at an early date *theou* was replaced by *Christou,* probably under the influence of 2 Cor 5:10 [B. M. Metzger, *A Textual Commentary on the Greek New Testament* (London: United Bible Societies, 1975), 531]).

6. See further ABD 2:76–77.

7. R. H. Hiers cites Pss 58:11; 96:10, 13; Eccl 11:9; 12:14; Isa 33:22; Ezek 11:8–11; Mal 3:5; *T. Benj.* 10:8–10; *1 Enoch* 91:7 (ABD 2:80).

8. The plural is a puzzle. The context suggests that the two in view are Enoch and Abel. But the same context distinguishes Abel's role in judging from Enoch's in recording. Some manuscripts read "him" instead of "them."

9. Translation by E. P. Sanders in J. H. Charlesworth, ed., *The Old Testament Pseudepigrapha* (London: Darton, Longman & Todd, 1983), 1:900.

10. Translation by N. Turner in H. F. D. Sparks, *The Apocryphal Old Testament* (Oxford: Clarendon, 1984), 412; Sparks does not include Recension B.

11. Sanders in Charlesworth, OTP 1:871–75; Turner in Sparks, AOT, 393–96.

12. Sanders in Charlesworth, OTP 1:890 n. 13a.

13. See, e.g., J. D. G. Dunn, *Christology in the Making* (2nd ed.; London: SCM, 1989), 152–53 and those cited there.

14. Dunn, *Christology,* 76–78.

15. Similarly, John 5:27 may reflect some influence from the Similitudes (*1 Enoch* 69:27); see further Dunn, *Christology,* 77–78.

16. Dunn, *Christology,* 90–91.

17. Mark 12:36 parr.; 14:62 parr.; Acts 2:34–35; Rom 8:34; 1 Cor 15:25; Eph 1:20; Col 3:1; Heb 1:3, 13; 8:1; 10:12–13; 12:2; 1 Pet 3:22. For bibliography, see Dunn, *Christology,* 309, n. 45.

18. Sanders in Charlesworth, OTP 1:890 n. 13c.

19. Dunn, *Theology of Paul,* #14.

20. Ibid., 467, 488, 491.

21. See, e.g., J. Reumann, *Righteousness in the New Testament* (Philadelphia: Fortress, 1982), index under "forensic sense of righteousness/justification."

22. See particularly K. P. Donfried, "Justification and Last Judgment in Paul," ZNW 67 (1976): 90–110.

23. One of the principal emphases in Dunn, *Theology of Paul,* #18.

24. See, e.g., 1 Sam 16:7; 1 Kgs 8:39; Pss 44:21; 139:1–2, 23; Prov 15:11.

25. Dunn, *Theology of Paul,* 314–15, 409–10.

26. On Paul's metaphors of salvation, see ibid., 231–32, 328–33.

27. The integration of Ps 110:1 with Ps 8:7 is a common *feature* of early Christian apologetic; see again Dunn, *Christology,* 108–9.

28. See further J. D. G. Dunn, *Romans,* WBC 38A (Dallas: Word, 1988), 85, 88–89.

29. See the details in Dunn, *Romans,* WBC 38B, 573–74, 638, and more fully in TDNT 4:196–214 and IDBS 735–36.

30. Particularly again *Pss. Sol.* 3:4–16; 7:1–10; 8:27–40; 13:4–11; also Wis 11:9–10; 12:22; 16:9–10. Paul seems to have such passages in mind when he speaks of Israel's "impenitence" and "hardness of heart" in Rom 2:5.

31. E.g., Isa 1:2–9; 5:1–30; Jer 2:33–35; 5:1–9; Ezek 7:2–27; 24:3–14; Hos 5:11–12; 6.5; Amos 7:4; 8:4–14; Mic 2:1–4; 3:9–12 (ABD 2:80).

32. E. P. Sanders, *Paul and Palestinian Judaism: A Comparison of Patterns of Religion* (London: SCM, 1977).

33. P. Stuhlmacher in a paper given at the Durham-Tübingen Symposium in Tübingen (September 1999) ("'Christus Jesus ist hier, der gestorben ist, ja vielmehr, der auch auferweckt ist, dar zu Rechten Gottes ist und uns vertritt' [Röm 8.34]").

34. F. Avemarie, *Tora und Leben: Untersuchungen zur Heilsbedeutung der Tora in der frühen rabbinischen Literatur,* WUNT (Tübingen: Mohr-Siebeck, 1996); also "Erwählung und Vergeltung: Zur optionalen Struktur rabbinischen Soteriologie," NTS 45 (1999): 108–26. Stuhlmacher's lecture (n. 33 above) suggests that Avemarie's work provides the possibility of *rapprochement.* "Weisung zum Leben und Lebens-Weise" was H. Lichtenberger's summary of Avemarie's findings in "Das Tora-Verständis im Judentum zur Zeit des

Paulus," in *Paul and the Mosaic Law,* ed. J. D. G. Dunn (Tübingen: Mohr-Siebeck, 1996), 7–23.

35. See P. Stuhlmacher, *Paul's Letter to the Romans* (Louisville, Ky.: Westminster John Knox, 1994), 46; he also notes that "nowhere in his extant letters does [Paul] draw a systematically rounded picture of the final judgment."

36. I have in mind a conversation with Friedrich Avemarie in September 1999.

37. Dunn, *Theology of Paul,* #18.

38. Ibid., #19.

39. See further ibid., 482–87.

40. Ibid., 497–98.

41. J. M. Gundry Volf, *Paul and Perseverance: Staying in and Falling Away,* WUNT (Tübingen: Mohr-Siebeck, 1990).

42. Moltmann, *Coming of God,* 250–55. Cf. T. Eskola, *Theodicy and Predestination in Pauline Soteriology* (WUNT; Tübingen: Mohr-Siebeck, 1998). Contrast Stuhlmacher: "For Paul there was no salvation possible in the case of a believer who impugns or repudiates the gospel (Gal. 1:8; 2 Cor. 11:4, 13–15; Phil. 3:18f.)" (*Romans,* 47).

II

*Vatican I, Vatican II,
and Catholic Theology*

3. Why We Still Need Theologians

Michael Heher

"How can we imagine how the things we call ideas
live in the world, or how they change, or how they
perish, or how they can be renewed?"
Marilynne Robinson[1]

It is generally assumed that we are coming to something new, that
we are becoming a global village, a place that will be everywhere by
not being anywhere specific; everyone will belong but to none in particular. At this crossroads, it is feared, the individuality of language and
culture will be swept away by something, well, technological and
"amalgamatious," ushering in a world as exciting as an airport lounge.

It is assumed that in this upheaval religion and theology will
become either syncretic or defiant; in either case, they will provide the
last bulwark opposing the reigning cosmology of moral indeterminism.
Either people will be heedless of where they are headed or they will
know with an unyielding intuition. With neither doubt nor faith, it will
be a wasteland.

I certainly cannot tell you if this is in fact what will happen. I
have no crystal ball; nor have I received an eschatological vision. But
I do have a report. If this new reality is yet to be firmly established, it
has nonetheless encamped in my parish of nearly five thousand families. Almost everyone here comes from somewhere else, transplanted
from the Philippines, Mexico, Korea, Nicaragua, Vietnam, El
Salvador, Kenya, and other places, living with each other and with
Anglos like me, who ourselves came to this area little more than a generation ago when it was still all milk farms and orange groves. My

parishioners don't share a common language or culture; we lack even a common continent or hemisphere of birth.

Conversations on the patio after Sunday mass are punctuated with references to trips across the country and across oceans, to telephone calls about the health of relatives and e-mail about the welfare of friends and associates around the globe. In the last few years, Zita, a parishioner, has returned to Manila several times to take her turn with her brothers and sister in caring for her ailing mother—and she is not unusual. Our housekeeper, Lydia, will fly to Guadalajara to do the same for her father in a few weeks. Others commute to the places of birth or family ties for marriages, for baptisms and first communions of children, for Christmas or even a special birthday. For many, home is more than one place and our parish is as much an intersection as a neighborhood.

We are mostly middle class, modestly well educated, and we live together in Cypress and La Palma, mid-sized suburbs of Los Angeles. We constitute what Pico Iyer has termed "a unified field of multiculture,"[2] but what we really have in common is this: our faith and this moment.

Our life is tied to another, floating above us in the air space of Los Angeles International Airport. All day and most of the night, passengers come in on jumbo jets from cities like Sydney, Hong Kong, London, and Milan as well as New York, Montreal, and Mexico City. Between these large planes, a smaller but more numerous fleet shorthauls passengers to and from nearer places like San Francisco, Las Vegas, Seattle, and Phoenix. Along the beach at night, the Pacific behind me, I watch the planes descending in parallel lines toward the north and south runways, spaced at uniform sixty-second intervals. It is possible that people in one of the planes above will introduce themselves to me next Sunday as new parishioners, replacing those moving on to somewhere else.

As I was packing my bags at the end of my days in Rome, Gerry O'Collins stopped by, as he often did on Mondays after finishing his duties as our house confessor. I told him, with disappointment, about the assignment my bishop had given me, a post I thought entirely unsuited to the theologian I had worked so hard to become. Gerry smiled at me with his characteristic sideways grin and said, "Ah Mike, you can do theology anywhere."

His response was meant, of course, to be encouraging and I was grateful for it; yet it lodges in my mind nowadays as a kind of theological declaration. For every Aquinas in Paris and O'Collins in Rome, lecturing to university students, you find an Augustine in Hippo and Newman in London, thinking hard amid ecclesial responsibilities and the controversies of the day. Yes, strong and useful theology is done almost *anywhere:* Paul while commuting; Chrysostom in exile; Anselm inside the cloister; Bonhoeffer within a Nazi prison. Theologians exist in time and space; we do human work forged of particular circumstance. The following, which I am surprised to see involves more my thought as a theologian than my exertion as a pastor, describes my circumstances.

Theologians speak and sing, we write and sketch, we prod and plead, we warn and lead so others may discover and embrace faith's good news. News is, by definition, a revelation addressed to a particular person or people at a given moment. It is not diffuse or general. As reflection on divine revelation, theology is generally understood to be, in large part, an act of culture; we think out of what we know and experience, and even what we know and experience about the mystery of faith enters us through the lens of our own particular culture. T. S. Eliot defined culture "simply as that which makes life worth living."[3] It specifies value. Each culture is a mode of appreciation and a limit of vision: value *this* and not *that*, caress *this*, run from *that*.

Theologians would prefer to meet faith at the cafe down the street without a culture, but she keeps a vow of poverty: here below, faith's great redemptive passion lives only in human expression. Like a dying fire hissing for oxygen, she begs. Can someone lend her a trustworthy recipe for unleavened bread? Who can tell her the secret to making a good red wine? To tell her parables, she must borrow language. She searches for music so the subtle ardor of her psalms can be felt. Who will shape stones into an altar for her? Who can apply rich color to her raiment? When faith summons her disciples, they will want to celebrate, but who will teach them which steps to dance? Faith will give them tasks but who will organize them? And when they dispute, as they surely will, how will order be restored? Who will suggest with what gifts one disciple might please the other? Without a people's culture, faith cannot grasp or give what she loves.

Except for cultists and millennialists, believers are an optimistic and idealistic group by and large; they want to believe creation and recreation, the *this* of earth and the *utter* of heaven, can unite in love, both transcendent and human. Theologians are more measured; they cite disturbing evidence of incidents, past and present. The marriage of faith's church and culture's state has led to crusades, inquisitions, intolerance, pogroms, exile, and ethnic cleansing nearly as often as heartfelt worship, holy fellowship, and generous dedication to the poor. It is not, in itself, a solution.

The history of the separation of church and state is briefer but no less rocky, as I know from experience. Some parishioners tell me that I am wasting my time supporting our various ethnic communities. "Face it, Father, you can't stop assimilation," they say. "It's 'the melting pot' that's made us the prosperous country we are. Those Hispanic kids will soon be surfers and rock stars. They're *here,* don't you see, not back in the old country? The best thing you can do for these immigrants is to get them up to speed as quickly as possible. Get them interested in baseball. Sign them up to become citizens. Have classes in English for the parents and keep our school open, even if you have to subsidize the tuition, so their children will get an educational leg up on the way to high-paying jobs. You know, the next Bill Gates is probably one of those Asian kids."

These are our Anglos and second-generation Mexicans, speaking from their experience. They may be right, but I hope not. The kind of assimilation that held sway in America during the great period of European immigration, from about 1870 until the First World War, had as its goal to help immigrants get quickly rooted in a new land and culture. And it worked. The church built an impressive array of schools and universities. With better education, generation after generation, offspring grew up to take better jobs than their immigrant parents. The bricklayer's son became a lawyer; the nurse's daughter, a university researcher. Families moved from rented apartments in the cities to owning homes in the suburbs. Then they sent the next generations off to the university. It was so successful that unprecedented numbers of them found a very comfortable piece of the prized "good life."

But many of them or their children or grandchildren, in embarrassingly large numbers, stopped regularly practicing their faith. There were, of course, many reasons for this decline, individual and communal, not the least of which were the upheavals and reversals of history and personal destiny. There were also terrible errors made by religious leaders like myself. Nevertheless, when I meet these people at wedding receptions or after funerals, I notice common threads. They are a congenial and well-dressed lot, confident in their success and very much at home in the world. They are good people, law-abiding and frequently quite refined, folks you would gladly recommend as trustworthy.

They compliment me on the way I conducted the ceremony and quickly tell me how glad or disturbed they are about the changes in the church. But their interest is a lace curtain of nostalgia, a curiosity to pass the time over lunch with an amiable priest and little more. Their engagement is fleeting. I see them next as they crowd our church for Christmas, Easter, or the next wedding or funeral to which they are invited. Many have become so comfortable that they no longer feel much need for anything as dire as salvation. I think of them often. Why have they settled for so little?

The same is happening among the new immigrants from Asia and Latin America. At a recent gathering of priests, we fretted over, once again, the sad state of *Quinceañera*, a ceremony marking the entrance into adulthood for young women at fifteen years of age. The energy and effort (and money) go into gowns, rented limousines, and the party afterward, not into the religious importance of the young woman's consecration to God. We have tried various schemes over the years to turn that tide, expending copious amounts of pastoral energy. The common belief was that *Quinceañeras* were "teachable" cultural moments, opportunities to evangelize the young woman and her family and friends. One of the priests described with pride the many hours he spends catechizing each girl and the attendants in her party. With admirable zeal he has been doing it this way for twenty years. But when a hard-nosed compatriot asked him how many of these young people he sees at church with any kind of regularity, he paused for a moment and considered the question, then looked up and said, "None that I can think of."

When I first arrived at the parish I asked advice of the leaders of our various ethnic communities as well as colleagues in similar parishes: How might I best shepherd such a diverse flock? Almost all of them told me: *Don't impose your own cultural biases on others. Respect the integrity of each of the cultures in your care. Listen carefully to their elders and do what they tell you. According to their own*

traditions, let each determine their agenda, organization, and forms of
leadership. You can't possibly know what's best for them.

In our parish we have been trying this approach. With respectful
egalitarianism, we gather our parishioners into smaller cultural communities—a little Managua, a little Saigon, a little Jalisco, a little
Cebu, and so on—scaled-down versions of the national parishes of old.
We foster their cultural celebrations, their feasts, and their ties to the
homeland. As the proportional number of Anglos dwindles, they will
form, I suppose, their own community as well. Through support for
each culture we hope each person finds a home among us.

In this undertaking, I am to be a caring bystander, sensitive facil-
itator, one who listens, watches, participates, and eats whatever is put
before him. I am not supposed to give direction, but these contacts fill
me with ideas and questions and worries, many worries. And so I have
not been following orders.

I am not at all sure the mother of Jesus, for example, should have
to live such a chameleon's life. On the solemnity of the Immaculate
Conception, I lead her tall porcelain figure, encircled by flashing elec-
tric stars and fat cherubs of clay, into the parish hall and begin the
Nicaraguan festivities with the jubilant question, "Quien causa tante
alegría?" A few days later I am up before dawn celebrating mass with
the pregnant mestizo image of Guadalupe at my side; after mass she
too is carried in procession to the hall, where there is warm *chocolate*
and *pan dulce*. Sometimes, if they get up in time and don't get lost,
mariachi musicians serenade her. In May, the Filipinos begin our *Festa*
ni Maria with a lengthy procession in which everyone—very well
dressed and ordered according to rank in their elaborate and impon-
derable pecking order—has a flower to place at Our Lady's feet. When
I finally reach the sanctuary, I crown the flower-bedecked, dark-
skinned statue from Antipolo with the help of one of several women
dressed in long white gowns.

Always serene and welcoming in her wildly different garb, Mary
possesses all the characteristics of the peoples who make up our parish:
she's got almond, oval, and deep-set eyes; she's slender and mighty;
her nose can be narrow, curved, or broad; her brows, wide, modest, or
troubled; she kisses with thin lips, is beautifully defined by her strong
jaw; her skin is every human color. She incarnates the diverse qualities
we love.

It is not surprising that Mary remains so popular in this time of global disequilibrium; she offers the considerable comfort of a mother's breast to those who feel adrift outside the predictability of native culture and land. "Culture shock" is an intense vertigo, like that which accompanies grief. When my parents died, I felt bereft, a house that had lost its foundations, a boat suddenly without anchor. Events felt beyond my control, whether or not they were. I became convinced that if something happened, I was powerless to undo it. Or if nothing happened, I was abandoned to an unknown fate. At times of travel and often enough here in our parish, I experience similar, though muted, dislocations and see them grip my parishioners as well. I know why the Israelites could not sing the songs of Zion in Babylon: it is poverty, pure and simple. Say what you want about poverty as a virtue, it is painful. And, without assistance, the natural inclination is toward withdrawal. *This is OUR virgin, and no one else's.*

But there is an angle by which these multiple images are farcical. Each group gets a Madonna in its own image and likeness, right down to the footwear and the trim on the halo, with little regard to whether or not she has anything in common with the woman revealed in the Gospels and described in theological tradition. The ceremonies, conducted operatically and without irony, suggest a sentimentality both preconscious and intimate. What one believes is unimportant so long as it is strongly felt. It's an old story: what faith inspires becomes changed or diminished or lost in a culture's seductive pageantry; the flow continues to impress and we don't notice the losses. The strongly felt faith on these feasts is not deeply experienced. A peak unrelated to valleys, it fades because it offers and requires too little.

I am puzzled that so many of my confreres carry out these rites with such equanimity or enthusiasm. Do they not feel as lonely as I do the following week when so many pews are again empty? Those brought in from the byroads and the highways are destined to be guests inside the wedding banquet, not bystanders merely peering in the window.

The argument is sometimes made that these immigrants are simple people and that they, needs be, express their faith in these simple ways. I find this both patronizing and untrue of my parishioners. People said things like this, generations ago, of my Irish ancestors, who turned out, by and large, to be sufficiently able to endure education, complexity, and the irony that brings an end to innocence but the beginning of wisdom. Rather, the failure of preachers, teachers, and pastors to provide an adequate passage toward greater complexity may explain why so many abandoned a too-simple faith as they settled and became more sophisticated in a new land. When they no longer wished to live as exiles, whom did they meet on the new road? It is argued that their prosperity made them worldly and secular; I think that came, when it did, after loneliness.

When I gathered with the Korean parents at lunch sometime ago, there was, as always, much awkwardness. Since I know virtually no Korean, they offered words from their modest English vocabulary to jumpstart our conversation. When we had exhausted our cross-cultural chitchat (it did not take long) I began to ask questions of their children, all of whom are fluent in English. I pointed at the various dishes their parents had prepared for our meal and asked them the Korean name for each of them. Some dishes they knew right away and politely raised their hands, hoping to be called upon. In Korean whispers they consulted their parents for the names of the ones they didn't know. If I judged their expressions correctly, the parents were pleased with our interaction. This was just the kind of experience they had hoped their children would have when they decided to enroll their children here.

But I had come to this luncheon on a mission. While the parents were busy clearing the tables, I told the children that I wanted to persuade their parents to be more involved in their schoolwork and asked them what we could do to make them feel more at ease in the school. There was a long pause and then one of them told me, "My parents think school is very important. The *most* important. It comes before anything else. But everybody speaks English here at the school. And the homework too is in English. They are embarrassed."

"Are you embarrassed too?" I asked.

She looked to be sure her parents were not near and then turned back to me. "Sometimes. Some kids think I sound funny because I have an accent." She looked over her shoulder again and then said to me very quietly, "Yes, I wish my mother could bring cupcakes or pizza to my classroom, like the other mothers, you know, to show my classmates that I am just like everybody else. But I don't mind. I don't want my mother to be uneasy."

If we are not to lose (or should I say abandon?) another generation, we must minister in and across cultures better than we have, but how? Certainly not by turning our colorful celebrations into earnest lessons. If I am tired of pious melodrama, I am more tired of preachers who harangue the presumably unfaithful. How can one who does not sufficiently *know* the faith be unfaithful to it? Before me stand not the unfaithful but the hungry.

Seamus Heaney says that "the movement is from delight to wisdom not vice versa," so I do not wish to embargo what has become known as "popular religiosity." Let's keep the images, the ceremonies and the music; let the processions snake through our neighborhoods as before (though the *Quinceañera is,* to me, a different case). But whatever we keep we need to make, among other things, deep enough to move people from visiting to communion with God (or his mother), in other words, to an ordinary life of faith like they lost when they left their home village.

Because many speak English, I hear better and feel more intensely the complexity of the circumstances of the children of immigrants, most clearly evident in our Vietnamese. The Vietnamese elders came to California after defeat in war neither for opportunity nor the promise of a better life but primarily because they did not wish to die at the hands of the Communists. Many, therefore, would prefer as much separation as possible from their American environment, especially to protect their children from its leveling influence. Their children, and now grandchildren, are very respectful of these elders. They admire their sacrifices and appreciate what their parents and grandparents have undergone but, like their Filipino and Korean classmates, they don't particularly want to follow their example. They attend Vietnamese language classes and youth activities, but they tell me it is more for the pleasure of being in each other's company than for the richness of their heritage. They complain that all the older generation does is bemoan their unsophisticated Vietnamese grammar and lowly vocabulary—the elders do not respect their hard-earned English fluency. These young people are right; fluency with the alien is the very thing that worries their elders.

These young people live in two worlds at the same time, much like many children of other immigrants. At home, there's an intimate, sometimes claustrophobic, world of the family, functioning very much as it did in their homeland. But outside the home, the required conduct is different, sometimes opposite. They don't know how to respond when teachers expect them to speak up with their own opinions. Why are they to declare themselves here when at home they have been trained to acquiesce? The teacher requires them to look her in the eye to show respect; out of respect, the elders require them not to.

When they get the chance, the young go to mass in English, the language in which they feel more comfortable and which they share with their growing number of non-Vietnamese friends. Like other teens, they adopt the spurious identities and roles that attract and protect them as outsiders among cultures. Some withdraw into a tight world of close friends; these often appear to be living their parents' dream: they get excellent grades, play in the band, win scholarships, and hold down part-time jobs. But listen when they give the valedictory address at high school graduation: they have no foreign accent. Close your eyes and you can imagine them blond. Their parents and grandparents notice too and worry intensely about even these successful ones. Despite their furious custody, their children have become Americans. With their elders, I doubt that their passion and energy are best employed in becoming the next Bill Gates.

A couple of years ago, Burt, a respected doctor in our Filipino community came to see me to tell me that some of our Filipino parents wanted to meet with me to discuss a number of disturbing incidents by which they concluded that our "parish" treated "Filipino children" poorly, that is, with prejudice and unnecessary harshness. I had already known about most of the incidents he described, having heard the other side of the story from trusted staff and parishioners who had been both surprised and disturbed by the parents' response. I told Burt that I viewed the incidents individually and did not believe the parents' conclusion was warranted. I did not tell him what I also felt—a little offended that he had not come to the defense of our parish. Did he too believe the parish was headed in the wrong direction?

"Burt, if they want to meet with me to hear an apology, I can't do that. I am not sure there is anything that our parish has to apologize for."

"Father Mike," he said, "I am here, like I said, to ask you to meet with them."

"We can meet, of course we can meet. But isn't that going to make things worse with more hurt feelings and angry resentments?"

Burt reiterated what he had said earlier, with the same measure of politeness and courtesy, which was annoying since it suggested that he had not been listening to what I had been saying. "You are the pastor," he added. "You show your concern by listening to them. And I believe," he said, looking at me directly, "they will all be interested in what their pastor has to say to them."

I doubted his rosy assessment; our last state would surely be worse than the first, and yet, to send him back without a meeting date would only confirm their judgment on our parish. When we settled on a time and place I thought Burt would leave; instead, he began holding forth, in very general terms, about matters Filipino. The material was modestly interesting, but why was he telling it to me? Burt saw my confusion and repeated his points in different ways until he saw that I was beginning to grasp his lessons, lessons I still felt were not germane to the matter at hand. When he finally left, I remember distinctly thinking, Now what was that all about?

I realize now that he had been trying to teach me, to prep me for the upcoming gathering. It would have been presumptuous for a Filipino to say, "Father Mike, let me give you some advice." One did not lecture a pastor. So, to suggest other options, Burt used indirection. He hinted by his stories and repeated certain aphorisms, hoping to lodge them in my mind for later use. He was also giving me alternatives to my usual responses. When I would object to a point, he would hint that certain habits needed changing. "Father Mike, that is true, of course," he would say, "but listen to what I am saying. This is *also* true…." He said none of this directly and I did not then recognize his goal; I thought he just liked to hear himself talk.

But at the parent meeting what he had said came to mind, unbidden and very welcome. Listening to the parents, I heard things in the way Burt had implied I might more usefully hear them. When I spoke, I said what I had intended to say but the ideas came out *translated*, sounding native and new at the same time. When I slipped back into old ways, he would gently interrupt, "Father Mike, I'm not sure everyone understands what you're saying." He would then say what I had said—without any loss of clarity or feeling—but more helpfully. As he spoke heads nodded in comprehension. He did the same translating for the parents when one would say something that was needlessly offensive. "Surely, isn't the main point you wish to communicate to Father Mike…?" At various well-timed points he would summarize what had been said and focus the discussion with an astute question. This was not only good diplomacy and accomplished group facilitation; he was the nurturing midwife to the birth of a cross-cultural relationship.

With his help, hard things that needed to be said were not only sent but received, in both directions. The meeting ended quite well, miraculously to my mind, with all of us committed to specific improvements. I tried to thank Burt for all he had done, but he only deflected my praise. And he was right. Individual achievement was nothing in comparison to the bonds that tie us together as a community, another of his lessons. He was showing me still how to watch over these parishioners, how I might preside.

Why theologians? Isn't this work for experienced pastoral ministers and experts in the social sciences? Why am I so eager for the help of theologians? Because culture is provincial; he likes the local wines and cheeses; given the chance, he progresses from language to dialect to idiom; he sits at home in his easy chair with gratitude. The work of pastors and social scientists is primarily in response to the demands of the *here* and *now*. Like St. Paul, someone has to remind them that salvation does not come from works. Theologians invite them and the flock to look up from their duties from time to time. Faith's home is heaven. She retires from the comfortable, sleeps lightly, eyes heavy with wanderlust. *Your* world is not *the* world, she whispers, which insists on being more, yet again more, and different, sometimes intensely and mysteriously more foreign than you can grasp or tolerate at once. Though it frightens, it draws you still; it has precisely what you didn't know you needed.

Faith has wings and theologians, like scripture scholars, are able to *translate* faith across the specificities of time and place, to reveal her in a culture without thereby imprisoning her. More than others, theologians chart her heavenly course in human life. Gerry O'Collins, for example, has spent much of his energy digging in the *Sitz im Leben* (setting in life) of the early days of the church, carefully raking its texts and artifacts to uncover what these disciples meant when they proclaimed the resurrection of Jesus to others of their generation. The meaning is not easily apparent to us, though it is of utmost significance—which is why O'Collins also attuned himself to the varieties of our own *Sitz im Leben*. His books are widely read because they can be trusted to preserve the ancient truth in words we can hear and be touched by. In this way he gives us a vibrant and trustworthy language for meaning and salvation, for evil and loss, even radiant words for the irony of righteousness and holiness. His theology has given us honest utterance.

What theologians have been doing for centuries across time is needed to cross current cultures and generations, across temperaments and aspirations—without loss of passion or import. If we want living faith to remain as catholic as redemption itself, theologians must help us distinguish it from every culture's tendencies toward comfortable inertia. I am not sure how this can best be done—perhaps it is an art more than a skill—but I think we may look for guidance from John Henry Newman in the attributes he ascribed to all living ideas. A living faith in translation conserves its past and remains true to its roots (what Newman called "preservation of type"), but it also possesses the capability of a "natural and necessary development." As life and people change, our expressions of faith develop a growing complexity. This makes catholicity but the dawning side of orthodoxy: obedient faith finds continuity with its foundational principles through a critical assimilation of meaning in later times and circumstances. It adheres with ancient roots but blossoms by means of the local nutrients. The authenticity of such development is exactly its "chronic vigor."[4]

Doing this *across* cultures presents a more complex problem. Where is specificity outside of culture? Is it found in our humanity, which we share beyond the affiliations of race or culture? Yes, but who determines the "human" among the competing claims of cultures? What is taken for granted in one place—polygamy, democracy, a caste system—is offensive in another. What is taken for granted in one faith—monotheism, animism, afterlife—is heretical in another. Discovering the human is precisely what we want to know.

I am not sure what will help us cross our many wide differences, but not to try to cross them is to withdraw, to foreshorten our hope in Christ. I suspect an indirect path may be required. This is where art and literature may have something to teach us. They seem, by the very specificity of their beauty, to cross borders easily. I do not believe in the ancient gods of the Greeks, for example, but Homer's *Odyssey* is still my story. I know little of ancient Chinese culture, but Chuang-tzu's poems resound mightily in my soul. I am completely taken in by the world created in Gabriel García Marquez's *Love in the Time of*

Cholera. Why? They do not define how I live, yet they describe more than adequately my condition.

Reading Exodus, *Gilgamesh,* Romans, Virgil, Dante, Twain, and Tolstoy conveys very different worldviews but a common condition: the longings that press us forward boldly toward the unknown and our failures to reach it. Gustave Flaubert suggested in a letter: "the highest and most difficult achievement of Art is not to make us laugh or cry, nor to arouse our lust or rage, but to do what nature does—that is, to set us dreaming."[5] Can you imagine the dreaming to be unleashed in our young Vietnamese if a poet/theologian like Ephrem or Hildegard were with them? If a latter-day John of the Cross were to journey among Mexican immigrants? Would Anglos recover their spiritual hunger if among them were a Gerard Manley Hopkins? With their unique blend of east and west, consider the character of the dreams Filipinos would discover, inspired by a Bernard of their own. Theologians have often been poets; our circumstances may require that to be either he or she must be both. If we are not to withdraw into fundamentalism, we'll likely need poems and stories that keep before our eyes our common condition, our rich life in the poverty of longing.

I don't know what will save us from a graceless future, but I believe the work of theologians and poets will be essential. When you look back, you see that, from the Council of Jerusalem forward, all our theological controversies were also culture clashes. The way out, to the extent that we have found our way out, has always been in an expansion of meaning and value beyond cultural or linguistic specificity. The faith is ever more not diffuse but concentrated. And when we have not found a way out, we have most often mistaken appearances for reality, to have specified *this* as the *utter.* The history of theology, like poetry, is a history of failure, as Aquinas well knew when he viewed his works as so much straw. Our theological statements are human approximations as we await the coming of the kingdom.

Instead of a gray future, our parish life leads me to submit that our world might find renewal in an increased delight in beauty through the opportunities our new technologies give us and a deeper shock at how much hatred and ugliness are also among us. In other words, we must regain our passion and not turn away—which is our greatest and easiest temptation. We may find ourselves involved then in communication of a very rambunctious kind, again made both easier and less incarnate by our technological advances. Then, we might find the courage to discover together, and perhaps indirectly—in the very living of it—the kind of community we can have as a neighborhood and a planet, how we can hold each other. In the end, though, we shall be restless still, like Augustine and like faith herself, and thereby united on that dawning horizon to which theologians have again drawn our gaze.

Notes

1. Marilynne Robinson, *The Death of Adam: Essays on Modern Thought* (Boston: Houghton Mifflin, 1998), 126.

2. Pico Iyer, *Tropical Classical: Essays from Several Directions* (New York: Alfred A. Knopf, 1977), 123.

3. T. S. Eliot, *Christianity and Culture* (reprint, San Diego: Harcourt Brace Jovanovich,1988), 100.

4. John Henry Newman, *An Essay on the Development of Christian Doctrine* (London: Longmans, Green, 1885), 55–75, 171–206.

5. Gustave Flaubert, "Letter to Louise Colet" (26 August 1853) in Francis Steegmuller, ed. and trans., *The Letters of Gustave Flaubert 1830–1857* (Cambridge, Mass.: Harvard University Press, 1980), 198.

4. The Meaning of Conciliar Dogmas

Francis A. Sullivan, S.J.

In his book *The Case against Dogma,* Gerald O'Collins raised an interesting question about the possibility of determining the meaning of dogmas that have been defined by councils.[1] His answer was that "it becomes difficult, if not downright implausible, to speak of 'the original meaning' of dogmas when we turn to conciliar pronouncements."[2] He reasoned that if one asked bishops as they left a council about the meaning of the dogma they had just defined, "they would all offer some paraphrase, but they would not say the same thing. Identical items in the conciliar documents would evoke from them differing paraphrases, reactions and interpretations."[3] From this he concluded: "From the outset conciliar dogmas display an ineradicable ambiguity and plurality of meaning. Some alleged 'original meaning' simply cannot be caught in a net of words. As regards Church councils, therefore, I want to register sharp dissent from the view endorsed by Lonergan (a) that there once was a single meaning, and (b) that we can ascertain it."[4]

O'Collins explicitly included papal infallibility, defined by Vatican I, among conciliar dogmas whose "one original meaning" is impossible to ascertain, on the grounds that the bishops who took part in Vatican I offered differing interpretations of what they had defined. Now there is no doubt that, in the years following the interruption of the council, bishops who had taken part in the council gave varying interpretations of this dogma. Klaus Schatz, S.J., who has published a lengthy study of the views expressed by the German-speaking members of the council "minority," has distinguished three groups among the bishops whose interpretations of the conciliar dogma are known.[5] The first he describes as "maximalists," among whom the author of the most extreme interpretation was Henry Edward Manning, archbishop of Westminster. The "center group," which included most of the "majority" who had voted in favor of the definition, offered interpretations that for the most part consisted merely in explanations of the terms used in the definition. The third group consisted of bishops of the "minority," who had voted against the definition of papal infallibility up to the last working session of the council and had absented themselves from the final solemn session in the presence of the pope. Every one of these bishops subsequently accepted the dogma, but in doing so, many of them offered interpretations that laid stress on elements in the conciliar document that had been introduced during the last phase of the council to meet some of their objections. The stress they put on those elements and the conclusions they drew from them made their interpretations considerably different from those of the majority.

O'Collins, then, quite rightly pointed out the fact that bishops who have taken part in a council will give differing interpretations of the dogma they have helped to define. However, does this justify the conclusion that conciliar dogmas can have no one meaning, and that therefore it is impossible to determine, for instance, what the dogma of papal infallibility really means?

One deeply concerned about the meaning of the Vatican dogma was John Henry Newman. I think it would be interesting to see how he would have replied to the question O'Collins has raised. Newman certainly knew that differing interpretations were being given of the dogma by bishops who had taken part in the council. He was not only aware of, but also profoundly distressed by, the interpretation given by Archbishop Manning in a pastoral letter published in October 1870.[6] Several years after the council, Newman also came to know a work written by Bishop Joseph Fessler, which was translated into English by Newman's friend Ambrose St. John with the title *The True and False Infallibility of the Popes: A Controversial Reply to Dr. Schulte*.[7] Bishop Fessler had been the secretary-general of the Vatican Council and had voted in favor of the definition of papal infallibility. His book replied to the hostile critique of the Vatican dogmas published by Dr. Schulte, professor of Canon and German law at the University of Prague. Fessler's work was presented to Pope Pius IX, who had it translated into Italian and gave it his approval as a faithful interpretation of the conciliar decrees. Newman came to know Fessler's book at about the same time that William E. Gladstone, prime minister of England, published his work *The Vatican Decrees in their Bearing on Civil Allegiance: A Political Expostulation.*[8] The interpretation of the Vatican decrees that Gladstone put forth was largely based on that given by Archbishop Manning in his pastoral letter.

Newman, therefore, was well aware of the fact that very different interpretations were being given of the Vatican dogma of papal infallibility, even by bishops of the majority, such as Manning and Fessler, who had voted in favor of its definition. To illustrate the difference between such interpretations, I shall quote a passage from Manning's pastoral letter, and one from Fessler's work against Schulte. Manning wrote:

> In like manner, all censures, whether for heresy or with a note less than heresy, are doctrinal definitions in faith and morals, and are included in the words *in doctrina de fide vel moribus definienda.* In a word, the whole *magisterium* or doctrinal authority of the Pontiff as the supreme Doctor of all Christians, is included in this definition of his infallibility. And also all legislative or judicial acts, so far as they are inseparably connected with his doctrinal authority; as, for instance, all judgments, sentences, and decisions, which contain the motives of such acts as derived from faith and morals. Under this will come laws of discipline, canonisations of Saints, approbation of religious Orders, of devotions, and the like; all of which intrinsically contain the truths and principles of faith, morals, and piety.[9]

With Manning's description of the scope of papal infallibility, one can compare that given by Bishop Fessler:

> The definition asserts that the Roman Pontiff, by virtue of the divine assistance, possesses the Infallibility promised to the Church in his doctrinal teaching only when he speaks *ex cathedra....* By this expression, then, *ex cathedra*, the gift of God's divine grace conveying Infallibility in faith and morals to the Roman Pontiff...is closely restricted to the exercise of his office as *Pastor* and *Doctor* of all Christians. The Pope, as visible head of the whole Church, is:
>
> I. The Supreme Teacher of truth revealed by God.
> II. The Supreme Priest.
> III. The Supreme Legislator in ecclesiastical matters.
> IV. The Supreme Judge in ecclesiastical cases.

He has, however, the gift of Infallibility, according to the manifest sense of the words of the definition, only as *supreme teacher of truths necessary for salvation revealed by God,* not as supreme priest, not as supreme legislator in matters of discipline, not as supreme judge in ecclesiastical questions, not in respect of any other questions over which his highest governing power in the Church may otherwise extend.... Accordingly, it is only as regards definitions of the Pope upon faith and morals, that the Council defines, as a proposition revealed by God, that they possess infallible certainty by virtue of the unerring divine assistance promised to the Pope in St. Peter, *i.e.* as the successor of St. Peter.[10]

Here we have two vastly different interpretations of the scope of papal infallibility, both given by bishops who took part in the work of the council and who voted in favor of the definition. Obviously, John Henry Newman had not taken part in the council. Faced with such contrasting interpretations given by bishops who did take part in it, did he find himself at a loss to know what the definition really meant?

The fact is that as soon as Newman had seen the text of the definition he felt confident that he knew what it meant. And as soon as he had seen Archbishop Manning's pastoral, he was confident that Manning's interpretation was not justified by what the council had actually defined. While Newman refrained from public comment on the Vatican dogma for four years (until he wrote his reply to Gladstone),[11] his private correspondence during those years contains abundant evidence of his conviction about the meaning of the definition. The following are some of the comments he made during the year after the council was adjourned.

I saw the new Definition yesterday, and am pleased at its moderation, that is, if the doctrine in question is to be defined at all. The terms used are vague and comprehensive, and personally, I have no difficulty in admitting it.[12]

You must not fancy that any very stringent definition has passed—on the contrary it is very mild in its tenor, and has been acted on by the Pope at least for the last 300 years.[13]

I agree with you that the wording of the Dogma had nothing very difficult in it. It expresses what, as an opinion, I have ever held myself with a host of other Catholics.[14]

Shortly after Archbishop Manning's pastoral appeared, Newman received a letter from a prominent member of the Westminster diocese, Lady Simeon, who wrote of her distress over the interpretation of the Vatican dogma that her Archbishop had proposed to the faithful of his diocese. Newman's reply contained the following very frank remarks on that subject:

> The Archbishop only does what he has done all along—he ever has exaggerated things, and ever has acted towards individuals in a way which they felt to be unfeeling…. And now, as I think most cruelly, he is fearfully exaggerating what has been done at the Council. The Pope is not infallible in such things as you instance. I enclose a letter of my own Bishop, which I think will show you this…. Therefore, I say, confidently, you may dismiss all such exaggerations from your mind, though it is a cruel penance to know that the Bishop where you are, puts them forth. It is an enormous tyranny.[15]

At this point one must ask on what grounds Newman felt so confident that his own interpretation of the Vatican dogma was correct and that Archbishop Manning was "fearfully exaggerating" the scope of papal infallibility. We find the answer to that question in the extensive notes Newman had been compiling on the controversial issues regarding papal infallibility during the five years prior to the Vatican Council.[16] He began compiling them with a view to responding to the objections that Edward Pusey had raised against this doctrine in his *Eirenicon,* but decided against replying to Pusey since, as he put in his notes: "I should not be writing against Pusey, but making a case against Ward, and every one would say so."[17] William G. Ward, a layman and editor of *The Dublin Review,* had for some years been putting forth a most extreme notion of the scope of papal infallibility. His view greatly distressed Newman, but he chose not to publish his criticism of it, as he did not wish to engage in public controversy with a fellow Catholic. On the other hand, Newman continued to study the issue and compile notes for the use of a younger priest of the Oratory, Ignatius Ryder, who in 1867 did publish a work critical of Ward's extravagant views.

From these private notes we are well informed about the grounds on which Newman based his confidence that he knew what the Vatican dogma meant, and that Manning was "fearfully exaggerating" its sense. The notes make it clear that Newman knew, from his wide reading of the standard Catholic theological manuals, that his understanding of the scope of papal infallibility was solidly based on the doctrine being taught at the Roman College by Giovanni Perrone, S.J., and elsewhere by other reputable Catholic theologians. In other words, Newman felt confident that his interpretation was based on the authority of the *schola theologorum,* that is, on what the great majority of approved Catholic theologians had been teaching and writing concerning the scope of conciliar and papal infallibility prior to Vatican I. The following passage of his notes is typical in this regard.

> Thus I am led to a more accurate discussion of the *Principle*—the Church has whatever infallibility she claims—the point being this: *what* is the token or evidence of her claiming it, viz.
>
> (1) either her saying a proposition is de fide
>
> (2) or marking it with an anathema, taking anathema in a vague sense as including censures (or some censures) under it. (Do the minor censures come under the word "anathema" is a question to be decided.)
>
> If, however, other tests *besides* de fide or anathema are to be admitted, this must be done on the authority of the *Schola*; which determines both the proof that a pronouncement is infallible or not, *and also* what the meaning of the pronouncement is.[18]

In confirmation of his view, Newman cites a passage of Perrone's Latin text, and comments: "In the first clause, Fr. Perrone lays down the condition which I first stated, viz. that there should be a declaration that a doctrine is *de fide*—and in the second its equivalent, viz. the *anathema*."[19]

It was, then, on the basis of his careful reading of the work of such highly regarded Catholic theologians as Giovanni Perrone that when Newman saw the Vatican definition, he felt confident he knew what it meant, because he knew how Perrone and others had been explaining the key terms the council had used, such as "*ex cathedra*," "define," "doctrine of faith and morals." On this basis, he also knew that the Vatican definition did not confirm the views of those like Ward and Manning, according to whom the scope of papal infallibility was so inclusive that every proposition listed in the *Syllabus of Errors* would have been condemned with papal infallibility. (The *Syllabus of*

Errors was a collection of eighty propositions that had been proscribed by Pope Pius IX in various documents such as encyclicals and allocutions between 1846 and 1864. The gravity of each condemnation could be determined only from the wording of the proposition and its context in the original papal document).

In a letter written to Lady Simeon on November 1, 1870, he wrote: "From what I heard at Rome, while the matter was going on, from almost the first authority, they hoped to get a decree which would cover the Syllabus, and they *have not* got it. They have only got *authoritatively* pronounced *that* which Fr. Ryder maintained against Mr. Ward."[20] Newman's judgment was confirmed by Bishop Fessler, who wrote: "Dr. Schulte assumes that the Syllabus, with all its eighty propositions, is one of those Papal definitions of doctrine of which the Vatican Council speaks in its fourth session. This assumption he has failed to prove. Dr. Schulte assumes it to be so as a fact, while the truth of the matter is, that this *fact* is called in question by the gravest theologians."[21]

While Newman was confident that he knew what the definition meant, and what it did not mean, he recognized that some details of its meaning needed clarification. In his view, this would be accomplished by Catholic theologians, who would weigh the merits of differing opinions and eventually reach a consensus as to the exact meaning of the terms used. An interesting expression of Newman's thought about this is found in a letter he wrote to an Anglican friend, Sir William Cope, who was giving serious thought to becoming a Catholic but was troubled by a number of questions concerning the precise meaning of the Vatican dogma. Newman wrote: "All these questions are questions for the theological school—and theologians will as time goes on, settle the force of the wording of the dogma, just as the courts of law solve the meaning and bearing of Acts of Parliament."[22] In the preface of his *Letter to the Duke of Norfolk,* Newman made this a basic premise of his reply to Gladstone. Expressing his judgment that the prime minister had "committed himself to a representation of ecclesiastical documents which will not hold." He declared: "None but the *Schola Theologorum* is competent to determine the force of Papal and synodal utterances, and the exact interpretation of them is a work of time."[23]

Newman was likewise confident that the interpretation of the Vatican dogma that Archbishop Manning had put forth in his pastoral letter "would not hold." One reason for writing his reply to Gladstone was that it gave him the opportunity to explain and justify a moderate interpretation of the dogma of papal infallibility, and thus to counteract the chilling effect he knew Manning's interpretation was having on many people, both Catholic and Anglican. There can hardly be any doubt about the fact that Newman's moderate interpretation, and not Manning's extreme one, has gained the consensus of modern Catholic theologians.

As an example of an interpretation of the doctrine of papal infallibility that, I believe, enjoys the consensus of modern Catholic theologians, I would cite the paper Avery Dulles contributed to the USA Lutheran–Catholic dialogue on "Teaching Authority and Infallibility in the Church." His paper is entitled "Moderate Infallibilism."[24] For Dulles, what is distinctive of "moderate infallibilism" is that it "asserts that papal infallibility, being limited, is subject to inherent conditions which provide critical principles for assessing the force and meaning of allegedly infallible statements." He further explains:

> Moderate infallibilism is contrasted with a kind of infallibilism which is described as "traditional" or, in more pejorative terms, as "absolutistic," "extreme," "fundamentalistic," or "hypertrophic." More neutrally, this other infallibilism is one that questions or denies the limitations and conditions emphasized by moderate infallibilists. An infallibilism of this second type may be found in the pre-Vatican I writings of William G. Ward, H. E. Manning, and Louis Veuillot, and in the post-Vatican I writings of J. M. A. Vacant, J. C. Fenton, and I. Salaverri.[25]

Veuillot, like Ward, was a Catholic layman, publisher of *L'Univers,* in which he campaigned for the definition of an extreme version of papal infallibility. Vacant, Fenton, and Salaverri were Catholic theologians who taught that popes could teach with infallibility not only in solemn definitions *ex cathedra* but also in the ordinary magisterium that they exercised in such documents as papal encyclicals.[26] Their opinion was strongly and effectively refuted by a number of other Catholic theologians, and the resulting consensus was confirmed by Vatican II, which clearly distinguished between the pope's ordinary magisterium and his exercise of the "charism of infallibility." Here we have a good example of Newman's confidence that questions concerning the precise meaning of the definition would, as time went on, be resolved by the work of Catholic theologians.

For Dulles, "moderate infallibilism" is characterized by the emphasis it places on the limitations and conditions to which the exercise of papal infallibility is subject. What is particularly to be noted in his development of this thesis is that "moderate infallibilism" takes into account not only the limitations and conditions that were acknowledged by Vatican I but also others that follow from sound principles of Catholic theology but were not mentioned in the conciliar definition.

Among these latter limitations and conditions, the first described by Dulles is that a papal definition must be in agreement with scripture and tradition. From this it follows that "a valid definition could not be in violation of the true meaning of the Scripture or contrary to previous infallible pronouncements."[27] The second is that a papal definition must be in agreement with the present faith of the church. From this it follows that authentic papal definitions will find an echo in the faith of the church and will therefore evoke assent, at least eventually. Dulles concludes: "If in a given instance the assent of the Church were evidently not forthcoming, this could be interpreted as a signal that the pope had perhaps exceeded his competence and that some necessary condition for an infallible act had not been fulfilled."[28]

The third condition is agreement with the universal episcopate. While recognizing that the pope in his infallible teaching is not *juridically* dependent on the assent of the body of bishops for the validity of his acts, Dulles points out that since the assistance of the Holy Spirit is promised both to the pope and to the bishops as a corporate body, it seems clear that they would not fail to assent to any valid papal definition of the faith. He draws the conclusion: "If the bishops with moral unanimity held the contrary, one would be put on notice that the conditions for a genuinely infallible act on the part of the pope might not have been fulfilled."[29]

The fourth condition Dulles describes as "sufficient investigation." Here one deals with a question on which the majority and the minority at Vatican I were deeply divided. The majority agreed that prior to issuing a dogmatic definition, a pope is morally obliged to undertake a serious investigation of the sources of revelation and of the faith of the church. The minority insisted that such investigation was not merely obligatory but objectively necessary, and that it should be mentioned in the definition as one of the conditions for a valid papal definition. The majority adamantly refused to allow such a condition to be mentioned in the definition, for fear that it would allow an appeal to be made against a papal definition on the grounds that the investigation had been insufficient. The most they would concede was the addition of a sentence noting that

> the Roman Pontiffs, according as the conditions of the times and the circumstances dictated, sometimes by calling together ecumenical Councils or sounding out the mind of the Church throughout the world, sometimes through regional Councils, or sometimes by using other helps which divine Providence supplied, have defined as having to be held those matters which, with the help of God, they have found consonant with the Holy Scripture and with the apostolic Tradition.[30]

In the aftermath of Vatican I, many bishops of the minority found in this sentence the help they needed to be able to give their assent to the dogma, insisting that what the popes had done in the past they would continue to do, and indeed could not fail to do. Dulles expresses his agreement with them, saying: "Perhaps in our day, thanks to a greater appreciation of the many ways in which the Spirit instructs the Church, we should recognize that adequate investigation of the sources of revelation is a true condition for an infallible teaching. This view, proposed by the minority at Vatican I, could, I believe, be integrated into a moderate infallibilism."[31]

> Dulles goes on to note that this position will be resisted on the ground that it might give rise to doubts as to whether a given definition enjoys the prerogative of infallibility. For some, the very essence of infallibility consists in the *a priori* assurance that if certain easily verifiable conditions are fulfilled, the definition may be regarded as unquestionably true. This, however, is to my mind an oversimplification.... In the majority of cases, the validity of a definition will not be a problem for the Church at large. But if grave and widespread doubts were to arise among committed Christians who are orthodox on other points, the definition would have to be treated as dubious and hence as not canonically binding. The consequence does not appear to me to be disastrous for the whole concept of infallibility."[32]

In 1974, when Avery Dulles presented the paper I have been citing, he did not claim that his understanding of "moderate infallibilism" already enjoyed a consensus among Catholic theologians. Undoubtedly some still have reservations about elements of it. In my opinion, however, this is the notion of papal infallibility to which the majority of Catholic theologians working today would subscribe. Several factors have contributed to its broad acceptance. One is the discussion occasioned by Hans Küng's book *Infallible? An Inquiry.*[33] Many Catholic theologians who took part in that discussion rightly criticized Küng's portrayal of infallibility as maximimalist and responded by defending a moderate interpretation. Another is recent serious study of the positions defended by the bishops of the minority at Vatican I, leading many scholars to the conclusion that their concerns were legitimate ones and that the Vatican dogma needs to be reinterpreted and "re-received" by giving their concerns the weight they deserve in our understanding of papal infallibility. The third is the realization that a moderate notion of infallibility is the only one with a chance of not being rejected out of hand by our partners in ecumenical dialogue. On this point, the Catholic members of the USA Lutheran–Catholic dialogue had this to say:

> There are certain understandings of infallibility which Lutherans, according to their own principles would evidently have to reject. For example, if Catholics were to teach that any papal statement issued with certain juridical formalities, regardless of its basis in Scripture and tradition and its consonance with the faith of the Church, could be imposed as a matter of faith, Lutherans would legitimately protest that the primacy of the gospel was being imperiled. But, as we have sought to show, such an understanding of infallibility would be a misrepresentation of the Catholic doctrine.[34]

In support of their position, the Catholic members of the dialogue could have invoked the authority of no less influential a Catholic theologian than Joseph Ratzinger, who, in his work *Das neue Volk Gottes,* spoke of the grounds on which questions could be raised about the legitimacy of a papal statement even if it seemed to meet the formal requirements of a definitive decision. He wrote:

> Criticism of papal pronouncements will be possible and even nec-
> essary, to the degree that they lack support in Scripture and the
> Creed, that is, in the faith of the whole Church. When neither the
> consensus of the whole Church is had, nor clear evidence from the
> sources is available, a definitive decision is not possible. Were
> one formally to take place, while conditions for such an act were
> lacking, the question would have to be raised concerning its legit-
> imacy.[35]

The moderate interpretation of the dogma of papal infallibility
current among respected Catholic theologians bears out Newman's
prediction that "theologians will, as time goes on, settle the force of the
wording of the dogma, just as the courts of law solve the meaning and
bearing of Acts of Parliament."[36] New questions can still arise, however, which will require further clarification of the meaning of the
dogma. Just recently the secretary of the Congregation for the Doctrine
of the Faith, Archbishop Tarcisio Bertone, has raised a new question
regarding the kind of statement in which the pope does not define a
doctrine but simply declares that it has been taught infallibly by the
ordinary universal magisterium.[37] Archbishop Bertone asserts that "a
papal pronouncement of *confirmation* enjoys the same infallibility as
the teaching of the ordinary, universal magisterium, which includes the
Pope not as a mere Bishop but as the Head of the Episcopal College."
There is no doubt that the agreement of the pope comprises an indispensable element in the consensus of the whole episcopal college,
teaching a doctrine as definitively to be held, and therefore participates
in the infallibility of the ordinary universal magisterium. The new
question is whether a papal declaration that a doctrine has been taught
infallibly by the whole college is itself an infallible statement. Here, I
suggest, is another challenge to Catholic theologians to "settle the
force of the wording of the dogma."

Notes

1. Gerald O'Collins, S.J., *The Case against Dogma* (New York/Paramus/Toronto: Paulist Press, 1975).

2. Ibid., 77.

3. Ibid., 78.

4. Ibid., 78–79. He refers to Bernard Lonergan's *Method in Theology* (New York: Herder & Herder, 1972), 325f.

5. Klaus Schatz, S.J., *Kirchenbild und Päpstliche Unfehlbarkeit bei den Deutchsprachigen Minoritätsbishöffen auf dem I Vatikanum,* Miscellanea Historiae Pontificiae, 40 (Rome: Università Gregoriana Editrice, 1975).

6. Henry Edward Manning, *The Vatican Council and Its Definition: A Pastoral Letter to the Clergy* (London, 1870). This was subsequently published, together with two other pastoral letters by Manning, in one volume, with the title *Petri Privilegium* (London: Longmans, Green, 1871).

7. Joseph Fessler, *The True and False Infallibility of the Popes: A Controversial Reply to Dr. Schulte* (New York: Catholic Publication Society, 1875).

8. William E. Gladstone, *The Vatican Decrees in Their Bearing on Civil Allegiance: A Political Expostulation* (London, 1874); now available in *Newman and Gladstone: The Vatican Decrees,* ed. Alvan S. Ryan (Notre Dame: University of Notre Dame Press, 1962), 1–72.

9. Manning, *Vatican Council,* 89–90.

10. Fessler, *True and False Infallibility,* 55–58.

11. John Henry Newman, *A Letter Addressed to His Grace the Duke of Norfolk on Occasion of Mr. Gladstone's Recent Expostulation* (London: B. M. Pickering, 1875); also available in *Newman and Gladstone,* ed. Ryan, 73–228.

12. Charles S. Dessain et al., eds., *The Letters and Diaries of John Henry Newman* (London/New York: Thomas Nelson, 1961–1984), 25:164.

13. Ibid., 25:170.

14. Ibid., 25:174–5.

15. Ibid., 24:230. The "letter of our own Bishop" to which Newman refers is probably that of Bishop Ullathorne of Birmingham, published in the *Birmingham Daily Post* of November 14, 1870.

16. These notes have been published by J. Derek Holmes in *The Theological Papers of John Henry Newman on Biblical Inspiration and on Infallibility* (Oxford: Clarendon Press, 1979).

17. *Theological Papers,* 112.

18. Ibid., 147.

19. Ibid., 105–6.

20. *Letters and Diaries,* 25:224.

21. Fessler, *True and False Infallibility*, 107.

22. *Letters and Diaries*, 25:447.

23. *Newman and Gladstone*, ed. Ryan, 76.

24. Avery Dulles, S.J., "Moderate Infallibilism," in *Teaching Authority and Infallibility in the Church*, ed. Paul C. Empie, T. Austin Murphy, and Joseph A. Burgess, Lutherans and Catholics in Dialogue 6 (Minneapolis: Augsburg Publishing House, 1980), 81–100.

25. Ibid., 82.

26. J. M. A. Vacant: *Le Magistère ordinaire de l'Eglise et ses organes* (Paris: Delhomme et Briquet, 1887); J. C. Fenton: "Infallibility in the Encyclicals," *American Eccleciastical Review* 128 (1953): 177–98; I. Salaverri, "Valor de las Enciclicas a la luz de la 'Humani Generis,'" *Miscelánea comillas* 17 (1951): 135–72.

27. Dulles, "Moderate Infallibilism," 87.

28. Ibid., 89.

29. Ibid.

30. Vatican I, *Pastor Aeternus* cap. 4; DS 3069.

31. Dulles, "Moderate Infallibilism," 91.

32. Ibid., 91–92.

33. Hans Küng, *Infallible? An Inquiry*, trans. Edward Quinn (Garden City, N.Y.: Doubleday, 1971).

34. *Teaching Authority*, ed. Empie et al., 57.

35. Joseph Ratzinger, *Das neue Volk Gottes: Entwürfe zur Ekklesiologie* (Düsseldorf: Patmos-Verlag, 1969), 144.

36. *Letters and Diaries*, 25:447.

37. *L'Osservatore Romano*, Dec. 20, 1996, pp. 1, 5; English ed., Jan. 29, 1997, pp. 6–7. See Francis A. Sullivan, S.J., "Recent Theological Observations on Magisterial Documents and Public Dissent," *Theological Studies* 58 (1997): 509–15.

5. Bishop Paul-Joseph Schmitt and Vatican II: Jesus Christ, the Fullness of Revelation[1]

Carmen Aparicio

Father Gerald O'Collins has dedicated much research and many years of teaching to fundamental theology. In his *Retrieving Fundamental Theology,* he explains what the Dogmatic Constitution on Divine Revelation, *Dei Verbum,* has meant for fundamental theology, that area of theology centered on revelation, its transmission, and its credibility.[2] He picks out elements from this constitution of Vatican II that show some notable changes in the way of understanding revelation since Vatican I. This change of perspective has opened new horizons for theology and, in particular, for fundamental theology.

Dei Verbum is a "Christ-centered" document, emphasizing the culmination of God's self-communication in the death and resurrection of Christ. By retrieving the centrality of Christ, *Dei Verbum* can appreciate the words and deeds that give revelation its sacramental character. That also entails recovering a sense of the historical economy of salvation: God has spoken in many ways through the prophets, and then in the fullness of time by means of his Son (Heb 1:1–2). *Dei Verbum* understands revelation to be self-revelation: God reveals himself and enters into communion with men and women. The divine self-manifestation aims at establishing a relation with each and every human being.

As we all know, the original document on revelation, *De fontibus revelationis,* did not get a warm reception by the majority of bishops at the council when it was discussed in November 1962. Its outlook and language were still far from what *Dei Verbum* would say in 1965.

Father O'Collins, in his work cited above, presents the valuable contribution made by Father Piet Smulders in bringing about this change of perspective. Besides having his impact on chapter 4 of *Dei Verbum*, a 1964 draft by Smulders helped shape chapter 1 of *Dei Verbum*. In that draft he presented revelation as God's gratuitous self-communication in Christ to human beings, and so introduced "self-communication" into the language of church councils.[3] Without playing down the input from Smulders, we should also note how right from the first session of the council some bishops intervened along the same lines in proposing changes in the presentation of divine revelation. One of them was Bishop Schmitt, who, among other things, asked for an emphasis on the centrality of Christ in the whole economy of divine revelation.

Bishop Schmitt, in one of a series of articles written for his diocese and published in the diocesan bulletin *Église de Metz*, mentioned how he felt when he discovered in the final text of *Dei Verbum* themes he had developed in his speech to the council on November 17, 1962, which had at that time provoked considerable criticism.[4] He cited a paragraph from that speech, which explained what it means to say that revelation culminates in Christ:

> The revelation of God culminates in Jesus Christ. He is the very Word of God addressed to human beings. He is the integral and definitive revelation of God. In Christ God exhausts his revelation. The words of Jesus and the apostles cannot be separated from the person and the life of Jesus Christ. They are only a prophetic commentary on the mystery of his life, death, resurrection and ascension. Those events are not merely the occasion of revelation; they constitute its proper object. (ÉGM III [1966]: 4)[5]

Why this insistence on underlining that Christ is revelation? We will see from what he contributed to the council's documents and from what he wrote in his diocesan bulletin the reasons for this constant insistence on the part of Bishop Schmitt. He himself would say that one of the principal fruits of the council was the deepening of our faith in Christ and its "only foundation," which is "revelation" (ÉGM III [1966]: 4).

THE PREPARATION FOR THE COUNCIL

To appreciate how Bishop Schmitt saw and experienced the council, we must first see how he reacted to the consultations that preceded it. In the volumes containing the responses sent to the Preparatory Commission, presided over by Cardinal Tardini, we find two responses from Bishop Schmitt. His first response, dated October 2, 1959,[6] does not stress the need to "return" to Christ with as much clarity as he would later show. But we do find here themes that would recur in his writings of those years as well as in his comments on the draft documents presented to the council. He recalled the concerns of his time and wanted the church to take into account the new world situation and provide valid and significant responses. He stressed three themes that bring us to the heart of the renewal proposed by the council: the supernatural end that awaits individuals and society, when everything will be recapitulated in Christ; the divine origin of the church in its mystery of faithful communion with the Trinity; and the mission of all the laity.

The second document from Bishop Schmitt during the preparatory stage of the council is a letter, which is undated and unexplained. It appears to respond to the Commission of the Council, after the draft documents prepared for discussion at the council had become known.[7] In it he proposed a new, Christ-centered document that would introduce the others and present "contemporary questions about the mystery of the Word Incarnate, about the function of Christ as Redeemer, and about the priesthood and grace of our Head." He also suggested presenting in outline a solemn profession of faith in Christ, so that the faithful could acknowledge him as the beginning and end of their redemption; the source and norm of all Christian renewal; the Way, the Truth, and the Life who directs everything and everyone; the One who illuminates and gives life to all.

As such, the proposal for a new, Christocentric document was not accepted. Nevertheless, this letter shows how Bishop Schmitt stressed the recovery of Christ's centrality, without which any renewal for the church and the life of Christians would remain superficial. The letter went on to suggest that all the council's documents, in their dogmatic and pastoral aspects, should consistently present our permanent relation with Christ, the Word Incarnate and Redeemer of all people. The letter ended by proposing that the Dogmatic Constitution *De fontibus revelationis* clearly states that divine revelation is essentially Christian, because everything tends toward Christ and comes from Christ.

Along with its significant emphasis on the centrality of Christ, this letter used a term that would frequently recur when the council's documents address the relationship between Christ and the church: "illuminate." The church must pass on to the whole world the light received from Christ. The mission of the church is to bring to all people the light of Christ.

The concerns expressed before the council opened in 1962 would take shape in the contributions that Bishop Schmitt would make to different documents during the four sessions of the council. He saw the fundamental consequences that Christ's centrality has for the life of the church and all Christians. Any fresh spiritual impulses depend on our relationship with Christ as Redeemer.

Beyond doubt, Bishop Schmitt was well informed about the theological renewal of his time. Although he did not mention many authors by name, his language and way of presenting his themes echo some of the most important works from those years.[8] Theologians of that time strove to recover the centrality of Christ and hence the need to relate all theological truths to him. This centrality of Christ comes from his being both the Revealer (or Word of God) and the definitive Revelation of God. Revelation, which is both intellectual and real, is communicated through all the words and actions of the whole Christ, who reveals his total person. He is the Truth, the eternal Truth, the only Truth. Hence, in Christ everything has already been revealed. Therefore, our incomplete human doctrines regarding revelation have meaning only in connection with the total truth of Christ.

Only from this point of view can we speak of the authentic development of dogma, a theme still in vogue after debates provoked by the modernist crisis. In taking up this issue, some authors wanted to interpret matters quite concretely. A very important article by Henri de Lubac, "Le problème du développement du dogme," took the object of revelation to be God's total action and presence to us in Christ.[9] Christ is the Revealer, the one who definitively shows us God, in a revelation of the divine mystery that is not only intellectual but also effectively real. Along the same lines Taymans D'Eypernon, in "Le progrès du dogme," identified revelation with Christ.[10] This same article contained a highly significant expression taken up by other theologians and by the pastoral writings of Bishop Schmitt: "In Christ, in effect, we attain the mystery of God and the mystery of man."[11]

Revelation reaches its goal when communion arises between God and human beings. In communicating himself, God also communicates what we become. This encounter leads to the commitment of faith, which entails meeting the Revealer and Revelation, believing Christ, and doing so in the church. In the church, with the help of the Holy Spirit, we receive the light to meet Christ, believe in him, and believe him. Thus there is a unity in the object of faith: Christ in the church. According to D'Eypernon, this is the immanent conscience of faith: believers know that they possess all in Christ, that Christ is all in all, and that Christ is the church.[12]

Let us recall here that God wants all people to be saved. Redemption is *the* gift God offers us through his Son, who is the fullness of salvation and the only source of eternal salvation for all men and women. Revelation and redemption cannot be separated.

This revelatory and redemptive centrality of Christ has its essentially trinitarian aspect. The definitive revelation of God in Christ brings us to the mystery of the Trinity, the specifically Christian God. The incarnation of the Word of God communicates the Trinity. In this connection Émile Mersch had proposed an interesting change in perspective that we find in Bishop Schmitt's writings: Christians know God because they know the Trinity, and not the contrary.[13]

The Council and the Pastoral Writings of Bishop Schmitt

Before studying Bishop Schmitt's concrete observations regarding the draft documents presented on the council floor, let us see how he communicated and lived this great ecclesial event in his own diocese.[14] A man of the church and for the church, he wanted to keep his diocese constantly and correctly informed about what was happening at the council. He knew very well that the renewal being asked of the church would require the authentic conversion of each person and every ecclesial group.

The leitmotif of his writings was the church, as it sees itself in Christ and allows itself to be guided, renewed, and always faithful to its founder and the mission it has received. The church has been founded to continue, under the light of the Holy Spirit, the mission of Christ to save all people. The church has received a marvelous treasure—the deposit of faith—which must be transmitted faithfully and at the same time with ever-deeper understanding. This challenge becomes more urgent in every era of profound change like the twentieth century.

For Bishop Schmitt, the council was a moment of grace in which the church wanted to respond to the question, What do you have to say about yourself? United in council, the church had to ask itself what it had done with the deposit of faith. To answer these and other questions, it needed to return to its foundation and mission in Christ, for only in Christ and from Christ would conversion be possible. Thus, renewal demanded looking at oneself and at the world, for which the church was the sign of salvation.

To return to the essence of the church, the council had to be Christ-centered. The church as a whole and all Christians in particular had to be convinced that their riches were found only in Christ. Here they could find the possibility of renewal, of conversion, of a recovered unity, and of being the sign of salvation for humanity and the world of today. Bishop Schmitt knew the church to be the Body of Christ, or the "total Christ," which works for salvation and is the actual form of the covenant until the end of the world. Yet the church is made up of men and women who need continual renewal and must return to Christ, the high priest and universal mediator between God and human beings. Bishop Schmitt wrote:

> Promised since the dawn of humanity and prepared for by patriarchs and prophets, Jesus, the awaited Messiah, appeared in the fullness of time.
>
> He is the only true prophet; he can speak of God to human beings and know fully what he is talking about.
>
> He is the living Good News. He lets us know the truth about God and the truth about human beings; he shows us God's loving plans for creation.
>
> He is the only true priest, the authorized Mediator between God and humanity. (ÉGM 18 [1963]: 2–3)

The church must proclaim Christ, the fullness of revelation; this obligation applies to all members of the church, for all are prophets and missionaries.

Another characteristic of the council stressed by Bishop Schmitt was the church's pastoral character. It must proclaim to all people today the truths that are always old and always new. This requires faithfulness and renewal, if the church is to be the sign of light and salvation to the world. The reason for the church's existence is its mission, and it will carry out its mission to the extent that it remains faithful to Christ.

The church must continue the mission of Christ by making known the love of the Father, reconciling everything in the Father, and proclaiming the good news of salvation. Bishop Schmitt wrote:

> The Church is Christ continued and propagated on earth down through the ages, under the dynamism of the Spirit. Her mission is to gather in Christ all human beings, the totality of each person, all civilizations, all technologies and all values. Nothing human should be foreign to her! Everything that makes up human beings and everything that human beings do belongs to Christ and should be incorporated in the Church. The Church needs all those values to be fully herself. For this Church, we are all responsible. (Pastoral letter for Lent, *L'Église de Metz à l'heure du Concile,* February 16, 1962, p. 33)

The church, Bishop Schmitt explained, "does not merely continue the work of Christ; she is Jesus Christ present today to humanity" (ÉGM 18 [1963]: 2). Hence the Christians must live rooted in Christ, because they are Christ living today. That is why for Christians there can never be any division between the things of God and the things of this world.[15] They are responsible for the earthly city without ceasing to be Christians. In the unity of Christian life, one assumes the double vocation of anticipating the kingdom and building the human city (cf. ÉGM 18 [1963]).

The church, in virtue of its mission, needs to look at the world: a world of new social situations presenting great consequences for forms of life and traditional values and bringing new questions to the human conscience, a world marked by atheism and unbelief. For Bishop Schmitt, the fact that Vatican II could be called in a world of atheism should not go unnoticed. He hoped that the council might offer principles for a Christian anthropology on which to build a new soteriology and ecclesiology (ÉGM 1 [1964]: 6; also 107 [1966]: 1–3). At the same time, the phenomenon of atheism could not leave him indifferent. Why in countries with a Christian tradition did so many men and women fail to believe? What stopped the church from being relevant today? Bishop Schmitt not only raised these and similar questions but also tried to find answers by analyzing causes and looking for solutions. He emphasized the general need for conversion and the call to dialogue. The church must enter into dialogue with a world in change, be questioned by it, and be close to people now living in unknown situations with new problems of conscience. Only then can the church give light to those who seek it. The church must rise out of its inertia and comfortable situation, leave behind the routine of its members, and abandon fear. Looking at the world with love, the church should recognize the unique value of every person. The church cannot forget its call to be the light of the world and ferment of the masses, proclaiming to everyone the message of salvation (ÉGM 1 [1964]: 5–9).

After 1965, Bishop Schmitt continued writing about the council and stressing the need to actualize the renewal that had begun. To do this one must understand its spirit and study its documents. Thus, in 1966 he devoted two series of articles to understanding Vatican II. In the first series, "A Council for Our Time," he presented some of the issues that had challenged the council and characterized its work.[16] Far from merely listing themes, he pointed out what each meant for the council and how each contributed to presenting the world with the new face of the church.

He began with those who participated in the council; they made Vatican II the first real "catholic" council. The presence of bishops of all races, cultures, languages, and civilizations "put to the Church of today the great questions of humanity in our times" (ÉGM 101 [1966]: 2). The church, "a small remnant" in a world more and more distant from God, has given testimony of its catholicity, which is not limited to mere geographic extension but is essentially "the power to embrace and set a value on everything" (ibid., 3). But what made the church's catholicity possible and fruitful was above all the fraternity lived out by the bishops at the council.

Along with the council fathers, a group of "Observers" shared in the council. The presence of members of other Christian churches was highly valued and appreciated; they offered a real sign of the way toward the unity of all those "who invoke the Triune God and confess Jesus as

Lord and Savior" (*Unitatis Redintegratio* 1). Their presence suggested that major obstacles to this unity had been overcome. They were a sign of a new mentality, for which "one can no longer raise a question in the Church without asking oneself: 'What do other Christians think? What does this mean for them?'" (ÉGM 102 [1966]: 2). The Observers provided help toward greater consciousness of the Catholic tradition and the profound demands of Catholic faith, to such a point that "the theology of the Church will be truly catholic only in the measure in which it integrates, in their right place, aspects of revelation which other Christian communities have particularly valued" (ibid.). Ecumenism cannot be reduced to extraordinary moments or to something that concerns just a few. On the contrary, Bishop Schmitt insisted, it involves the entire church and all of the church's life. One sees signs of the road already taken, but one must continue to walk along it.

The other three articles from Bishop Schmitt refer to characteristics of our time that had an impact on the development of the council. Vatican II took place at a time when the church had been happily separated from political power and had become more aware of its missionary role. The church wanted to renounce both the tendency toward power and the temptation to evade the world. The church wanted to look at the world's values with the eyes of the gospel, dealing with the big problems that concern governments and afflict humanity—war, hunger, threats to human dignity, social injustice, and religious oppression. The church could not and cannot forget that its mission demands that it too must say its word here (cf. ÉGM 2 [1962]). The church does not ask governments for privileges, but asks "the freedom to believe and preach her faith, the liberty to love her God and serve him, the liberty to bring to human beings her message of life" (*Message of the Council to Those Who Govern,* cited in ÉGM 103 [1966]: 5).

Bishop Schmitt responded to those who said that the declaration on religious liberty would cause a theological revolution: such liberty already belongs to the patrimony of the church. He wrote:

> The mission of the Church is to challenge all people and to announce their Savior. But conversion to Jesus Christ can only be the deed of a free person; it is the personal response of someone to the appeal of a personal God, the acceptance of the totality of a liberation which concerns the whole human being. One cannot force people to encounter the living God, by imposing from the

outside the most interior event that there is. It is a question of
respect with regard to God. It is a question of respect with regard
to human beings. (ÉGM 103 [1966]: 5)

The church cannot cease to proclaim the gospel, but the church
cannot impose it. The church asks for religious liberty for its members,
and at the same time the church commits itself to respect that liberty in
all human beings. Above everything else, this right must be safe-
guarded and all means taken so that everyone can find the truth without any kind of obstacle being put in the way.

By renouncing all temporal power, the church is aware that its
only wealth is the gospel, knowing that "in the life of the Church as in
that of Christ, actions explain words, and often deeds come before dec-
larations. They engage the Church in an irreversible evolution" (ÉGM
103 [1966]: 6). We will be judged not by our intentions but by our
actions.

Apropos of the world interest created by the council, Bishop
Schmitt inquires about the reasons for that. No single cause, he suggested, sparked the interest, but among the possible reasons, we should
note that the council allowed itself to be touched by the world and
chose the most profound and contemporary questions posed by the
world. In particular, it took seriously the power of modern means of
communication. The council gave public opinion the place it deserves
and tried to do everything necessary to facilitate good information and
communication (cf. ÉGM 105 [1966]).

Our age, Bishop Schmitt recognized, is marked by atheism,
which is a mutilation because it deprives persons of the transcendent
dimension in their relationship to God. It is also an answer to and a
rejection of caricatures of God, false images of a God far from humanity and the world. It also rejects any flight from temporal responsibilities. But in reality, authentic faith is not being denied. Faced with the
phenomenon of atheism and the reductionism of many Christians,
Bishop Schmitt asked: How can we love an inhuman God or adore a
God who is too human? (cf. ÉGM 107 [1966]: 1–3).

The God of the philosophers alone is not in position to reply to the
questions of contemporary human beings. They are hungry, more
or less consciously, for the God who is perceptible to the heart as
much as to reason, for the God who walks with them on human

roads, for the living God revealed in Jesus Christ. No faith beyond
the faith in God made man can reply totally to what human beings
of the twentieth century expect. (ÉGM 107 [1966]: 2)

This is what the church wants to propose to all people: Christ. To
resolve the problem of atheism, the church invites Christians to dialogue, commitment, and collaboration, but above all to be witnesses
with their lives. As Bishop Schmitt had already said on many other
occasions, only those who have encountered Christ will be authentic
witnesses. Hence the remedy for atheism:

> It is not necessary then to seek another remedy for atheism
> beyond profound renewal in the teaching of the Church and the
> witness given by Christians. Thus every one will see that faith in
> God, so far from alienating human beings, frees them and makes
> them achieve their full human stature. How would a Christian
> have the right to neglect the earthly tasks that the God-man him-
> self did not disdain? That is why the Pastoral Constitution [on the
> *Church in the Modern World*] invites believers and non-believers
> "to work together in building up this world in which they live
> together." Thus it will be seen in practice that God and human
> beings are not rivals and that what agrees with one does not rob
> the other. (ÉGM 107 [1966]: 3)

The second series of articles, on "The Spirit of Vatican II," was
written with the purpose of promoting the spirit of the council. Bishop
Schmitt was convinced that the most important results had been not
decisions but changes in mentality and spiritual renewal. In these articles, he presented the spirit that guided the attitudes and reflections of
the council, the profound causes that made these changes possible.[17]

The first thing, he noted, is the spirit of faith. Without the deepening faith that guided the work of the council, nothing would have
been possible. Renewal would have been simply "a change of facade."
The council needed to face the problems, hopes, and anxieties of
people today. This led the council to a first conclusion: faith is not a
batch of abstract truths. The council considered the quality of our faith,
its motivations, expressions, and content; it faced the Word and called
attention to the place of the Word in Christian life.

The church knows well that it is one thing to accommodate the
deposit of faith and another to adapt its formulations. In examining

itself and its mission in the world, the church has rediscovered that it must be continuously at the service of the Word. For this reason, in order to understand Vatican II, it is necessary "to grasp faith's essential relationship to the God of revelation, which is inseparably biblical and historical, and finally to the God of the incarnation, Jesus the Messiah and Son of the living God" (ÉGM 109 [1965]: 5).

Faith seeks a greater understanding of revelation. That is why the council's work developed by accepting St. Anselm's classical definition of theology: *fides quaerens intellectum*. The council never stopped searching. Recalling the words Pope John XXIII spoke at its opening (October 11, 1962), Bishop Schmitt said that in this search the church united in council did not wish—and could not wish—to change its foundations in its creed and constitution. It simply wanted to understand better the treasure of revelation and at the same time express it better for people today. In this work, the collaboration between theologians and bishops was of great importance: those themes of theological renewal that had advanced the most were those the council also advanced.

Obviously, the spirit of inquiry is not free of ambiguities, but, as Bishop Schmitt argued, that is no excuse for renouncing it. One has to find a balance, which is necessary for the church to be faithful in its mission of conserving faithfully the deposit of faith and progressing in its understanding of faith. Both elements are required, in order to be faithful to the gift of revelation.

BISHOP SCHMITT'S SPECIFIC CONTRIBUTIONS TO THE COUNCIL DOCUMENTS

Bishop Schmitt did not speak very often on the council floor, but in all his speeches we find elements that help us understand his fundamental presupposition, which in a certain way guided them all: the desire to recover the centrality of Christ.

Because of its theme, the first of his interventions also interests us most: the observations he made during the first session of the council on the draft document *De fontibus revelationis*. The council debated and severely criticized this draft for its academic style, its lack of pastoral and ecumenical sensibility, and so forth. Even before the council discussions had begun, alternative drafts were in circulation. One of these, supported by practically all the Central European bishops' conferences—*De Revelatione Dei et Hominis in Iesu Christo,* prepared principally by Karl Rahner and Joseph Ratzinger, and in which Bishop Schmitt also collaborated[18]—offered a vision of a Christ-centered revelation. Interestingly, this draft showed a strong similarity to *Gaudium et Spes,* both in its themes and in its way of presenting matters.

In a speech during the Twenty-First General Congregation, Bishop Schmitt referred to the draft in general rather than to any specific point in it.[19] He proposed guiding principles for a new draft. It should consist of an introduction, followed by three parts: all revelation consists in the person of Christ, who is the very revelation of God; Christian revelation is the good news; this good news responds admirably to the needs of today's apostolates. Let us look at each point in turn.

Introduction

Guided by a pastoral interest and a missionary consciousness, Bishop Schmitt affirmed that new developments in biblical theology, patristics, and catechesis highlight some aspects of revelation and faith in a way distinct from their treatment by earlier councils, particularly Trent and Vatican I, even though what these councils said continues to be valid. He did not offer an analysis of the situation, as Vatican II would do in the introduction to *Gaudium et Spes*, but he simply affirmed the fact. Faced with new changes, Vatican II should not adopt a defensive posture but rather "proclaim a genuine, very open and very fundamental understanding of the Gospel." To achieve this, Bishop Schmitt made three proposals that, according to his judgment, ought to comprise the main thread of the new draft.

All Revelation Consists in the Person of Christ, Who Is the Very Revelation of God

The first proposal called for a return to Christ, for he is the Revealer and the Revelation of the Father. He is the fullness of revelation in the sense that "God's intention from eternity had Christ as its goal." God has revealed himself from the time of creation and has been present throughout the history of the chosen people; he has made a covenant with his people and has revealed himself at the fullness of revelation in Christ; Jesus Christ is the fullness of revelation, because "he is the very Word of God to men and women; he is God's revelation." Christ has taught us supernatural truths, but in that all his humanity, all his life, and above all his death and resurrection are divine revelation. In Christ we can know what God wants from creation, from humanity, and from history: "In the person of Christ, God has been manifested in history: that is to say, the revelation that God is for human beings and that human beings are in the presence of God."

After a first part, in which we find synthesized the most salient points of the contemporary theology of revelation, Bishop Schmitt moved to another point that also had an important place in the theological discussion of that day: "the development of dogma." He followed the same line as Henri de Lubac and Taymans D'Eypernon: with Christ, God has already said his definitive word. With him, revelation has reached its perfection, but the church "does not cease to scrutinize the inscrutable riches of the mystery of the Word incarnate." This deepening has to be made in the light of the only Redeemer; in the light of the person of Christ; in the light of his life, death, resurrection, and ascension.

Christian Revelation Is the Gospel

As we have already seen, one of the issues that concerned Bishop Schmitt was the phenomenon of disbelief and the fact that many Christians believe only in a "weak" way. Analyzing the causes of this new collective phenomenon, he saw the danger of reducing Christianity to an ideology. Therefore, he emphasized the need to recover the complexity of revelation, and not see it as a mere collection of truths.

The primary finality of revelation is salvation, and not a mere answer to "questions of our intelligence." Teaching is something one cannot ignore, "but there is never doctrine without the Gospel of salvation. Christian truth is not only intellectual, but it also actualizes the knowledge and reality of the mystery of supernatural life." According to Bishop Schmitt, this means that Christian revelation is an economy of salvation: the Word of God is an action. That is why he could say in this same passage, "it is dangerous to separate, on the one hand, the salvific acts of Christ, from the words of Christ and the admonitions of the Apostles, on the other hand."

The Gospel Responds Admirably to the
Necessities of Today's Apostolates

In his pastoral writings, Bishop Schmitt always insisted that the return to the essence of the church cannot be separated from its mission. This point clearly appears in the third part of his 1962 intervention, where he spelled out the exigencies of what he had just expressed. What moved him to make this third proposal was the fact that many Christians know by memory the doctrinal truths of our faith but have not encountered Christ. For him the church's mission helps to provoke this personal encounter with Christ and make it live. Faith is possible only through such an encounter: "Christ is the only one who moves people to faith. Converting to Christ, the faithful confess that Christ is the coming of God and his kingdom, Lord and judge of the living and the dead." One must convert to Christ, but one must be converted in one's heart. Only in this way "will the faithful be witnesses of Jesus Christ."

In a 1963 Easter letter to his diocese, Bishop Schmitt reproduced nearly this entire text.[20] The tone was more pastoral, and we find some new paragraphs or more developed ideas that help us understand the depth of his proposal to the council. In particular, we can discover two reasons why he made this contribution to the council. In the introduction to his Easter letter, he referred to the goal of the Constitution *De fontibus revelationis:* "The conciliar debates on the relations between Scripture and Tradition risk relegating to second place that essential and very traditional truth, that the true, unique and total source of revelation is Jesus Christ" (ÉGM 15.4 [1963]: 1).

Along with recovering Jesus Christ as the only and total source of revelation, Bishop Schmitt offered another reason that corresponded to his wish that the council might be a moment of renewal—conversion for the whole church (the title of his letter was already significant in this regard). These proposals would help prepare an encounter with Christ, our Easter, and our conversion to him.

The theme of the first point is more developed, perhaps because he had to cut short his speech to the council. He was reminded that he was using up all the time at his disposal.

In his 1963 letter he added a paragraph in which, using an expression from Paul's Letter to the Galatians, he introduced the theme of revelation in the Old Testament: "The slow spiritual maturation of humanity converged towards Christ: he appeared in the fullness of time, and is the center of history." This further point highlighted the mission of Christ as savior and revealer. As savior he fulfills and carries out redemption; as revealer he gives us an understanding of our salvation.

We recalled above how the theology of those years was recovering the importance of moving from Christ to the Trinity. In the text that Bishop Schmitt read on the council floor, he simply stated that Jesus Christ reveals to us the intimate life of God. However, in his 1963 pastoral letter he explained it in this way: "It is Jesus who makes us know that God is Father, a Father who loves us; that God is Son, a Son who sets himself to seek us out; that God is Spirit, a Spirit who gives us life" (ÉGM 15.4 [1963]: 4).

In brief we can recognize briefly the central idea in Bishop Schmitt's first contribution to the council debates. He synthesized divine revelation, which he saw as a happening, an action of God in creation, in history, and in humanity directed toward salvation. This historic manifestation of God comes to its fulfillment and definitive completion in Christ, God with us.

Christ is at the same time Revealer and revelation. Everything in him is a revelation of God: his life, his works and words, and above all the mystery of his death, resurrection, and ascension. In Christ and with Christ the total and definitive manifestation of God is fulfilled in history: he allows us to know God himself, and in him the mystery of human beings. That is to say, in Christ we are able to know what God is for human beings, and what human beings are for God.

Although revelation has reached its fullness in Christ, the church does not cease to scrutinize the riches and depths of this mystery. It is to be noted that Bishop Schmitt speaks of mystery in the singular, the characteristic usage of Vatican II, and not of mysteries in the plural as we find in the text of Vatican I.

The later contributions of Bishop Schmitt to the council did not repeat what he said in 1962, but followed the same line of thought. It can be said that his first intervention formed the presupposition. From it, one sees with more clarity the meaning of all his other contributions, which result from the centrality of Christ in the life of Christians and the church.

During the council's second session (1963), in the debate on the draft proposal for a document on ecumenism (AS II/6, 162–65).[21] Bishop Schmitt spoke concretely of the episcopacy's special mission in dealing with ecumenism. He mentioned above all religious liberty, as presupposed in order to reach the desired unity. He called attention to the responsibility that all the members of the church have in this regard, particularly the bishops because of the mission they have received. The bishops have the obligation of collaborating in all that is at their disposal to achieve unity among Christians. But along with this urgent duty, he called attention to the need to avoid the dangers of irenicism, relativism, or accommodation of the revealed truth. The bishops must be vigilant so that the deposit of faith should be integrally preserved, in fraternal discipline and in the celebration of the sacraments, since the work for ecumenism does not exempt them from "preserving, defending and advancing the true deposit and the integrity of the divine tradition."

In this 1963 intervention we are given a key to the prospective changes being made in fundamental theology, which follow along the lines of Bishop Schmitt. He had asked that the presentation of doctrine might be clear, so that all might understand it and know how to interpret it (AS I/3, 184–87).[22] "The bishop, like the prophet and doctor of the Word of God, must not defend revealed truth as much as preach it positively, in a way apt for the concrete life of his audience, explaining it each time with greater clarity" (AS II/6, 164). This will allow the time of apologetics to give way to the moment of the truth.

In the council's third session, Bishop Schmitt spoke twice, once about the formation of the clergy and once in reference to what was to become *Gaudium et Spes*. Without doubt, the theme of formation was a priority in his pastoral work—concretely the formation of priests in the seminary as well as throughout their life. In this respect, it is interesting to see the formation program proposed for his diocese,[23] which takes into account the different stages in pastoral work as well as in the development of persons. It is no coincidence, then, that he would have something to say about what would become the council's document *Optatam Totius*.

Aware that the council's adaptation would depend in great part on the priests, he made an observation concerning faith education in the seminaries. Interestingly, he was occcupied not so much with providing the necessary means for making the seminarians aware of the council as with the need to get to the foundation of the Christian and priestly vocation. Again, the axis of his theme was the centrality of

Christ, this time in life of the person. The formation of priests has to be made by consolidating their faith, a faith centered in Christ and necessary if they are to go forward even when things are against them:

> The seminarians will be formed in a solid faith,...a faith that is centered in the death and resurrection of Christ, who is the Alpha and Omega, the Lord of the centuries. Thus those who dedicate their lives can say with the Apostle: "I know in whom I have put my trust." With this faith, the Lord will always and everywhere "nurture," even when one might have to live among infidels and be subject to many trials and tribulations. (AS III/8, 27)

One has to educate, Bishop Schmitt insisted, toward a missionary and ecclesial faith, which will aid one in carrying on dialogue with the world and which, thinking with the church and in the church, can move others to this same faith in their hearts. Over and above the required theological studies and formation in prayer, one has to take into account the demands of our time and the questions of our contemporaries. Therefore, along with science, where one must include human sciences, one has to learn to listen, to know, to discern the immutable elements that respond to the human condition, and to discern the signs of the times and the meaning of the events through which God speaks.

These requirements for priestly formation bring us to another document that, without doubt, attracted the attention of Bishop Schmitt—the Pastoral Constitution *Gaudium et Spes*.[24] In his first intervention on this document, he called attention to its opening words, "Of this time." If, on the one hand, the missionary impulse has moved the church not to separate itself from the world (something that has not always been achieved), the new developments of our time have produced new human beings. Bishop Schmitt asked two questions: What is the new development in the world? How must the church situate itself in this new development?

The first question he answered by pointing out some of these developments. Among other things, he mentioned the phenomenon of atheism and the urgency of elaborating a Christian anthropology.

He answered the second by pointing out the attitude of the church in the face of the world. The church has to be a presence, and this will be achieved through friendship and the spirit of poverty, so that the gospel might be present. The scope of the gospel goes beyond the questions the world asks. The church has to be the light in the world, and for this it has to have a positive attitude toward the world.

In this intervention Bishop Schmitt asked that *Gaudium et Spes* present in a clearer and more positive fashion that which the church receives from the world. This is necessary if the church is to acquire a greater consciousness of itself, to express better its message, and to fulfill better its mission. Everything that contributes to the good of humanity and of the world cooperates with God's project.

Bishop Schmitt knew well that sincere dialogue with the world would free us from many things, but he was also aware that only in this way would the church recover its essence and purify itself of all that had stained it over time. The world is not only the place of the church's mission, but in it the church collaborates in the work of Christ's salvation.

Bishop Schmitt ended his contributions to *Gaudium et Spes* with a brief conclusion in which he went beyond Vatican I's dichotomy between natural knowledge of God and supernatural revelation: "the Christian God of salvation is the same God of the creation of humanity and of history."

CONCLUSION

In the light of Vatican II and subsequent theology, it is easy to see the profound meaning of Bishop Schmitt's contributions. Without Christ, everything evaporates or remains superficial. To say that Christ is the fullness of revelation is to say that in him alone and in his light can we get close to the mystery of God and of human beings.

But how to return to Christ? How do we situate ourselves and how can we find him? Father O'Collins, in his work cited at the start of this chapter, introduces three methods for doing theology. The first one is driven by a passion to find the truth. One goes to the sources of Christian tradition; one dialogues with other disciplines. In this style reason predominates. The second method is attuned to the contemporary situation, above all, where persons approach mystery through the last times of the earth and human history. They go to the prophets of the Old Testament, who denounce the situations of injustice, a condition necessary in order to return to God. The third method focuses on divine beauty. People consult the great men and women of prayer.

They approach mystery from the religious expressions of ritual and prayer.

O'Collins presents such a synthesis as an ideal as well as a challenge for anyone who approaches the mystery of God. Bishop Schmitt has given us his attempt at such a synthesis. Through the texts studied, we have detected a cycle in his approaches: between reflection and the pastoral ministry, and between the spiritual life and commitment in the world. He reflects, labors, studies, and debates, but never forgets the questions and anxieties of the men and women who surround him, the people whom God has entrusted to his care. He communicates the fundamental certainty of his life: Christ and only Christ can give meaning to our existence.

Notes

1. Bishop Schmitt (1911–1987) led the diocese of Metz (France) from 1958 to 1987. As well as the observations he signed with other bishops (principally French bishops), he presented some *animadversiones* during the sessions of the council: on the constitution *Dei Verbum* (CG XXI, in *Acta Synodalia Sacrosancti Concilii Oecumenici Vaticani II* [AS] 1/3, 128–31); on the decree *Unitatis Redintegratio* (CG LXXVI in AS II/6, 162–65); on the decree *Optatam Totius* (CG CXXIII, in AS I II/8, 27–30); on the constitution *Gaudium et Spes* (CG CVIII, in AS III/5, 406–8; CG CXL, in AS IV/3, 116–18).

2. Gerald O'Collins, S.J., *Retrieving Fundamental Theology* (Mahwah, N.J.: Paulist Press, 1993).

3. Ibid., 52–54.

4. *Église de Metz* (hereafter ÉGM) III (1966): 4. The translations will be my own.

5. This makes reference to his Easter Message of 1963, "Conversion à Jésus," in ÉGM, April 14, 1963.

6. *Acta et Documenta Concilio Oecumenico Vaticano II apparando* (AD) II/I, Città del Vaticano 1960–1969, 323–25; hereafter referred to as AD.

7. This commission had been created by Pope John XXIII to coordinate drafts at the preparatory stage. The letter in question is found in AS *Appendix*, 301.

8. The theology of those years is well described by T. Citrini, *Gesù Cristo Rivelazione di Dio* (Venegono Inferiore: Seminario Arcivescovile, 1969).

9. Henri de Lubac, "Le problème du développement du dogme," RSR 35 (1948): 130–60.

10. Taymans D'Eypernon, "Le progrès du dogme," NRT 81 (1949): 687–700.

11. Ibid., 694.

12. Ibid., 692–93.

13. Émile Mersch, *La théologie du corps mystique,* vol. 2 (Paris-Brussels: Desclée de Brouwer, 1946), 52.

14. For this we depend on the diocesan bulletin ÉGM of those years, in which Bishop Schmitt wrote about the council or because of the council.

15. This will be one of the most serious issues examined by *Gaudium et Spes* (no. 23). We should remember that when Bishop Schmitt wrote in these terms, no drafts of GS had yet been submitted to the council.

16. This series comprised five articles in ÉGM: "Un Concile pour notre temps," 101 (1966); "La présence des observateurs: une grâce," 102 (1966): 1–3; "Un Concile libre," 103 (1966): 3–6; "Un Concile bénéficiant d'une

audience mondial," 105 (1966): 1–3; and "Le premier Concile à l'heure de l'athéisme,"107 (1966): 1–3.

17. "Un esprit de foi," ÉGM 109 (1966): 30–35; "Esprit de recherche," ÉGM 110 (1966): 1–3; "Un esprit d'équilibre," ÉGM 111 (1966): 1–5.

18. R. Burigana, *La Bibbia nel Concilio* (Bologna: II Mulino, 1988), 110.

19. AS I/3, 128–31.

20. Easter Letter: "Conversion à Jésus-Christ," ÉGM 15.4 (1963): 1–3.

21. A part of this text was not read on the council floor but was submitted in writing to the secretary.

22. Bishop Schmitt makes an allusion to this intervention in ÉGM 105 (1963): 3.

23. Pastoral letter (in preparation for the diocesan synod) "Pour un renouveau des études pastorales," ÉGM 15 (1965): 1–25.

24. AS III/5, 406–8 and *AS* IV/3, 116–18. In two articles in ÉGM he published his two conciliar contributions to this document: "L'Église et le monde," 7 (1965): 1–3, and "Dialogue de l'Église et du monde," 17 (1965): 1–4.

6. *Dei Verbum* Developing: Vatican II's Revelation Doctrine 1963–1964

Jared Wicks, S.J.

Gerald O'Collins presented in 1985 a key element in the genesis of the doctrine of revelation in Vatican II's Dogmatic Constitution *Dei Verbum*.[1] Going beyond his account of how the preconciliar Catholic notion of revelation as *locutio Dei* was in 1962 first broadened to include revelation in events and deeds, this study will treat developments of 1963–1964 by which *Dei Verbum's* opening chapter came to present revelation as personal, historical, and Christocentric in its realization and salvific in its central content.

THE COUNCIL'S RETURN TO WORK ON REVELATION

A revised text on divine revelation came out of the Mixed Commission in late spring of 1963, and many council members submitted written comments, both critical and constructive, on this draft.[2] Nonetheless, this *Textus prior* was not discussed during the Second Period of the Council in 1963, but Paul VI put it back on the agenda for the Third Period.[3] Stimulated by the pope's announcement, the bishops sent in more suggestions for improving the text of 1963, and in March 1964 the Doctrinal Commission entrusted a work of revision to a subcommission of seven council members and twenty-four *periti*, presided over by Bishop André M. Charue of Namur. This body divided itself into two sections: the first, headed by Archbishop Ermenegildo Florit of Florence, set out to revise the initial chapters on revelation and its transmission; the second, under Bishop Charue, had to amend the chapters on biblical inspiration and interpretation, the Old and New Testaments, and the role of scripture in the life of the church. All revisions were to rest on contributions made by the council members as these were accepted by the subcommission. Archbishop Florit's section thus became the agent for developing the doctrine of divine revelation in spring 1964 on the basis of comments from seventy-five individual council fathers and sixteen regional or national episcopal conferences.[4]

Under Archbishop Florit the initial study and preparation of a revised draft text on revelation were entrusted to the *peritus* Father Pieter Smulders, of the Maastricht theologate of the Dutch Jesuits. He studied the bishops' comments and, after consulting twice with Bishop Joseph Heuschen (Auxiliary of Liège) and the Belgian *periti* L. Cerfaux and A. Prignon, formulated an emended draft in late March and early April 1964, completing a text with explanatory comments on April 12, which he then sent to Father Umberto Betti, the secretary of the Florit section.[5] The full subcommission on revelation met in Rome April 20–25, 1964, making revisions of Smulders's draft, especially to abbreviate his explanations of the new text. In early June the Doctrinal Commission approved the new draft. On July 3 the council's Coordinating Commission declared ready for the council fathers this *Textus emendatus,* which now contained the six chapters of the eventual *Dei Verbum.* It was mailed out to the council members as a sixty-four-page booklet, giving in parallel columns the texts of 1963 and 1964, with appended *relationes* on the sources of the changes and on the reasoning underlying the new formulations. The council's Third Period opened September 14, 1964, and on September 30, Archbishop Florit presented to the council members the new chapters 1 and 2 on revelation and its transmission.

THE RENEWED DOCTRINE OF REVELATION (1964)

In the development of *Dei Verbum,* chapter 1 sailed on smoothly from September 30, 1964, to the promulgation of the constitution on November 18, 1965.[6] The drama of this later period concerned the relation of tradition and scripture (chapter 2, *Dei Verbum* 8–9), the inerrancy or truth of scripture (chapter 3, *Dei Verbum* 11), and the historical character of the Gospels (chapter 5, *Dei Verbum* 19). On revelation itself (preface and chapter 1, *Dei Verbum* 1–6), *modi* of the bishops were accepted but these polished and fine-tuned the text that had already gained wide approval in the form produced by the revisions of spring 1964.

In the following pages, I will treat some fourteen emendations introduced by Father Smulders or the Florit subcommission in the formulation of chapter 1 on divine revelation in the *Textus emendatus* of spring 1964. My concerns are to highlight the new traits ascribed to revelation, to identify the episcopal contributors of these formulations and to relate the reasoning behind their acceptance by Father Smulders and the subcommission for introduction into the text.

1. The *Textus prior* of 1963 had already opened by citing 1 John 1:2–3 in order to connect the council's doctrine of revelation to the apostles' experience of hearing and seeing Jesus, whom they in turn proclaimed in order to lead believers to communion with the Father and Son. One member, Archbishop Raul Silva Henriquez (Santiago, Chile), had noted that the opening paragraph was not explicit on the pastoral intent of the constitution. To remedy this lacuna, during the April 1964 meetings the passage stating the scope of the text (*"genuinam de divina Revelatione ac de eius transmissione doctrinam"*) was expanded by the subcommission with a formulation of its aim and purpose in words based on St. Augustine's *De catechizandis rudis:* "so that the whole world by hearing may believe, by believing may hope, and by hoping may love."[7]

2. The *Textus prior* had followed Vatican I's *Dei Filius*, chapter 2, by beginning its account of revelation itself from the impotence of human natural reason to know the mysteries of the Trinity and our vocation to share in the divine nature (2 Pet 1:4). As requested by three episcopal interventions, Father Smulders changed this to a positive citation of Rom 1:20 on the knowledge of God possible from creation, which revelation then transcends. But the Charue section excised even this reference, to give clear priority to God's initiative in revealing himself (*"Placuit Deo...seipsum revelare..."*). What prevailed was the critique by Bishop Paul Seitz (Kon Tum, Vietnam) of a tendency to begin numerous council schemas from the human aspect instead of from dogmatic data. Father Smulders noted Seitz's critique of the *Textus prior* (*"laborat anthropocentrismo"* and it begins with what

humans cannot do), which the subcommission then applied more rigorously to give revelation an unambiguously theocentric character.[8]

3. A major innovation in the conciliar account of revelation was introduced in the Smulders draft on what God reveals regarding his salvific plan and purpose: "*...et 'notum facere nobis sacramentum voluntatis suae'* (Eph 1:9), *quo homines per Christum in Spiritu Sancto accessum habent ad Patrem* (cf. Eph 2:18) *et ad divinae naturae consortium vocantur* (cf. 2 Pet 1:4)." Father Smulders explained laconically that this reformulated from Ephesians what *Dei Filius* had termed the "eternal decrees" of the divine will, but the innovation was in fact more than terminological.

Among the general lines of revision desired by numerous bishops was a development of the salvific content of God's revelation as a call to communion with the Divine Persons. Bishop Seitz situated revelation in realizing God's intention to make believers participants in the life of the divine trinitarian family. Bishop Amédée Lefevre (Rabat, Morocco) had found the *Textus prior* so focused on the intellectual aspect of revelation that it excluded the dimension of "real" revelation. He called for highlighting how revelation is primarily and essentially salvific, aiming to lead us to share in the Christian mystery. The French bishops of the Apostolic Region of Bordeaux stated that the proper object of revelation is to allow us to participate in God's salvific plan. Archbishop Silva Henriquez insisted on indicating the "*valor salvificus veritatis revelatae eiusque aspectus dynamicus,*" along with the essential relation between revelation and redemption.[9] Father Smulders's work as *peritus* was to supply the Pauline phrases on God's *mystērion* which captured the intent of the bishops on revelation as salvific and leading to personal communion with the Trinity, as the text of 1 John 1 had already indicated in the draft's opening lines.

4. Among the criticisms of the *Textus prior,* numerous council members said it dealt more with the revelation of truths about God than with God revealing himself. Two of these critics touched a central nerve by calling for a personalistic conception of revelation and faith. Bishop Arthur Elchinger (coadjutor of Strasbourg) declared that the times call for a vital, biblical, and personal doctrine, so as to revivify the faith of Christians. Bishop Joseph Satowaki (Kagoshima, Japan) stated that revelation is a manifestation of the love of God for humans, in the form of "*allocutio, collocutio, vel contactus personalis et vitalis*

Dei cum hominibus."[10] To give expression to this desire, Father Smulders expressed the nature of revelation in biblical terms as personal encounter, as passed substantially into the final text of *Dei Verbum:* "Through this revelation, therefore, the invisible God (cf. John 1:18; Col 1:15; 1 Tim 1:16) out of the abundance of his love addresses humans as friends (cf. Exod 33:11; John 15:14–16) and lives among them (cf. Bar 3:38), admitting them to personal communion (*societatem*) with Father, Son, and Holy Spirit."

5. In his *relatio* on the emended text, Father Smulders noted sixteen interventions calling for recognition that revelation occurs not only through spoken words but also through historical deeds and events. To these, Smulders added the point that in Hebrew *dābār* ("word") refers both to utterance and expressive action. The new text followed closely a formulation offered by the bishops of Indonesia: "This revelation occurs not only through words addressed to humans, but also through deeds *(gesta)* done in the history of salvation, in such wise that the authority of the words is confirmed by the works *(opera)* and the mystery contained in the works is made manifest by words."[11]

The interrelation of words and deeds in revelation drew the attention of others in the subcommission, and in late April 1964 the Smulders text was developed into the form that eventually entered the promulgated text of *Dei Verbum.* This involved (i) speaking of the comprehensive *"oeconomia"* of revelation; (ii) intertwining the modes of its realization: *"gestis verbisque intrinsece inter se connexis"*; (iii) expanding the role of God's actions in history to manifesting along with confirming the doctrine and realities signified by the words; and (iv) adding that the words first announce the works before throwing light on their mystery. On the basis of this text, Archbishop Florit supplied a term in the Aula on September 30, 1964, which facilitated understanding of the new text, by reference to the "sacramental" nature of revelation, because of the interrelation of actions and words.

6. The *Textus prior* had concluded its skimpy opening paragraph on the object of revelation itself by stating that in revelation the truth about God and man shines forth *(illucescit)* for us in Christ. The bishops felt that more should be said. Archbishop Jean Julien Weber (Strasbourg) held that revelation manifests divine mysteries, the inner life of God, and so Father Smulders had the sentence open with *"intima veritas."* Archbishop Silva Henriquez insisted that revelation

is about the history of our salvation, and so Father Smulders specified the "truth" as *"de homine eiusque salutis."* Numerous bishops
called for more emphasis on the centrality of Christ, such as Bishop
Seitz (*"la Révélation attient son sommet en la personne du Verbe
incarné"*), Bishop Elchinger (in scripture Christ is *"la révélation en
sa plénitude"*), and Bishop Luigi Carli of Segni, Italy (truth shines
forth in Christ because he is *"plenitudo et recapitulatio totius divinae
revelationis"*). So, Father Smulders added, *"qui non solum mediator,
sed et summa totius revelationis existit* (cf. John 17:1–3; 1 Cor 2:2; 2
Cor 3:16—4:6)," and explained that what is said here will be developed subsequently in a historical perspective on revelation in and by
Christ.[12] In late April the subcommission made a terminological
change, substituting *"plenitudo"* for Father Smulders's *"summa,"* and
added references to John 1:14, 17; 14:6; and Eph. 1:3–8, giving the
intervention of Archbishop Weber as the source.[13] Thus, the revelation doctrine of *Dei Verbum* began to take on its christological concentration.

7. The next numbered paragraph of the *Textus prior* treated revelation before Christ from the fall down through God's dealings with
Israel in preparation for the gospel. I note here only two changes in the
text of spring 1964, although more could be said about the shaping of
this section.[14] One point that drew fire from council members was the
1963 statement that after the fall God immediately restored the order
of salvation (*"mox restauravit ordinem salutis"*). The objections were
diverse, across a span from the unchanging divine purpose to the definitive "order" only given in Christ. Father Smulders chose to substitute
a more personalist form suggested by Bishop John. J. McEleney
(Kingston, Jamaica), that after the fall God's promise of redemption
immediately stirred human hearts to hope for salvation, for which
Father Smulders added a reference to the *protoevangelium,* Gen 3:15.[15]

On his own, Father Smulders noted that while the *Textus prior* of
1963 spoke of the election of Abraham with a view to blessing all generations, it did not mention God's revelation in this context. So he
added the principal points of God's self-revelation to Israel through
Moses and the prophets: the one God, a provident Father, and a just
and merciful judge. The subcommission added a fourth aspect, namely,
the promise that stirred expectation of a Savior to come. Also, the title
of this paragraph, eventually *Dei Verbum* 3, became *"De evangelicae*

revelationis preparatione," which underscores that Vatican II considers all revelation as culminating in Christ and the gospel.

8. The *Textus prior* had treated the revelatory work of Jesus Christ in two numbered paragraphs. No. 3 had affirmed that in Christ and through the Holy Spirit's work in the apostles, divine revelation reached its ultimate and definitive realization. No. 4 treated the manner of revelation in Christ, namely, by teaching his divinity and also by works and events, especially his resurrection, which render credible the mystery expressed in the teaching.

Two interventions, by Archbishop Florit and the Indonesian bishops, proposed inverting these topics and unifying them in a single number, so as to treat first how Christ reveals, doing this more amply, before affirming the ultimacy of revelation in Christ.[16]

Father Smulders supplied a new title to this unified paragraph, "*De Christo revelationis consummatione,*" in which the subcommission substituted the concrete term "*consummatore.*" This responded to the more general desire to highlight the person and works of Christ as revelatory, for which Bishops Seitz, Elchinger, Carli, and Weber were noted in (6), above. In addition, the bishops of Provence called for a stronger affirmation that Christ is the primary source of revelation, just as much in his life, death, and resurrection as in his teaching. The Indonesian bishops underscored that Christ's deeds reveal "*qualis nobis sit Deus,*" that is, merciful to sinners and offering the bread of life. Abbot Christopher Butler (Downside Abbey, president of the English Benedictine Congregation) referred to John 14:9, concluding that in Christ the Father manifests himself perfectly.[17]

9. To express that Christ is the summit of revelation, the new formulation began with a citation of Heb 1:1–2, as urged by Bishops Weber and Silva Henriquez. To this Father Smulders added Gal 4:4 on the Son being sent "in the fullness of time," as suggested by the bishops of Central Africa, but the latter text was excised by the subcommssion in order to make an immediate transition from God's speaking (Hebrews) to what John 1 attributes to the Word. This had been laconically suggested by the bishops of Provence: regarding revelation by Christ, one should refer to John 1:1–16, for "*Ipse est verbum Dei.*" Father Smulders made explicit what John 1 says about the Word, to give reasons why the Incarnate Word is the consummation of revelation: in him all is created, he enlightens every person, he dwelt

among us, and he tells about the inner depths of God. The last point, based on John 1:18 and 1 Cor 2:10, came from Archbishop Maurice Baudoux (Saint Boniface, Canada).[18]

10. Continuing on Christ as revealer, Father Smulders inserted a phrase from the *Letter to Diognetus* that Christ was sent as "*homo ad homines,*" to say concisely what Bishop Seitz had declared ("*Dieu s'est révélé en adressant son Verbe aux hommes, qui leur parla leur langue propre et selon ce qu'ils pouvaient en recevoir*"). The continuation was Johannine, referring to Christ's words and deeds, with a citation suggested by the Indonesian bishops, "*verba Dei loquitur*" (John 3:34), and their paraphrase of John 5:37 and 17:4 on Jesus completing the work given him to do by the Father.[19]

To lead this statement to its climax, the new text referred to the particulars of the Christ-event, which the *Textus prior* had done, but now they appeared not simply as proofs of Christ's teaching but first as themselves having revelatory significance. Numerous bishops had called for such a role for Christ's "words and works, signs and miracles, especially his death and glorious resurrection from the dead, and his whole person."[20] In the comments of the council members, Fr. Smulders had before him numerous ways of concluding this line of teaching. He chose a dense phrase about Christ that passed into the final version of the constitution, "*revelationem complendo perficit,*" similar to the wording used by five French council members.[21] To this was coupled the apologetical role of Jesus' deeds in support of his revealed message and teaching, "*ac testimonio divino confirmat,*" which had been the sole concern of the *Textus prior,* and which the bishops wanted to see complemented but not excluded.

This christological concentration of revelation grew from the seedbed of the "French approach" in the First Period of 1962 to the views prevailing in the preparatory drafts distributed on the eve of the council, *De fontibus revelationis,* and *De deposito fidei pure custodiendo.* The French bishops opted to call for thorough revision, not total rejection, of *De fontibus,* with the addition of an opening section on revelation itself. The latter should transform *De deposito,* chapter 4, in the light of revelation in salvation history and in the person of Christ. This strategy can be seen in passages of the 1962 interventions of Cardinal Achille Lienart (Lille), Archbishop Maurice Guerry (Cambrai), Bishop Paul Schmitt (Metz), Bishop Georges Hakim (Melchite diocese of

Akka, Israel), Archbishop Gabriel Garrone (Toulouse), Bishop Alfred Ancel (auxiliary of Lyon), and Bishop Pierre Veuillot (coadjutor of Paris).[22] In the later comments on the *Textus prior,* the christological center of revelation was expressed by several, but most forcefully by Bishop Arthur Elchinger in four dense paragraphs on *"Le Christ, source et contenu de la Révélation."*[23] This, then, is the background of the passage, eventually in *Dei Verbum* 4, extending from the citation of Heb 1:1–2 to the climactic *"[Ipse Christus] revelationem complendo perficit."* This affirmation is anticipated in Dei Verbum 2, on Christ as *"mediator simul et plenitudo totius revelationis,"* and it then echoes in *Dei Verbum* 7, as already in the *Textus emendatus,* about Christ, *"in quo summi Dei tota revelatio consummatur."*

11. To bring the new text on revelation in Christ to its initial completion, Father Smulders expressed the content of what Christ communicates to the world as he brings revelation to its summit and recapitulation: "namely (*nempe*) that God is with us (cf. Matt 1:23) to liberate humans from the darkness of sin and death (cf. John 8:32) and raise them to eternal life." With a slightly different word order and without the scripture references, this went into the *Textus emendatus* and on to *Dei Verbum* 4, where the beneficiaries of God's saving work, "humans," are actualized as *"nos."* This text completes the content of revelation, first explicitated in the emendation treated in (3) above, and is substantially what the Indonesian bishops had suggested in the text their *peritus* Smulders had helped draft. It satisfied as well Bishop Baudoux, the minority of five French bishops, Bishop Tabera Araoz, and Archbishop Lorenz Jaeger (Paderborn, Germany), who had all called for a declaration of the saving work and message of Christ beyond the limited revelation of his divinity in the *Textus prior.*[24]

12. We recall that the *Textus prior* had stated first about Christ that his revelation and religion (*"Christianismus"*) were ultimate and definitive. Father Smulders placed this at the end of the revised christological paragraph, but in biblical terms. He formulated the truth as what Christians "before whose eyes Christ has been set forth" (Gal 3:1) believe about the "Christian economy," namely, that it will never pass away (cf. Matt 24:35), basing the modification of *"Christianismus"* on texts from the bishops of Provence and Central Africa.[25] This economy is "ultimate and definitive," beyond which no further public revelation is expected, as in the *Textus prior.* To maximize

biblical expressions, Father Smulders added a modifying phrase, "before the final revelation of our Lord Jesus Christ (1 Cor 1:7)," in line with several episcopal desires that an eschatological note not be lacking in the council's christocentric doctrine of revelation.[26]

At this point there occurred a significant refusal of an episcopal recommendation, namely, that the new draft adopt the traditional statement that revelation was closed with the death of the Apostles. Bishops Carli and Seitz had wanted this, but Father Smulders argued that this would raise the debated question about the relation between the revelation given by Jesus before his ascension and what the Apostles received later from the Holy Spirit. The subcommission modified the *relatio* on the refusal, stating that a reference to "closure" would require further explanation and that the text already gave the reason for this, namely, that in Christ revelation reaches its summit (*"consumatur"*).[27] This position made possible the consideration, for example, by G. O'Collins, of revelation both in its expressive summit in Jesus Christ and in its ever-present actuality, as indicated in *Dei Verbum* 8, 21, and 25.[28]

13. The *Textus prior* had passed from revelation in Christ to restate Vatican I on the revelation of "natural truths" connected with the supernatural mystery of participation in divine life. Then its final paragraph treated faith, for which God's grace must open the mind to revelation and move the heart to acceptance. Father Smulders proposed the inversion of these passages, since revelation directly invites to faith, while the natural truths are a corollary of revelation.

For the revised text on faith, Father Smulders provided a new title, *"De fide revelationi assentiente,"* in which the subcommission substituted the more generic participle, *"praebenda."* In the paragraph itself, Smulders inserted changes to develop more fully the nature of faith, in correspondence with the preceding fuller doctrine of revelation, as requested by several bishops. He related faith personally "to God who reveals," not simply to "revelation."[29] He incorporated Vatican I's descriptive definition of faith as "the full submission of intellect and will to God who reveals," as asked for by the bishops of Central Africa, and added "the voluntary assent to the truth revealed by God," in line with interventions by Archbishop William Conway (Armagh) and Archbishop Silva Henriquez (who had said *"oboeditio fidei...est actus eminentissimae libertatis"*).[30]

A fuller statement follows on the grace of faith, *"praeveniens et adiuvans,"* through a complex of interior gifts of the Spirit, who works in the heart to give "joy and ease (*suavitatem*) to all in consenting to and believing the truth," based in part on suggestions of the German-speaking and Scandinavian bishops and Abbot Butler, and on Father Smulders's own selection of the terms *adiuvans* from Trent and *suavitas* in consenting from the Second Council of Orange.[31] Apparently on his own, Father Smulders added words based on John 6:44, on coming to Christ only by the "drawing" by the Father, which, however, the subcommission excised from the *Textus emendatus*. The same body did add a specific dimension of the Spirit's way of eliciting faith, *"mentis occulos aperiat,"* which suggests the thesis proposed early in the century by Father Pierre Rousselot, S.J.[32] Both Father Smulders and the subcommission left intact the final lines on faith in the *Textus prior*, in reference to the Holy Spirit's ongoing work in believers to promote their deeper understanding of revelation, on which Smulders's *relatio* stated that this refers both to individuals and to the ecclesial community of faith.

14. Where the *Textus prior* had entitled its penultimate paragraph, *"Veritates naturales cum revelatione connexae,"* and then contrasted a strict mystery with the truths of the natural order, Father Smulders kept the title for the reworded but not substantially modified paragraph that now concludes the doctrine of revelation itself. But the subcommission noted the incongruity and simplified the title to *"De veritatibus revelatis."*

Instead of keeping the more theological wording of the *Textus prior,* Father Smulders made over the paragraph following a suggestion of Abbot Butler that it follow closely *Dei Filius* of Vatican I, which the Smulders *relatio* said would simplify discussion by the council members: *"ne oriantur discussiones infinitae,"* as on grace and natural reason, "virtually revealed" truths, and the assent to the truths given as corollaries of God's word of salvation.[33]

Father Smulders proposed keeping the lines of the *Textus prior* that had concluded that revelation not only opens the path to our supernatural end (changed by Smulders to "eternal life") but also conveys principles by which one understands life in this world and can live accordingly. In a change that in retrospect appears questionable, the subcommission decided to excise these lines from the *Textus emendatus,* explaining that this theme now pertains to *Schema XIII,* which became the Pastoral Constitution *Gaudium et Spes.*[34]

CONCLUDING REFLECTION

The emendations introduced into the draft text on revelation in 1964 expressed, at times eloquently, the desires of numerous council members. First, they asked that revelation be presented as God's personal address, as treated in (3) above; second, that revelation be portrayed as historical and indeed "sacramental," not just verbal, as indicated in (5) above; and, third, that revelation be understood and taught as concentrated and recapitulated in the person and work of Jesus Christ, who radiates the truth about God and human salvation, as seen in (6), (8), (9), and (10) above.

We can further appreciate how revelation according to *Dei Verbum* opens the way to believers' participation in the light, love, and movement of life through Christ, in the Spirit, toward the Father, as Father Smulders supplied a passage based on Eph 2:18, noted above in (3). This is more than an I–Thou personal relation, for it looks to envelop the believer in dynamic and saving communion with the triune God of revelation.

Also, topic (11) introduced the engaging formulation of the content of revelation in Christ, which has not received adequate attention after the council. Beyond stating that Christ completes and recapitulates God's word, this passage gives this word definite contours. Christian revelation finds normative expression in the message that God is with us as Emmanuel, working for our liberation from sin and death and our passage to eternal life. The Paschal Mystery is climactic in realizing God's revelation and redemptive salvation, but it is more, since the salvation proclaimed has the very form and structure of Christ dying to free the captives and rising to be the firstborn of many conformed to his passage to new life.

Through this study one grows in esteem for the council members who offered the revisions. One recognizes as well the competent theological work of the redactors, who studied and selected from the episcopal interventions. The people of God were well served at this moment of a crucial doctrinal development, as shown in the archives and *Acta* of Vatican II. The council's doctrine of revelation is thereby freshly open for a present-day re-reception.

Notes

1. "At the Origins of *Dei Verbum*," *Heythrop Journal* 26 (1985): 5–13; also more concisely in *Retrieving Fundamental Theology* (New York/Mahwah, N.J.: Paulist, 1993), 57–63. O'Collins shows the key development of late November 1962, when the newly formed Mixed Commission accepted a draft formulation on revelation to Israel "*verbis et gestis,*" which entered no. 14, on the Old Testament in the second conciliar draft on revelation, the *Textus prior,* which went out to the council members on April 22, 1963. Below I will relate how this notion passed into *Dei Verbum's* account of the whole of divine revelation.

2. This commission combined members of the council's Commission on Doctrine and the Secretariat for Promoting Christian Unity. Its work on revelation in 1962–63 is narrated in chapter 3 of Riccardo Burigana's history, *La Bibbia nel Concilio: La redazione della costituzione "Dei Verbum" del Vaticano II* (Bologna: Il Mulino, 1998), 171–218. Burigana gives in his appendix the initial form of the *"Prooemium"* on revelation itself, which was then simplified before going out to the council members. What they received is the first draft given in synoptic presentations of the four texts (three drafts and *Dei Verbum* itself) of 1963 to 1965. The comments by the council members are found in the volume of *Acta Synodalia* and the book of Gil Hellín referred to in n. 4 below.

3. Closing Address of the Second Period, December 4, 1963; *Acta Synodalia Concilii Vaticani II,* Vol. II, Part VI (Vatican City: Typis Poliglottis Vaticanis, 1973), 566–67; and *Acta Apostolicae Sedis* 56 (1964): 36. J. Ratzinger saw this decision as steering the council away from an ecclesiological monism, by engaging it with God's act of communication under which the church ever remains a listener to God's Word. Herbert Vorgrimler, ed., *Commentary on the Documents of Vatican II,* 3 vols. (New York: Herder & Herder, 1969), 3:162.

4. These numbers, along with the makeup of the two subcommissions, were given in the *Relatio generalis* of the *Textus emendatus* of 1964. *Acta Synodalia Concilii Vaticani secundi,* Vol. III, Part III (Vatican City: Typis Poliglottis Vaticanis, 1974), 109–10, 123; also in Francisco Gil Hellín, ed., *Concilii Vaticani II Synopsis: Constitutio dogmatica de divina revelatione Dei Verbum* (Vatican City: Liberia Editrice Vaticana, 1993), 2–6 (hereafter cited as Gil Hellín). From this point on, I treat only revelation itself. The genesis of chapter 2 of *Dei Verbum,* on tradition, scripture, and magisterium, has been related exhaustively in U. Betti, *La trasmissione della divina rivelazione* (Rome: Pont. Athenaeum Antonianum, 1985).

5. Father Smulders related something of his work in "Zum Werdegang des Konzilskapitel 'Die Offenbarung selbst,'" in E. Klinger and K. Wittstadt, eds., *Glaube im Prozess: Christsein nach dem II. Vatikanum,* Festschrift K. Rahner (Freiburg/B.: Herder, 1984), 99–120. The Smulders council papers are now in the Katholiek Documentatie Centrum, Nijmegen, with texts from his revision work of 1964 in Smulders's Folder 11H. My further references to his work are based on the papers of this folder, which I consulted in June 1999 with the help of Dr. Willem Dings.

6. R. Burigana treats the developments of 1964–65 in chapters 4 and 5 of *La Bibbia nel Concilio,* 255–434.

7. Silva Henriquez: *Acta Synodalia,* III/III, 797; Gil Hellín, 477. During the Third Period, Cardinal Julius Döpfner questioned the exalted claim of this passage regarding a doctrinal exposition on revelation and scripture, but the Doctrinal Commission stated that since *Dei Verbum* is logically the first of all the council documents, its *Prooemium* may use elevated terms because it introduces the whole corpus of Vatican II's constitutions and decrees (Gil Hellín, 13). My references to commission explanations and responses to *modi* are taken from the useful edition of Gil Hellín.

8. Paul Seitz: *Acta Synodalia,* III/III, 877; Gil Hellín, 384. Archbishop Florit, presenting the new text in the Aula on September 30, made reference to revelation having an "*indolem primariam theocentricam*" (ibid., 491). Only in 1965, when it dealt with votes *placet iuxta modum,* did the commission further express this theocentrism by giving the constitution its opening words, "*Dei verbum religiose audiens et fidenter proclamans....*"

9. Seitz: *Acta Synodalia,* III/III, 876; Gil Hellín, 383. Lefevre: *Acta Synodalia,* III/III, 848; Gil Hellín, 423. Bishops of the Region of Bordeaux: *Acta Synodalia,* III/III, 899; Gil Hellín, 437. Silva Henriquez: as in n. 7 above. Bishop Lefevre's reference to "real" revelation shows influence of an article of E. Schillebeeckx in *Lumen Vitae* 46 (1960): 25–45, translated as "Revelation-in-Reality and Revelation-in-Word," in *Revelation and Theology* (New York: Sheed & Ward, 1967), 33–56.

10. Elchinger: *Acta Synodalia,* III/III, 829; Gil Hellín, 387. Satowaki: *Acta Synodalia,* III/III, 874; Gil Hellín, 397f.

11. Indonesian bishops: *Acta Synodalia,* III/III, 914; Gil Hellín, 431. Along with being a *peritus* of the Doctrinal Commission, Father Smulders was also a theological consultant of the Indonesian episcopal conference, some members of which had been his students in Maastricht.

12. Weber: *Acta Synodalia,* III/III, 886; Gil Hellín, 411. Silva Henriquez: as in n. 7 above. Seitz: as in n. 8. Elchinger: as in n. 10. Carli: *Acta Synodalia,* III/III, 818; Gil Hellín, 354. Bishop Carli's formulation was mentioned neither

in the Smulders *relatio* nor in what accompanied the *Textus emendatus* given to the council members.

13. Weber: as in n. 12.

14. The German-speaking and Scandinavian bishops had called for a more universal statement of God's offer of salvation and revelation: *Acta Synodalia,* III/III, 906; Gil Hellín, 415. But the expression of this in the new draft and in *Dei Verbum* was so reserved that it led to critical commentaries from diverse viewpoints, e.g., by Karl Rahner and Joseph Ratzinger. To treat this issue in Vatican II itself, one would have to present the Rahner-Ratzinger "antischema" of 1962, *De revelatione Dei et hominis in Iesu Christo facta,* which circulated widely among the council members and *periti.*

15. McEleney: *Acta Synodalia,* III/III, 851; Gil Hellín, 435.

16. Florit: *Acta Synodalia,* III/III, 834; Gil Hellín, 457. Indonesian bishops: *Acta Synodalia,* III/III, 914; Gil Hellín, 431.

17. Bishops of Provence: *Acta Synodalia,* III/III, 898; Gil Hellín, 374. Indonesian bishops: *Acta Synodalia,* III/III, 914; Gil Hellín, 432. Abbot Butler: *Acta Synodalia,* III/III, 813; Gil Hellín, 463.

18. Weber and Silva Henriquez: as in nn. 12 and 7 above. Central African Bishops: *Acta Synodalia,* III/III, 892; Gil Hellín, 389. Bishops of Provence: as in n. 17. Baudoux: *Acta Synodalia,* III/III, 805–6; Gil Hellín, 391.

19. Seitz: as in n. 8 above. Indonesian bishops: as in n. 16.

20. Among others, the Indonesian bishops, as noted in n. 17 above. Also, Bishop Arturo Tabera Araoz (Albacete, Spain): *Acta Synodalia,* III/III, 881–82; Gil Hellín, 447. Also Bishop Luis E. Henriquez Jimenez (auxiliary of Caracas): *Acta Synodalia,* III/III, 839; Gil Hellín, 481.

21. Others had said of the events, *"mysterium ostendit"* (Indonesian bishops), *"mysteria divina recondita manifestant"* (Tabera Araoz), *"manifestant credenti gloriam Filii Dei"* (Archbishop L. Jaeger, *Acta Synodalia,* III/III, 844; Gil Hellín, 471). But the most suggestive formulation (*"Eius opera...perficiunt et suo modo iam manifestant ipsum salutis mysterium"*; *Acta Synodalia,* III/III, 889; Gil Hellín, 398) was submitted by a minority group of five bishops of French origin, including Marcel Lefebvre, formerly archbishop of Dakar, Senegal, but in 1963 superior general of the Congregation of the Holy Spirit.

22. Lienart: *Acta Synodalia,* I/III, 32f.; Gil Hellín, 196f. Guerry: *Acta Synodalia,* I/III, 99–101; Gil Hellín, 246. Schmitt: *Acta Synodalia,* I/III, 128–30; Gil Hellín, 260–63. Hakim: *Acta Synodalia,* I/III, 152f.; Gil Hellín, 276f. Garrone: *Acta Synodalia,* I/III, 188–91; Gil Hellín, 300f. Ancel: *Acta Synodalia,* I/III, 203–4; Gil Hellín, 311–13. Veuillot: *Acta Synodalia,* I/III, 285–87. Bishop Schmitt concentrated on Christ as God's revelation in his

very person, as is treated in C. Aparicio's article in this volume. Bishop Veuillot offered a new opening section on revelation, composed by Father Jean Daniélou, which Archbishop Garrone then contributed to the Mixed Commission in late November. The approach of the French bishops has been identified and studied in the dissertation of B. Cahill, published as *The Renewal of Revelation Theology (1960–1962),* Tesi Gregoriana, Serie Teologia, 51 (Rome: Gregorian University Press, 1999).

23. Elchinger: as in n. 10 above.

24. Indonesian bishops: *Acta Synodalia,* III/III, 914–15. Gil Hellín, 432. Baudoux: as in n. 18 above. The French group: as in n. 21. Tabera Araoz: as in n. 20. Jaeger: *Acta Synodalia,* III/III, 843–44; Gil Hellín, 471.

25. Provence: as in n. 17 above. Central African bishops: as in n. 18 above. The two biblical texts were supplied by Father Smulders himself, but only the reference to Matthew 24 was approved by the subcommission for the *Textus emendatus.*

26. Among those pointing to eschatological revelation were the bishops of western France: *Acta Synodalia,* III/III, 901; Gil Hellín, 376. Also, the French minority of five, as in n. 21 above, along with Bishop Antonio Bagnoli (Fiesole, Italy): *Acta Synodalia,* III/III, 803; Gil Hellín, 404. This was also one of many recommendations made in the text of the bishops of the German-language area and Scandinavia: *Acta Synodalia,* III/III, 907; Gil Hellín, 415, which also offered at some length its preferred way to state the finality of revelation in Christ. Archbishop Lorenz Jaeger sent in a more concise statement, namely, that no more intimate divine communication can possibly be given than that realized by the Incarnate Word and indwelling Spirit of God (*Acta Synodalia,* III/III, 843; Gil Hellín, 471). Father Smulders elaborated this with five New Testament texts in his *relatio,* noting how this would prepare the later treatment of apostolic and ecclesial tradition, but he concluded that such an explanation, although valuable, would go beyond the concision marking other points of revelation doctrine in the developing text.

27. The completion of revelation with the apostles is an antimodernist doctrine of the decree *Lamentabili* (1907; DS 3421). Carli: *Acta Synodalia,* III/III, 819; Gil Hellín, 355. Seitz: *Acta Synodalia,* III/III, 877; Gil Hellín, 384. This refusal was challenged during the Third Period by Cardinal Ernesto Ruffini (Palermo) and Archbishop Armando Fares (Catanzaro, Italy), but the Doctrinal Commission held its ground, stating that to speak of the "closure"of revelation would introduce complications from a variety of perspectives (Gil Hellín, 34).

28. G. O'Collins, "Revelation Past and Present," in *Vatican II: Assessment and Perspectives,* ed. R. Latourelle (New York/Mahwah, N.J.: Paulist, 1988), 1, 125–37. Also published in *Retrieving Fundamental Theology* (see n. 1 above), 87–97.

29. The German-speaking and Scandinavian bishops: *Acta Synodalia,* III/III, 907; Gil Hellín, 416. Tabera Araoz: *Acta Synodalia,* III/III, 882; Gil Hellín, 448. Jaeger: *Acta Synodalia,* III/III, 844; Gil Hellín, 471. Silva Henriquez: *Acta Synodalia,* III/III, 798; Gil Hellín, 478.

30. Conway: *Acta Synodalia,* III/III, 825; Gil Hellín, 396. Silva Henriquez: *Acta Synodalia,* III/III, 796; Gil Hellín, 476. The latter text also proposed a more ample view of faith, closely based on the recommendation of the German-speaking bishops, with Pauline and Johannine passages: *Acta Synodalia,* III/III, 798; Gil Hellín, 478. Based on a later intervention of the German-speaking and Scandinavian bishops during the Third Period (*Acta Synodalia,* III/III, 146–47; Gil Hellín, 533), a more personal trait entered *Dei Verbum* 5, on faith *"qua homo se totum libere Deo committit."*

31. German-speaking and Scandinavian bishops: as in n. 29. Butler: *Acta Synodalia,* III/III, 813; Gil Hellín, 464.

32. In a conversation in Frankfurt in early 1967, Father Otto Semmelroth told the author that he was responsible for this modification, which passed into *Dei Verbum* 5, and that the recognition of Rousselot was intentional.

33. Butler: *Acta Synodalia,* III/III, 813; Gil Hellín, 463.

34. The *relatio* justifying this excision is given in Gil Hellín, 44. Had the passage been kept, *Dei Verbum* would have expressed a theme of Pope John XXIII's inaugural discourse of 1962, namely, that the church is steward of truths enlightening all spheres of life. It would also have shown the little-noted coherence of *Dei Verbum* and *Gaudium et Spes,* since the latter does develop a revelation doctrine in the light of which one can live human life to the full. On this, see C. Aparicio, *La Plenitud del Ser Humano: La Revelación en la "Gaudium et spes,"* Tesi Gregoriana, Serie Teologica, 17 (Rome: Gregorian University Press, 1997).

7. Globalization: Discovery of Catholicity

Karl H. Neufeld, S.J.

Since Vatican II fundamental theology has undergone many changes. With the constitution *Lumen Gentium* the council gave for the first time dogmatic status to discussion of the church—a subject traditionally dealt with in fundamental theology. Later on, revelation was given new emphasis by the Dogmatic Constitution *Dei Verbum,* even if the question of revelation would become the heart of further developments in fundamental theology.[1] It seemed to many that the apologetic mind that had marked thinking in fundamental theology before the council, especially since the antimodernistic struggle, had discredited the discipline and even had made it obsolete. This left the impression that apologetics were no longer necessary and even ran counter to the ecumenical spirit so much in favor after the council. What remained, as some were strongly convinced, was to consider and rely on other disciplines such as fundamental exegesis, fundamental moral theology, fundamental catechetics, and so on. But many felt that treatment of the church still demanded attention in fundamental theology and that real problems were being overlooked. Developments in the contemporary world required consideration of a new foundation of religion, a consideration of Christian faith and church in the context of today.

QUESTIONS AND DIMENSIONS

Fundamental theology must be more than a simple introduction to other disciplines or just a preparation for theology. In addition, new difficulties emerged as fundamental theology attempted to respond to insights that had arisen since the early 1970s. Because of the varying contexts, the responses to these insights were often very diverse. It was then that, together with R. Latourelle in Rome, Gerald O'Collins published in the early 1980s *Problems and Perspectives of Fundamental Theology* (Italian, Brescia: Queriniana, 1980; English, New York: Paulist, 1982), a representation of various viewpoints from all over the world.

Certainly a new image of fundamental theology was the central point, but before it could be dealt with, the contemporary situation needed to be sketched out. Some colleagues described their work since the council. Others attempted to show that classic fundamental theology was not out of use as many had thought. At the same time there were indications that difficulties of another type were bursting onto the scene, even if the official end of the Communist system was not yet foreseen. With the newly developed dialogue, that is, conversations in order to clear up differences with better understanding, people began to see changes and great differences in attitudes. With the collapse of Communism in 1989 a new era in the development of conditions for fundamental theology began. In a certain sense apologetics again seemed necessary.

How should fundamental theology respond to these new conditions? The first step required updating dictionaries,[2] with articles outlining the prevailing status of key terms of theological discussion. Even here the need to reformulate fundamental theology was evident from both the inside and the outside, the result of theological discussion and a new, changing situation. When people ask about the main topics discussed in this evolution they find, above all, responses linked to diversity as well as a basic need for unity. This experience led to the issue called "globalization." For Christians, the task receives a new emphasis and a certain urgency from the call for dialogue with other religions and from the differing presuppositions in the modern theology of religions. Here it is sufficient to mention the name of John Hick. In the German-speaking world, the confrontation came with new interpretations of the "postmodern" period, which followed certain ideas coming from France and was marked by questions directed to fundamental theology. At the same time the memory of the Holocaust has inspired further writings by critics of fundamental theology as it has been done up to now. The principal effort seems to be on the level of the so-called learned consideration of Christian truth, often involving specialized methods in academic centers. This should not be surprising if we are aware of the world in which we live; fundamental theology cannot be done outside the concrete framework that influences the world and theology itself.

In looking at all these questions and possibilities, one could conclude that there we need several different fundamental theologies to deal with the various tasks given here or there. Without denying such a diversity, fundamental theology for the first time serves the unity of theological thinking by providing the tools for such a reflection. Currently, globalization gives great importance to fundamental theology's task. Some think that globalization simply coordinates given facts without relating them internally to the whole, or, as is often said, the sum of the parts. But most people are aware that globalization is more than the result of an addition. Fundamental theology needs to ask how best to show and to explain its starting point, and how best to provide the basis for belief and for theology. As an example, liberation could ask for foundations corresponding to its particular reflection on faith. Likewise fundamental theology in an Asian context needs to be considered a necessary element for a theology that must consider the great religions of that part of the world, which has only a small number of Christians. The propositions of African theology similarly must take into account the traditions experienced by people of that continent. It seems that only countries bordering on the North Atlantic look at the task in a more general way; but when we examine this impression we find the presuppositions of the Western world so intertwined that a dialogue between the different aspects of fundamental theology as just described cannot even begin.[3]

In particular, we see this diversity when we take into account interreligious dialogue and the question of a plurality of theologies of religions.[4] Each religion has its own foundations and bases, that is, its own way to consider the data and deal with them. What, then, could be the common elements necessary to have a meaningful dialogue? Without doubt, Christian faith has its orientation in the truth of the gospel and in the faith of believers gathered in the church, the mediator of tradition. But these realities are not possible outside of concrete cultures, which are necessary only on a second level: being a Christian does not require as a first condition that one become a Jew or a Greek or a Roman; the Lord can touch all people in their own situations, wherever they live. To become a believer in Christ is not connected with this or that privileged culture, but with the current context. It is the universal sense of catholicity that we understand in Christian language and that of globalization when we speak of it in contemporary thought.

In view of these observations, the way we consider new questions like those just raised with regard to fundamental theology seems obvious. We cannot continue simply with habitual reflection on faith; after the collapse of Communism the current world scene calls for new judgments and other analyses. In today's world the need for apologetics in the traditional sense does not exist as it did before. Controversies, polemics, and apologetics have all had their time because they all derived from premises that determined the form of the answers. This does not deny that such elements still have some importance, but they do not respond to the needs of today's world.

THE ACCESS

The first great task for fundamental theology is offering informed experience as a basis for a reflection that meets the needs of being a Christian today. There is also the issue of its being a basis for faith in a responsible and conscientious way, something that looks new but has been taken for granted for a long time. This comprises not only the right starting point but also the first of many steps leading in the right direction.

In the contemporary world the first difficulty lies in finding a foundation for Christian belief that both leads to an encounter with Jesus Christ and also provokes the assent of faith. Since traditional religious culture is lacking more and more today, the result is a fragmentary knowledge of the gospel, but no understanding of the person of Jesus and his whole message. Consequently people seek answers about this or that element but not about the gospel as such, that is, Jesus Christ revealed. Our faith is not a faith of words, of miracles, of parts—we believe in Jesus Christ or we are not believers at all. The whole New Testament speaks of the encounter with Jesus as the Christ. Seeing that understanding it remains simple and difficult at the same time. We need to understand the difficulties of men and women in order to discover and make this foundation available to them. Where basic experiences are absent, where principal terms have no meaning, where it is impossible to adequately formulate the meaning of life, where people are unable to insert themselves into a larger understanding of reality, the spiritual foundation must be learned anew.

Previously many of these things seemed self-evident. But the scene has changed profoundly. Normally we make a distinction between the end and the path leading to it. In the Fourth Gospel John tells us that Jesus declared himself: "I am the way, the truth and the life" (John 14:6). Surely he is the way leading to the Father, but he is the way. And without this way there is no access to the Father, or in other words, no access to Christian faith.

The New Testament has already formulated the question of the "way" along with concrete indications for reflection. The formulation could lead to the idea that there is only one way to God. This is true if, at the same time, we realize that this one way comprises different and limitless possibilities and remains open to every person. The absoluteness of the Christian claim does not exist without this universal openness. Finding this open door is the task of the invited people, and it is possible that not all find it without difficulty; there are differences here as everywhere in human life, but these differences do not exclude someone definitively. Continuing research constitutes the logical next step. Investigating the foundation of faith always includes the community of faith, which helps not only the community as a whole but also its individual members. The great challenge of the incarnation lies in the fact that Jesus Christ is concretely united to God and to us as word-flesh.

Here the diversity of creation takes part in the mission of Jesus Christ, a possibility that can also alter the true sense of the mission. Error and sin are not excluded—facts that theologies must always consider—but misuse does not abolish the possibility of good use. And so this worldly part of us is both served by Christ's mission and serves it. When diversity receives coherence and orientation, it shows the possibility that it does not mean absolute decay and destruction. Of course, it is not always easy to see how this orientation works, and new models need to be formed. But these new insights mean that building the foundation remains a duty and is sometimes hard work. On the other hand, by going in this direction we note those experiences that give hope and security, support, and surety. To speak about the foundation is not enough, even if the discourse about such a theme has its basis in experience itself. In our times we need a sensitivity of this kind in order to take responsibility in choosing the direction of the gospel. Sensitivity allows us to speak about this experience to others and to witness the dynamic of this evolution, or better, of this new life. Each new step on the way discloses more deeply the foundation; it deepens our convictions and introduces us more into the bond uniting us with Jesus Christ in the world of God and the world of men and women

It is an invitation; there is no compulsion. On one hand it means that there is grace; on the other that there is freedom. And this also has consequences for reflection, for we cannot count on fixed reasons and deductions. A formulation must say something personal, which depends more on other factors than on some type of constraint. Our thinking and speaking must consider this if we are to keep in mind the real nature of what happens.

The spiritual recognition of God's grace-filled freedom and of men's and women's free reactions challenges any reflection on faith. It is always difficult to consider something open-ended, not determined. In this regard analyzing both the gospel and the response of the believer to the invitation or call, which respects the responsibility of the hearer, best serves the way of truly grasping the importance of Christianity. Here is another starting point on which to base fruitful diversity. Taking the gospel as invitation will lead the hearers to find out what promise they follow. The dynamics of a search characterize the whole movement. In searching practically, the foundation shows itself not only as a door or an entrance, but as a path, that is, a living process.

FUNDAMENTAL THEOLOGY—TO WHAT END?

Until recently fundamental theology very often was presented as a general sort of foundation of theology and even as a justification of faith valuable for all situations. But today's climate of interreligious and intercultural dialogue raises difficult questions about this assumption. In a certain sense fundamental theology had been even more closely linked to spiritual and cultural presuppositions than other disciplines in the field of reflection on faith. Responding to actual challenges, fundamental theology remained dependent on those who attacked the faith and those who defended it. These efforts show many connections with Western philosophy and history, with the mentality of a time and place, even if the results were formalized and abstracted in order to generalize its contribution. The consequences often seemed to be false ideas about a more or less presumed universal value of an elaborated instrument. The impression is not simply false, since it remains a principal task of fundamental theology to assure the possibility of a common foundation for the greater unity of the Christian world. But at the same time the diversity is not out there somewhere, but takes part in the contribution of fundamental theology itself. Here a responsible distinction is needed, which until now has not yet appeared, been elaborated, or practiced. Let us make some simple distinctions to justify this claim.

The title of this article refers to the worldwide process of globalization and tries to bind it to the Christian aim of catholicity. Fundamental theologians, conscious of their duty and also of given situations, must take up this task knowing the specific risk of such an enterprise.

The searched result—that is the first condition—cannot consist in an even greater abstraction or more complex model that presupposes all which must be avoided, since this form of reflection is to be treated universally. By going back to the very roots of the gospel and Christian faith, we can arrive at a basic formulation and method that supports different types of responses demanded by different churches in our multicultural world. It is clear that such a *retour aux sources* must be attempted also in concrete situations in which churches find themselves so that those who engage themselves in this manner know and take into account these conditions. In this sense the question of Jesus becomes decisive and remains—posed in the right manner—the source of how the invitation should be understood as well as all that goes with it.

The history of theology of the last few centuries shows the errors of false questions and essays on this topic. Such impasses are possible; people are not forced to lose themselves. We can try again, but in another way. And we must do so for the common foundation of Christian faith worldwide to operate effectively by gathering together what seems to be the Christian creed existing in a variety of situations and circumstances.

The second condition requires finding in the development of openness the yet-to-be-discovered richness of Christianity diversity; here the ecumenical sense will help us see and judge what is constructive and what is destructive. This openness enables people to say yes, but also to say no when necessary. In this way fundamental theology becomes an art of distinction and decision. Self-criticism will also be needed, but aims to offer a formulation of what a reflection of Christian faith today can be and should be. Likewise men and women who wish to live as Christian believers cannot be overlooked. The openness mentioned above includes respecting persons and personal relations.

And so the third condition consists in taking seriously interreligious dialogue and all that is needed for it. Of course this is not the direct task of fundamental theology but a necessary preparation for it. Today we know quite well the importance of such preparation for spiritual struggles and for dialogue and communication in general. This condition takes in far more than exchanges between representatives of different religions. If it works it could be offered as an approach to many problems, tensions, confrontations, and so on. The question of power and how to deal with it is central. The fall of a great power has shown its importance and significance especially as minor nations tried to fill up the gap instead of trying to overcome the superficial order of mere power and finding a new manner of being together corresponding to the dignity and rights claimed for men and women today. Between the theoretical aims and the daily reality of human relations there remains great opposition, even contradictions. The field of interreligious dialogue could be a training camp for suggesting the right changes. Fundamental theology, in preparing this field, in correcting it, and in helping people use it according to the declared aims, could provide valuable experiences and suggestions for the wider difficulties in our world.

The main purpose of fundamental theology is to enable believers to have a conscious understanding of their being Christian and to continue to reflect on their faith. This must be communicable not only to justify their beliefs but also for witness and proclamation. This also provides the starting point for elaborating theology in all its disciplines to serve people with better understanding and deeper insight. The feedback will influence faith itself, shape its development, and show how it can be inserted into our contemporary world. As a public reality, Christian faith will not only reach and change the individual or groups, but believers will be convinced that their faith is important for public order and will realize that special conditions of communication must be observed. These conditions involve both cultural and spiritual realities whose influence simply cannot be predetermined, as well as a mutual exchange that looks at the nature and the role of all the factors involved.

The end of fundamental theology is therefore not just a term but rather a process leading to the term, with room for all to enter this movement as necessary and helpful elements, including thinking people. Perhaps the reader has been wondering why, after the publication of the recent encyclical *Fides et Ratio,* this factor has not yet been mentioned. But all elements must be considered in dealing with this question. Thinking Christians and some initial steps have led us today to make such an effort—something that needs to be explained in clear manner. Fundamental theology has become very aware of the changes of the last generation, especially in the last few years. Our awareness could be fragmentary, our evaluation might be hazy, but the lesson appears with doubt: no longer can we do fundamental theology outside of concrete times and places.

SOMEONE DOING FUNDAMENTAL THEOLOGY

To honor Gerald O'Collins we can conclude by remembering that he came from Australia and received training in the United States and Great Britain before taking up his main work in Rome, without losing contact with the other parts of the world he knew. This personal experience of globalization has had practical effects on his theological contribution, always closely linked to the lived faith of people. His great involvement in widespread publications of the English-speaking world shows how he deals with such themes. Theology in the service of the people of God has thus gained in this way the new dimensions we have just explored.

The challenge of Rome in such a situation seems a very old one: What are the sense and signification of catholicity? Do we not find here some very important factors in order to take the globalization of today as our proper task in light of the many specific possibilities Christianity has learned and gained throughout the ages? We cannot say that the task is completed. Perhaps we must even recognize that only the first step has been taken and there remains very much to do. It does not matter as long as there is hope that the church is pursuing the right course.

Notes

1. See G. O'Collins, *Theology and Revelation* (Notre Dame, Ind.: Fides, 1968), and in *Vatican II: Assessment and Perspectives 1* (New York: Paulist, 1988), 125–37.

2. See G. O'Collins, *A Concise Dictionary of Theology* (New York: Paulist, 1991); idem in *The Encyclopedia of Religion,* ed. Mircea Eliade (New York: Macmillan, 1987); and in *The Anchor Bible Dictionary,* ed. David Noel Freedman (New York: Doubleday, 1992).

3. It is not so important to give examples here because they can be found without great difficulty. But it remains decisive that there is no common model allowing a simple comparison.

4. Another contribution to this volume, for example, deals with John Hick's Christology and Gerald O'Collins's response.

III

Fundamental Theology and Spirituality

8. Society, Academy, and Church: Who Can Read the Bible?[1]

Nicholas King, S.J.

> But rich he was of holy thought and werk.
> He was also a lerned man, a clerk,
> That Christes gospel trewly wolde preche.
> > Geoffrey Chaucer, *The Canterbury Tales,*
> > General Prologue, 479–81

Gerry O'Collins (can someone so perennially youthful really be seventy?) would certainly be highly embarrassed at the application to him of Chaucer's admiring lines about the "poor parson," carefully contrasted with his robust predecessor and fellow pilgrim, the "Wife of Bath." Yet in his writings Gerry has not only for many years given us fine scholarship, accessibly presented, but he has also, especially in his writings on spirituality (to which more than a few of us are indebted[2]), testified that good theology involves a faith commitment. He bridges the gulf between learning and life. Another chasm that, apparently effortlessly, he likewise bestrides, is the one between theology and the study of scripture. In both these respects Gerry is a prophetic figure, challenging the rest of us to reunite spirituality and doctrine, exegesis and dogmatics.

In almost any of his writings in systematic theology, what I find striking is a rare quality among theologians: his surefootedness when he speaks of scripture. First and foremost, he knows the text well and has made it his own; he speaks authoritatively of the several evangelists, for instance, and knows their differences *from the inside;* he stays in close touch with modern biblical scholarship. And then he makes up his own mind.[3]

Like Joseph Fitzmyer and the late Raymond Brown, O'Collins finds his place firmly in both academy and church. This does not mean that all scholars would agree with him (for no two scholars ever agree on anything for more than about a week), nor that all representatives of the institutional church would happily accept everything he says (for such people earn their salaries by worrying about the implications of what scholars say). He belongs, nevertheless, fairly and squarely in the people of God. He is also, of course, a thoroughly pastoral person, wholly at home in modern culture (witness his constant citations of recent novels and films), and knows that as well as church and academy there is also that amorphous mass called society to consider when pondering the reading and the meaning of the Word of God.

Not all readers of the Bible nor all students of theology have Gerry O'Collins's easy familiarity with these disparate fields; so it seemed good to attempt a discussion of them and to blink myopically into the future, to see if the way ahead might lead to their rapprochement. As one who for a decade now has been reading the biblical texts in various modes in the rich and vibrant South African context, or set of contexts, I should like to share with readers something of those different contexts. This means that this contribution will be form-critically rather odd, partly resembling something with scholarly pretensions and partly having an autobiographical feel to it.

I want to argue, first, that the different "constituencies" of South African Bible readers and the different approaches they take to the text all tend in the direction not of confusion but of enrichment, and, second, that this enrichment is possible only because "there is something about the Bible." There are, I know, atheist and agnostic friends of mine who will shift irritably at this proposition, but this essay is for Gerry O'Collins and not for them. In it I shall say something first about the different constituencies of Bible readers and then about the different ways of reading the Bible that make for such a rich and apparently confusing mix. I argue that the church is the privileged site for reading the Bible, although it is not quite as simple as that.

THE DIFFERENT "CONSTITUENCIES"

We have spoken already of society, church, and academy. There is a certain imprecision about our use of such terms. *Society* is rather hard to define, but as a heuristic or working definition, I shall occasionally use the word to mean South Africans at large, whatever they do or believe. More often, however, it will refer to Bible readers who are not (in some sense or other) church leaders or biblical "experts." The term is intended to remind us that the Bible is in the public domain, is part of the cultural baggage of the West, and has played its part (albeit an ambiguous one) in the recent history of Africa. Society tends to use the phrase "the Bible says..." in a literalist way and to look with misgivings on biblical readers both in church and in the lecture hall.

By *church* I mean the community and communities of believers that have handed down the scripture; this group, for whom the Bible is "the church's gift to itself," sees itself as belonging to a community that "owns" the text. Presumably all church readers of the Bible belong also in society, and at least some also are members of the academy. Nevertheless, and for the reason of this explicit assertion of ownership, this group makes a particularly important claim when the Bible is discussed. They will also use the phrase "the Bible says...," but probably in a different way from society.

The third group, which I am calling the *academy,* is unlikely to employ this phrase at all. These have learned the languages of the Bible and studied the background from which it emerged. Some biblical scholars are, of course, members of churches, and some are not; of those who are, at least some find themselves offering quite different readings of biblical texts in the pulpit and in the lecture hall. This group is no more homogeneous than the other two, and tensions can exist between those academics who are and those who are not believers.

At all events, the main point is clear: there are groups of potential readers of the Bible in this country, each of whom may have a different agenda. The differences between them may conceal (at times barely conceal) a squabble for power. We should not deceive ourselves: there is power in the Bible, and we human beings tend to behave rather oddly when faced with the means to power.

THE DIFFERENT WAYS OF READING

In addition to the different sorts of people who may be classed as readers of the Bible in this country and elsewhere, there are also different ways of reading the Bible. Here I do not primarily refer to the "ordinary reader" who picks up the scriptures and reads, but to the "expert reader" who has read or written and thought about "how to read" and has an awareness of the philosophical complexity of the deceptively simple process that we call "reading the Bible."

The first way of reading, the one on which most of us cut our *bibelwissenschaftlich* teeth, is the historical-critical method, including at least—though its boundaries are somewhat fluid—source and form criticism, perhaps also textual criticism, and, more lately on the scene, redaction criticism. What this method, or collection of methods, seeks to establish may be lumped together as "what the original meant." This approach to reading the Bible has been of considerable importance in South Africa. The Dutch Reformed Churches very sensibly insist on seven years of study for their ministers, including a good working knowledge of Greek and Hebrew; and they have looked to the best of German scholarship in the course of their training. The result has been a delayed-action impact on their congregations, and it has helped to prepare the Afrikaner people for a new way of looking at South African society.

At least four other approaches to reading have had a good deal to say to Bible readers in South Africa.[4] The first, *liberation hermeneutics,* has been of immense importance for a small number of readers, especially during the time of the struggle against apartheid.[5] This way of reading the text enables readers to resist unjust authority without feeling that they are disobeying biblical injunctions,[6] and asserts that God is actually on the side of the marginalized and the oppressed. For such readers, the phrase "the Bible says" introduces the possibility of liberation from an oppressive situation[7] by reading texts "through the eyes of the poor," and the desire to change the structures of an unjust society. Liberation hermeneutics has spawned a variety of offspring, sometimes lumped together as "advocacy criticism,"[8] which privileges the vantage point of the "poor and marginalized," including women, and thereby makes the important point that all theology is "interested."

The second is *reader-response criticism,* which has posited the reader as an active source of meaning. This has the effect of putting a question mark over the historical-critical methods, shifting the emphasis away "from the origins of texts, the world that produced the text."[9] Here the reader says to her- or himself, "I construct the meaning." This way of reading rests on an obvious fact, though it may take it too far, that a text does not come alive until it is read. The reader has an active part to play, and the writer surrenders control and has no further rights over the marks he or she makes on paper.

The third is *postmodernism,* whose stance before a text could be caricatured as "it might mean anything at all." The problem here is that nobody quite knows what the postmodernist approach is (perhaps that is the point). Certainly no one ever defines it, except in terms that leave one gasping for meaning. Very sensibly, Gerald West contents himself with the following allusive dance around the idea: "all is uncertainty, all is unstable; all is not as it has seemed. Difference and deconstruction foreground the particular and the partial."[10] For all the uncertainty, it probably suits well the fractured culture of modern South African urban life, both the townships, where traditional customs have been forgotten and family life destabilized, and the wealthy suburbs that have ceased to be clearly defined territories of particular tribes. In both settings, people reflect nostalgically that "we knew where we were in those days." Both postmodernist culture and postapartheid South Africa are charged with a sense of loss of meaning, which conceals the yearning, misplaced as it may be, for "the old values." Both, likewise, point implacably to the impossibility of turning back the clock.

The fourth is what West calls *enculturation hermeneutics.* This way of reading asks, How is the Bible received, or how can it be received, in my culture? It fits well the current situation of South Africa, with its twelve official languages and even greater multitude of cultures ("in Africa," the saying goes, "the culture changes each time you cross a river"). This can be described in two metaphors: the more optimistic one is that of the "rainbow nation," which remains serviceable, even though it is used too readily and has become a cliché; less optimistic is that which sees different cultures as "tectonic plates," which rub up against each other and have seismic impact on the societies where they meet. Inculturation is a tricky art; it is as old as the gospel itself, though the word was coined, apparently by the Thirty-second General Congregation of the Society of Jesus, only in 1975.[11] African cultures on the whole find themselves more at home in the biblical world than European ones do, so African readers have much instruction to give Western readers.[12] Our cultural background affects the way we read. Inculturation is a constant challenge, and African readings never fail to resist the European package in which biblical reading is sometimes wrapped. The fact is that the gospel challenges all cultures in which it is proclaimed. Inculturation does not assume that "my culture" is a static concept, unaffected by the *Zeitgeist* or the changes that history begins.

A WAY OUT OF THE CONFUSION?

What I write here is, therefore, intended partially as a contribution to a debate that rages, in the light of this confusion of role players and ways of reading, in university common rooms in Europe and America and is not unknown even in the gentler atmosphere of South African universities. The field of biblical studies in these universities seems sometimes to find itself trapped between a nether and an upper stone. There are two ways in which it can find itself in this uncomfortable bind. In both cases, one of the two stones is the heavy affirmation that "the Bible says," and the other is the lighter, and apparently subversive, "but what *does* the Bible say?"

The first case highlights the clash between an uncritical and a postcritical reading of the text, between what is sometimes called "fundamentalist literalism" and the insights hard won through the last two centuries of academic biblical study. This clash will most characteristically present itself as one between the "simple faith" of theology students who want to learn more about God and the rather more complex position of a modern scripture scholar who may or may not have a faith commitment.

The second case is apt to occur within biblical studies departments in universities and to consist of the clash between lecturers who have a denominational allegiance and those for whom the biblical texts are an object of academic study in principle no different from the Ras Shamra tablets or the *Shepherd of Hermas*.

Both cases raise a question of ownership and of power. I recall hearing, and to some extent sympathizing with, a very distinguished semitist complaining about the lamentable standard of Hebrew attained by the group that he classed, with dismissive contempt, as "theologians," who made themselves acquainted with only so much Hebrew as they needed to jump through their theological hoops, while his whole life was given over to a passion for Northwest Semitic languages and the light shed on the development of these languages, including Biblical Hebrew, by certain well-known archaeological discoveries in the course of the present century.

Despite my sympathy with the student of Semitics, I should like to suggest, rather against the current trend, that standing in the continuous living tradition that uses the Bible in prayer and worship gives believers a privileged position for understanding the texts that compose the Bible, because "there is something about the Bible." Insofar, therefore, as there is a clash between the academy and the church as privileged readers, I fall on the side of the latter. And I think that there is a clash. If a professor mentions over coffee in the senior common room that Jesus Christ is everything to him or that the resurrection is the center of his faith, the academy shifts in its seat, uneasy and embarrassed, for that is the question to be resolved, not the starting point.

ACADEMY VERSUS CHURCH?

This position needs to be hedged and fenced around with a good many qualifications. The academic clearly does have some rights over the text. Believers espouse many even quite persistent traditions that have no real continuity with biblical origins, and a fair-minded nonbeliever with a profound knowledge of the biblical languages is probably in a better position to know what the text may originally have meant, or what it could not possibly have meant, than an uncritical literalist dependent on a translation into his or her own language.

The academic has worked hard on the text, crafting day and night to make it yield its secrets, and comparing it with related texts in the same or other languages. One could argue that the academic biblical scholar has something of the same rights over the text as the explorer who plants the country's flag on hitherto unknown territory. One must avoid intellectual colonialism here, of course, for no one "owns" the text any more than nineteenth-century explorers who claimed parts of Africa on behalf of European powers could be said to "own" the land so demarcated. Nevertheless they do have authority of a kind when it comes to interpreting the text.

The church reader, however, also has rights. The New Testament as a canon simply did not exist until the end of the fourth century,[13] and makes no sense except as a collection of texts made by the community of those who regarded themselves as disciples of Jesus. The texts are intended to shed light (in each case a very different sort of light) on the mystery of who Jesus is and what the implications of Jesus' identity are for those who wish to be his disciples.

This is what lies behind the hermeneutical approach associated with the name of Brevard Childs, often called "canonical criticism."[14] This essay does not examine the merits of this approach, though I think it has both strengths and weaknesses;[15] all I should like to do here is point to an unconscious assumption on the part of those who uncritically espouse the historical-critical method that their approach is value-free and therefore potentially more apt to reach the original meaning. No interpretation is value-free, and postmodernism has taught us not to be too optimistic about "original meanings."

Can we referee between the conflicting claims of church and academy? Philip R. Davies, pillar of the Qumran academy, has argued in a slight but interesting, if at times mischievous, work that we do not need to.[16] Davies, if I understand him correctly, is very much of the academy and no longer a believing member of the church. He argues that "the difference of interest between church and academy is…not really a problem to either side."[17]

At the heart of his case is the useful distinction between two different kinds of discourse. The church studies the text with a "confessional" agenda, while the uncommitted academician is free of those restraints. Davies offers an interesting analogy on the distinction of discourses. "Discourses are like currencies, they may have an intrinsic value, but they are used mostly to permit the exchange of goods between persons within a society and between societies." Here, however, is the rub for the church reader: "A confessional currency has no intrinsic value and is non-exchangeable. It is a soft currency which is unable to be negotiated outside its own country."[18] So Davies argues that we should distinguish between "scripture," which is Bible study done from a confessional direction, and "biblical studies," which is not. At one point it seems that "scripture" is to biblical studies as astrology is to astronomy and alchemy is to chemistry.[19]

There may well be an important point here, although perhaps too strongly expressed.[20] If we were to take this with absolute seriousness, then no believing student of the biblical text could ever manage a conversation with one who had no such faith commitment. There are different priorities for a believer who reads or studies the biblical texts; but the thread of the argument is stretched to the breaking point when Davies says that "the end point of the discipline of 'scripture' is the definition or clarification of the theology of a particular religion...the ultimate object of this discipline is integration within the broad contours of theology," and that its conclusions "are circumscribed in advance by credal considerations." This seems to drive a somewhat meretricious wedge between the two forms of discourse. A believer, after all, and a nonbeliever can have a perfectly sensible discussion about Ugaritic verb forms or Western noninterpolations; in academic discourse in general, the conclusions are of less importance than the journey toward them, the method of traveling, and the stations on the way. Davies seems to argue that not believing in a god makes one a more appropriate exponent of academic biblical studies. Presented in this form, his argument provides a good example of why we need to distinguish between forms of discourse. We did not have to speak of them before the wedge was driven between church and academy by Enlightenment rationalism; speech about discourses reflects a pluriform intellectual world, where Christian belief is simply one option among others. There is no point in lamenting this state of affairs; it is a fact and is not to be wished away. We may, however, resist Davies's implicit claim that his form of discourse is superior to the other.

It seems to me that the boot may be on the other foot and that it is possible to argue that confessional approaches to the text of the New Testament are on surer footing and that the believing reader is in his or her own territory in a way that is simply not the case for an unbelieving scholar, no matter how competent. Certainly the New Testament (if we may indulge in a convenient fiction) appears so to believe, for hardly any of its twenty-seven documents makes any pretense at being comprehensible other than against a background where the Old Testament is authoritative. Not only is each addressed to the community of believers, but it was the community of believers who, in the course of several centuries and not without a good many bitter battles, decided that these texts were what the community wanted to say to itself about Jesus and about discipleship. This is so, even though the collection of documents reflects an impressive diversity of views.[21]

Nor is the case weakened by the admission that the New Testament has a tendency to challenge the reader rather disconcertingly.

Indeed the "church reader" who approaches the text expecting to find in its lines something to assist in the living of his or her faith commitment may be better positioned to answer the challenge than the scholar for whom it is simply another text, and who does not expect to find herself addressed about the proper conduct of life. The fact is that the New Testament and what Christians call the "Old Testament" are, if we may leave aside the lack of agreement on what precisely constitutes them, the "church's gift to itself." What determines the New Testament texts to be collected under this catch-all (or catch-some?) rubric is not that they were written by apostles, for they were not; nor that they were dictated by the Holy Spirit, for inspiration is a more complicated idea than such an expression would suggest, and divine causation in principle differs from the ordinary link between effect and cause. What proclaims these documents as "New Testament" and denies that label to other similar documents is, quite simply, the church. That church has, moreover, an unbroken tradition of using the texts to feed its private devotions and its public celebrations, not to mention its theological formulations. So in an important sense the church has proprietary rights over the Bible. At the same time, of course, the "divine discomfort" that scripture induces means that the community of believers will do well to treat the Bible with the same circumspection that the owners of a Rottweiler tend to accord their watchdog.

This will, of course, seem an odd line of argument to South Africans, for the greater number of Bible readers in this country have always done their Bible reading from the point of view of a Reformed ecclesiology. As a result, the scriptures have been taken, if one may caricature slightly, as "a hot-line from God" rather than as the product of a community. This view has two further implications: first, such a reader evinces considerable unease when faced with claims from authority—even, or especially, church authority—about "how to read the text."

Second, a reader for whom the text is simply a given will feel likewise thoroughly uncomfortable with the claims of academic readers of the text and may restively mutter that biblical professors are "undermining the faith." They are not (or need not be) doing anything of the kind, of course, only pointing to one or two facts about the transmission of the text from the first pen on papyrus (presumably that of Paul or his amanuensis in 1 Thessalonians) to the deceptively permanent-looking copy of the New Testament in a modern translation that I can hold in my hand. The "Bible" is not quite so secure a phenomenon as we tend to suppose; even establishing the reference of the term is trickier than it might seem at first sight. Do we, for example, mean the Jewish Bible or the Christian Bible? If the latter, do we refer to the tradition, for the Old Testament at any rate, that broadly follows the Masoretic Text or the one that includes also the books embraced by the Septuagint? Once you have sorted that out, which text are we to adopt, and which translation (this deceptively simple question already, of course, conceals an option about the text)?

THE CLAIMS OF SOCIETY OVER THE BIBLE

The "game" of Bible-reading is therefore more complex than it initially appears. The "Bible" is not easily tied down. Worse still, at least two players in the game skirmish for control. A third contestant, moreover, cannot in this country (and probably in most other places also) be excluded from the field. This country has just experienced its second democratic election, a dull affair in comparison with the heady excitements of 1994, but one, nevertheless, in which 84 percent of the electorate took part, and 96 percent of the voting public pronounced themselves satisfied. We can attribute some part of the success of the first election, and perhaps of the second also, to the fact that in all sections of South African society there are those for whom Bible reading is important, and whose lives are actually affected by what and how they read therein. We may call this rather varied constituency "society," provided that we remember that it is an amalgam of several different and, as to their biblical interpretation, differing groups of people.

Two points about them, however, are important for our quest. First, they will tend to resist, even if only unconsciously, the claims of church and academy to any kind of absolute domination over the biblical text. Second, their reading will tend to be "fundamentalist" or "precritical." This will be the case, even if they are from those sections of South African society for whom the Bible is not normative. Their claims are not, at all events, to be ignored.

WHO HAS RIGHTS OVER THE BIBLICAL TEXT?

So we are presented with a somewhat fluid situation. The Bible itself is evidently more impalpable than we had supposed; at least three sorts of readers claim rights over it, and there are at least five (and in fact a good many more, *quot homines, tot lectiones*) ways of reading it.

Faced with this fluidity, what is the hapless South African reader to do? First, I suggest, note that there is "something about the Bible." This will not do for a thoroughgoing postmodernist stance, suspicious of any claims that sound absolute or exclusive. But it seems to me to be the case, and if that is so, then we may have (however reluctantly) to say "so much the worse for postmodernism."

Second, and in a much more deconstructionist vein, we shall have to admit that all three "readers" can lay claim to a piece of the action. More importantly, each of them can ask awkward questions of the other. Society can challenge church and academy's proprietorial pretensions; church can ask the other two about transcendent values and encourage them to explore their own spiritual dimensions and to open up to God; academy can turn its expertise as a torch in dark places, and gently indicate "but you can't say that," when the other two make preposterous claims. All three can challenge the power plays of the other two.

Third, we can learn that all five ways of reading that I have mentioned, and the many others that I have not, provide us with different colored lenses through which to read the text, and so to delve deeper into the different worlds the biblical text reveals. It would follow from this that no single "lens" has any absolute claim; each of them, however, can enrich the reader's encounter with the text.

THERE IS SOMETHING ABOUT THE BIBLE

To say so much is an admirably correct piece of 1960s liberalism (though most of the reading methods I have mentioned are much younger children). I should like, however, to take matters a little further, by way of my statement, maddening as it must be to readers of various persuasions, that "there is something about the Bible." So far, I have not succeeded in saying what this mystical "something" is, but an analogy may help. Visitors to holy places such as Nongoma, Mecca, the Jewish, Christian, and Muslim sites in the Holy Land, or the grotto at Lourdes, experience something they would find hard to explain or even rationally justify. What matters about these places is not what may or may not have happened there, but that people have prayed there. Eliot catches the idea in "Little Gidding":

> ...You are here to kneel
> Where prayer has been valid.

I should like to attempt my own contribution, distilling my experience of the last ten years in South Africa, certainly the most exciting years of my own life and very possibly the most exciting in the country's entire history. The gist of it is this sense of "something about the Bible," an untamed power or a numinous quality that was less evident to me when I first came to the country, or when I learned the aseptic rigor of the historical-critical method with its white-coated votaries. We had in those distant years a good grasp of the Bible's complexity and studied 1QMilḥamah with the same relish as the Carmen Christi; but we had no sense of the Bible's raw power. Ten years in South Africa have taught me something of that and have underlined the importance of the church as a site for reading the Bible; for if you venture into a cage of hungry tigers, you are better off doing it in the company of a professional tamer of tigers.

The following points sum up the experience of studying and teaching New Testament in two seminaries over the last ten years, together with certain other commitments not directly related to the teaching, that has led inexorably in this direction. I offer them not because my experience is unusual but because it may be typical of Bible readers in this country in these days. My aim is not to demonstrate apodictically this assertion of "something about the Bible," but to indicate some markers on a journey.

1. It no longer seems possible to view the text of the New Testament as a solid datum, nor the "intelligent attentive reading" that I seek to encourage in my pupils as a "search for the objective original meaning." This says no more than what many biblical scholars have been thinking for quite a while now; nevertheless, it is a Copernican revolution whose implications may not have been fully apprehended in the academy. Obviously one needs to enter a caveat here: a discovery about Aramaic morphology, for example, such as those yielded by the

scrolls from the Qumran Caves or the Wadi Murabba'at, are *objective* in the sense in which we once used the term with regard to the meaning of the texts. Nevertheless, the general point will stand: Bible reading is not quite like scientific investigation, and we ought no longer to sustain the pretense that it is.

2. It follows from the above that reading the text is no longer an empiricist's rigorous search for the truth, on the model of the scientist's investigation of natural phenomena. The reading I succeed in doing these days is that which is required for teaching; and my teaching has the rather less austere objective of liberating the text[22] and letting it sing.[23] This is, I think, something I have learned from my African students; or perhaps it was just the context.

3. The context has itself changed in these years. Students in the late 1990s read the text quite differently from their predecessors at the beginning of the decade. When the 1980s ended, "grand apartheid" still ruled the scene, and it was obligatory (not that I felt remotely inclined to resist) to read the text in a political and liberationist sense. Nowadays, with South African society far more visibly in a state of transition, students tend instead to look for solid rocks of systematic theology and scripture on which to build safe houses; so their readings tend to be more settled than open to an excitingly uncharted future. I may need to challenge this attitude; I do not know—I simply observe that this is so. It does at least demonstrate the effect of context on Bible reading.

4. I have also for some years now written a weekly column that offers reflections on the readings appointed for the Sunday Eucharist in Catholic (and certain other) churches for the following Sunday. I perform this "popularizing" task by reflecting on my own translation of the prescribed texts, including the too-often neglected Psalms, and linking the whole to help ordinary Christian worshipers make sense of their Monday morning lives in their particular context. The results, both approval and at times intense anger on the part of readers, suggest that the remarks hit some kind of target and that the Bible is powerfully at work, especially perhaps when a particular rendering shocks by its unfamiliarity. The assumption underlying this activity is that intertextuality between different biblical books is a good thing, in principle different from relating other literary products to each other.

5. Pastoral work of various kinds has also fed into this sense of

the Bible's potency. There is a rural parish, high in the Zululand hills, which in the early part of my time in this country saw many, far too many, political killings and house burnings and "cleansing" of people who were deemed to be of the wrong political persuasion, on no grounds other than that they lived on that side rather than this of the main road that divided the parish. My work there consisted of no more than presiding at mass on certain Sundays and endeavoring to share, in halting Zulu, what the biblical readings seemed to say to those in this situation not of their own making, trying to give meaning and hope. Nowadays in the same parish the young men are being slaughtered by AIDS rather than gunshots and stabbings, and the Bible has something to say in that situation too. The work in this parish took only a tiny proportion of my time; the effect on me was incalculable.

6. There has been other extra-curricular activity as well: retreats and spiritual direction and the endeavor to listen to people's fragility in their journey toward God, finding for them some biblical sustenance, then listening awestruck as a text spoke to their situation; Bible study groups, where anxious people asked how it was possible to carry on living in South Africa today and found an answer of a sort in the Word of God; a nearby boys' school and the attempt to make sense of Sunday or weekday readings for hardy adolescents with their minds on rugby and girlfriends. All this work underlined the portentous capacity of the biblical text to leap off the page and stand challengingly before the reader, "large as life and twice as natural."

7. My current job involves teaching students for the Catholic priesthood in a seminary that is largely residential. This produces at least the following three tensions:

- The tension between giving the students a serious academic grasp of scripture and training them to be "breakers of the word" in their future ministry. A colleague incessantly (and correctly) reminds me "we are not trying to produce little academics, but pastoral ministers."
- The need (in the ugly but effective expression) to "walk one's talk" in such a situation. In a residential institution everyone knows everyone else's hypocrisies far too well. So there is an uncomfortable tension between what one preaches or teaches and what one lives.

- The tension, common in all educational establishments, between the young and those in authority, complicated, as everywhere in South Africa, by the question of race. In all these tensions the Bible has, I have learned, something powerful to offer by way of healing and help.

8. Nowadays I find biblical conferences rather tedious. I make this confession with some shame. In the course of a decade I have attended such gatherings in at least three countries and listened dutifully to a good many lectures. I have admired the competence of those who lectured, and, at least occasionally, the illumination they shed on difficult texts or crucial questions. Yet even apart from the intermittent whiff of smoke-filled rooms and academic politics, I have wondered whether a treatment of "The Body as Strategy of Power in Religious Discourse" (to take a title virtually at random) really helps unleash the Bible's power into the human situation. More precisely, it has sometimes seemed to me that scholars can labor under a "tyranny of method."[24] It is not that I think method unimportant; one of the advances in biblical scholarship of the last couple of decades (even, I suppose, of the last couple of centuries) has been an alertness to the complexity of the hermeneutical event. Nevertheless, the Bible is written to be read (or heard), absorbed, and lived, and at times our academic preoccupations can seem no more than an evasion of the challenge. Preoccupation with method owes perhaps too much to the model of biblical scholarship as scientific investigation. I recall how, during a recent sabbatical when I was catching up on all that I had not had time to read in a rather narrow field of New Testament studies, a septuagenarian academic of some distinction would come up to me after a morning in the library, rubbing his hands and asking, "Well, young man, what have you discovered that is new today?" I admired his youthfulness of spirit, but balked at the assumption that biblical studies operates like paleo-botany.

FINAL WORDS

This is not a conclusion, for that would imply an ending; this is very much a beginning. The reflection on ten years of teaching and listening to the New and Old Testaments in South Africa has underlined for me that biblical studies involve a "rich mix" of role players and ways of reading; the way ahead has something (I am conscious that I have not achieved an appropriate precision of thought on what this "something" might be) to do with abandoning the understanding of the biblical text as *terra incognita,* to be scientifically mapped and measured. It has, furthermore, a good deal to do with the Bible understood as a live, if dormant, and unmistakably powerful animal. It has become clear to me that the strange and variegated collection of ancient documents that we call the Bible has not lost its power.

This should not be taken as an attempt to disparage the work of the last two centuries: critical biblical scholarship has not tamed the text, only opened up new horizons of meaning that act as a backdrop to the Bible's power. Similarly, the fact that colonizing imperialists used the Bible has not robbed it of a place in African culture.

There is a further aspect to this matter. In the last half-century, it is not putting it too strongly to say that the Catholic Church has rediscovered the Bible. This will have implications, which have not, I think, yet become fully clear, both for the inner life of the church and for its external relations, the ecumenical journey on which it is irreversibly set. When I disagree with colleagues from the Dutch Reformed tradition about the reading of a particular text, it is far more likely to be on methodological[25] than on confessional grounds.

Both of our churches, however—and this may be particularly true for a large organization of centralizing bent, such as the Roman Catholic Church—must be prepared for the Bible's power to challenge us, or to "turn around and bite us." Both the DRC and the Catholic Church have felt the teethmarks in recent years.

The reading of the Bible is still, therefore, partly an academic enterprise, one in which I have not ceased to believe and which should be rigorously pursued. Second, though, Bible reading in this country takes place in a particular context, that of a society undergoing the most momentous transition to a future that is as yet unclear; and the Bible actually has something to feed into that process. Yet, finally, the community of believers is the privileged *locus* for reading the inherited scripture; the words on the page hold a power that is beyond the church's control and yet is its inheritance.

So, finally, we rejoin the work of Gerry O'Collins, expressing to him the wish *ad multos annos.* Specifically I wish for him that he will continue to show us how to reintegrate what the Enlightenment has unhappily divided, the spiritual life from the study of theology and the study of theology from the attentive reading of scripture. Psychologists tell us nowadays that "compartmentalization" is a defense mechanism; all unconsciously, I fear, we may be using this intellectual apartheid to block the demands of God. It is time to stop and listen.

Notes

1. Part of this chapter has appeared in *Grace and Truth* 16, no. 2 (1999): 4–21, and is reproduced here by kind permission of the editor.

2. For example, G. O'Collins, *Experiencing Jesus* (London: SPCK, 1994).

3. G. O'Collins's *Christology* (Oxford/New York: Oxford University Press, 1995) and *The Resurrection of Jesus Christ* (published in England as *The Easter Jesus*) are outstanding examples of what I mean.

4. Usefully outlined in Gerald West, "Reading the Bible and Doing Theology in the New South Africa," in *The Bible in Human Society—Essays in Honour of John Rogerson,* ed. Daniel M. Carroll, David J. A. Clines, and Philip R. Davies, JSOT Supplement 200 (Sheffield: JSOT Press, 1995), 445–58.

5. See, e.g., Allan Boesak, *Comfort and Protest: Reflections on the Apocalypse of John of Patmos* (Philadelphia: Westminster, 1987).

6. An instance would be Jonathan Draper, "Humble Submission to 'Almighty God' and Its Biblical Foundation: Contextual Exegesis of Romans 13:1–7," *Journal of Theology for Southern Africa* 63 (June 1988): 30–55.

7. One thinks primarily of apartheid, but see also F. A. van Jaarsveld, "The Afrikaner's Idea of His Calling and Mission in South African History," *Journal of Theology for Southern Africa* 19 (June 1977): 16–28.

8. For this term, see Raymond Brown, *An Introduction to the New Testament* (Garden City, N.Y.: Doubleday 1997), 27–28, and, for the variety, Simon Maimela and Adrio König, *Initiation into Theology* (Pretoria: J. L. van Schaik, 1998), 1–4.

9. West, *Reading the Bible,* 446.

10. Ibid., 447.

11. See Stuart Bate, *Inculturation and Healing* (Pietermaritzburg: Cluster Publications, 1995), 294 n. 10.

12. As an experiment, I suggest that a reader from a Western culture discuss the Samaritan woman in John 4 with an African reader.

13. For a forthright statement of this point, though not tending in the same direction as the present essay, see Pieter J. J. Botha, "Words, Worlds, Works: Making our Way With New Testament Scholarship," *Religion and Theology* 5, no. 1 (1998): 35–58.

14. For a useful introduction, consult Brevard Childs, *Introduction to the Old Testament as Scripture* (Philadelphia: Fortress, 1979).

15. For the strengths, see Brown, Introduction, 42–44. For weaknesses, the remarks by Philip R. Davies (*Whose Bible Is It Anyway?* [Sheffield: Sheffield Academic Press, 1993], 28–35) are very perceptive.

16. Davies, *Whose Bible*. Chapter 5 of this book, which is a characteristically clear and attentive reading of the Genesis material on Abraham, comes into the category of mischief.

17. Ibid., 13.

18. Ibid., 34.

19. Ibid., 22.

20. Two dense volumes that debate with Davies are Francis Watson, *Text, Church and World* (Edinburgh: T. & T. Clark, 1994), and idem, *Text and Truth* (Edinburgh: T & T Clark, 1997).

21. See James Barr, *The Semantics of Biblical Language* (London: Oxford University Press, 1961), for a demonstration of this important point.

22. For the general idea, see Nicholas King, *Setting the Gospel Free* (Pietermaritzburg: Cluster Publications, 1995); and *Whispers of Liberation* (Mahwah, N.J.: Paulist, 1998).

23. This creative idea comes from Robert Murray, *Exegesis and Imagination* (London: University of London, 1988), 10.

24. On this point, though this phrase is not his, see now David Jobling, *1 Samuel* (Collegeville, Minn.: Michael Glazier Books, 1998), especially pp. 23–27.

25. Methodology is not, you see, wholly rejected.

9. "Knowing" Jesus: Do Theologians Have a Special Way?

William Reiser, S.J.

> Several times [in this book] I have taken issue with those who entertain the ambition of adopting a neutral, non-partisan approach to theology and similar fields. I still endorse strongly what I put forward years ago: that personal commitment and critical reflection can and should mutually support each other.... In the particular discipline of Christology, to be confessional involves some claim to "know" Jesus.[1]

That a Christian thinker should feel called upon to render an epistemological "apology" for the fact that his mind cannot divorce itself from his faith is perhaps a sign of the times. Among academics, the issue appears most acutely today in various efforts to differentiate theology from religious studies.[2] The academic study of religion, with all the resources of the historical, social, and behavioral sciences, proceeds along its own carefully defined and closely defended track. Theology is often viewed as the business of seminaries, divinity schools, and identifiably Christian universities. The firm emergence of spirituality as a distinct discipline within the study of religion, however, suggests that the study of religion is always going to be more than a matter of mind. Moreover, the steady emergence of spirituality as distinct from (but a presupposition for) every Christian theology suggests further that serious reflection on living faith obeys an intentionality that is ultimately nonconfessional.[3] The theologian, in other words, walks with *all* men and women who seek God, no matter what their religious tradition or confessional location; such accompanying belongs to his or her vocation. Searching for God, consistently and wholeheartedly, creates its own kind of communion.

NO PROFESSIONAL DISTANCING FROM FAITH

For many—indeed, perhaps for most—of those who teach and practice theology, the normal conversation partner is not the academy but the believing community. They write for students of theology, for believers across the spectrum, and for other theologians. In obedience to a tradition that dates back to Justin Martyr, theologians also address themselves to those outside the community of faith, following the apostolic instruction: "Always be ready to make your defense to *any-one* who demands from you an accounting for the hope that is in you; yet do it with gentleness and reverence" (1 Pet 3:15b–16a).[4] The tools and methodologies theologians use should be as sophisticated and varied as those employed by researchers and writers in other academic disciplines. In this sense, theology follows recognized canons of scholarship. One cannot fault historians for not being theologians, even when the subject of their investigations is Christian origins and the figure of Jesus. But one could fault theologians who failed to take that historical research into account and to develop a theology that takes history seriously, for in some sense the Word became history long before it became flesh.

Yet even while theologians examine the meaning and act of faith, they do not phenomenologically bracket the reality of God either from the life of the community or from their own lives. To be more specific, even while researching the figure of Jesus—a figure both human and historical, and mediated by devotional, liturgical, and doctrinal traditions—theologians do not mentally or physically separate themselves from their confessions and from the religious experience of believing communities. The theologian must "know" Jesus; otherwise the theologian cannot speak meaningfully to the church. If a theologian were to insist on standing outside the circle of faith in order to reflect on the mystery of God, then one could argue that the theologian had stepped beyond the possibility of any real knowledge of that sacred reality that solicits the most profound human reflection. The research and writing that follow would necessarily represent, at least from the community's point of view, an epistemological distortion. The idea of professional or academic distancing, the notion of the neutral, scientific observer, is based on a mistaken view about how knowing happens. The oversight proves disastrous in the matter of knowing God.[5]

Perhaps these remarks do nothing more than draw out the significance of Bernard Lonergan's insight that the foundations of theology are the authentically converted theologian.[6] And since conversion is an ongoing process in one's life, a process truly determinative of the sort of person we become and absolutely inseparable from the way we perceive, think, evaluate, and decide, it necessarily affects every stage of the unfolding of one's theology. As knowers, we are already performers. A Christian theologian could study and write about Buddhism intelligently without being a Buddhist, but I do not think the theologian could write about it meaningfully unless he or she was already a believer, that is, a religious person confidently immersed in his or her own spiritual tradition.

THE THEOLOGIAN'S SPIRITUALITY

What intrigues me, however, is not what differentiates theology from religious studies, or the confessional from the academic, for I take the difference to be largely epistemological. More interesting from a theological point of view is the spiritual development of the individual theologian. The more sustained one's engagement with the mystery of God, the more likely one is to reach a level of insight that occasionally transcends Christian theological understanding itself. This ought not to be surprising. After all, learning is by nature a self-transcending process. Scholarly endeavor, in opening new areas of inquiry, pushes the frontiers of the community's self-understanding forward. This pushing forward is inevitable, given the fact that the church is constantly engaged by its past and always facing the challenging circumstances of the present. The Paul who wandered through the temples of Athens, for example, could never have envisioned the serious, respectful dialogue with the religions of the world taking place today. The church has learned important lessons about the mystery of divine revelation from its long missionary experience. Or again, the bishops and theologians who wrote and commended to the church the documents of the Second Vatican Council walked on theological terrain scarcely conceivable to those who gathered at Vatican I. In the meantime the church had learned important lessons about history, liturgy, the biblical texts, democratic aspirations, and modern culture. What is referred to as the development of doctrine is essentially the development that takes place within human understanding—the self-transcending process of learning taken to the institutional level.[7]

But the point we were following was not so much about the process of learning as the consequence of sustained engagement with the mystery of God. And here it is not enough just to recall the well-known words about his theological accomplishment that Thomas Aquinas uttered toward the end of his life. However inadequate the language we use to talk about God and the mysteries of faith, language matters. It was the *Word*, after all, that became flesh and thereby cast human discourse itself in a new light. Language is revelatory, no matter how provisional it is, no matter how much like straw our discourse might sometimes taste.

Ideally, something happens to men and women who spend most of their waking hours thinking about what the community believes and who share fully the community's experience of the mystery that has taken up its dwelling among them. Deepening understanding of the mystery one has been contemplating for many years does not lead to displacing or relativizing one's religious tradition, or even to going beyond it in some gnostic fashion. Rather, one's religiousness shifts to a new key. One increasingly apprehends Christian faith with the nondiscursive insight of the mystic. One feels oneself belonging, as I remarked above, to a communion of God-seekers wider than one's particular confession. One discovers, in keeping with Luke 6:36, that compassion is the ultimate human attribute and that solidarity is its sacrament. Indeed, the difference between where a theologian "is," spiritually speaking, at the outset of his or her vocation and where the theologian winds up after many years of reflection on the whole Christian mystery may be roughly analogous to the difference between the discursive and unitive ways. The theological mind makes its own ascent to God. Looking back on one's life, one might even reflect: "I was a believer then and I am a believer now. But the way I am a believer now is so markedly different from the way I believed then, that I wonder if I was formerly a believer at all!"[8] In purely descriptive terms, perhaps we have here another way of approximating the distinction between religious studies and theology.

WHAT MIGHT IT MEAN TO KNOW JESUS?

Can someone teach the Gospels, let alone do Christology, who does not know Jesus? The Gospels, after all, are about him; the very existence of the Gospels points to a community of faith committed to proclaiming Jesus' name and his life, and convinced of his abiding presence in their midst. One can, needless to say, study and exegete the scriptural texts without believing in them. But of what interest are those ancient texts in and of themselves? Apart from communities whose lives are informed and continually animated by those writings, the texts would be consigned to departments of Jewish and Hellenistic antiquities.

What then does it mean to "know" Jesus? Setting quotation marks around the word "know" simply acknowledges the obvious. The historical figure Jesus of Nazareth died two thousand years ago; one cannot, therefore, know Jesus the way one usually comes to know another person. We do come to know people from the past through stories others have told us about that person, as when one generation in a family passes along its memories and reminiscences to another. We can even come to know individuals through historical research. A scholar could study and come to know, for instance, Ignatius Loyola or Abraham Lincoln. Yet such knowing is different from what we learn about someone from daily living and interaction, although even in this case we may not really know another person as well as we think.

From a New Testament perspective, knowing *Jesus* could never be solely an intellectual or cognitive enterprise, because truly to know Jesus is to experience God's salvation. This is the central Christian claim. Knowing Jesus becomes a short formula for describing salvation itself. Knowledge, like love, is a way of participating in the very being of another. Thus to participate in the being of Christ is to share his Spirit. That would be the rich meaning of Paul's words, "I want to know Christ and the power of his resurrection and the sharing of his sufferings by becoming like him in his death" (Phil 3:10). *Knowing* Christ, *experiencing* the divine power at work in his being raised from the dead, *sharing* the mission which brought him to the cross, and thereby *becoming* more like him each day: such would be the ingredients of the Pauline formula. The same christological concentration lies at the heart of the second week of the *Spiritual Exercises* of St. Ignatius

Loyola with its recurring prayer for "interior knowledge of the Lord" ("*demandar conoscimiento interno del Señor*" [#104]).[9]

KNOWING JESUS ENTAILS A RISK

Discipleship always carries the potential of a full share in the sufferings of Christ. Being with Jesus, the apostles quickly discovered, could land them in bad company or in hostile territory. It was one thing for Jesus to sit at table with tax collectors and other public sinners or with people whose poverty forced them into a permanent state of ritual impurity, but rendering oneself liable to the same charge by closely following Jesus was quite another. It was one thing for Jesus to be labeled a drunkard and a glutton, but wouldn't that make his companions susceptible to the same ugly judgment? Sailing off with Jesus sounds inviting, until we recall that at least one voyage took the disciples through the eye of a storm and landed them in hostile, demon-infested Gentile territory. Peter would later discover that following Jesus could exact the highest price (John 21:18–19). So too would Stephen and James and Paul and then innumerable others.

Even for theologians, knowing Jesus can be dangerous. One thinks of Dietrich Bonhoeffer or Ignacio Ellacuria. But in addition to the theologian-martyrs, there are the theologians whose work brought them at one time or another to cross the limits of the church's understanding of itself and the gospel entrusted to its care—Edward Schillebeeckx, Karl Rahner, or Bernard Haring—witnesses of another sort. More recently, one thinks of Gerald O'Collins's own spirited defense of Jacques Dupuis, whose work on interreligious dialogue—the theological fruit of his cultural location for many years in India—had prompted a Vatican investigation.[10] Doing theology has its risks. It also invites a number of tensions into a theologian's life *qua* believer, which means that theologians too may find themselves needing spiritual direction.

The root of nearly every tension in a believer's life arises from the fact that our ultimate loyalty is to God. The Spirit of God characteristically exposes those areas of our lives where that loyalty may be compromised in one way or another. For a Christian theologian the implications are simple but far-reaching. One's *ultimate* loyalty is not to the church or to scripture or to the scholarly community or to human reason or even to the gospel portrait of Jesus. Important as they are to the life of faith, these things must always remain temporary and provisional; Christian hope reaches beyond them, to the city in which there will be no temple (Rev 21:22), where charismatic gifts disappear and only love remains (1 Cor 13:8–10). One's ultimate loyalty is to the mystery of God, or, more precisely, to the mystery of God in Christ revealed through the Spirit. That mystery transcends even the historical form of the figure Jesus of Nazareth.

It would be an imprecise use of language to respond here that Jesus after all *was* God, without giving any further explanation. The equation would be imprecise because it overlooks the clear scriptural fact that Jesus himself related to that mystery in his prayer and during the whole of his ministry. It was God who called Jesus, and it was the Spirit of God that empowered him to preach and heal. Or, to put things a little differently, trinitarian faith protects the Christian community against naively substituting Jesus for the Father, the Holy Mystery that stands behind creation, redemption, and the raising of the dead to life. Jesus did not glorify himself; God did that. Christ can be proclaimed as "all in all," the dynamic principle of renewal that tears down the barriers dividing us from one another (Col 3:11), but this proclamation has to be placed alongside another one equally striking: "[There is] one God and Father of all, who is above all and through all and in all" (Eph 4:6).

What this loyalty of mind and heart guarantees is, first, that the theologian does not become trapped by confessional differences; and that, second, the theologian can think of God even beyond the categories of Christian self-understanding. Love of God, deploying itself supremely in a person's life, does not relativize religious traditions; rather, love of God moves us to humility and to respect for everything that is sacred. Religions certainly deserve to be understood, but comparing them does a disservice to the mystery of the self-revealing God we believe in. Christian thinkers have learned two important facts. First, divine self-communication is not uniform; and, second, because God's entering into human lives is always a gift, one must tread carefully when approaching the study of traditions other than one's own. To fail in this regard might lead to profound irreverence. To know Jesus is to understand the etiquette of religious dialogue.

I have no intention of discussing here what happens when, as a result of their research and reflection, theologians finds themselves in disagreement with the church's pastoral magisterium on a particular issue; that matter has already been sufficiently addressed in both popular writing and technical studies.[11] The underlying tension may even be endemic to the theological enterprise itself, a particular instance of the wider phenomenon of resistance to new thinking, something that prompted Jesus to conclude that new wine demands new wineskins (Mark 2:22). It may also be the problem of how new ideas are to be shared, critiqued, and then communicated to wider publics. Needless to say, those who educate (whether pastors or theologians) have to be prepared to face the resistances in people's minds and wills. The process of teaching and learning generates a particular form of asceticism: to teach without forgetting that, in matters touching upon God, one is forever a learner; to think and to teach without being intimidated by the understandable defensiveness of others; to suspect the integrity of one's own theological reflection when one's own practice does not conform to the message of Christ; to have the humility to admit that one could be wrong and the magisterium correct; and so on.

Knowing Jesus implies that the central features of the gospel story have certain parallels in our own lives. Ultimately Jesus was rejected by the religious leadership of his people because of an unswerving fidelity to his experience of God. Some theologians can relate to this. All Christian scholars have to be ready to endure the isolation that comes from seeing what others do not yet see. And they should anticipate that, in the end, their most costly efforts to reflect on matters of faith are destined to pale before the mystery that God is. Finally, while thinking about God is the mind's way of praying, the story of Jesus teaches us that there is no way to think about the God Jesus knew without thinking about the historical fortune and circumstances of God's people.

FIVE COGNITIONAL ELEMENTS

Claiming to know someone from the past presents us with a distinctive challenge as we endeavor to explain to others what we believe. I would suggest that "knowing" Jesus involves at least five elements. One comes to know Jesus from (1) immersion in the community of faith, that is, insertion into the life of the church, especially through its liturgical expressions of belief; (2) immersion in Christian scripture, especially the Gospels; (3) insertion into the Christian ascetical experience, that is, being a person who seeks God, discerns, and prays in communion with others; (4) insertion into the Christian doctrinal and aesthetic traditions, that is, the church's creeds and art forms; and (5) existential insertion into the life of God's people, particularly the histories of communities of suffering.

That each of these elements (particularly the first four) appears in the work of Gerald O'Collins is abundantly evident from his writings; the fifth is more prominent in the work of Johann Baptist Metz. Taken together, however, they account for how any one of us comes to know Jesus. Through hearing *and through preaching* the word, through everyday contact with devout men and women, through the stories of holy women and men who have preceded us, through the history of the church's own scholarship, through lifelong participation in the liturgical life of the people of God, through one's own prayer and graced efforts to follow Jesus risen, and through unyielding attentiveness to "the joys and the hopes, the griefs and anxieties of the men and women of this age," the theologian as a believer comes to know Jesus.[12]

I italicized the phrase *through preaching* in order to draw attention to a particular mode of knowing Jesus risen that may be experienced by many of those who regularly preach and explain the gospel before believing communities. It is obvious that sincere and informed preaching can so move those who listen that they really encounter Jesus. Thus the force of Paul's words: "But how are they to call on one whom they have not believed? And how are they to believe in one of whom they have never heard? And how are they to hear without someone to proclaim him?" (Rom 10:14). What may be less obvious, however, is that the one who stands before others and preaches the gospel "knows" Jesus in the very act of preaching about his life and death. I believe this knowing to be a manifestation of the Spirit distinctive of the experience of the minister of the gospel and a singular blessing for theologians who preach. The experience of the one who preaches provides further confirmation of the real presence of Jesus in the biblical word.

KNOWING JESUS AND DOING THEOLOGY IN SOLIDARITY

Among the five elements involved in coming to know Jesus that I listed above, the last one merits special consideration. It may be that coming to know *anyone,* and not just Jesus, normally entails some measure of risk. A couple pronouncing their marriage vows makes a great act of faith in one another. In solemnly committing oneself to another, one steps into an emotional and spiritual unknown, for men and women do not reveal themselves to one another all at once (indeed, they cannot), but only over a period of time. Yet all the more so in the case of knowing Jesus must it be said that we do not know him all at once, and indeed that we cannot, for two reasons. First, because the practice of discipleship, like any major lesson of our lives, is not mastered overnight. And second, because some desires and capacities in us have to develop and mature in order for us to be able to relate to Jesus for who and what he is.

In any deep relationship, we gladly embrace all that is wonderful and attractive about another person (or, in the case of a Christian under vows, a religious community). But we also have to be prepared to embrace things that may one day cause us to suffer. The same holds true for knowing Jesus. We eagerly accept the good news of God's salvation, together with the enormously attractive human qualities that the evangelists attribute to Jesus. We make our own God's preferential love for the poor and downtrodden, sacramentalized in the incarnation; and, like the first disciples, we at least desire to be able to set aside everything in order to follow the Son of God. But here knowing Jesus takes a turn away from our familiar patterns of experience. Sooner or later we will have to realize that Jesus brings the world itself into our lives—the world created and loved by God, the world to which Paul himself felt nailed (Gal 6:14), with all its beauty and all its burdens. No path to God in Christ takes a detour around the world.[13] Communion, solidarity, and compassion are quintessentially evangelical. To know Jesus, then, is to know his people. To know Jesus crucified is to pray, think, and live out of an effective solidarity with victims of poverty, injustice, and violence. To know and love *one* victim is to know and love *all* of them.[14]

The significance of this mode of knowing Jesus cannot be overstated. To the degree that any of the five elements is missing from a person's life, one's knowledge of Jesus will be skewed or even truncated. Jesus can be reduced to being solely a historical figure, or inflated to mythological proportions, or imprisoned by thoroughly private piety, or made distant and abstract by overemphasizing christological doctrine, or frozen in cultic imagery and language. Jesus can even be so identified with the poor that hope as a theological virtue evaporates and Christians with financial resources grow either disaffected from the gospel or chronically guilt-ridden; and the poor themselves are no longer challenged to face their own need for conversion. Nevertheless, solidarity with the suffering poor (for not all human suffering is caused by poverty, exploitation, and the abuse of power) defines a special mode of knowing Jesus.

Ignatius Loyola's vigorous practice of poverty was not an idle exercise in imitation of a Francis of Assisi and other Christian heroes. Ignatius learned experientially the elemental principles of evangelical living. Those experiences were absolutely essential to his coming to know Jesus.[15] Like Paul, Ignatius found his prayer "to know Christ and the power of his resurrection" answered. And for those who want to make them today, the Ignatian *Exercises* prove fruitful to the degree that they excite profound religious desires to imitate Jesus. Yet desires alone are not sufficient. Desires must lead to practice, for it is in the practice of discipleship that knowledge of Jesus is finally attained.

In other words, how can theologians speak of Jesus who became poor for our sakes if they have never actually had to face poverty themselves, or if they do not faithfully accompany men and women who endure severe financial hardship? How can they write meaningfully of the Jesus who ransomed us if their *only* experience of being ransomed is an interior one, a sense of having been inwardly released from the power of sin? They may never have been in prison, but theologians might be enabled to understand the mystery of Jesus as redeemer better if they have worked to help others win back their freedom, taking to heart the exhortation "Remember those who are in prison, as though you were in prison with them" (Heb 13:3). How do we grasp the Jesus who was rashly judged, laughed at, and accused of working in league with the prince of demons, if as Christian thinkers we have never had personally to endure such things? Will the theologian's manner of relating to Jesus, the rejected and humiliated prophet, be largely noumenal; or will it arise from encountering injustice and being outraged over dehumanizing economic policies and unfair social arrangements? Perhaps those who have reminded us most forcefully of this point have been Latin American theologians such as Jon Sobrino, Enrique Dussel, and Gustavo Gutiérrez. The vitality of theology depends above all on the theological community's insertion into the world of the poor. Their experience not only serves as a corrective lens as we read and study what Jesus referred to as "good news to the poor" (Luke 4:18); the experience of the poor chastens any rhetoric about salvation that skirts around the concrete realities from which the poor in particular need deliverance.

Again, Paul's prayer about wanting to know Jesus through sharing in his sufferings is germane here. Knowing Jesus and being called to proclaim him were two sides of the same experience. Furthermore, there was no way to be an apostle without completing in one's own life what was lacking in Jesus' afflictions (Col 1:24).[16] Paul's recounting of what he had already endured for the sake of the gospel in 2 Corinthians 11–12 confirms that his prayer was granted. Paul's suffering *qua* apostle was eschatological; he had been privileged to share in the "cup of suffering" (Mark 10:38) of Jesus himself, God's righteous servant. It is important for us, however, to adjust this eschatological perspective in terms of our nonapocalyptic understanding of history. The sufferings endured by the servant of Second Isaiah, by Jesus, and by Paul (and, we must presume, by the other apostles) were brought on by social, cultural, and political circumstances. Suffering can never be abstracted from its concrete sources within real human communities that stand in need of divine deliverance here and now. For this reason every generation of disciples is invited to drink from the "cup of suffering," that is, from the pain and ongoing crucifixion of God's people. When God's people are no longer being crucified, then (and only then) will the cup finally have been drained.

The Pauline idea about completing the afflictions of Christ—about drinking from the cup of suffering—bears on the way theologians come to know Jesus. Partial or regional theologies are probably not only unavoidable; they are demanded by the process of inculturation. The more deeply theologians insert themselves into particular cultures and communities, the more their theology is going to reflect their social location and even a certain conceptual partiality. Overall, the result is a Christian theology more diverse, more incarnational, and from a purely aesthetic standpoint more interesting. Nevertheless, that very partiality can obscure an important reality. It can prevent us from seeing the *whole* Christ. And following the thread contained in the Pauline text, I do not think it would be off the mark to suggest (in this context) that "whole Christ" means the historical suffering of *all* God's people, and in particular the sufferings of those without anyone to defend them except God: the poor, the landless, those imprisoned by circumstances beyond their control; the victims of genocide, ethnic cleansing, and secret massacres. The theologian needs to keep this whole Christ constantly in view, no matter what the specific topic being studied and developed. Every specific question we consider as theologians needs to be thought through with one eye on that cup of suffering which still needs to be drained. One knows Jesus in knowing the human, historical totality and thereby sharing in the Lord's cup.

CONCLUSION

The expression "to know Jesus," like so much of Christian discourse, clearly requires explanation. Do theologians enjoy a special mode of access to Jesus? If the question means, Do scholars have tools at their disposal for interpreting the ancient Christian scriptures which many believers simply do not have?, the answer could be yes, but it would not be all that consequential. A skilled mechanic, for example, understands a car engine better than most owners, but that does not make mechanics better drivers. Nevertheless, knowledge of scriptural texts can be liberating and spiritually stimulating, not only for theologians but for all believers. Opaque words, like opaque symbols, interfere with the Lord's being really present to us. Ideally, one would like to imagine, the privilege of devoting the major part of one's life, along with one's intellectual and spiritual energies, to the work of theology ought to translate into a distinctive pattern of holiness. From a strictly epistemological viewpoint, the ways by which any of us comes to know Jesus are basically the same. No one simply by virtue of his or her Christian calling can lay claim to a more intimate knowledge of Jesus than another believer might have. That some among us enjoy a clearer understanding of the Jesus story must surely be granted. However lovingly Ignatius Loyola contemplated the scenes of the Gospels, there were dimensions of the scriptural texts that his imagination was not able to reach. Today, however, we know more about the Gospels literarily, historically, sociologically; we do not, of course, know everything.

Indeed, we have more accurate historical information about the life and times of Jesus than did Jerome or Augustine, but do we know

Jesus "better?" Do we know Jesus "better," say, than Ignatius? Indeed, might we even possess more accurate historical knowledge about the life and times of Jesus than Paul did? Although the questions may sound presumptuous, they can help to illustrate why what theologians do is so important to the church. If we take knowing Jesus in its soteriological sense, then obviously the question breaks down. Experiences of salvation and grace cannot be compared in terms of "better" or "worse." Christians today are not more "saved" than Paul or Peter or Mary Magdalene or Martha, but neither were *they* more "saved" than we are simply because they were Jesus' contemporaries.

On the other hand, if we take knowledge of Jesus in terms of historical understanding, then, yes, we enjoy important insights that generations before us have not possessed. In this case, modern biblical studies have enabled us to overcome the scandal of historical distance. We may be living two thousand years after Jesus, but the span of centuries hardly seems conceptually overwhelming to those men and women today who want to follow a "real Jesus," not a Jesus made-up to appear like one of us, but a Jesus with a real history, a human being fully inserted into the social and cultural space into which divine providence placed him. Biblical scholarship has been a great blessing to the church, while the ongoing appropriation of that scholarship by theologians testifies to the enduring presence of the Spirit of Jesus. Hans Urs von Balthasar once wrote that "serious research can enrich faith in the person of Jesus provided that it does not depart from the attitude of faith but applies itself to show how the strands of tradition (whose elements were formed by the faith of the first Christians) come together, penetrate each other and acquire distinct forms."[17] For a Christian theologian, history becomes a theological category and historical research plays a graced role in understanding revelation.[18]

Notes

1. Gerald O'Collins, *Christology: A Biblical, Historical, and Systematic Study of Jesus* (New York: Oxford University Press, 1995), 322–23.

2. See Francis Schüssler Fiorenza, "Theology in the University," *Council of Societies for the Study of Religion Bulletin* 22, no. 2 (1993): 34–39; Donald Wiebe, "On Theology and Religious Studies: A Response to Francis Schüssler Fiorenza," *CSSR Bulletin* 23, no. 1 (1994): 3–6; and Fiorenza's response in the same issue. Also Delwin Brown, "Academic Theology and Religious Studies," *CSSR Bulletin* 26, no. 3 (1997): 64–66; and in the same issue, Arvind Sharma (ed.), "On the Distinction between Religious Studies and Theological Studies," 50–68. Related to this issue, see Alan G. Padgett, "Advice for Religious Historians: On the Myth of a Purely Historical Jesus" in *The Resurrection,* ed. Stephen Davis, Daniel Kendall, and Gerald O'Collins (New York: Oxford University Press, 1997), 287–99.

3. On the relation between spirituality and theology, see James Matthew Ashley, *Interruptions: Mysticism, Politics, and Theology in the Work of Johann Baptist Metz* (Notre Dame, Ind.: University of Notre Dame Press, 1998), 1–26; and Mark A. McIntosh, *Mystical Theology: The Integrity of Spirituality and Theology* (Malden, Mass.: Blackwell Publishers, 1998), 3–38. See also Sandra M. Schneiders, "The Study of Christian Spirituality: Contours and Dynamics of a Discipline," *Christian Spirituality Bulletin* 6, no. 1 (1998): 1, 3–11.

4. All the scriptural quotations I have used here are taken from the New Revised Standard Version (NRSV).

5. A believing Christian can certainly be engaged in the study of religious phenomena within or outside of one's own religious tradition, just as men and women of faith can devote themselves to the serious study of any discipline—anthropology, sociology, psychology, history, and so on. In all cases, however, I believe that self-consistency demands an integration of reason and faith. But not all study moves to the same end; not all thinking is contemplative or "pious" in Heidegger's sense (see Martin Heidegger, *The Piety of Thinking,* trans. James Hart and John Maraldo [Bloomington, Ind.: Indiana University Press, 1976]).

6. Speaking about religious, moral, and intellectual conversion with respect to theology's foundations, Lonergan wrote: "The threefold conversion is, not a set of propositions that a theologian utters, but *a fundamental and momentous change in the human reality that a theologian is.*" (*Method in Theology* [London: Darton, Longman & Todd, 1972], 270, emphasis added).

See also Avery Dulles, *The Craft of Theology* (New York: Crossroad, 1992), 53–68.

7. Since it was Gerald O'Collins who suggested to Paulist Press that I write about dogma for their What Are They Saying About series, a kind of followup comment might be in order here. Much of the resistance to the very idea of doctrinal development at the beginning of the twentieth century arose from an inability on the part of some theologians and bishops to think of human history and divine revelation together. The notion of doctrinal development, like Karl Rahner's notion of the anonymous Christian, served as a bridge idea. Rahner's celebrated expression helped us to resolve the problem of salvation outside the church when as yet we could not appreciate the presence of grace in non-Christian religions. Ecumenical theology and interreligious dialogue have gradually displaced Rahner's idea. Similarly, the notion of the development of dogma enabled us to accommodate our theology to the massive work undertaken by historians over several centuries. Once historical-critical and other methods found their way into the theological mainstream, however, thanks to modern biblical studies, and once we learned how to view our liturgical and doctrinal traditions historically, the notion of dogmatic development, which had allowed us to "bridge" the categories of revelation and history, became far less crucial.

8. The opening chapter of Marcus J. Borg, *Meeting Jesus Again for the First Time* (New York: HarperCollins, 1994), captures an aspect of this experience. Of interest too is Jürgen Moltmann, ed., *How I Have Changed: Reflections on Thirty Years of Theology* (Harrisburg, Pa.: Trinity Press International, 1997).

9. San Ignacio de Loyola, *Obras Completas,* ed. Ignacio Iparraguirre, S.J., and Candido de Dalmases, S.J. (Madrid: Biblioteca de Autores Cristianos, 1982), 233.

10. Letter to *The Tablet* (12 December 1998): 1650. The Dupuis book is entitled *Towards a Christian Theology of Religious Pluralism* (Maryknoll, N.Y.: Orbis Books, 1997).

11. See *Cooperation Between Theologians and the Ecclesiastical Magisterium: A Report of the Joint Committee of the Canon Law Society of America and the Catholic Theological Society of America,* ed. Leo J. O'Donovan, S.J. (Washington, D.C.: Catholic University of America, 1982). See also Congregation for the Doctrine of the Faith, *Instruction on the Ecclesial Vocation of the Theologian* (Washington, D.C.: United States Catholic Conference, 1990); and Francis A. Sullivan, "The Theologian's Ecclesial Vocation and the 1990 CDF Instruction," *Theological Studies* 52, no. 1 (1991): 51–68.

12. Luke Timothy Johnson identifies and develops a number of these

points in *Living Jesus: Learning the Heart of the Gospel* (New York: HarperCollins, 1999); see chapters 2, 3, and 4.

13. This is the main idea of a book I published entitled *To Hear God's Word, Listen to the World* (New York: Paulist, 1997). See also William Reiser, "Solidarity and the Reshaping of Spirituality," *The Merton Annual* 11 (1998): 97–109.

14. The idea is richly developed by Gil Bailie in *Violence Unveiled: Humanity at the Crossroads* (New York: Crossroad, 1995), 30–41.

15. The story of Ignatius's experiences with poverty can be found in his autobiography or, perhaps better, "reminiscences." See *Saint Ignatius of Loyola: Personal Writings,* trans. Joseph A. Munitiz and Philip Endean (London: Penguin Books, 1996), 1–64.

16. The meaning of this text is not self-evident. James D. G. Dunn comments: "Foreshadowed [in this text] is the apocalyptic thought that there is an appointed sum of suffering that must be endured in order to trigger (as it were) the final events of history…; the thought then is that the death of Christ has (as it were) activated the first trigger, but those sufferings are not yet complete, otherwise the second and final trigger would have been activated too" (*The Epistles to the Colossians and to Philemon: A Commentary on the Greek Text* [Grand Rapids: Eerdmans, 1996], 116).

17. Hans Urs von Balthasar, *Does Jesus Know Us? Do We Know Him?* (San Francisco: Ignatius, 1983), 65. I do not think we should be harsh on those Gospel critics who approached the texts as historical critics rather than as theologians. Their work forced theologians to familiarize themselves with contemporary hermeneutics, literary theory, and methods of research, which made possible a fresh reading of the biblical texts. The result has been the emergence at the end of the millennium of a theology increasingly scriptural, historical, liturgical, and pastoral.

18. Indispensable but not exclusive. Francis Schüssler Fiorenza writes: "Roman Catholic theology has to seek a reflective equilibrium among diverse sources and norms. These include a mutual counterbalancing, between historical reconstructions of Jesus as the historical root and center of Christian faith and the diverse receptions of Jesus throughout the history of Christianity, from its presentation in the Gospels to its lived practice in the lives of saints, its proclamation, and its liturgy, and to present theological and ethical reflection upon the practice of Christianity as involving retroductive warrants" (*Proceedings of the Forty-Ninth Annual Convention of The Catholic Theological Society of America* [June 1994]: 99).

10. Spiritual Direction in Dialogue with Fundamental Theology

Dominic Maruca, S.J.

During the past forty years, I have been engaged in the practice and teaching of spiritual direction. In various parts of the world I accompanied literally thousands of priests, religious, and members of the laity during their spiritual journey. Many of these I also initiated into the art and science of spiritual direction. Gerald O'Collins was an unfailing help in these pastoral and academic endeavors. His companionship, astute observations, and writings enabled me to minister to others with greater sensitivity and understanding.

In my contribution to this Festschrift I propose to do three things: (1) illustrate how Gerry enabled me to guide directees as they negotiated various transitions in their lives, especially as they struggled with "negative" experiences such as suffering and death; (2) review how the practice of spiritual direction has taken on different forms over the past forty years; and (3) report on the emerging form that this ecclesial ministry is assuming, moving from pedagogy back to its earlier form of mystagogy, in order to meet the challenge of the third millennium.

Let me first clarify how I understand the terms of the title. I understand *spiritual direction* as primarily directing a disciple's attention to the Spirit, the principal director. It is the role of the Spirit to nurture deep communion and reveal what God wishes to communicate. The human director provides ways to safeguard that communion and to authenticate presumed communications. I use *fundamental theology* in a restricted sense, as the disciplined reflection on divine revelation received and grasped by faith. By *dialogue,* I mean inquiring conversation that seeks not a definitive solution to specific problems but a general *modus procedendi,* a way to walk in faith from clarity to clarity.

NEGOTIATING TRANSITIONS IN LIFE

Numerous persons have come to me over the years because they were struggling to make a transition in their personal or professional lives. Like St. Augustine, Dante, and St. Ignatius Loyola, they found themselves at mid-life in the midst of a dense wood. Some had already looked to the disciplines of psychology and sociology searching for a new sense of identity and purpose in life. These disciplines had been able to clarify the dynamics of what they were enduring and to provide them with statistical data situating them within their cohort of persons passing from one stage of life to another. But they felt that something was missing. They needed a spark to enkindle the dry data of information, a fresh breeze that could fan into flame the dying embers of life. They turned to spiritual direction in the hope of finding such inspiration.

I regularly put into the hands of such seekers Gerry's slim volume *The Second Journey.*[1] This modest book exemplifies the wisdom of the old adage: Minds are molded and hearts are moved not by abstractions but by models! Without fail Gerry's reflections uplifted their spirits. By providing a new perspective for understanding and interpreting their situation, he encouraged them to resume their pilgrimage with renewed hope and enthusiasm. This did not surprise me, since in our Catholic tradition bibliotherapy has long been recognized as God's preferred approach to healing and transformation. Suffice it to recall the experience of St. Augustine when he heard the mysterious voice in Milan chanting "Tolle, lege!" or St. Ignatius reading Ludolph the Carthusian's *Life of Christ* and de Voragine's *Lives of the Saints* while convalescing at Loyola. Each of us is *homo viator,* a traveler walking through the darkness, proceeding from clarity to clarity, with hope that the mystery will eventually become luminous. When we complete one stage we must take up the challenge presented by the second—or third—stage of our journey. This is the only way we can ultimately reach the goal of our pilgrimage. Gerry's book regularly occasioned a rebirth of hope. My directees thanked me for introducing them to such a genial and wise guide.

COPING WITH FAILURE, SUFFERING, DEATH

On various occasions I discussed with Gerry the mystery of how God deals with us through a dialectic of presence and apparent absence. This perennial question has engaged the minds and hearts of believers down through the centuries. Some scholars view the history of the Israelites as a process of light alternating with darkness.[2] God's people believed firmly that he accompanied them in their journey, befriending all who sought him with humility, faith, and love. But there were times when God seemed distant from them: hidden, silent, withdrawn, elusive, even totally absent. His ways definitely are not our ways (Isa 55:8). Believers have often made their own the question Gideon asked the angel of the Lord: "If the Lord is with us, then why is it that all this is happening to us now?" (Judg 6:13). (This story of Gideon, I might remark in passing, was a favorite passage of Don Pedro Arrupe, General of the Society of Jesus.) When apparently abandoned to the power of enemies or caught in a storm, it should not surprise us that the Lord's disciples have cried out: "Awake! Why do you sleep, O Lord? Rise up!... Why do you hide your face...? Rise up, help us! Redeem us as your love demands" (Ps 44:24–27).

I had the opportunity to consider with Gerry a striking incongruity. Most of us find it naturally gratifying to think that we have been given the mission to herald the gospel, to serve as active agents in building up the human community. As long as we exercise our natural powers and can see palpable evidence that our activity is transforming the world we find it easy to see the manifest will of God. We find it consoling to acknowledge God as present in our lives when he appears as someone concerned, caring, and compassionate, someone commissioning us to collaborate with him energetically.

Why is it that we seem reluctant to acknowledge that God can be just as present when we are assailed by what Pierre Teilhard de Chardin called the "passivities of diminishment?"[3] When negative experiences such as failure, illness, declining health, and ultimately death, deprive us of control over our lives and destiny, we find it difficult to acknowledge that the hand that hurts may also be the hand that will heal. We willingly recognize God revealing himself in "peak" experiences, when we are bathed, as it were, in the light of Mount Tabor. But when we find ourselves enveloped in the darkness of

Calvary, we cry out, "My God, my God, why have you forsaken me?" (Mark 16:34).

I told Gerry that I needed help in meeting what I considered the supreme challenge in guiding and accompanying others: how to help them recognize that God could be inviting us to an even deeper communion in such "negative" experiences; that God might be communicating his will for us most clearly when it does not coincide with what our nature would prefer. Gerry's theological writings, in which he extended the locus of encounter with God's Word to the entire range of human experience, proved especially illuminating. They provided the light many directees needed in order to interpret positively their experiences.

In a key chapter entitled "Revelation Past & Present," Gerry summed up recent church teaching on divine revelation.[4] He demonstrated that both in the documents of the Second Vatican Council and in many important postconciliar statements, revelation was understood as indeed a complete, definitive, and unrepeatable self-communication of God through Jesus Christ. Yet this official teaching also called revelation a present reality that is repeatedly actualized here and now. These complementary forms of revelation—*past,* which Gerry and his colleagues also referred to as "foundational, originating, or independent," and *present,* also called "actualized, participant or dependent"— provided a perspective that enabled us to address a broad spectrum of urgent contemporary issues.

Our traditional approach to discerning God's will focused on contemplating the mysteries of Jesus' earthly life.[5] By observing and considering what Jesus and those around him had said and done, we might recognize that God extends an invitation for us to follow and do likewise. Gerry indicated how a more comprehensive understanding of revelation as both past *and present* could supplement this traditional approach. By stressing actualized revelation we could become more aware of the dynamic presence of the Risen Christ in our lives; we can recognize the Holy Spirit's active power as both the bearer of tradition and the inspirer of new initiatives. We develop a deeper appreciation of the mystery of time and of our faith as a free response to God's personal self-communication. I continued to encourage directees to contemplate the mysteries of Jesus' earthly life, as St. Ignatius had directed, for those mysteries are still normative for genuine discernment of God's will for us today. Complementing this retrospective exercise was the need to read the signs of our time and consider whether God was revealing new prospects for our mission.

Many were accustomed to identifying prayer with what they did while they were dwelling on sacred scripture, kneeling at their prie-dieu, or relishing the presence of the Lord in a chapel. Extending the possibility of communion and communication with God throughout the entire range of actual human experience enables us to remain contemplatives even amid our activity. As persons learned to recognize God's actual presence in situations they had previously viewed as totally devoid of the light of his presence, they experienced renewed faith and a sense of peace.

They perceived that the sacrifices demanded of us by circumstances over which we have no control can often invite us to enter more deeply into the Paschal Mystery of Jesus.

> In the days when he was in the flesh, he offered prayers and supplications with loud cries and tears to the one who was able to save him from death, and he was heard because of his reverence. Son though he was, he learned obedience from what he suffered, and when he was made perfect, he became the source of eternal salvation for all who obey him, declared by God high priest according to the order of Melchizedek. (Heb 5:7–10)

With this appreciation of extended divine revelation in mind, suffering and death can be discerned as revelatory moments par excellence. We know in theory that the identity and destiny of every human being is bound up with the identity and mission of Jesus Christ. The difficulty seems to be in reducing theory to practice. I found a single verse from the Gospel according to John especially helpful: "I came from the Father and have come into the world. Now I am leaving the world and going back to the Father" (16:28). This descending-ascending movement captured by Johannine Christology describes the destiny of every Christian, the path each of us must walk. All culminates in an exodus and return to the Father. Accepting this destiny is a test for all of us.

Many came for direction feeling depressed not because of what they were enduring personally but because of their growing awareness of the distress others were suffering. The media bring into our living rooms the faces of millions of victims of natural disasters, such as floods, famine, and earthquakes. We can view at first hand the consequences of war and other human-made calamities: millions of refugees, racial injustices, political inequities. How were they to deal with this enigma of evil? It seems so senseless, utterly unintelligible. They could, of course, consult philosophical and theological analyses that have addressed the problem of evil down through the centuries; the language of such works, however, was usually remote from their lived experience. The theories put forward did not touch them where they lived. Could I suggest another approach, they asked, one that would not only address this problem objectively but also penetrate to the mysterious depths of their hearts?

On such occasions I recommended Gerry's personal reflections on suffering and evil, especially his early work *The Calvary Christ.*[6] This rich essay enabled many to experience the mystery of the passion and crucifixion of Jesus with renewed intensity. Gerry gave them a new perspective from which to view both what Jesus Christ had done for them and what he might be inviting them to endure for others. Many told me that as a result of their reading they had developed a new sense of commitment and dedication to their Christian vocation.

So much for concrete examples of how Gerry's wisdom helped me meet specific practical challenges in spiritual direction. Now let's consider how the practice and theory of spiritual direction has changed over the past forty years to illustrate how Gerry's writings in fundamental theology have made a distinct contribution.

THE DEVELOPMENT OF SPIRITUAL DIRECTION:
FROM A FORMAL TO A FUNCTIONAL APPROACH

The basic or underlying challenge that we faced in the decades following the Second Vatican Council, as I have already indicated, was helping persons broaden their understanding of divine revelation. Gerry's reflections, occasioned by ongoing dialogue with his colleagues in fundamental theology, enabled many of us directors to meet this complex challenge.

To begin, we should recall the cultural and theological context in which spiritual direction was being given. We who had been formed prior to the Second Vatican Council had received a traditional theological training. The prevailing mind-set we shared was what Bernard

Lonergan has called a classicist worldview.[7] Most who sought or gave spiritual direction saw themselves as persons entrusted with guarding and transmitting divine revelation. We viewed revelation primarily as divinely authoritative teaching, inerrantly proposed as God's Word by the Bible, tradition, and official church teaching. The model of revelation most favored was what Avery Dulles has termed "propositional."[8] These creedal statements enjoyed a cognitive clarity, objectivity, and stability that enabled us to guide our charges with enviable assurance and confidence.

Similarly, our preferred model of Christology was the descending approach of St. John's Gospel, fostered by the school of Alexandria. Our favorite image of the church was that of an institution, emphasizing structural permanence. These models were neat and tidy. The world they reflected was fixed and predictable.

In such a context, spiritual direction was understood and practiced as a deductive science, an extension of ascetical-mystical theology. The point of departure was the body of doctrinal truths revealed by God and enshrined in scripture, tradition, conciliar teachings: creation, elevation to the supernatural state, the fall and its consequences, redemption and its effects, and so on.[9] From these revealed dogmatic truths, as interpreted and articulated by theological reflection, we could deduce the unchanging essence of perfection: it was universal, remaining the same in all cultures throughout history. From this immutable essence directors could deduce principles that would obtain always and everywhere, that could be applied to every concrete, particular instance. Tried and tested ascetical practices were prescribed as normative for Christian living: for example, penance, abnegation, mortification, conformity to God's will, the practice of theological and cardinal virtues. Laws were formulated that had to be observed if a person wished to progress through the purgative and illuminative to the unitive stage. As long as these principles were honored and put into practice faithfully, persons could surmount all obstacles to perfection, walk securely, and ultimately scale the summit of perfection.

The role of the spiritual director was primarily that of a pedagogue—to communicate the body of timeless truths revealed by God, enshrined in the Bible, treasured by the church down through the centuries. The director was to exhort disciples to embrace those truths by applying them faithfully to daily life. Since the ideal was a lofty one, failure could be anticipated: the director was to stand by and encourage disciples to get up and strive again to climb toward that summit of perfection.

This classicist approach had many advantages: the doctrinal truths were certain; the line of reasoning that established the essence of perfection and the absolute principles deduced therefrom was cogent and coherent; the practices had been tried and tested by masters of spirituality; they were proposed as proven means of advancing toward sanctity. Such models favored the values of stability and security, highly prized in a world of uncertainty and insecurity. Since Jesus had revealed himself as the Way, the Truth, and the Life, it was relatively easy for a director to guide seminarians, religious, and priests: they simply had to prolong Christ's threefold office as pastor, prophet, and priest within the church. Everything was clear and foreseeable.

But in the wake of the Second Vatican Council a new context emerged, one characterized by greater sensitivity to issues of social justice and to the gradual pace of human development. Attuned to the opening words of the Pastoral Constitution on the Church in the Modern World, persons coming for direction definitely shared and experienced "[t]he joys and the hopes, the griefs and the anxieties of the men of this age, especially those who are poor or in any way afflicted." As a result they frequently found themselves caught up in conflicts of one kind or another. In this respect they provided a mirror reflection of the world around them. They were often disoriented, disenchanted, despondent.[10] They were crying out for help. They were not intent on striving for perfection conceived as a remote idealistic goal, but on making sense of what was happening to them and to their church. They had no interest in the formal approach to perfection that looked good on paper; they wanted a functional spirituality, one that would actually work for them. They sought a clearer sense of identity and a more focused mission in life.

The role of spiritual directors underwent a significant shift. The world no longer was fixed and predictable; it was characterized by pervasive change and tentativeness. We had to learn to live with ambiguity. Whereas the focus of spiritual direction had once concentrated narrowly on explicitly religious activities, such as formal prayer, penance, mortification, and the like, its scope became more comprehensive. In the aftermath of the Second Vatican Council, our challenge lay in recognizing the wider horizon of spiritually significant experiences. The classicist worldview, which had prevailed for centuries, was gradually replaced by a historical mindedness that began not with the abstract nature of perfection but with the concrete individual reality that exists in time and is involved in an ongoing process of change and development. We turned to the theological community for light. They did not fail us.

Theologians reminded us of other models of divine revelation to complement the propositional model, for example, historical, mystical, dialectical, and symbolic. The ascending approach to Christology favored by the school of Antioch regained widespread favor alongside the descending model. Ecclesiologists gave us various models of the church to supplement the institutional, for example, Mystical Communion, Sacrament, Herald of the Word, Servant of Humanity.[11]

The *formal* approach to spiritual direction was gradually supplemented by a more *functional* strategy. Instead of proceeding deductively from doctrinal principles to the nature of perfection and then to tested ascetical practices, the functional approach proceeded inductively by asking a series of questions: What is the experiential situation in which we find ourselves? (E.g., confused by liturgical and catechetical changes, differences of opinion on vital moral issues culminating in intractable polarization, frustration, and anger?) If so, more questions followed: Can we analyze and identify the factors causing this tension? (E.g., are there opposed images implicit in the fixed positions? Are these images occasioning misunderstandings, compounded by lack of communication skills?) What then should be our pastoral procedure? (E.g. ascetical dialogue, shared prayer, tentative experiments?) Can we preserve reverential continuity with our past and courageously revise our *modus procedendi* in order to assume creative responsibility for the future?

In effect, spiritual directors were asked to assume a new role. Instead of listening to the recital of a laundry list of spiritual successes and failures, he or she was asked to listen to what a fellow pilgrim perceived and interpreted as actualized divine revelation based on their integration of sacred scripture, liturgical celebrations, and involvement in historical events. Together, director and disciple engaged in dialogue seeking clarification of God's revealed will. They had to monitor continuously their disciples' response of faith. The experience and wisdom enjoyed by directors led them to confirm a presumed actual revelation or advise caution, sometimes moderating the intensity of their enthusiasm, at other times encouraging them to move ahead boldly.

Moreover, as the behavioral sciences revealed the gradual nature of human development, the complexity of human motivation, the fragility of our will, and the unpredictability of human behavior, spiritual directors had to respect these findings of psychology and sociology. By availing themselves of what these disciplines taught about the dynamics of the human person, directors were able to relieve directees of morbid guilt, help them scale down unrealistic expectations, refashion expectations into realizable goals, and come to a more realistic self-understanding and self-acceptance. They based their approach on the time-honored principle, "Grace elevates and builds on nature, it does not destroy it." The benefits of integrating psychology and spirituality led many directees back to a therapeutic model that was popular in the early church. Others, however, sounded a warning: we must avoid a reductionism that would effectively marginalize the spiritual dimension of human life.[12]

CONTEMPORARY CHALLENGE:
REDISCOVERING THE ROLE OF MYSTAGOGUE

As we enter the third millennium, the challenge facing spiritual directors seems to be shifting once again. Some of us are still asked occasionally to accompany contemplatives in their life of extraordinary prayer or to guide and support seminarians and religious in their vocational choices. But most directors are now being called upon to assist pastors and their staffs as they progress and lead their congregations more deeply into the Paschal Mystery. As Aidan Kavanagh has expressed it, we are all being called into the continuing conversion that is ecclesial life together. He reminds us that the Rite of Christian Initiation of Adults understands initiation as a sustained and closely articulated process, a "transition that brings with it a progressive change in outlook and style of life, which should become evident by a gradual evolution over a period of time (*OICA,* 19:12, quoting the decree on missions, *Ad Gentes,* of the Second Vatican Council para. 13)."[13]

Mark McIntosh reminds us that "[t]he ancient technical term for teaching that does not merely speak about the divine mystery but helps to lead others to a participatory understanding of it themselves

is *mystagogy*."[14] Many others attest that spiritual directors are rediscovering their primary role as "teachers and guardians of mystery."[15]

Inasmuch as a mystagogue is one who leads us into the depths of
the Paschal Mystery by walking beside us, he or she cannot merely
point out the path to be taken and then remain at a distance monitoring
progress; no, he or she must walk that path with us, sharing in the common Christian experience of being pilgrims. The goal toward which we
all are traveling is not a lofty ideal floating high above the details of
daily life, an abstraction called perfection; rather it is the actualization
of what we once experienced ritually in baptism. Dying and rising are
realized in our day-to-day living together with Christ.

A mystagogue is to be a contemplative theologian, bearing in mind
that a contemplative mentality denotes an abiding *mystical consciousness* rather than an isolated *mystical experience*. This is not a matter of
a rare event that may connote altered states—visions, locutions, raptures
and the like. Such a contemplative mentality must be an integral part of
spiritual directors in their lifelong spiritual journey. The words of
Evagrius Ponticus, so dear to the heart of Gerry O'Collins, come to
mind as an apt description of a mystagogue: "If you are a theologian you
will truly pray; and if you truly pray you are a theologian."[16]

Being a prayerful person necessarily moderates how a spiritual
director views his or her fellow pilgrims. Gregory the Great observed
that the key to compassion for others is a contemplative spirit.[17] If
directors accompany their directees, honestly trying to live the truth in
love, they will know that we must wait patiently for God's grace to
lead us forward at our own pace and in God's good time. As we grow
in experiential assurance of living the truth, we become more serene in
bearing witness to it. We learn that truth is invitational, not coercive.
Simply by being itself, truth bears witness to itself, attracting minds
and hearts. It doesn't have to overwhelm by force. It is gentle, respectful, reverential. Such a spirit characterizes the true spiritual director.

CONCLUSION

It has been my experience that in accompanying fellow pilgrims
along our common Christian journey to the Father, we directors need
the continuing help of fundamental theologians. The questions we ask
are the perennial ones: How can we recognize divine initiative as gen-

uine? By what criteria do we discern authentic revelation? In monitoring presumed revelation from God, how can we provide assurance that a directee is on the right path, moving from clarity to clarity, through the enveloping darkness?

On one occasion I discussed with Gerry at some length the mystery of alternating darkness and light in relation to our religious faith. (At the time I was serving as a theological consultor with the Congregation for the Causes of Saints; we were considering the Cause of Cardinal Newman.[18]) Gerry helped me to deepen my understanding of this mystery as we considered how God provides sufficient light to make our faith reasonable but not so much as to overwhelm us and replace faith by rationalistic certainty. Throughout our earthly pilgrimage God calls us to walk humbly with trust and confidence, not with some arrogant complacency based on human power alone. We must be willing to accept our human condition as always in transition. As we cope with the existential demands of concrete reality the willingness to move forward from clarity to clarity, in faith and hope must become a permanent characteristic.

This mystery of walking in faith amid alternating shadows and light has had great significance for me as a spiritual director. It brings together many of the themes I've treated in this paper, serving as a conclusion for my dialogue with Gerry and other fundamental theologians. In the tradition of St. Ignatius Loyola,[19] I've seen my role as that of helping fellow pilgrims move forward continuously while maintaining their equilibrium. I've done so by monitoring the fluctuating moods they experienced as they tried to discern and respond progressively to God's will. I've encouraged them in time of darkness and distress by reminding them to remain firm in the decisions made previously when they were surely being guided by God's light. Conversely, in time of euphoric success, I advised them to remain humble, temper their enthusiasm, avoid precipitous decisions, recognize the danger of delusion.

As we enter the new millennium the world may be passing through a time of fear comparable to that which gripped the general populace of Europe toward the end of the fourteenth century. That fear was due in part to the devastation caused by the black death. Our present fear is being occasioned in part by many natural disasters (earthquakes, floods, hurricanes), but even more so by widespread terrorism, political oppression, and other human-made calamities. I frequently call to mind Julian of Norwich's well-known dictum that all will be well.[20] What I say to those coming to me seeking some kind of assurance is what I have come to appreciate from my dialogue with fundamental theology: We simply don't know what the future holds; what we do know is that the One who holds the future in his hands is Lord and Savior, our brother and companion. Remembrance of blessings in the past serves as the basis for our hope in the future. *Procedamus in pace.*

Notes

1. Gerald O'Collins, *The Second Journey* (New York: Paulist, 1978; Leominster: Gracewing, 1995). By way of contrast, cf. William Bridges, *Transitions: Making Sense of Life's Changes* (Reading, Mass.: Addison-Wesley, 1980).

2. Roland de Vaux, "The Presence and Absence of God in History According to the Old Testament," in *Concilium,* vol. 50 (New York: Paulist, 1969), 7–20; cf. Arthur Gibson, *The Silence of God: Creative Response to the Films of Ingmar Bergman* (New York: Harper & Row, 1969); Josef Pieper, *The Silence of St. Thomas: Three Essays* (Chicago: Regnery, 1957); Samuel Terrien, *The Elusive Presence: Toward a New Biblical Theology* (San Francisco: Harper & Row, 1978).

3. Pierre Teilhard de Chardin, *Le Milieu Divin: An Essay on the Interior Life* (London: Collins, 1960), 52–95.

4. Gerald O'Collins, *Retrieving Fundamental Theology: The Three Styles of Contemporary Theology* (New York: Paulist, 1993), 87–119; and *Fundamental Theology* (New York: Paulist, 1981), 32–113. His concern was to refine, in dialogue with his colleagues, the theological complexity presented by this magisterial teaching of ongoing revelation. He shows how present revelation *actualizes* the living event of the divine self-manifestation but does not add to the "content" of what was completely and fully revealed through Christ's life, death, resurrection, and sending of the Holy Spirit. Revelation continues to be an actual encounter, but this living dialogue adds nothing to "the divinely revealed realities," which essentially amount to Jesus Christ crucified and risen from the dead. My concern was to utilize this distinction in guiding the priests and religious coming to me for spiritual direction, to broaden their understanding of how God was dealing with them. See also Yves Congar, *I Believe in the Holy Spirit,* II (New York: Crossroad, 1997), 30, 32.

5. St. Ignatius Loyola, *Spiritual Exercises,* nos. 261–312.

6. Gerald O'Collins, *The Calvary Christ* (Philadelphia: Westminster, 1977). See also *The Cross Today: An Evaluation of Current Theological Reflections on the Cross of Christ* (New York: Paulist, 1978); and *Experiencing Jesus* (New York: Paulist, 1994).

7. Bernard Lonergan, "The Transition from a Classicist World-View to Historical Mindedness," in *A Second Collection: Papers by Bernard J. F. Lonergan,* ed. William Ryan and Bernard Tyrrell (Toronto: University of Toronto Press, 1996), 1–5. I trust that most readers are familiar with this distinction; my references are quite schematic. See also William V. Dych, *Thy*

Kingdom Come: Jesus and the Reign of God (New York: Crossroad, 1999), 1–11.

8. Avery Dulles, *Models of Revelation* (Garden City, N.Y.: Doubleday, 1983); idem, "Faith and Revelation," in *Systematic Theology Roman Catholic Perspectives,* vol. 1, ed. F. Schüssler Fiorenza and John P. Galvin (Minneapolis: Fortress, 1991), 92–104.

9. See the indices of Adolphe Tanquerey, *The Spiritual Life: A Treatise in Ascetical and Mystical Theology* (Tournai: Desclée, 1930); or Joseph de Guibert, S.J., *The Theology of the Spiritual Life* (New York: Sheed & Ward, 1953).

10. James Gill, S.J., M.D., "Despondence: Why We See It in Priests," *Medical Insight* 1 (Dec. 1969): 21–32.

11. Avery Dulles, *Models of the Church* (Garden City, N.Y.: Doubleday, 1974).

12. Irénée Hausherr, *Spiritual Direction in the Early Christian East* (Kalamazoo, Mich.: Cistercian Publications, 1990); William Barry and William Connolly, *The Practice of Spiritual Direction* (New York: Seabury, 1982); Gerald May, *Care of Mind, Care of Spirit: A Psychiatrist Explores Spiritual Direction* (New York: Harper & Row, 1982); idem, *Will and Spirit: A Contemplative Psychology* (New York: Harper & Row, 1983).

13. Aidan Kavanagh, "Christian Initiation in Post-Conciliar Roman Catholicism: A Brief Report," in *Living Water, Sealing Spirit: Readings on Christian Initiation,* ed. Maxwell E. Johnson (Collegeville, Minn.: Liturgical Press, 1995), 1–10, at 5.

14. Mark A. McIntosh, *Mystical Theology: The Integrity of Spirituality and Theology* (Malden, Mass.: Blackwell, 1998), 27. The context illumines his remark: "…religious perspectives have recovered a fundamental assumption of earlier eras; namely, that living, practical involvement in reality…is a prerequisite for true insight in conceptualization…a holistic and participative approach that involves a person in some personal existential contextualization of the material. If the reality I desire to speak of is no 'object,' indeed does not exist as one of the items of the universe, but is rather the answer to the question why there is a universe at all rather than nothing, then it would be the case that the most adequate truth-telling would attempt to guide one into participative encounter with that reality, not to offer an impossible series of descriptive propositions about it…. what is most mysterious is not the divine being per se but precisely the infinite self-giving of God which is the fundamental characteristic of the divine Trinity and is enacted in history in the life, death and resurrection of Jesus" (pp. 24–27, 41).

15. *Mistagogia e direzione spirituale,* ed. Ermanno Ancilli (Rome: Teresianum, 1985), especially, "Dalla mistagogia alla psicoterapia: la

direzione spirituale ieri e oggi" (pp. 9–51); "La mistagogia della Chiesa" (pp. 163–245); and Shaun McCarty, "Spiritual Directors: Teachers and Guardians of Mystery," *Presence: The Journal of Spiritual Directors International* 4 (1998): 7–15.

16. Evagrius Ponticus (346–399), "On Prayer," in 60, PG 79:1180B.

17. Gregory the Great, *Regula Pastoralis,* Part II, chap. 5 (PL 77:32B–34B). See also the doctoral dissertation of Austin Doran, "Contemplation and Compassion in the Life of the Pastor" (Pont. Univ. S. Thomae, Rome, 1990).

18. Venerable John Henry Cardinal Newman, "The Humiliation of the Eternal Son," *Parochial & Plain Sermons,* vol. 3 (London: J. G. & F. Riverton, 1837), 172–89, at 183: "Before He came on earth He was infinitely above joy and grief, fear and doubt, pain and ignorance; but afterwards all these properties and many more were His as fully as they are ours. Before He came on earth, He had but the perfections of God, but afterwards He had also the virtues of a creature, such as faith, meekness, self-denial. Before He came on earth He could not be tempted of evil; but afterwards He had a man's heart, a man's tears, and a man's wants and infirmities. His Divine Nature indeed pervaded His manhood, so that every deed and word of His in the flesh savoured of eternity and infinity; but, on the other hand, from the time He was born of the Virgin Mary he had a natural fear of danger, a natural shrinking from pain, though ever subject to the ruling influence of that Holy and Eternal Essence which was in Him."

19. *Spiritual Exercises,* nos. 314–36.

20. "Jesus said: Sin is necessary, but all will be well, and all will be well, and every kind of thing will be well. In this naked word 'sin,' our Lord brought generally to my mind all which is not good, and the shameful contempt and the direst tribulation which he endured for us in this life, and his death and all his pains, and the passions, spiritual and bodily, of all his creatures…. When the judgment is given, and we are all brought up above, we shall then clearly see in God the mysteries which are now hidden from us. And then shall none of us be moved to say in any matter: Lord, if it had been so, it would have been well. But we shall all say with one voice: Lord, blessed may you be, because it is so, it is well; and now we see truly that everything is done as it was ordained by you before anything was made" (Julian of Norwich, *Showings,* trans. from the critical text with an intro. by Edmund Colledge, O.S.A., and James Walsh, S.J., Long text, 27th and 85th chapters [New York: Paulist, 1978], 225, 341).

11. Docility to the Holy Spirit and the Call to Follow Jesus: Catherine of Siena "In Dialogue" with Gerald O'Collins

Donna Orsuto

In the Creed the Holy Spirit comes as the third divine person who is the object of the profession "I/we believe in."...The divine Spirit makes things possible and makes things happen: personal faith, the forgiveness of sins, the life of the sacraments, the whole church's basic fidelity to the original message of and about Christ, fresh insights into and new applications of that message, and loving communication between individuals and groups where all communication seems to have broken down. Everywhere God's Spirit is at work, humanizing and divinizing people within and beyond Christianity.[1]

Gerald O'Collins, S.J., *Believing: Understanding the Creed*

... without this guide, we cannot go on.[2]

Catherine of Siena, *Epistolario, lettera* 335

At first glance, the suggestion of any similarity between the Jesuit priest Gerald O'Collins (b. 1931) and the Dominican laywoman Catherine of Siena (1347–1380) may seem somewhat surprising. Not only are they persons of different centuries, but also, as history has shown, the Jesuits and the Dominicans have not always agreed on theological matters. Further, their style of writing is quite diverse: the well-read Gregorian University professor has a crisp systematic way of doing theology that has attracted thousands of students from every continent. The woman mystic and Doctor of the Church, Catherine of Siena, with her more affective and intuitive approach, uses symbols

192

and images to communicate the depths of God's love manifest in Jesus Christ. And yet, despite the diversity between Gerald O'Collins and Catherine of Siena, they share some common ground.

This Jesuit priest and Dominican laywoman have a decidedly christological focus to their writings. Even a quick perusal of the ample bibliography of O'Collins's books and articles reveals a persistent emphasis on the "person, being and doing of Jesus Christ."[3] Catherine of Siena's 26 *Prayers* and 381 *Letters,* and *The Dialogue* are also clearly christological. In fact, when she was named Doctor of the Church in 1970, Paul VI called her "the mystic of the Incarnate Word, above all of Jesus Crucified."[4] Without a doubt, the christological focus of O'Collins and Catherine of Siena offers important insights for Christian theology and spirituality. Indeed, any authentic Christian theology or spirituality must have as its center the person of Jesus Christ. Not only are we called to imitate Christ, but we are beckoned to enter into a profound union with Christ that transforms our lives.

Another commonality between the two is that the Holy Spirit does not figure prominently in their writings. O'Collins does have some eloquent passages about the Holy Spirit in his many articles and books, particularly those published in more recent years. For example, in his 1995 *Christology: A Biblical, Historical and Systematic Study of Jesus,* the final chapter on "The Possibility of Presence" focuses on a Christology of Presence that serves as a thread linking the soteriological mysteries and includes the activity of the Holy Spirit within and beyond the Christian community.[5] Yet the author himself admits that, taken as a whole, his writings have a more christological than pneumatological focus. Similarly, when compared with Catherine's references to the Father and the Son, the Holy Spirit seems to be given only scant attention in her writings.[6] Still, a rich experience and understanding of the Holy Spirit underlies all that Catherine says and does.

In this essay, I propose to engage Gerald O'Collins in a dialogue with Catherine of Siena about her understanding of docility to the Spirit and the call to follow Christ. This is obviously not an exhaustive study of the Holy Spirit in Catherine's writings, for such a task would be far too ambitious in such a short space. What I hope to do, quite simply, is explore some key insights that Catherine has about the Holy Spirit and ask how these can be applied to the call to follow Christ. Catherine specifically sees this conformity to Christ as intimately intertwined with openness to the Spirit's transforming presence. The main purpose of this essay is to describe the dynamic activity of the Spirit in this transformation and to ask how she complements in some way the writings of Gerald O'Collins.

THE TRANSFORMING PRESENCE OF THE SPIRIT

To effectively live the Christian life one must discern the Holy Spirit's presence. Without a doubt, the Spirit is present in the world, in our lives, in ways beyond our hopes and expectations, working more than we do and far better than we are.[7] Specifically, with regard to Catherine of Siena's writings, Mary Ann Fatula notes:

> Catherine recognizes the Holy Spirit not only as the "burning charity" of God, but also as the very person of mercy, the largesse and kindness that reaches down to human weakness with a love gone mad with excess. To our fear and selfish love the Spirit brings the fire of God's own charity, a love so profound and free that those touched and inflamed by it participate in the very abyss of the trinitarian life. The Spirit's fire gently heals our disordered desires, and, like dew, waters what is sterile in our hearts, giving us renewed desire for God. The Spirit's warmth and life extend to all creation, for we who have known the Spirit's mercy must become inevitably a sacrament of mercy to others.[8]

With such an insight into the activity of the Holy Spirit, it is no surprise that Catherine includes docility to the Spirit's lead as a vital part of responding to the call to follow Jesus. When reflecting on the importance of the Spirit in her life, she simply states, "without this guide we cannot go on" (L. 335, 5:110).[9] It is in the Spirit that we receive the courage to follow Jesus, who is the Way, the Truth, and the Life (John 4:16).

THE SPIRIT AT WORK ON CALVARY AND IN THE LIVES OF BELIEVERS

Catherine of Siena recognizes the universal action of the Spirit at work in all creation, but she focuses specifically on the Spirit's role in the passion of Jesus. Using symbolic language, she explains:

...for love, that is, the Holy Spirit, sustains all things. The Holy Spirit is the light that banishes all darkness, the hand that upholds the whole world. In that vein, I recall his [the Holy Spirit] saying not long ago, "I am the One who upholds and sustains the whole world. It was through me that the divine and human natures were brought together. I am the mighty hand that holds up the standard of the cross; of that cross I made a bed and held the God-Man fast to it." He was so strong that if the bond of charity, the fire of the Holy Spirit, had not held him; the nails could never have held him.[10]

Where there is love, Catherine discerns the Spirit's fiery presence. For her, however, love is not sentimental but costly, and the extent of God's expansive love for us is manifest most poignantly in what happened to Jesus on the cross, particularly through the shedding of his blood. Catherine of Siena's enthusiasm about the blood of Jesus may be somewhat distasteful for contemporary thinking, but as Gerald O'Collins notes in a reflection on blood symbolism in general, "[as] a symbol touching the human-divine relationship, it exemplifies wonderfully well the 'frightening and fascinating' mystery *(mysterium tremendum et fascinans)* that we encounter in God."[11] Too often contemporary theologians and biblical translators have dismissed as insignificant or have even outrightly ignored blood symbolism when focusing on the passion. In doing so, perhaps they lose something of great significance with regard to our redemption.[12]

One dimension of Catherine of Siena's blood symbolism is the integral connection she sees between the shedding of Christ's blood and the work of the Holy Spirit in the passion. According to Catherine, "there is no blood without fire" (L. 80, 1:35),[13] In fact, as Suzanne Noffke comments, "each attribute of the Spirit is attributed also to the blood, and so the blood is charity, mercy, generosity, compassion, liberation, 'because the blood was shed out of love.'"[14] Thus, it is no surprise that in one of her letters, Catherine says: "O gentle fire of love! You have given us as a servant, as laborer, the most merciful free-flowing Holy Spirit, who is love itself! He is the strong hand that held the word nailed fast to the cross. He crushed the tender body and made it yield blood powerful enough to give us life" (*Letters* 55, 1:171–72).

In a special way, the Spirit enfolds into trinitarian love those who suffer or who are forsaken. This is illustrated in Catherine's most famous letters where she expresses this assurance to a certain young Perugian, most probably Niccolò of Toldo, who was executed in Siena around June 1375. She courageously accompanied this man to the place where he was beheaded. After she received his head into her hands, she movingly describes the mystical experience she had at that moment:

> Then was seen the God-Man as one sees the brilliance of the sun. [His side] was open and received blood into his own blood— received a flame of holy desire (which grace had given and hidden in this soul) into the flame of his own divine charity. After he had received his blood and desire [Jesus] received his soul as well and placed it all-mercifully into the open hostelry of his—side. Thus First Truth showed he was receiving him only through grace and mercy and not for anything he had done. With what tenderness and love he awaited that soul when it had left his body—the eye of his mercy toward it—when it came to enter into his side bathed in its own blood, which found its worth in the blood of God's Son.
>
> Once he had been so received by God (who by his power was powerful enough to do it), the Son, wisdom and Word incarnate, gave him the gift of sharing in the tormented love with which he himself accepted *his* painful death on the cross in obedience to the Father for the welfare of the human race. And the hands of the Holy Spirit locked him in. (*Letters* 32, 1:110–11)

Again, Catherine's attempt to find words to describe this intensely mystical experience may seem somewhat awkward to Christians at the beginning of the twenty-first century. Yet the underlying thought she expresses is not dissimilar from contemporary reflection on the crucifixion. For example, Gerald O'Collins notes that a trinitarian understanding of the passion should bring us beyond the first Good Friday.

> When crucified between two criminals, Jesus ended as he had lived—in solidarity with society's victims rather than with society's successes. He had proclaimed his Father's coming kingdom to the poor, the mourners and the hungry. Jesus' crucifixion not only dramatized the beatitudes which he had preached, but also disclosed a privileged place where we should expect the self-revelation of God—among the world's failures and victims. Among those who are forsaken (and even mercilessly destroyed)

by their fellow human beings and look forsaken by God, we can expect to find in a special way the presence and power of the Father, Son and Holy Spirit. As the setting for the self-communication of the triune God, the passion of God remains a piece of unfinished business. It continues in the whole history of human suffering.[15]

The passion does indeed bring us beyond the first Good Friday because of God's love manifest there. Catherine of Siena's mystical language may lack the sophistication of contemporary theological expression, but the kernel of the message is the same. By entering into the pierced side of Christ she finds a way to describe the power of Christ's redemptive love for the forsaken. She perceives this love at work through the presence of the Triune God—Father, Son, and Holy Spirit—in the death of Niccolò of Toldo.

THE COMING OF THE SPIRIT AND JESUS' PROMISED RETURN

In less dramatic ways, Catherine of Siena encourages all believers to welcome the Spirit's coming and to be transformed by that experience. In her main work, the *Dialogue*, she explains explicitly how the descent of the Spirit at Pentecost is also a trinitarian event that continues to have an impact on followers of Jesus. In the following passage from the *Dialogue,* which is structured as a dialogue between God the Father and Catherine, she weaves her reflections around Jesus' promise to his disciples that he would return (John 16:28): "He said he would return and he did return. For the Holy Spirit did not come alone, but with power from me the Father and with the wisdom of the Son and with his own mercy. So you see, he returned, not in the flesh but in his power, to firm up the road of his teaching."[16] The coming of the Spirit guarantees that Jesus not only *was* the way for the first disciples; he continues to be the way for those who follow him today.

Using the symbol of the bridge, Catherine explains that after Jesus ascended to the Father, the "living bridge" was taken away, yet Christ's presence is assured in the church, because of its trinitarian foundation. This is explained in the *Dialogue*, where once again the Father is the subject:

> So first I made a bridge of my Son as he lived in your company. And though that living bridge has been taken away from your sight there remains the bridgeway of his teaching which as I have told you is held together by my power and by my Son's wisdom and the mercy of the Holy Spirit.... So now as much as before, through his teaching as much as when he was among you, he is the way the truth and life—the way that is the bridge leading to the very height of heaven. (*Dialogo* 92.79)[17]

If Jesus continues to be the way, how concretely do Christians follow Jesus today? The response to that question can be found in some of the practical advice that Catherine gives in some of her letters.

THE HOLY SPIRIT AND THE INTERIOR CELL

For Catherine, the disciples waiting in the upper room at Pentecost symbolize the attitude necessary for receiving the Holy Spirit and thus for following Jesus. In a letter to Urban VI, she says, "[The disciples] after much vigilant, humble, and continual prayer...were filled with the strength of the Holy Spirit.... It seems that with this they teach us how we can receive the Holy Spirit. How? By entering in the house of self knowledge" (L. 351, 5:188). Receiving the fullness of the Spirit does not imply that the Spirit somehow does not already dwell within us; rather it means that we allow the Holy Spirit to transform our lives and lead us into a deeper conformity to Christ crucified.

Catherine explains this in one of her letters to Monna Giovanna di Corrado Maconi. The context of this letter is important for understanding the message. Giovanna was the somewhat possessive mother of Stefano Maconi, who was not only one of Catherine's closest disciples but also her friend and secretary. Monna Giovanna had apparently written to Catherine complaining that her son spent too much time away from home. In fact, she had good reason to complain because at the time she wrote the letter, Stefano was once again far from home, this time with Catherine in Avignon.

Catherine responds to this complaint in her gentle, yet no-nonsense manner: "I Caterina, servant and slave of the servants of Jesus Christ, am writing to you in his precious blood. I long to see you making your home in the cell of self-knowledge, so that you may attain perfect love for I know that we cannot please our Creator unless we love him, because he is perfect love and wants nothing but love" (*Letters* 73, 1:226). Further in this letter, she links this perfect love with the Holy Spirit. Catherine explains that in the cell of self-knowledge, Monna Giovanna will encounter "the gentle mercy of the Holy Spirit, the aspect of God that gives and is nothing but love. Whatever the Spirit does is done because of love" (ibid.).

The cell of self-knowledge is an interior and constant awareness of one's own nothingness and God's goodness. Catherine's teaching on this interior cell has its roots in an experience she had early in her life. When at one point she was deprived of her room, the Holy Spirit inspired Catherine to make a cell within her own heart—a place where she could remain uninterruptedly.[18] As Catherine matured, this became a constant theme in her writings, most particularly in her letters. In this interior space she came to a profound knowledge of God and of herself. From this interior space she received the truth and knowledge necessary to embrace more effectively her responsibilities in the world. As Catherine once told her spiritual director, Raymond of Capua, when he felt burdened by too much work: "Build yourself a cell within your heart, and never put your foot outside it."[19]

Catherine tells Monna Giovanna that in this cell of self-knowledge she will discover her own nothingness: all is gift and grace given to us with boundless love from God. This is a foundational theme in Catherine's writings. As Noffke notes, "The essence of Catherine's message lies in the one central truth that God Is of himself and all else, of itself, is Not. It is instructive to note that Catherine refers to the root of sin not simply as 'self-love' *(amore di se)* but as 'selfish self-love' *(amore proprio di se)*."[20] Specifically, in this letter Catherine explains that the practical consequence of this knowledge, the result of this docility to the Spirit in the life of Giovanna, will be a more "perfect love," a love purified of all selfishness. In other words, as she is "on fire with divine charity" or "blazing love," she will be more conformed to Christ crucified. This is the work of the Holy Spirit. In a final barrage of images, Catherine concludes her letter:

> So up dearest mother! I don't want you sleeping any more in irresponsibility and sensual love. No, with boundless blazing love get up and take a bath in Christ's blood, hide in the wounds of Christ

crucified. I'll say no more. I'm sure that if you live in the cell I've been talking about you will discover none other than Christ crucified. Tell Corrado to do the same. Keep living in God's holy and tender love. Gentle Jesus! Jesus love! (*Letters* 74, 1:228)

To summarize, this letter emphasizes three points. First, the Holy Spirit, who is love par excellence, brings about conversion, moving Monna Giovanna gently from imperfect to perfect love. One practical result is the purification of relationships. In Monna Giovanna's situation, docility to the Spirit means becoming less possessive, less selfish, and more detached in her relationship with Stefano. It is the Spirit who brings about this loving freedom. Second, Catherine shows that in the midst of everyday life in the world, one can experience the gentle mercy of the Holy Spirit. There is an interior cell where one can grow in self-knowledge and knowledge of God. Finally, the end result of the Spirit's action is to help Monna Giovanna live her life in greater conformity to Christ crucified.

THE ROLE OF THE SPIRIT IN PROCLAIMING CHRIST IN THE WORLD

According to Catherine, docility to the Spirit, as symbolized by waiting in the interior cell, also leads one into active service of others. After the disciples received the Spirit, they left the upper room and fearlessly preached the good news. They were not afraid to suffer and they went forth boldly (*Dialogo* 74.189; Noffke 74, 137). Since the Spirit is the bond of love between the Father and the Son, we experience the Spirit as love. Indeed as Paul notes in his letter to the Romans, "The love of God has been poured in our hearts through the Holy Spirit which has been given to us" (Rom 5:5). That love liberates us from fear. This is well expressed in the First Letter of John: "We know that we are living in him and he is living in us because he lets us share his Spirit.... We ourselves have known and put our faith in God's love for us.... In love there can be no fear, for perfect love casts out fear" (4:3–18).

The Holy Spirit not only casts out fear but also envelops desires and enables the Christian to live a life of boldness in prayer and service. An incident in Catherine of Siena's life illustrates this point. When she first joined the Dominican lay tertiary group, the Sisters of Penance, instead of embracing their active lifestyle of service to the poor and sick of the city, Catherine lived in solitude. She lived in her own home and left only to share in the liturgy and to see her spiritual director. This went on for three years and was a time of intense mystical experiences of union with Christ that culminated in the mystical marriage, a transformative and unitive encounter with Christ of the highest sort. This was followed by a call from God to go out and serve others. From every indication, Catherine resisted this call because she felt that it would separate her from the deep union she had experienced with Christ during these years of solitude. Yet she obeyed and discovered that even in the midst of an active life, she could find Christ.

What enabled Catherine to accept this call was perhaps a profound experience of the Holy Spirit. In a revealing passage in the *Dialogue* Catherine explains what she considers the grace of Pentecost, an experience of perfect love: "[The Father is speaking] Now it remains to say how one can tell that a soul has attained perfect love. The sign is the same as that given to the holy disciples after they had received the Holy Spirit. They left the house and fearlessly preached my message by proclaiming the teaching of the Word, my only begotten Son...." Further on she hears the Father say to her,

> I gave her a share in this love, which is the Holy Spirit within her will by making her will strong to endure suffering and to leave her house in my name to give birth to virtues for her neighbor...for *the fear that she had of not showing herself lest she lose her own consolation is gone. After she has come to perfect, free love, she lets go of herself and comes out as I have described.* (*Dialogo* 74.190)[21]

Is this passage somewhat autobiographical? Though a difficult passage to translate, which may leave it open to other interpretations, I think we have a hint of Catherine's own struggle. The experience of the Holy Spirit described here gave Catherine of Siena the strength to leave her cozy yet Christ-filled solitude and courageously embrace his call to serve others—in Siena and beyond the walls of the city.

LIFE IN THE SPIRIT

For Catherine, the Holy Spirit actively works in the great and small details of her life, always prompting her to greater docility to

God's providence, ever leading her to a deeper communion with the Trinity. She perceives that this happens not only in her own life but also in the lives of others. This is amply demonstrated in her letters, in which she coaxes others to be more receptive to the prompting of the Spirit. In this regard, the number of letters written to laypersons where she mentions the Holy Spirit is noteworthy. From Elizabeth, the Queen Mother of Hungary, to Bernabó Visconti, one of the most notorious scoundrels of her time, Catherine exhorts women and men to "be set ablaze with the gentle loving fire of the Holy Spirit" (*Letters* 40, 1:13).[22] It is likely that some people who received a letter from Catherine would have been just as happy not to hear from her! Nevertheless, this does not stop her from encouraging them to be receptive to the Spirit's action. Finally, Catherine also acknowledges the work of the Holy Spirit in those around her, especially in her confessors, whose ministry in the sacrament of reconciliation is to "baptize in the Spirit."[23]

The interior transformation wrought by the Spirit had a concrete effect in Catherine's life, and so it does in the life of every Christian. Paradoxically the Spirit led her at the same time into the cell of self-knowledge and out into the world in loving service of God and neighbor. Though the references to the Holy Spirit are few compared with the constant focus on Christ in Catherine's writings, they have a theological centrality that would be hard to overemphasize. It is in the Spirit that Christ effected our redemption, and it is through that same Spirit that Christ continues to work in us. The Spirit who descended on the community gathered in the upper room is a life-giving force that enabled the first disciples, and all Christians, to go forth boldly and be authentic disciples of Christ in the world.

CONCLUSION

I began this essay by stating that Catherine of Siena and Gerald O'Collins coincide in a common christological focus and in a paucity of references to the Holy Spirit in their writings. This lack of emphasis on the Holy Spirit, however, does not imply a lack of appreciation of the Spirit's role in salvation history. I mentioned references to the Holy Spirit in O'Collins's works at the beginning of this essay. In more detail, I have explored Catherine of Siena's teaching on the Holy Spirit, specifically with a focus on the theme of following Jesus. Now I raise the question: Does Catherine's teaching on the Holy Spirit complement the writings of O'Collins in some way? In a certain way she does. As this essay has shown, Catherine develops practical insights regarding docility to the Spirit as an important element for following Jesus.

At the end of his book *Interpreting Jesus,* O'Collins states that the credibility of the Christian message requires something more than solid scholarship about the person of Jesus, his death and resurrection. He argues:

> It is not so much right theory about him as loving discipleship which establishes that "Jesus is Lord" (1 Cor. 12:3). In brief, there has never been such a thing as a purely theoretical Christology. All beliefs about Christ come from the practice of a genuinely Christian life and in turn should nourish such a life. To improve Christology we need both better scholarship and better discipleship. But ultimately the discipleship will prove more significant than the scholarship. We have to pay the price for Christology. It is only when we suffer, act and pray with Christ that we will truly know who he is as Son of God and Savior of the World.[24]

Clearly Catherine of Siena's insights on the Holy Spirit are not written as a scholarly treatise. They do offer, however, insights into the role of the Holy Spirit in the lives of those desiring to become better disciples of Jesus and thus "improve Christology." This contribution is not to be underestimated for, as O'Collins has noted here, discipleship may ultimately prove more important than scholarship. In fact, in the postmodern world in which we live, words and theories seem to have lost their compelling force. John Paul II describes the situation well in *Redemptoris Missio:* "People today put more trust in witnesses, than in teachers, in experience, than in teaching, and in life and action than in theories" (RM 42). The witness of "loving discipleship" may impact on a contemporary understanding of Jesus in ways beyond our expectations.

"Loving discipleship" involves coming to know Christ by participating in his life. "True knowledge of Jesus comes only through being converted and following him."[25] The scholarly contributions of Gerald O'Collins put a personal challenge to his readers. It is not a new challenge, for it is the "real drama and essential issue raised by the Gospels: Am I willing to put my whole life—with all its fears and hopes—into the crucified hands of Jesus?"[26] Like O'Collins, Catherine teaches that loving discipleship is costly. Her writings complement those of Gerald O'Collins by giving practical insights into how to live Christian discipleship. Specifically, this essay has focused on her conviction concerning the activity of the Holy Spirit in bringing about the interior tranformation that enables one to follow Jesus. Catherine was right when she said "without this guide, we cannot go on!" (L. 335, 5:110) because life in the Spirit is the only option for those who want to respond fully to Jesus' call: "Come, follow me."

Notes

1. Gerald O'Collins and Mary Venturini, *Believing: Understanding the Creed* (Mahwah, N.J.: Paulist, 1991), 133.

2. *Le lettere di S. Caterina da Siena,* ed. Piero Misciattelli (Florence: Giunti, 1940), letter 335, volume 5, 110. Hereafter, we will use the abbreviation L. 335, 5:110.

3. Gerald O'Collins: *Christology: A Biblical, Historical, and Systematic Study of Jesus* (Oxford: Oxford University Press, 1995), 1.

4. Paul VI, "La spirituale esultanza," AAS 62 (1970): 676. The Catherinian scholar Giuliana Cavallini notes: "Even a cursory reading of the *Dialogue* can show the primary relevance of Christ and his doctrine in Catherine's thought: his presence marks both the opening and the solemn conclusion of the book, and the book is centered on the teaching of Christ-the-bridge. Catherine normally begins her letters 'in the name of Christ crucified' and closes them in that of 'sweet [gentle] Jesus'" (*Catherine of Siena* [London: Geoffrey Chapman, 1998], 67–68). See also Mary O'Driscoll, "Catherine the Theologian," *Spirituality Today* 40 (spring 1988): 4–7.

5. O'Collins, *Christology,* 317.

6. The paucity of references to the Holy Spirit in Catherine's writings led G. Getto to say that the mysticism of the Holy Spirit is rather neglected in Catherine's writings (*Saggio letterario su S. Caterina da Siena* [Florence: Sansoni, 1939], 123). In recent years, however, other scholars have shown that in fact, though the Spirit is not mentioned often, Catherine does have a profound perception of the work of the Spirit. See particularly the following articles: Y. Congar, "Le Saint-Esprit dans le prières de Sainte Catherine de Sienne," in *Atti del Congresso internazionale di studi cateriniani, Siena— Roma, 24–29 aprile 1980* (Rome: Curia generalizia, O.P., 1981), 76–92; Domenico Abbrescia, "Lineamenti cateriniani per una vita secondo lo Spirito," ibid., 266–96.

7. Carlo Maria Martini, *Tre racconti dello Spirito,* Lettera pastorale per verificarci sui doni del Consolatore (Milan: Centro Ambrosiano, 1997), 11.

8. Mary Ann Fatula, *Catherine of Siena's Way* (London: Darton, Longman & Todd, 1987), 180.

9. Similarly in L. 168, 3:52, she says, "I write...with desire to see you filled with divine grace and the light of the Holy Spirit, as I see it, without this light we cannot go on."

10. *The Letters of Catherine of Siena,* trans. Suzanne Noffke (Binghamton, N.Y.: Medieval & Renaissance Texts & Studies), letter 29, 1:103 (hereafter *Letters* 29, 1:103). It is curious that the Holy Spirit is the sub-

ject here. As Noffke mentions, probably this letter is recounting an experience that Catherine had during prayer. "[T]he context, and even more the whole body of Catherine's writings, clearly indicate that the Holy Spirit is the speaker—a most unusual feature in Catherine's recorded experiences. Throughout this letter, Catherine identifies charity with the Holy Spirit" (p. 306 n. 4).

11. Gerald O'Collins, "Our Peace and Reconcilation," *The Way* 22 (1982): 120.

12. O'Collins notes: "When contemporary theological works deal with the suffering and death of Jesus, they regularly fail to discuss how he made peace *through the shedding of his blood upon the cross.*" Further on, O'Collins ponders: "I wonder whether Biblical translators and theologians are losing something of great significance when they play down or even ignore the blood of Jesus shed for us on Good Friday" (*Interpreting Jesus* [London: Geoffrey Chapman/Mahwah, N.J.: Paulist Press, 1983], 162).

13. Written to Master Giovanni Terzo. Suzanne Noffke also makes reference to this in *Catherine of Siena: Vision through a Distant Eye* (Collegeville, Minn.: Liturgical Press, 1996), 26.

14. Noffke, *Vision through a Distant Eye,* 27.

15. O'Collins, *Interpreting Jesus,* 95–96.

16. Caterina da Siena, *Il Dialogo,* ed. Giuliana Cavallini (Siena: Edizioni Cantagalli, 1995), chapter 29.80. The English translation is from an earlier edition of *Il Dialogo* edited by Cavallini (1968): *Catherine of Siena, The Dialogue,* trans. with an introduction by Suzanne Noffke (New York: Paulist, 1980), 70. In this case and throughout this essay, I have carefully checked the translation against the 1995 critical edition, but found nothing to adjust.

17. Noffke, *Dialogue,* 70. Though the translation of this passage is quite difficult, Noffke's solution of translating "*il ponte e la via della dottrina*" as "the bridgeway of his teaching" seems to be the best solution in English.

18. Raymond of Capua, *The Life of Catherine of Siena,* translated, introduced, and annotated by Conleth Kearns (Dublin: Dominican Publications, 1980), par. 49, 46–47.

19. Ibid.

20. Suzanne Noffke, "The Dialogue: A Window on St. Catherine's Vision," *Dominican Ashram* 2 (March 1983): 12–20.

21. Noffke 74, 137 (italics mine). There is a problem with this last sentence, as Noffke remarks in n. 95 "because the true reference is unclear from the context: '*Ma poi che sono venuti all'amore perfetto e liberale, escono*

fuore per lo modo detto abbandonando loro medesimi.'" Manuscript S omits *abandonando loro medesimi.*

22. See the following references for other examples of how Catherine invokes the Holy Spirit to inspire persons to particular actions: L. 8, 1:30; L. 15, 1:50; L. 28, 1:101; L. 29, 1:108.

23. Catherine uses this expression with reference to the sacrament of reconciliation in one of her prayers. See *Le orazioni*, ed. Giuliana Cavallini (Rome: Edizioni Cateriniane, 1978), 34; *The Prayers of Catherine of Siena*, ed. and trans. Suzanne Noffke (New York: Paulist, 1983), 38. She says: "When you [Jesus] parted from us, you did not leave us orphans, but you gave us your vicar, who gives us the baptism of the Holy Spirit, and not once, as we were washed once by the baptism of water, but he is constantly washing us by holy penance and the cleansing of our sins." This is a rather interesting association of baptism of the Spirit and confession. Yet as Cavallini notes in her comment on this prayer in the critical edition (p. 34 n. 23), it is more understandable in the context of Matt 3:11: "he will baptize you with the Holy Spirit and with fire." As we have noted above, the Spirit as fire comes to purify and transform the soul. This is certainly a characteristic of the grace received in the sacrament of reconciliation as well.

24. O'Collins, *Interpreting Jesus,* 207.

25. Ibid.

26. Gerald O'Collins, *What Are They Saying about Jesus?* rev. 2nd ed. (New York: Paulist, 1983), 78.

12. The Church as Easter Witness in the Thought of Gerald O'Collins, S.J.

William Henn, O.F.M. Cap.

Gerald O'Collins has not devoted many writings explicitly to ecclesiology. Nevertheless, his publications about themes that generally fit under the category of fundamental theology often contain insights into the origin, nature, and mission of the church. Perhaps because he does not intend to focus on the church, but rather to describe it in relation to other topics, such as revelation, hope, tradition, or the interpretation of scripture, his insights can strike one as having a welcome freshness and originality. He is certainly no "ecclesiocentrist"; yet the church plays an important role in his theology. In the following pages, I would like to lay out some of the insights about the church that are woven throughout his extensive bibliography.

Faith and the Church as the "Place" of Revelation

Already one of Gerald O'Collins's earliest books, *Theology and Revelation* (1968), announces many of the leitmotifs concerning the church that will recur throughout his work.

The apostles, the official witnesses of Christ's resurrection, provide the bridge from him to humanity. To them God is revealed in his Son; their mission is one of proclaiming this revelation. Peter stands up "with the eleven" (Acts 2:14) to preach the revealing event that is Christ's death and resurrection, made known with the sending of the Holy Spirit. This proclamation shapes the church, building the community of those who believe in Jesus as the Lord. To all the apostles we can apply the words of 1 John 1:2–3: "the life was made manifest, and we saw it, and testify to it, and proclaim to you the eternal life which was with the Father and was made manifest to us…so that you may have fellowship with us; and our fellowship is with the Father and with his Son Jesus Christ."[1]

What immediately comes into bold relief here is the centrality of the proclamation of Christ's death and resurrection for understanding the church. The church is shaped by this proclamation; it is the community of those who believe in Jesus as Lord, risen from the dead. Faith comes from hearing the proclaimed word (Rom 10:17; Gal 3:5).[2] Thus the church, as the fellowship (*koinōnia,* communion) of believers, is truly born of the word (*creatura verbi;* cf. 1 Pet 1:23 and *Lumen Gentium* 9). Her mission is to proclaim this word.

Thus, the church is "the 'place' of revelation" (*Theology and Revelation,* 66–69). This way of understanding the church allows one to grasp also the sacramental nature of the community. Just as revelation consists of both word and deed (cf. *Dei Verbum* 2), so the church is not only the place to hear the word through the proclamation of scripture, preaching, catechesis, official teachings, creeds, patristic writings, and the works of theologians, but also the place where this word must become actualized in the lives of people today.

It is not enough, for example, for people to read or hear the scriptures. The scriptural witness must be actualized and made concrete in the given situation by the church seeking the proper human word through which revelation may be reenacted. Christ promised his church that "the Holy Spirit…will bring to your remembrance all that I have said to you" (John 14:26), but the Spirit does not simply assist the members of the church in refreshing their memories of past events. Under the guidance of the Spirit they can make present, interpret, and help others to experience the ongoing reality of revelation in Christ (*Theology and Revelation,* 66–67).

The sacraments are part of the saving economy by which revelation becomes actualized in the lives of believers. The community of believers in turn becomes an instrument by which God's saving revelation effectively reaches and transforms those who are not yet believers in Christ. After acknowledging that God's will to save all human beings implies that God reaches out to touch those millions who have heard little or nothing of Jesus, O'Collins reflects on the role of the church in this history of salvation.

> ...it is necessary to insist that the church is the divinely estab-
> lished place of revelation and has the authentic means by which
> the divine disclosure is transmitted in all its fullness. At the same
> time the church is more than merely the normative place where
> revelation is renewed and transmitted. However mysteriously, it is
> involved wherever the divine revelation becomes an actuality for
> individual men. (*Theology and Revelation,* 70–71)

The relation between the church and those who do not believe in Christ
will be taken up again on other occasions when O'Collins addresses
the fullness of revelation and the universality of redemption in Jesus
Christ.[3] Here it may suffice to point out, first of all, that the category
of "fullness," which is used in comparing the church with non-
Christian religions, appears quite congenial to Vatican II's affirmation
that "[i]n [Christ], in whom God reconciled all things to himself (2
Cor. 5:18–19), men find the fullness of their religious life" (*Nostra
Aetate* 2). Second, O'Collins seems to recognize an instrumental role
for the church in relation to the salvation not only of those who explicitly belong to her but also, in a very mysterious way, of those who do
not. This echoes the council's description of the church as the "universal sacrament of salvation" (*Lumen Gentium* 48).

Finally, *Theology and Revelation* does not neglect the trinitarian
framework for understanding the church: "It is the Spirit who determines the inner nature of Christian existence in which by faith, hope
and love and prayer we recognize God our Father made known to us
through his Son.... It is this same Spirit who builds into a unity those
who believe in the manifestation of Jesus as the Lord (1 Cor 12:3ff.)"
(*Theology and Revelation,* 44). This "unity of believers," whose existence is stamped by their relation with the Triune God, is the church.
These believers are "witnesses," whose testimony *(martyria)* can be
heroic, even unto death. A recurrent theme in O'Collins's writings is
the appreciative recognition of the inspirational witness of Christians
from the past and the present,[4] especially those who have offered their
lives for their faith.[5] Among this crowd of witnesses, the apostles are
"official witnesses to Christ's resurrection," and among them, Peter
has a special role.

The church has always been convinced that the apostles enjoy a
unique role as true witnesses. Their special function as "founding
fathers" carries with it a special guarantee. Their trustworthiness affects

not merely their proclamation of the revealing event in Christ but also their further interpretation on the basis of meditation and reflection under the Holy Spirit. "The church is in a sense already there as soon as the Lord appears to Peter and he gathers about him the other apostles (Lk. 24:34; 1 Cor. 15:5)" (*Theology and Revelation*, 47). Thus O'Collins here recognizes the importance of apostolic and even Petrine ministry in relation to the founding and the ongoing life of the community.

The church is born of the Easter proclamation; its mission is to proclaim the gospel and occasion its actualization in the authentic witness of believers, who form a community guided by an apostolic ministry within which Peter plays a special role. All of this can be gleaned from O'Collins's first book of theology. This ecclesial vision will be further developed and complemented by additional themes appearing in later writings.

THE CHURCH OF HOPE AND LOVE

Theology and Revelation was published in what turned out to be the revolutionary year of 1968. In harmony with the spirit of the day, O'Collins gave a series of lectures later that year at the Weston faculty of theology, in which he sought to relate Christianity to that understanding of human hope which is expressed in the writings of such secular authors as Marx, Engels, Bloch, Mao Tse-Tung, and Freud. This gave O'Collins the opportunity to return once again to theme of the church, now under the title "The Pilgrim People."[6]

The theme of hope allowed O'Collins to reflect more explicitly on the historical nature of the church as a pilgrim, which moves through the constantly changing circumstances of time and place, which knows the discouragement of failure and sin, and which continually strives to bring to fruition in the world the values of the kingdom of God. Christians do not fault Marxists for hoping for a better life. Rather they are disappointed because the secular hope is "too small" for the human heart. "The Church is the union of those who believe in the future coming of the Lord and hope for a kingdom of God which will transcend every kingdom of man" (*Man and His New Hopes*, 106). To enter the church is "to join oneself to the history of promise" (Acts 2:39); the values that belong to the church constitute "a program of hope"; the ultimate criterion for discerning what is best of the many ecclesial traditions and for discarding what is harmful or irrelevant is the extent to which a tradition "serves the hope of the Church" and enables persons "to complete their process of Christian growth" (*Man and His New Hopes,* 103).

The community of those who believe in Christ is also distinctive because of the unconditional love that its transcendent hope makes possible. The inescapable problem facing the secular humanist is death. If one has faith and hope in Jesus Christ, the crucified one whose great love moved him to give his life for his friends (John 15:13) and whom God did not abandon but rather raised from the dead (Acts 2:24), then love unto death does not remain a perplexing riddle. The death of the noble and faithful martyr is not an absurdity. O'Collins comments: "For its part Christian hope offers the possibility of being effective in an unconditional love. Jesus, the preacher of the coming kingdom, was also a preacher of love and a martyr of love" (*Man and His New Hopes,* 107). O'Collins sees the unity of Christian hope and love nicely conveyed by St. Paul, whose First Letter to the Corinthians pairs one of the New Testament's most inspiring statements about hope (chapter 15) with what many would consider its most memorable hymn about love (chapter 13). This letter furthermore stipulates many of the concrete demands of love, such as the requirements to resolve spiritual and legal quarrels, to practice charity toward the more needy members of the community, and to avoid sexual immorality. 1 Corinthians 10–11 allows O'Collins to touch upon the relation between the church and the Eucharist, the celebration of which reinforces the deep connection between faith, hope, and love. The Eucharist situates the church in time between the first and second comings of Christ; it is a constant reminder of the church's pilgrim and missionary status.

The Last Supper both initiated and foreshadowed the messianic banquet of God's final kingdom. In the celebration of the Eucharist Christians continue to anticipate the end even by recalling the past. They proclaim the death of the Lord *until he comes* (1 Cor 11:26). The Eucharist is a meal of missionary hope celebrated in the mode of memory (*Man and His New Hopes,* 111).

Thinking about the church within the context of human hopes naturally draws O'Collins to consider the church's role in "the world." In contrast to the Isaian image of all nations streaming toward Jerusalem (2:2–3), the more operative image for the Christian community in its pilgrimage through time is that of the missionary mandate with which Matthew's Gospel closes: "Go and make disciples of all nations" (28:19).

The church has always been a minority in the world. It must ever renew its consciousness of being a *missionary* minority, not a frightened minority that withdraws in a spirit of self-protection. Its commitment in and for the world is no optional, extramural activity. Through its members the church should be at the front of political and economic life, with Christians forming the real extra-parliamentary opposition. They constitute a revolutionary movement proclaiming a gospel that endangers the evil values of contemporary society and such social, political, and economic structures as embody those values (*Man and His New Hopes,* 112).

Thus, the consideration of the church in light of Christian hope has complemented and enriched the image emerging from O'Collins's first sketch. Now more attention is given to the historicity of the church, in such a way as to highlight its nature as a community of hope and love, which gathers to celebrate the Eucharist in memory of Jesus and in anticipation of his final return, and which commits itself to struggling for the transformation of the world according to the gospel values of the kingdom of God.

LATER REFINEMENTS FROM WRITINGS ABOUT THE PASCHAL MYSTERY, CHRISTOLOGY, AND FUNDAMENTAL THEOLOGY

The ideas we have so far considered from O'Collins's first two theological books furnish us with his fundamental approach to the church. Roughly speaking, they seem to parallel the first two chapters of *Lumen Gentium,* which concern, respectively, the mystery and the history of the church. From this point on O'Collins's publications center, more often than not, (1) upon the Paschal Mystery and Christology, and (2) upon fundamental theology. While not focused on ecclesiology, these writings often contain insights that further nuance O'Collins's view of the church. Because of the limits imposed on the present essay, I can only briefly list a few of these refinements here.

1. The texts on Christ's death and resurrection and on Christology develop several themes important to ecclesiology. First of all, from more of a methodological perspective, O'Collins's various studies of

the Paschal Mystery call attention to the fact that Christian faith and doctrine find their center in the event of Jesus' death and resurrection, which reveals the love constitutive of the very being of the Triune God (1 John 4:16). Any teaching about the church will be more adequate and credible to the extent that it relates what it says about the Christian community explicitly to this christological and trinitarian center. A second theme that was announced in his earlier writing, but which now is deepened, is the theme of Jesus as a martyr. Already in *Man and His New Hopes,* O'Collins had proposed a new ecclesiological saying — *extra crucem nulla ecclesia*—to emphasize that the hope of the church cannot be isolated from the cross of its founder (p. 109). Now O'Collins's vivid meditations on Jesus' experience in facing his own death bring home the challenge that believers must "in their flesh complete what is lacking in Christ's afflictions for the sake of his body, the Church" (Col 1:24).[7] A third theme from the christological writings that could well contribute to ecclesiology is that of discipleship. Many of O'Collins's publications invite readers to come to know Jesus in a personal way (for example, *A Month with Jesus* [1978]; *Finding Jesus: Living through Lent with John's Gospel* [1983]; *The People's Christmas* [1984]; *Experiencing Jesus* [1994]; and *Focus on Jesus* [1998]). Recalling Avery Dulles's addition of the model "community of disciples" to the revised version of his very popular *Models of the Church,* one can easily imagine how O'Collins's reflections about knowing Jesus could contribute much to a well-rounded ecclesiology.

2. In the area of fundamental theology, O'Collins has contributed helpful reflections about three of the major themes discussed by Vatican II's Dogmatic Constitution on Revelation, *Dei Verbum:* magisterium, tradition, and scripture. Each also sheds light on how O'Collins views the church. His work on the magisterium balances the church's need for shared doctrinal statements with the historical conditionedness and subordination to revelation of official teachings.[8] His two books on the creed, *Friends in Faith* (1989) and *Believing: Understanding the Creed* (1991), enjoy an ecclesiological relevance as contemporary commentaries on some of the most important "formulas of faith" that foster church unity. A similar ecclesial dimension can be found in O'Collins's reflections about tradition, which recall some of the many ways in which tradition is constitutive of the very life of the community. The question of discerning the normative tradition among

the many traditions handed on over the centuries is an ecclesial task that engages the entire church: theologians, ordained ministers, and the whole people of God, guided by the *sensus fidei* or supernatural "sense of the faith."[9] Here the church appears as a dynamic community journeying through history and eliciting the active involvement of all of its members, according to the gifts and competencies of each. Finally, O'Collins's essays about scripture present the Bible as the book of the church that can only be adequately read and interpreted within an ecclesial context (see, e.g., the last two chapters of *Fundamental Theology*, 225–59). Several of the ten principles that he and Daniel Kendall offer in their recent book on interpreting the Bible have a distinctive ecclesial tonality (see *The Bible for Theology*, 8–39). For example, scripture must be "actively listened to" within the ecclesial contexts of liturgy, commitment to justice, and academic pursuit of truth (principle 2). Or again, the living community of faith with its classic creeds provides an indispensable framework for understanding the biblical text (principle 3). These recent theses reaffirm that insight from O'Collins's earliest writings that the church is a community born of the Word of God whose identity is intimately bound up with the reception and proclamation of that Word.

When he examines the scriptures precisely about the topic of the church O'Collins comes up with his most distinctive ecclesiological proposal: that we find the key for understanding the primacy of Peter in the New Testament as well as for grounding a continuing ministry of primacy in the church by a successor to Peter in the fact that Peter was the first official witness to Jesus' resurrection from the dead.[10] O'Collins demonstrates that many exegetes, not only Catholics but especially those belonging to other Christian communities, concur that Peter's prominence in the New Testament closely relates to his being the first official witness to the resurrection ("Peter as Easter Witness," 1–8; *The Bible for Theology*, 124). O'Collins shows that Catholic theology has tended to propose as biblical foundation for the primacy the "big three" Petrine texts from Matthew 16 ("you are Peter and on this rock I will build my church"), Luke 22 ("I have prayed for you...strengthen your brothers in faith"), and John 21 ("feed my lambs; feed my sheep"), to the neglect of 1 Cor 15:5; Luke 24:34; and Mark 16:7, which tell of Peter's primacy or importance as witness to the risen Lord. O'Collins frankly acknowledges that being first witness to the resurrection is only one of the ways the New Testament portrays Peter and welcomes a careful listening to the full biblical evidence. That said, the Easter witness of Peter can rightly be considered the most important scriptural testimony about him, first of all, because the resurrection is at the very heart of the Christ-event and the subsequent birth of the church and, second, because many of the other Petrine themes from the New Testament can be read in an "Easter" key. On these two points O'Collins's own eloquent words are clear:

> In place of speaking more vaguely of the divine truth, the Gospel and Christian faith, we should talk more specifically. The heart of that faith involves accepting as true the good news that the incarnate and crucified Son of God has risen from the dead in the power of the Spirit. Thus the doctrine of the Trinity points to and gathers up the self-revelation of God communicated through Christ's resurrection (understood in the light of the prior mysteries of Creation, Incarnation and Crucifixion and the "posterior" mysteries of Pentecost and the Eschaton).... This resurrection gathered the final community of faith whose members live their sacramental and Christian lives in expectation of the coming kingdom.... It is only if we give this kind of correct weight to Christ's rising from the dead that we can appreciate both the privilege and responsibility implied in Peter's being its primary official witness. ("Peter as Easter Witness," 15–16)

Among the variety of Petrine images presented by the New Testament, O'Collins individuates the following: fisherman or missionary (Mark 1:16–18; Luke 5:10), shepherd (John 21:15–17), rock (Matt 16:18; see Eph 2:20), repentant sinner (Mark 14:72), and martyr (John 21:18–19; see 13:36). While these cannot be reduced to the single image of Peter as Easter witness, still they each can be related in a special way to Peter's encounter with the risen Lord.

In the opening chapters of Acts, Peter's missionary "fishing" takes the form of proclaiming the resurrection. The shepherding vocation comes from the risen Christ. Peter's role as "rock" receives its legitimation from the crucified and risen Jesus, who is the "living stone," the "cornerstone," and the "stone of scandal" (1 Pet 2:4–8). Peter's repentance comes with the passion, death, and resurrection of Jesus (Luke 22:61–62; 23:49; John 21:15–17); he will suffer a martyrdom in the service of the risen Lord (John 21:18–19) (*The Bible for Theology,* 123–24).

O'Collins has occasionally expressed disappointment that his proposal of Peter's Easter witness as foundation for a Petrine ministry of primacy in the church does not seem to have been widely received or to have sparked much interest.[11] I suspect that, in addition to the reasons for such reticence that O'Collins himself mentions,[12] one other explanation may also account for this hesitancy. Most theologians would probably agree that, for an ecclesial structure to be considered in some way normative, it must derive from the will of God. Anything merely "of human institution" may well be useful for a given period of history, but could hardly be thought of as indispensable. Here we touch upon the ancient question of *ius divinum,* which, in quite different terminology, can be divined already in Clement of Rome's concern that the Corinthians follow the guidance of their ministers because their office had been established by the apostles, who in turn had been chosen by Christ, who himself had been sent by the Father (see *Letter to the Corinthians,* 42). For this reason, Catholic thought appealed to Matthew 16, seen as the promise of a special ministry to Peter by Jesus before his death, and John 21, seen as the conferral of that ministry after his resurrection, as having the advantage of demonstrating a certain "divine intentionality" with regard to the primacy. Can a similar divine purpose be seen in the selection of Peter as primary witness to the resurrection, to that event standing at the very center of the faith that unites all Christians in one community of hope and love? I do not see why it cannot. Peter's experience of the risen Lord (who, after all, would have chosen to appear to Peter and to entrust to him the role of primary official witness to the resurrection) need not be seen a matter of sheer accident. His subsequent leadership of the apostles in proclaiming a unified testimony to the risen Lord could well be seen as part of God's intention for the foundation and ongoing structure of the church.

CONCLUDING APPRECIATION

What a rich vision of the church has emerged in this survey of a few of the writings of Gerald O'Collins! The present commentator is particularly struck how these ecclesiological reflections exemplify what *Unitatis Redintegratio,* 11, says about the "hierarchy of truths." There is a center or heart to the Christian proclamation and to Christian faith. It is that center around which the whole liturgical year of the church turns, when during the Easter vigil, new members join together with those who are already part of the communion to proclaim with joy: "Jesus is risen from the dead." O'Collins' theology quite intentionally places the origin, nature and mission of the church in direct relation with the center of Christian faith. This makes for the beginnings of an ecclesiology that is evangelical and missionary, and thus well suited to the task of "new evangelization," for which so many have expressed hope at the dawn of the third millennium. Moreover, this ecclesial vision gives promise of being unusually helpful in the path toward Christian unity. By showing how ecclesial doctrine can be related to the center of the faith, O'Collins points the way toward greater agreement about questions that have proven to be so divisive in the past, such as ministry and primacy.

Not intending to produce a full-fledged ecclesiology, there are themes he touches upon only rather lightly and which merit further development, such as the sacramentality of the church. Nevertheless, one cannot but marvel at the basic solidity and completeness of his ecclesiological vision, which enjoys an attractive credibility for being so well integrated with the central mysteries of Christian faith. He has gotten to the heart of the matter and, in his characteristic style, as I hope the quotations included in this essay show, done so with great heart. One feels in his reflections on the church that excitement of the first Easter, conveyed so well by the evangelist:

> They said to each other, "Did not our hearts burn within us while he talked to us on the road, while he opened to us the scriptures?" And they rose that same hour and returned to Jerusalem; and they found the eleven gathered together and those who were with them, who said, "The Lord has risen indeed, and has appeared to Simon!" Then they told him what had happened on the road, and how he was known to them in the breaking of the bread (Luke 24:32–35).

Notes

1. Gerald O'Collins, *Theology and Revelation* (Notre Dame, Ind.: Fides, 1968), 45. Future quotations from this and all other works by O'Collins, once the full data of publication have been given in a note, will appear simply as title and page number within parentheses in the text. O'Collins will again make use of these verses from the first letter of John in his extensive exploration of the meaning of revelation, entitled "The Divine Self-Communication," which is chapter 3 of *Fundamental Theology* (London: Darton, Longman & Todd/Mahwah, N.J., Paulist, 1981), 53–113, at 60.

2. See the fine chapter 5 on faith entitled "Experiencing the Divine Self-Communication in Faith," of *Fundamental Theology,* 130–60, which comments on these Pauline texts (pp. 139–40).

3. See, e.g., "Christ and Non-Christians," in *Fundamental Theology,* 114–29; and "Universal Redeemer," in *Christology: A Biblical, Historical and Systematic Study of Jesus* (Oxford: Oxford University Press, 1995), 296–305.

4. I am thinking here, for example, of the stories recounted in *The Second Journey* (New York: Paulist, 1978); or the conversations between young people and O'Collins on the contemporary meaning of the creed in *Friends in Faith: Living the Creed Day by Day* (New York: Paulist, 1989).

5. For example, these words appear at the beginning of one of O'Collins's more recent works: "This book is dedicated to the memory of many Jesuits who, since the Second World War, have been killed in Bolivia, Lebanon, Rwanda, El Salvador, Zimbabwe, and other parts of the world. Through their ministry and death, they witnessed to their faith in the One, who as the way, the truth, and the life forms the heart of the biblical story. We know ourselves to have been blessed by these companions and by a host of other twentieth-century Christian men and women who have given their lives in witness to what they read and treasured in the scriptures. Their heroic example interprets the biblical text with a power that far outstrips any theories and principles that we might develop. But if our words can throw a little light on the integrity of their deeds, we will be more than satisfied" (from G. O'Collins, S.J., and D. Kendall S.J., *The Bible for Theology: Ten Principles for the Theological Use of Scripture* [Mahwah, N.J.: Paulist, 1997], 3).

6. This is the title of chapter 5 of these lectures, which together were published the following year under the title *Man and His New Hopes* (New York: Herder & Herder, 1969), 103–12.

7. I am thinking here especially of texts such as the chapters "Jesus the Martyr" and "Jesus on the Run" from *The Calvary Christ* (Philadelphia: Westminster, 1977), 1–39.

8. See his *The Case Against Dogma* (New York: Paulist, 1975), and "Shared Statements of Faith," which is chapter 6 of *Fundamental Theology,* 161–91.

9. See "Tradition: The Ecumenical Convergence and Common Challenge," and "Finding the Tradition within the Traditions," in *Fundamental Theology,* 192–224; and "Criteria for Interpreting the Traditions," in *Problems and Perspectives of Fundamental Theology* (New York: Paulist, 1982), 327–39.

10. See "Peter as Easter Witness," *Heythrop Journal* 22 (1981): 1–18; and (with D. Kendall) "The Petrine Ministry as Easter Witness," in *The Bible for Theology,* 117–30. Another study that explores the biblical witness about the church was O'Collins's contribution to an ecumenical symposium held at the Centro pro Unione, Rome, in November 1995, entitled "Did Apostolic Continuity Ever Start? Origins of Apostolic Continuity in the New Testament," published in *Louvain Studies* 21 (1996): 138–52. This was reworked and appears again as "Leadership and the Church's Origins," in *The Bible for Theology,* 101–16. For the sake of brevity, I will discuss only the proposal about Petrine ministry, which is more distinctive to O'Collins. Under his direction, this theme was explored in a very fine doctoral thesis by William Thomas Kessler and published as *Peter as the First Witness of the Risen Lord: An Historical and Theological Investigation* (Rome: Editrice Pontificia Università Gregoriana, 1998).

11. For example, "We expect the proposal we have made in this chapter, more than those made in previous chapters, to meet with resistance or simple silence" (*The Bible for Theology,* 129).

12. O'Collins mentions the following reasons why Catholic theologians have passed over the importance of Peter's Easter role ("Peter as Easter Witness," 14–15): until recently the resurrection has not played so prominent a role in Catholic theology; Peter's Easter witness may not sufficiently distinguish him from the other resurrection witnesses; the Easter witness does not easily lend itself to establishing a primacy of "jurisdiction"; and it has been misinterpreted to suggest that Peter's witness was in some way the cause of the Easter faith of the whole community. He reiterates some of these reasons in *The Bible for Theology,* adding the further explanation that it is simply very difficult for thinkers to shift from some favored passages (Matt 16; Luke 22; John 21) and symbols (fisherman, shepherd, rock, penitent, martyr) to others (1 Cor 15:5; Luke 24:34; Peter as Easter witness) (pp. 129–30).

13. The Church in the Context of the Kingdom of God

John Fuellenbach, S.V.D.

The kingdom of God and its relationship to the church have been the topic of numerous theological discussions since Vatican II. One of the recurring questions in this context has been the following: Is the church now here on earth *identical* with the kingdom in history or is the kingdom a broader reality than the church, although preeminently present in it? The following pages offer a few thoughts on what a *nonidentification* of the kingdom in history with the pilgrim church means for the church's self-understanding and its mission today. In his *Following the Way* Gerald O'Collins has drawn on twenty-four parables from Jesus to shape a spirituality of the kingdom.[1] My article aims to develop something similar, but much in focus of the world and church.

THE CHURCH IN RELATION TO THE WORLD

The first question we have to ask is: What is the relationship among kingdom, church, and world? Whenever the church in its history was closely identified with the kingdom now present in history, the church's relationship with the world was portrayed accordingly. The world was the object the church had to act upon or influence. The church itself was the active subject. Such deliberations always focused on the internal reality of the church and affirmed its self-sufficiency in relation to the world. The question asked was simply: What can the world do to build up the church?

Since Vatican II the question has been reversed. Now people ask: What can the church do to make the world a better place to live?

Theologically this is based on the insight that the kingdom of God is meant for the world and that the church must see itself and its mission in the service of the kingdom. The kingdom is not only the future of the church but also the future of the world. In God's plan of salvation we cannot separate the church from the world, as Yves Congar saw so well years ago:

> In God's unitary design the Church and the world are both ordered to this Kingdom in the end, but by different ways and on different accounts. Church and world have the same end, but only the same ultimate end. That they should have the same end is due to God's unitary plan and the fact that the whole cosmos is united with man in a shared destiny. That they should have only the same ultimate end prevents a confusion that would be bad for the Church, as raising a risk of dissolving her own proper mission in that of history, and bad for the world, as raising the risk of mis-understanding and hindering its own proper development.[2]

The Pastoral Constitution on the Church in the Modern World (*Gaudium et Spes*) from Vatican II presents this new understanding of the relationship between the church and the world. After recognizing the world's legitimate autonomy, the council asserts that the church must consider itself part of the total human family, sharing the same concerns as the rest of humankind. Articles 3 and 92 state that just as Christ came into the world not to be served but to serve, so the church, carrying on the mission of Christ, seeks to serve the world by fostering unity among all people. The advantage of such a view of the church in its relationship to the world lies in these points:

1. It helps the church turn away from an exaggerated concern about its own internal affairs and to look at the world for which the kingdom is meant. The important thing for the church is not to withdraw into itself and reduce itself to a small group that keeps its distance from the world. The church must take part in constructive action and liberation.
2. The church, viewed in this way, can give hope to a world stricken by war, injustice, and hatred, by pointing constantly to the coming kingdom meant for the whole world and having appeared already in Jesus Christ. The church gives meaning to

the small services everyone can do for a better world, a world of justice, peace, and unity. For every good work done in this world means building up the kingdom that is coming.

3. This view underlines the principle that *diakonia,* which includes the struggle for a new social order, is as essential to and even as constitutive of the mission of the church as are proclamation and sacramental celebration.

The kingdom demands the transformation of all human reality, and the church must be an "agent" of this transformation.

THE CHURCH IS NOT IDENTICAL WITH KINGDOM OF GOD NOW

The Second Vatican Council described the church as the mystery of Christ. In the church is realized the "eternal plan of the Father, manifested in Jesus Christ, to bring humanity to its eternal glory." Here the church is seen in connection with the "bringing about of the secret hidden for ages in God" (Col 1:16; see Eph 3:3–9; 1 Cor 2:6–10). Therefore the church has to be seen in this broad perspective of God's plan of salvation, which includes all human beings and creation as a whole (see 1 Tim 2:4; Rom 8:22ff.). The most comprehensive symbol for God's plan with creation is the biblical phrase *kingdom of God.*

The kingdom aims at transforming the whole of creation into its eternal glory, and the church must be seen and understood in the context of this divine intentionality. The church's essence and mission make sense only in this setting. Its mission is to reveal through the ages the hidden plan of God to lead all humankind toward its final destiny. The church must see itself entirely in the service of this divine plan meant for the salvation of all creation.[3]

Nowhere do the Gospels identify the group of disciples around Jesus with the kingdom of God. The text often used for such identification is the parable of the Tares and the Wheat (Matt 13:24–30). But the "field" in this parable is not the church but the world, as the interpretation of the parable clearly states: "The field is the world" (Matt 13:38). The parable teaches about the kingdom that invades history without visibly interrupting the present structure of this world. Good and evil will exist side by side, and only in the future, when the kingdom will come in fullness, will there be a separation of both.

Jesus' mission is addressed primarily to his disciples. To them it belongs; they will celebrate it and be in it. But this special proximity of the group to the kingdom does not turn them into a closed society. The church has no monopoly on the kingdom of God. Citizenship in the kingdom never means a privilege but always a summons to solidarity with people, particularly with those excluded and discriminated against.[4]

One of the chief temptations for the church in history is to claim the kingdom for itself, to take over the management of the kingdom, and even to go so far as to present itself as the realized kingdom of God vis-à-vis the world. The kingdom of God is not the kingdom of the Christians.

God has inaugurated the kingdom in the world and in history. He did so in two stages. First, the kingdom was inaugurated through the earthly life of Jesus, his words and works; yet it was fully inaugurated through the Paschal Mystery of Jesus' death and resurrection. This kingdom, present in history, must now grow through history to reach its eschatological fullness at the end of time. The council clearly accepted this distinction between the kingdom present in history now and the eschatological fullness still to come (see LG 5, 9). But the question not clearly answered is whether the council also made a clear distinction between kingdom and church.

There are two questions to be asked. First, did the council identify the kingdom of God in history with the pilgrim church, or did it consider the kingdom of God in history a reality broader than the church and extending beyond its boundaries? Second, is the kingdom of God in its final fulfillment identical with the church in its eschatological fullness, or does the kingdom again extend beyond the church while at the same time embracing it?

A number of theologians still hold that a close analysis of the relevant texts of *Lumen Gentium* (3, 5, 9, 48) would show that in Vatican II the kingdom of God remains identical with the church, be it with the historical reality of the kingdom now or with the eschatological fulfillment where the church will find its fulfillment as well.[5]

This view can be found in the Final Document of the International Theological Commission in 1985. Once again the distinction between the pilgrim church in history and the heavenly church in its eschatological fullness is made, but the document continues to identify, on the one hand, the kingdom of God in history with the pilgrim church and, on the other hand, the eschatological fullness of the kingdom with the heavenly church. On the first aspect the document has this to say: "It is clear that in the Council's teaching there is no difference so far as the eschatological reality is concerned between the final realization of the Church (as consummata) and of the Kingdom (as consummatum)."[6]

On the second aspect, the documents comment: "Belonging to the Kingdom cannot *not be* belonging—at least implicitly—to the Church.[7] The commission, however, does adopt the theological phrase, "the Church, sacrament of the Kingdom," although the council did not use this expression.

While one may still have some doubts as to whether the council maintained an identity of church and kingdom, in the encyclical *Redemptoris Missio* we can find a clear distinction between the church and the kingdom of God in their pilgrimage through history.

> An analysis of the recent document of the central teaching authority would show that the Encyclical *Redemptoris Missio* is the first to distinguish clearly—while uniting them—the Church and the Reign of God in their pilgrimage through history: the Kingdom present in history is a broader reality than the Church; it extends beyond her boundaries to embrace the members of the other religious traditions.[8]

Once again the question is: Did Jesus identify the kingdom with the group of disciples, or did he see the kingdom as being broader than the group that became the church after his resurrection? Jesus understood his mission first and foremost in the context of Israel's mission. He saw himself as "being sent to the house of Israel" and not to the Gentiles. His instructions to the disciples were: "Go nowhere among the Gentiles and enter no town of the Samaritans but go rather to the lost sheep of the house of Israel" (Matt 10:5–6). He came to restore Israel to make it once and for all what it never managed to become, the true covenant partner.[9]

Yet in some instances in the Gospel Jesus oversteps the boundaries of Israel. Jesus made the kingdom present through his miraculous healings and exorcisms (see Matt 12:25–28; Luke 4:16–22). The Gospels tell us that he healed those who did not belong to the people of Israel (see Mark 7:24–30; Matt 15:21–28). These miracles signify therefore that the kingdom is operative and present among the pagans as well. Thus Jesus did not identify the kingdom with the "movement" created by him and destined to become the church.[10]

In the letters of St. Paul the kingdom of God is seen present under a new form, that of the kingship of the risen Christ in which it is realized, but as extending not only to the church but also to the whole world. In Col 2:10 and Eph 1:10 the kingship of Christ also extends not only to the church but to the entire world: Christ is the head of the world and of the church; but only the church is his body (Col 1:18; Eph 1:22; 4:15; 5:23). Church and world should be seen as two concentric circles, whose common center is Christ. The kingship of Christ as the presence of the kingdom in history extends to the whole world, visible and invisible.

> [The] Kingdom of Christ is...a more comprehensive term than "Church." In the Christian's present existence on earth his share in Christ's Kingdom and his claim to the eschatological Kingdom...find their fulfillment in the Church, the domain in which grace of the heavenly Christ are operative.... But Christ's rule extends beyond the Church...and one day the Church will have completed her earthly task and will be absorbed in the eschatological kingdom of Christ or of God.[11]

A considerable number of theologians hold, therefore, that the Catholic Church in Vatican II did separate itself from any identification with the kingdom in history now. The theological basis for doing so is seen in the council's definition of the church as a "Sign *(Sacrament)* of the Kingdom" (LG 9). Since God's saving grace can never be bound exclusively to a sacrament, one has to accept that the kingdom is still broader than the church. Such a separation is indirectly expressed in article 5 of *Lumen Gentium* and in article 45 of *Gaudium et Spes*. Richard McBrien sees in this separation of kingdom and church a major achievement of Vatican II. He comments:

> The nature and mission of the Church are always to be understood in relationship and in subordination to the Kingdom of God. This principle is expressed in article 5 of *Lumen Gentium* and again in article 45 of *Gaudium et Spes*. It replaces what was perhaps the most serious pre-Vatican II ecclesiological misunderstanding, namely, that the Church is identical with the Kingdom of God

here on earth. If it is, then it is beyond all need for institutional reform, and its mission is to bring everyone inside lest salvation elude them.[12]

Avery Dulles, who seems to favor a distinction between the glorious kingdom of God and the church admits, however, admits that such a distinction creates some difficulties with regard to the council's view of God's plan for the whole of creation.

> If one looks on both the kingdom and the Church as existing proleptically within history and definitively at the close of history, it becomes more difficult to see how they differ. With regard to the final phase it must be asked—is the consummation of the Church something different from the definitive arrival of the kingdom of God? The Pastoral Constitution on the Church in the Modern World makes the point in article 39 that "all the good fruits of our nature and enterprise produced on earth in the Spirit of the Lord and in accord with his command" will be found again, in a purified and transfigured form, in the final kingdom. This text seems to imply that the world itself, in all its secularity will be transformed in Christ. It then becomes very difficult to distinguish between the glorified Church and the transformed cosmos. Perhaps one should say that the heavenly Church, as the place where Christ rules in the assembly of the saints, will be at the heart of the center of the ultimate kingdom. The new heavens and the new earth, while they may include more than the transfigured Church, will serve to mediate and express the blessed life of the redeemed.[13]

In conclusion we can say: Not all theologians agree on the nonidentification between the kingdom in history and the pilgrim church. But it is equally justified to hold that—based on the magisterium's own teaching *(Redemptoris Missio)* and on the view of a considerable number of exegetes and theologians—a nonidentification is an accepted position in the church today.

The Kingdom of God as Present in the Church

Although the kingdom in history cannot be identified with the church, that does not mean the kingdom is *not* present in the church.

The encyclical *Redemptoris Missio*, while acknowledging the difference between the kingdom and the church, is very much concerned
that the church should not be seen and treated as separated from the
kingdom: "One may not separate the Kingdom from the Church. It is
true that the Church is not an end unto herself, since she is ordered
towards the Kingdom of God of which she is the seed, sign and instrument. Yet while remaining distinct from Christ and the Kingdom, the
Church is indissolubly united with both." (18)

The kingdom makes itself present in the church in a particular
way. We can say that the church is an "initial realization" or a "proleptic anticipation" of the plan of God for humankind, or in words of
Vatican II, "She becomes on earth the initial budding forth of the
Kingdom" (LG 5). One explanation of how kingdom and church are
not identical and yet intimately related could be presented as follows:

In the New Testament we find two sets of ideas connected with
the kingdom of God. First, in the Old as well as in the New Testament,
the kingdom is mostly understood as God's sovereignty or kingly rule.
It is perceived as a dynamic concept and means God's active rule
over all reality but particularly at the end of time. It is all-embracing
but still provisional, still to come in all its fullness. This strand is the
most dominant and can be found in all the writings of the Bible. It
expresses clearly God's intention to save all human beings and the
whole of creation.

Second, there is, however, also a strand in the message of Jesus
that understands and portrays the kingdom in spatial terms, as a terri-
torial reality. This is expressed in sayings like these: one can enter the
kingdom (Matt 5:20; 7:21; 18:3), and one can be thrown out of it (Matt
8:12). There are keys of the kingdom (Matt 16:18–19). The kingdom
is compared with a house into which people are invited, and so on. This
strand of the message of Jesus is largely new but pervasively present
in his kingdom message.

These two strands create a tension that is fundamental in the New
Testament.[14] While they help us to understand better the world in relation to the kingdom, they certainly could help us also clarify the tension between church and kingdom. They indicate that while the kingdom is a reality that embraces all creation, God still has bound it in a
particular way to a particular group in space and time now. Dulles

makes a similar observation by seeing the symbol kingdom in the New Testament as referring to reign and realm.

> The term *basileia* in the Greek New Testament frequently means kingship (reign) but it sometimes must be translated as kingdom (realm). The two concepts are inseparable. Christ's kingship or lordship implies a community over which he reigns—in other words, a kingdom. Conversely, the concept of the kingdom always implies a king. Several different expressions such as "kingdom of God," "kingdom of heaven," "kingdom of the Son," and "kingdom of Christ" are used almost interchangeably in the New Testament, and the differences of nuance among them need not concern us here.[15]

It is the kingdom present now that creates the church and keeps it constantly in existence. The church is therefore the result of the Spirit, who makes God's final saving intentionality (kingdom) effectively present as the true source of the community called church. "The Kingdom creates the Church, works through the Church, and is proclaimed in the world by the Church. There can be no Kingdom without the Church—those who have acknowledged God's rule and there can be no Church without the Kingdom; but they remain two distinguishable concepts: the Rule of God and the fellowship of men."[16]

The most common solution for solving this tension between kingdom and church sees the church as a *means or sacrament* of the kingdom through which this plan of God with the world realizes itself in history (LG 8, 48). Yet it has to be admitted that the council did not use the phrase *"Church as sacrament of the Kingdom."* We should never separate the kingdom from the church, since after all, the church is God's chosen instrument for his kingdom here on earth.

One more general theological argument for saying that the kingdom of God, which Jesus brought irrevocably into this world through his life, death, and resurrection, is now also found outside the church is based on the incarnation and ultimately on the resurrection. In the resurrection, the limitations of Jesus' earthly existence are gone. In him matter has been transformed into the state of the new creation. Christ is, in his risen body, the world to come. He, therefore, assumes a new global relationship with reality as a whole: he is present in creation in a new way.

As the future of the present world, Christ relates to creation in a new way. The whole world belongs to him not only on the basis of creation (Col 1:1–15; John 1:1–14) but also now on the basis of its transformation in the resurrection of his body into the new creation. We cannot limit the presence of the new creation to the church only. This all-pervasive presence of the kingdom of Christ in the world makes itself visible not only in the church but also in historical movements outside of the church. This was expressed by the International Ecumenical Congress of Theology in São Paulo (Brazil 1980) in these words:

> The coming Kingdom as God's final design for his creation is experienced in the historical process of human liberation. On the one hand, the Kingdom has a utopian character, for it can never be completely achieved in history; on the other hand, it is foreshadowed and given concrete expression in historical liberations. The Kingdom pervades human liberations; it manifests itself in them, but it is not identical with them. Historical liberations, by the very fact that they are historical, are limited, but are open to something greater. The Kingdom transforms them. Therefore, it is the object of our hope and thus we can pray to the Father: "Thy Kingdom come." Historical liberations incarnate the Kingdom to the degree that they humanize life and generate social relationships of greater fraternity, participation and justice.[17]

The encyclical *Redemptoris Missio* acknowledges the working of the kingdom outside the church by seeing there the "values of the Kingdom of God" concretely lived: "It is true that the inchoative reality of the Kingdom can also be found beyond the confines of the Church among people everywhere, to the extent that they live 'Gospel values' and are open to the working of the Spirit who breathes when and where he will" (20).

THE RELATIONSHIP OF THE CHURCH TO THE WORLD AND OTHER RELIGIOUS TRADITIONS

The real value of a nonidentification of the kingdom in history with the pilgrim church shows itself in the face of two theological problems and their solution. First, how is God's saving will related to this world and its development? And, second, how is this saving will concretely present in other religious traditions?

First, in the context of social justice, the distinction between kingdom and church connects the historical liberation of the oppressed in this world with the eschatological kingdom still to come in fullness at the end. It shows how the work for justice and liberation inside and outside the church is intrinsically linked with the kingdom present now, since the ultimate goal of the kingdom of God is the transformation of all reality.

Second, in interreligious dialogue the kingdom symbol furnishes the theologian with a broader perspective to enter into dialogue with other religious traditions. If the kingdom is the ultimate goal of God's intentionality for all humanity, then the question is no longer how these other religious traditions are linked to the church but rather how the kingdom of God was and is concretely present in these religions.

The church itself, while accepting the distinction between the church and the kingdom in principle, has been very eager lately to assure that both are not to be pulled apart, be it in liberation theology or in interreligious dialogue. Some theologians, particularly in India, are at the moment afraid that we are heading toward a crypto-identification of church and kingdom once again. In the words of Felix Wilfred:

> Since certain trends in liberation theology and in the theology of religions seemed to highlight the reality of the Kingdom at the expense of the Church and to distance themselves from the Church, the reaction (of the official Church) has taken the form of barring any access to the Kingdom except through the Church. Or to put it in another way, instead of understanding the Church in relation to the mystery of the Kingdom, this trend wants to understand the Kingdom of God in terms of the Church, and indeed turn the Church itself into the Kingdom.[18]

If such a trend gains the upper hand in Catholic theology today, one of the most powerful sources for the renewal of the church and its theology could be seriously stifled. Kingdom theology provides us, on the one hand, with a way to relate to this world and its destiny productively and, on the other hand, with a way to enter into a more open and creative dialogue with other religious traditions and ideologies.

Therefore, Wilfred insists that we have to be on our guard not to allow such an identification once again as subtle as it may be. The church is not the kingdom now, since the kingdom makes itself felt outside the church as well. The church's mission is to serve the kingdom, not take its place.

There are three dangers:

1. If church and kingdom are seen to be so closely connected that an identification takes place, the result is an abstract and idealistic image of the church cut off from real history and its traumas.
2. If church and world are identified, the result is that the image of the church is secular and mundane, and a constant conflict with the powers of the world cannot be avoided. This has been called "the 'secularist temptation' when the Kingdom of God is consciously or unconsciously identified with some earthly goal or other, and the goal of the Kingdom of God is entrusted to the care of the Church."[19]
3. A church totally centered on itself, out of touch with the world and the kingdom, becomes a self-sufficient, triumphal, and perfect society not recognizing the relative autonomy of the secular sphere.

According to Leonardo Boff, "these dangers are theological 'pathologies' that cry out for treatment; ecclesiological health depends on the right relationship between Kingdom—World—Church, in such a way that the Church is always seen as a concrete and historical sign (of the Kingdom and Salvation), and as its instrument (mediation) in a salvific service to the world."[20] The correct alignment of these terms is highly important: kingdom—WORLD—church.

THE CHURCH, THE "UNIVERSAL SACRAMENT OF SALVATION," AS MEDIATOR OF THE KINGDOM

With regard to the salvation of non-Christians, the following question still arises: If the kingdom as God's universal will to save all people is active outside of the church, is this activity still mediated through the church or in a way that is independent of the church? The answer varies according to whether one identifies the kingdom now with the pilgrim church or not.

Those who maintain a distinction between kingdom and church argue as follows: Pope John Paul in *Redemptoris Missio* (10) teaches that "for those people (non-Christians), salvation in Christ is accessible by virtue of a grace which, while having a mysterious relationship to the church, does not make them formally part of the church, but enlightens them in a way which is accommodated to their spiritual and material situation. This grace comes from Christ."

This text is seen as clearly rejecting *ecclesiocentrism*. The necessity of the church for salvation is not such that access to the kingdom is possible only through the church. One can partake in the kingdom of God without being a member of the church and without passing through the church's mediation of the kingdom.[21] Theologians who take this stand in no way deny that the salvation of any human being is based on Christ's death and resurrection. For them all grace is Christocentric. They hold that God's saving grace in Jesus Christ reaches the non-Christian not directly through the church but by circumventing the church "in ways only known to God."

Theologians who identify the kingdom on earth now with the pilgrim church cannot accept this position. For them all saving grace passes through the church; otherwise the church could not be called "the universal sacrament of salvation." They base their view on a careful reading of the main documents of Vatican II, maintaining that one cannot deduce from these documents that the church in Vatican II made a distinction between the kingdom present now in history and the pilgrim church here on earth. Their arguments are the following:

The council describes the church as being by its very essence the *universal sign of salvation*. The description, which holds a prominent place in the Dogmatic Constitution on the Church (*Lumen Gentium* 48), is quoted both in the Decree on the Church's Missionary Activity (*Ad Gentes* 1) and in the Pastoral Constitution on the Church in the Modern World (*Gaudium et Spes* 45). By sacrament the council means a symbolic reality established by Christ, a sign that contains and confers the grace it signifies. The church, therefore, is not merely a cognitive sign, making known something that already exists, but an efficacious sign that brings about the redemption to which it points. Since the church is seen as a universal sacrament, that is, as "*an instrument for the redemption of all*" (LG 9), we must assume that the salvation of all human beings does in some way depend on the church. The church is involved in the salvation of all who are saved (LG 16). Whatever faith or belief people may confess, we must assume that the grace that saves them is in a *mysterious way* linked to the church. They are, in the words of the council, through this grace *ordered* to the church. That means the saving grace they receive outside the church gives the recipients a positive inclination toward the church, so that all who live by God's grace are in a certain sense affiliated with the church.[22]

The question that arises now is: Does the church simply save by being the reality toward which people are oriented, or does the church act deliberately to bring about the salvation of such persons? The perception of the church as "a universal instrument" of salvation (LG 1) suggests that the church is actively at work in the salvific process; however, it does not explain by what activities the church accomplishes this result.

Francis Sullivan puts the question this way: "In what way can the Church be said to exercise an instrumental role in the salvation of all those people who apparently have no contact with the Church?" Referring to the encyclical *Mystici corporis* of Pius XII, the teaching of the council (Constitution on the Liturgy [*Sacrosanctum Concilium*, 83]), and the eucharistic prayers, Sullivan sees the church mediating salvation to non-Christians through prayer and intercession. It can therefore be said that the church, at least by means of intercessions, especially during the Eucharist, prays and offers Christ's sacrifice for the salvation of all people. Thus the church's intercessory mediation extends to all who are being saved. In Sullivan's own words:

> On the basis of the teaching of the Council, and the eucharistic prayers which reflect this teaching, we have sound reason for affirming that because of the Church's role as priestly people, offering to the Father with Christ the High Priest the sacrifice from which the grace of salvation flows to the whole world, the Church is rightly termed the universal sacrament of salvation in the sense that it plays an instrumental role in the salvation of every person who is saved.[23]

Those who hold the first position would not deny that the church's prayer and the celebration of the Eucharist mediate God's grace for the salvation of all people, but they would not regard these as the only way the salvation wrought in Christ can and will reach people.

THE TWOFOLD MISSION OF THE CHURCH

One more important point can be made that flows from a non-identification of the church with the kingdom. If God's kingdom is operative outside the church, then the church's mission of proclaiming and celebrating the kingdom now present in history can be understood as twofold.

The church's ultimate goal is to serve the kingdom and to lead humankind to its final destiny. Wherever the kingdom shows itself in the world the church must help to promote and to bring it to its fullness. The mission of the church in the service of the kingdom is therefore basically a twofold one.

First, we are called to make God's kingdom present by proclaiming its presence in word and sacrament. This happens through the creation of Christian communities in which God's kingdom shines forth like a symbol, a sign, or a parable, where its presence can clearly be discerned and where its final goal appears like a foretaste of what is to come in fullness in God's own time. The disciples in such communities are to celebrate the presence of God's kingdom in their midst and let themselves be set on fire again and again. This happens especially when they remember the Lord in the table fellowship of the Eucharist. The kingdom can therefore never be separated from the church, which, after all, is God's chosen instrument for his kingdom here on earth. The following quotation might sound strong but it is certainly correct:

> The Kingdom is, of course, far broader than the Church alone. God's Kingdom is all-embracing in respect of both points of view and purpose; it signifies the consummation of the whole history; it has cosmic proportions and fulfills time and eternity. Meanwhile, the Church, the believing and active community of Christ, is raised up by God among all nations to share in the salvation and suffering service of the Kingdom. The Church consists of those whom God has called to stand at His side to act out with Him the drama of the revelation of the Kingdom come and coming. The Church constitutes the firstling, the early harvest of the

Kingdom. Thus, though not limited to the Church, the Kingdom is unthinkable *without* the church. Conversely, growth and expansion of the Church should not be viewed as ends but rather as means to be used in the service of the Kingdom. The Church, in other words, is not a goal in and of itself; but neither is it—as some at present would seem to imply—a contemptible entity that should feel ashamed of its calling and seek its redemption in self-destruction. The keys of the Kingdom have been given to the Church. It does not fulfill its mandate by relinquishing those keys but rather by using them to open up the avenues of approach to the Kingdom for all peoples and all population groups at every level of human society. It makes no biblical sense whatever to deny, as many do, that the upbuilding of the Church everywhere in the world is a proper concern of the proclamation of the good news of the Gospel; and it is high time for a forthright repudiation of such nonsense.[24]

Second, we can see that neither Jesus nor his Spirit has abandoned the world; they continue to be present and active among people. In us, the community of believers and followers of Jesus, his action, which is present everywhere, acquires a visibility and a symbolic reality. Because of this, we are called and sent into the world to serve and to promote the ongoing action of Jesus and the Spirit. From here follows the second dimension of our mission: to be at the service of, and to promote in a collaborative way, God's own continuing action in the world and among people who do not actively share our faith.

If the church community "feasts" on the presence of God's kingdom in its midst most intensely in the Eucharistic meal celebration, then there must also be a "feast" aspect in the church's second missionary task. We are, therefore, called to promote "feasts" where people of all races and cultures sit together and enjoy each other's company in life-giving relationships and genuine compassion. It is precisely here that God's kingdom makes itself felt and can be experienced as present in the midst of human affairs.

The two "feast" aspects are interrelated ways of pursuing the goal of mission, the realization of the "new heaven and the new earth," that God promises to all peoples. One could say that in getting actively involved in promoting God's transformative action in the world the church community will build itself up as an authentic symbol of and witness to that action.[25]

If the kingdom of God is operative anywhere in the world and not just in the church, then our mission is to witness to this presence and to "sniff it out," raise people's awareness of it, and celebrate it where it makes itself present. If we share Jesus' mission of proclaiming and bringing God's kingdom into the world, then that very kingdom demands of us these two ways of witnessing to God's kingdom actively present anywhere in our midst.

Notes

1. Gerald O'Collins, *Following the Way* (London: Harper Collins, 1999).

2. Yves Congar, *Lay People in the Church* (London: Bloomsbury Publishing, 1957), 88.

3. W. Pannenberg, *Theology and the Kingdom of God* (Philadelphia: Westminster, 1977), 72–75.

4. Jan Milic Lochman, "Church and World in the Light of the Kingdom of God," in *Church—Kingdom—World: The Church as Mystery and Prophetic Sign,* ed. Gennadios Limouris, Faith and Order Paper 130 (Geneva: World Council of Churches, 1986), 6.

5. J. Dupuis, "Evangelization and Kingdom Values: The Church and the 'Others'" *Indian Missiological Review* 14 (1992): 4–21. See also idem, *Towards a Christian Theology of Religious Pluralism* (Maryknoll, N.Y.: Orbis Books, 1997), 330–57. In this chapter Dupuis has much to say about the kingdom and the church.

6. M. Sharkey, ed., *International Theological Commission: Text and Document 1969–85* (San Francisco: Ignatius, 1989), 300–304, at 302.

7. *Theological Commission,* 303.

8. Dupuis, "Evangelization," 8.

9. G. Lohfink, *Jesus and Community* (London: SPCK, 1985), 75–148.

10. Dupuis, "Evangelization," 10.

11. R. Schnackenburg, *God's Rule and Kingdom* (New York: Herder & Herder, 1968), 301.

12. R. McBrien, *Catholicism* (London: Geoffrey Chapman, 1984), 686.

13. A. Dulles, "The Church and the Kingdom" in *A Church for All People,* ed. E. LaVerdiere (Collegeville, Minn.: Liturgical Press, 1993), 17–18.

14. P. Kuzmic, "The Church and the Kingdom of God: A Theological Reflection" in *The Church: God's Agent for Change,* ed. Bruce J. Nicholls (Flemington Markets, Australia: Paternoster Press, 1986), 61–63.

15. Dulles, "Church and the Kingdom," 14.

16. G. E. Ladd, *The Present of the Future: A Revised and Updated Version of Jesus and the Kingdom* (Grand Rapids: Eerdmans, 1974), 277.

17. In *Tensions Between the Churches of the First World and the Third World,* ed. Virgil Elizondo and Norbert Greinacher (New York: Seabury Press, 1981), 83.

18. Felix Wilfred, "Once again…Church and Kingdom," *Vidyajyoti* 57 (1993): 6–24, at 10.

19. Lochman, "Church and World," 59.

20. Leonardo Boff, *Church, Charism and Power: Liberation Theology and the Institutional Church* (London: SCM, 1985), 1–2.

21. J. Dupuis, *Jesus Christ and the Encounter of World Religions* (Maryknoll, N.Y.: Orbis Books, 1991), 6.

22. A. Dulles, "Vatican II and the Church's Purpose," *Theology Digest* 32 (1985): 344–45.

23. Francis A. Sullivan, *The Church We Believe In* (New York: Paulist, 1988), 128.

24. Johannes Verkuyl, "The Biblical Notion of Kingdom: Test of Validity for Theology of Religion," in *The Good News of the Kingdom: Mission Theology for the Third Millennium,* ed. Charles Van Engen, Dean S. Gilliland, and Paul Pierson (Maryknoll, N.Y.: Orbis Books, 1993), 71–81, at 73.

25. M. Amallados, "New Faces of Mission," *UISG Bulletin* 99 (1995): 21–33.

14. Roads to God:
An Australian Exploration in Fiction

Michael Paul Gallagher, S.J.

"Love" is an exhausted word, and God has been
expelled by those who know better, but I offer you
the one as proof that the other still exists.

Patrick White[1]

Among the many references to the creative arts in Gerald
O'Collins's writings, the following can serve as an introduction to the
theme of this essay: "Religious elements within the *cultural* sphere
may not so much have disappeared as relocated.... Do we dismiss as
aberrant exceptions...modern authors who raise genuinely religious
questions, even if they are often negatively disposed towards religious
answers?" And he goes on to argue that far from being secularized, the
arts, cinema, and literature of today often explore spiritual and even
Christian themes "obliquely and covertly."[2]

In this light it seems fitting to choose Patrick White (1912–1990),
Australia's only Nobel laureate for literature, and to study his unusual
exploration of religious themes. These pages will concentrate on a
cycle of seven of his novels, which appeared over a twenty-year period
starting in the late fifties, arguing that they constitute a unique theodicy, in the sense of defending the authentic mystery of God against its
impoverishment by both religion and the dominant culture. Although
White's version of theology may be heterodox and eccentric, he seems
a perfect example of the "relocation" of religious concerns and of the
"oblique" wavelength of literature—as indicated in that O'Collins text.

RELIGIOUSLY OBSESSED NOVELIST

White has often been recognized as perhaps the most religiously obsessed of major novelists since the World War II. Many literary critics have highlighted this dimension:

> The view of man and his world which underlies White's novels is religious in its basic orientation.[3]
> "Religious" may be an odd term to use for one who has written so scorchingly about religion and religious people as White, but "religious"...seems to be the only word adequate to White's intention.[4]
> An age-old spiritual drama . . . is being played out in the midst of a predominantly secular world where most people are unaware of the issues involved. White has seized these issues [and] placed them at the centre of his work.[5]
> In an exploratory and wholly undogmatic sense White can be said to be a "religious" novelist.[6]

More recently a similar consensus is echoed by some more specifically theologically writers:

> From his earliest writings onwards, his themes have had to do with the search for God and the struggle to overcome the self.[7]
> According to the popular perception in Academe, Western literature apparently ceased to bother about God, faith or transcendence after 1900. This is not true of White.[8]

In spite of such general agreement on the religious dimensions of White's fiction, nobody seems to have noted the unity of the seven novels under scrutiny in these pages. Hence what is offered here can claim to break new ground in the study of White's theological horizons.

In his biography of White, David Marr recounts an episode around Christmas of 1951, when the novelist slipped into a pool of mud. At first he started to curse God but then, as a later letter commented, "faith began to come to me."[9] This moment of almost comic conversion led to the religious themes that came to the fore in the seven novels explored here. In White's own words "I set out to find a secret core, and *The Tree of Man* emerged."[10] Although White occasionally attended Anglican communion in these years, and although he was at times attracted to

Catholicism, his overall religious position is best summarized by Marr as "a believer without any formal faith."[11] Two years before his death White wrote a short credo: "I am coming to believe, not in God, but a Divine Presence of which Jesus, the Jewish prophets, the Buddha, Mahatma Gandhi and Co., are the more comprehensive manifestations." He went to on voice his admiration for Catholic mystics, including the "Teresas, John of the Cross, Thomas Merton," and indeed all "humble everyday saints created for our consolation."[12]

UNPROFESSED SOURCES OF FAITH

Even though the author's intention is somewhat despised within certain circles of literary criticism, it is fascinating to find White himself openly acknowledging his religious horizons.

> I suppose what I am increasingly intent on trying to do in my books is to give professed unbelievers glimpses of their own unprofessed factor. I believe most people have a religious factor. ...The churches defeat their own aims, I feel, through the banality of their approach and by rejecting so much that is sordid and shocking which can still be related to religious experience.[13]

This revealing statement establishes a number of traits of White's religious approach: the function of his fiction as challenging superficial unbelief; its critique also of church mediating faith as lacking in depth or as naively avoiding the actualities of evil; his own inclination to seek "religious experience" in unusual and even ugly aspects of human behavior. In an interview of three years later, White admitted that he had ignored his own "religious tendencies" until *The Tree of Man,* the first of the novels proposed here as constituting his religious cycle: "I have tried to convey a splendour, a transcendence, which is also there, above human realities. From *The Tree of Man* onward...I wanted to suggest my own faith in these superhuman realities. But of course it is very difficult to convey a religious faith through symbols and situations which can be accepted by people today."[14]

Later in the same interview he suggests even more strongly that one of his aims as a novelist is to make people aware of the roots of mystery latent and neglected within them and which can be forced into shyness by the dominant culture: "I believe that most people, if they are honest with themselves, have in them the germ of a religious faith, but they are either too lazy or too frightened, or too ashamed intellectually to accept the fact."[15]

Against this background there can be little doubt that Australia's most famous novelist deserves the attention of those working in fundamental theology, especially of those drawn toward frontiers of dialogue between culture and faith. More precisely, these pages hope to demonstrate that White embodies a prophetic sense of the darker and more demanding aspects of religious faith. The cycle of seven novels to be examined here began with *The Tree of Man* in 1956 and ended with *A Fringe of Leaves* in 1976. Hence White's main creative energies over a twenty-year period were devoted to a deepening exploration of the cost of genuine faith, frequently presenting this richer vision in sharp contrast with complacent versions of established religion.

NOVELS OF THE LATE FIFTIES

The Tree of Man centers on the marriage of Stan and Amy Parker from youth to old age, and while it evokes the twists and turns of their outer life together, a major strand concerns their "fluctuations of belief" (TM, 66) as experienced differently by the man and by the woman. The novel is explicitly concerned with their quest for God through the evolving experiences of a lifetime and focuses especially on the costliness of arriving at a moment where God is at last glimpsed by Stan even in a "jewel of spittle" (TM, 476).[16] Ironically, this scene of being "illuminated" is provoked by the intrusion of a young evangelist, acting as a "steam roller of faith" (TM, 475). In fact twenty years later there was to be an exactly parallel visit from a naive preacher toward the end of *A Fringe of Leaves*. At both the beginning and the end of this cycle of novels, White satirizes what he saw as the imaginative poverty of much church religion. As will be seen, the positive rhetoric of his fiction gives priority to less superficial dimensions in the adventure of faith: its mysteriousness and difficulty of attainment, its emergence from within the intense flux of a person's emotional life, and the fragility and momentariness of any experience of God in this life.

The Tree of Man inaugurates White's cycle of religious novels with a hymn of negative theology. Stan is described at an early stage as having "been brought up in a reverence for religion, but he had not yet needed God" (TM, 35). The interior plot traces the awakening of that need in him and his hope that he may "eventually receive a glimpse" (TM, 416). The text of the novel is studded with such expressions in order to dramatize the long road from the "wooden prayers" and "absence of signs" during his "years of drought" (TM, 295, 392, 297) toward the threshold of "true knowledge…telling him of the presence of God" (TM, 186). The final stage of his story leads him to a "great tenderness of understanding," whereby he can see "the most sickening incidents of his life" with immense clarity and compassion (TM, 476). Even from this brief account, *The Tree of Man* clearly represents a celebration of the human potential to wait for God through deserts of emptiness. Although White is sardonic in his dismissal of surface living and of surface believing, the positive thrust of his fiction defends the possibility of reaching "that final clarity and strength which can acknowledge the immensity of belief" (TM, 275).

Voss (1957) continues to emphasize the difficulty of the surrender of faith, but it differs from its predecessor in its vocabulary, which is more overtly theological and specifically Christian, and in its more explicit attention to atheism. The story involves a man–woman relationship but of a different order than in *The Tree of Man*. When Voss, the explorer and Nietzschean man of will, first meets Laura, she has recently decided that she is no longer a religious believer and has left behind her "fuzz of faith" (V, 9). But this incipient unbelief is strangely reversed through her contact with his intense pride and his wish to become God. In contrast with his extremism, she discovers her Victorian crisis of faith to be merely "intellectual vanity" (V, 89) and she enters on a deeper journey toward authentic faith.

Laura's initially shallow rationalism is one of three forms of unbelief explored in this novel. A second is the more assertive self-will represented by Voss himself, a position Laura gradually undermines through love, leading him to a sense of humanity, humility, and ultimately of Christ. As Laura voices it in her illness to an uncomprehending doctor, "when man is truly humbled, when he has learnt that he is not God, then he is nearest to becoming so" (V, 387). A third form of unbelief, and a target for White's irony in later novels, concerns the mediocrity and "almost mystical banality" of Australian middle-class society (V, 61). Indeed *Voss* may be said to have three locations of the struggle between belief and unbelief: the consciousness of Laura, who has to lose her older faith in reason if she is to "receive revelations" (V, 160); the explorations, inner or outer, of Voss in the desert, finding that he "had in him a little of Christ, like other men" (V, 445); and the practices of bourgeois existence that deaden religious hunger unless somehow "the curtain of illusion" is "tweaked" (V, 430). All three forms of unbelief here are versions of the "old illusion of self-importance" (V, 332), differing in that they belong to reason, will, or world. In the narrator's words, in one of his few moments of direct commentary, "only a few stubborn ones will blunder on, painfully, out of the luxuriant world of their pretensions into the desert of mortification and reward" (V, 74).

The narrative strategies of this novel are designed to lead the reader along that same road, or at least to "tweak" his or her curtain of secularist shallowness. The very technique of the fiction is geared toward establishing a nondiscursive level of consciousness. Through counterpointing scenes of desert and superficial society, it promotes an alternative and nonrationalist epistemology. It evokes extremes of suffering and of surrender, so as to prepare the reader for the insight finally voiced by Laura: "Perhaps true knowledge only comes of death by torture in the country of the mind" (V, 446). Through the sheer eloquence of his fiction White insists that any serious pursuit of religious questions has to transcend predictable levels of commonplace living and commonplace religion. In ways reminiscent of Newman's method in his university sermons on faith and reason, White's literary strategy in *Voss* is to transform the disposition of his readers.

VISIONARY ALTERNATIVES

Where *The Tree of Man* was concerned to reveal the extraordinary behind the ordinary, and where *Voss* focused on the collapse of pride in order to reveal basic humanity and ultimately Christ, *Riders in the Chariot* (1961) explores visionary knowledge as a valid form of truth. The four central characters represent four different spiritual traditions: Jewish mysticism (Himmelfarb), Christian love (Mrs. Godbole), childlike intuition (Miss Hare) and artistic sensibility (Alf

Dubbo). Together they represent a powerful "relocation" (the O'Collins term already mentioned) of religious consciousness. These four figures forge a way of wisdom that survives inner and outer betrayal. Their coming together finally in one symbolic scene (a death on Good Friday of a crucified man) suggests a convergence of four different paths of spirituality toward the cross.

As always White's emphasis falls on the purgative way of arriving at deeper reality. In Mary Hare's words, "eventually I shall discover what is at the centre, if enough of me is peeled away" (RC, 52). Once again one finds the typically Whitean defense of religious horizons (rather than creeds), but this theodicy is now set against a background of greater evil and opposition than previously. Indeed White's narrative tone toward both the "armour of disbelief" (RC, 395) of conventional religion and the "immense plains of complacency" in the secular culture is harsher than before. This is voiced by Mrs. Rosetree, shocked out of her smallness by the suicide of her husband: "There is also the power of evil, that they tell us about…and we forget, because we are leading this modern life—until we are reminded" (RC, 450). This novel seems to move between two poles. On the one hand it evokes a demanding level of spiritual awareness where "everything, finally, was a source of wonder, not to say love" (RC, 457). On the other hand it seeks to deconstruct satirically a world that "will not tolerate the truth, at least in concentrated form" (RC, 466). As this cycle of novels progresses, White's characteristic stance becomes more and more clear: through the power of fiction he contrasts true and false forms of religiousness as well as forces his readers to face their possibly superficial secularism.

The contrast of dispositions underlying belief and unbelief is a more overt concern in White's next novel, *The Solid Mandala* (1966), which recounts the lives of twin brothers Waldo and Arthur Brown. Their parents had rejected their own Baptist background and brought up the boys in "intellectual Enlightenment" (SM, 145). Indeed their father had burnt *The Brothers Karamazov*, because he was afraid of the "bits he understood" and "the bits he didn't understand were worse" (SM, 199). Waldo, the clever son, is portrayed as sinking into bitterness and hatred, whereas Arthur, who is something of a simpleton, becomes a repository of hidden love: "It had been proved, Dad had already told them, that everything…ignorant people refer to as the supernatural, is non-existent. Waldo was proud to know. He would have liked to go permanently proud and immaculate, but his twin brother dragged him back repeatedly behind the line where knowledge didn't protect" (SM, 46). Again and again Waldo's cold "knowledge" is contrasted with his brother's compassionate "understanding." Even the narrative structure of the novel mirrors the conflict between these two dispositions, because the story is first narrated from the point of view of Waldo before shifting to the perspective of Arthur. This latter part reaches its climax when Arthur dances in order to "reveal" the religious vision he has discovered and lived: "Even in the absence of gods, his life, or dance, was always prayerful" (SM, 265).

Throughout *The Solid Mandala* White evokes a realm of religiousness unknown to rationalism and often forgotten by religion. He is less concerned with creeds than with the source of religious faith in a certain spiritual receptivity and sensibility. In the words of one commentator, this novel deals with "the nature of redemption" and with the question of whether love is strong enough to heal an inherited self-hatred.[17] As already indicated, this cycle of seven novels seems to have a double focus—to make real through his fiction a more worthy wavelength of religious wisdom and at the same time to expose the barrenness of both unbelief and belief in their merely cultural forms.

In *Riders in the Chariot* the hope of the artist, Alf Dubbo, was that "he might dare eventually to clothe the formless form of God" (RC, 353). This is also true of Hurtle Duffield, another painter who is the central character in *The Vivisector* (1970). Initially he can conceive only of a cruel God, "God the Vivisector" or "the Divine Destroyer" (TV, 307, 336). Through the agony of his art he tests his hypothesis about the "ugliness and cruelties" of existence, only to find himself drawn in a different direction later in his life, "because love is subtler, more elusive, more delicate" (TV, 408). His hope becomes "to find some formal order behind a moment of chaos and unreason" (TV, 517). While the art experts speak glibly about his being involved in "God paintings" (TV, 589), Duffield himself enters a contemplative passivity of "being painted with, and through" (TV, 614). He dies, on the final page of the novel, having painted a brilliant indigo that is equated with God in his consciousness. This novel thus traces a tortuous road to one moment of illumination before death, exactly as in *The Tree of Man*. It also dramatizes a difficult conversion of heart from hostility to acceptance as in

Voss. White's fictional strategy throughout this cycle is to expose his readers to the "dangers of mystery" (TV, 307), inviting them into a powerfully nonconceptual world of searching, beyond the "sheer intricate activity...which made God unnecessary" (TV, 365). In this way both the themes and the techniques of this sequence of novels combine to authenticate fundamental religious questions in a new way.

EMBRACING AMBIGUITY

This pattern continues, but in a totally different setting, in *The Eye of the Storm,* published in 1973, the year White was awarded the Nobel prize for literature. Here Elizabeth Hunter unites a destructive temperament with visionary gifts, and, like Duffield, she arrives at an experience of the "endless" at the moment of death (ES, 532). The plot centers on the bedside of the elderly and wealthy Mrs. Hunter as she nears her end, and her daughter Dorothy voices at one stage a major theme of the book: "could anything of a trancendental nature have illuminated a mind so sensual, mendacious, materialistic, superficial as Elizabeth Hunter's?" (ES, 570). The answer of the novel is a powerful affirmative, highlighting the co-presence of falsity and sanctity not only in the main character but in the whole universe. Mrs. Hunter thinks of herself as "human and consequently flawed" and yet hopes to be "shown the inconceivable something" she had always sought (ES, 526). Her key memory is an occasion when she escaped death by happening to be in the eye of the storm and there "had experienced transcendence" (ES, 199): "she could not contemplate the storm for this dream of glistening peace through which she was moved" (ES, 409). In this instant she came to know herself "to be a detail of the greater splintering" (ES, 90); from then on "she would have liked to experience a state of mind she knew existed, but which was too subtle to enter except by special grace" (ES, 15).

The novel explores this paradox of a flawed mediator of grace, embodied in Elizabeth Hunter, and in doing so it has much in common with White's previous works. Where it breaks new ground, however, is in its notably more inclusive attitude toward even the more superficial characters in the story. In place of the harsh tone of earlier novels, several of the lesser figures here are shown as having "inklings of transcendence" (ES, 427). Thus Mrs. Hunter has a particular impact on one of her nurses, Flora Manhood (surely a significant name). Flora oscillates between a "scientific" unbelief and wanting to give "closer attention" to God (ES, 523, 530); under the influence of Mrs. Hunter she comes to hope that her "emptiness" might be "filled with understanding" (ES, 534). Flora later comments: "She understood me better than anyone ever. I only always didn't like what she dug up out of me" (ES, 554).

In this way *The Eye of the Storm* shows White developing a new sense of grace as utterly gratuitous, as involving a journey of slow purification, and as embracing with compassion the ambiguities of the human heart. Mrs. Hunter has an even deeper impact on her senior nurse, Mary de Santis (again the name seems noteworthy). Mary becomes conscious of her "need to worship" and of the "mystery that was already there," in spite of her agnostic father, who tried to "commit her to unbelief" (ES, 162–63). Indeed Mrs. Hunter's role as awakener of mystery continues after her death. At the end of the novel Mary de Santis undertakes the nursing of a deeply embittered and "entombed" young girl and wonders how she could convey to her "the beauty she herself had witnessed, and love as she had come to understand it" (ES, 588). This novel is marked by a more hopeful implicit theology of redemption and of arriving at faith. Existence, like Mrs. Hunter's house, is sometimes envisaged in terms of "blatant echoes of downright lies, together with hints of the exasperating, unknowable truth" (ES, 274). But through the process of erosion of the ego in the course of the novel, the truth comes closer and more knowable: in Mrs. Hunter's case "age forced her to realize she had experienced more than she thought she had at the time" (ES, 584). One could argue that these novels offer a fictional counterpart to Karl Rahner's explorations of mystagogy, of moments of unrecognized but crucial grace in every life. Moreover, as suggested earlier, the rhetoric of White as narrator seems designed to bring his secular readers to acknowledge at least the possibility of such spiritual encounters.

In the final book of the series, *A Fringe of Leaves* (1976), human love enters as a key witness for the defense of mystery. The two epigraphs that White chose for this novel are indicative of a new focus and serenity in his theodicy. From Simone Weil he quotes, "If there is some true good in man, it can only be unknown to himself," and from Louis Aragon, "Love is your last chance. There is really nothing else on earth to keep you there." The novel tells of the outer and inner adventures of Ellen Roxburgh as she is led, in quasi-Pauline terms, from law to freedom and from conventional religion into grace and love. Set in the 1830s, the plot centers on her ordeals of shipwreck and captivity by natives, and then on her rescue by Jack Chance, an escaped convict, whom she comes to love. The interior plot involves a conflict between two images of God—as accusatory and as healing. At an early stage Ellen was disturbed by a gold "riband" in a church proclaiming "Lord God of Hosts" (FL, 95). Later, and after much suffering and guilt, she arrives at the predictable Whitean moment of grace: in a makeshift chapel she finds another riband with "GOD IS LOVE, in the wretchedest lettering, in dribbled ochre," and here at last "peace of mind" descends on her (FL, 352–53). Unlike earlier visionaries, Ellen is portrayed as returning to ordinary existence, as being set free to love and be loved. Moreover, the process whereby she learns trust is shown as something other than an interior experience. The liberation of her humanity from fear and guilt is both the condition and the consequence of her religious conversion—her movement from the desolation of worshiping "a supreme being . . . by rote" (FL, 222) to the consolation of being enclosed in silence "like a beatitude" (FL, 353). However, the novel does not end with that glimpse of grace; unlike previous books, this moment becomes the threshold for a human relationship, depicted simply as "sharing a secret" (FL, 365) of fragile humanity. The implicit theology here is more incarnational than before, and the implicit spirituality is more gradualist.

VINDICATING MYSTERY

These pages have avoided precise theological judgment of Patrick White's religious stance. It would be easy to diagnose a certain elitist gnosticism, or tendencies toward a merely eclectic sense of spiritual consciousness. An obvious pitfall of discussing his writings in this way is to oversimplify the dense texture of his narratives and to treat them almost like parables. For the theologian dealing with imaginative literature, a constant temptation is not only to press one's own categories too quickly on the ambiguities of a literary text, but to view its relevance too exclusively in terms of explicit content. In this case one neglects the central process of reading the text. The unique contribution of imaginative art lies in that experience rather than in any paraphrasable message. Indeed to underline experience in this way is perfectly in tune with many of the articles that Gerald O'Collins wrote for *The Tablet* over the years and with his frequent explorations of frontier areas between spirituality and theology.

The hope of these pages has been to establish that Patrick White is one of the great literary vindicators of religious mystery in this century. He starts from a sense of deep dismay over how the dominant culture can stifle human depth and how average religious forms can fail to meet spiritual hungers. His intuition is that the crucial battleground of faith has shifted from discursive arguments to the prereligious zone of human interiority. The costly journeys toward light, dramatized in this sequence of seven novels, can challenge fundamental theology in its task to do justice to the human and cultural ground for the hearing of the Word.

Notes

1. Patrick White, *The Twyborn Affair* (London: Jonathan Cape, 1979), 426.

2. Gerald O'Collins, *The Theology of Secularity* (Dublin/Cork: Mercier Press, 1974), 19.

3. Patricia Morley, *The Mystery of Unity: Theme and Technique in the Novels of Patrick White* (Montreal: McGill-Queen's University, 1972), 1.

4. William Walsh, *Patrick White's Fiction* (London: Allen & Unwin, 1977), 124-25.

5. Peter Beatson, *The Eye in the Mandala—Patrick White* (London: Elek, 1976), 167.

6. Mark Williams, *Patrick White* (London: Macmillan, 1993), 99.

7. Emyr Vaughan Thomas, "Patrick White and the Purification of Atheism," *Theology* 101 (1998): 36.

8. George Watt, "Patrick White: Novelist as Prophet," *Literature and Theology* 10 (1996): 273.

9. David Marr, *Patrick White: A Life* (London: Jonathan Cape, 1991), 281.

10. Ibid., 284.

11. Ibid., 451.

12. *Patrick White Speaks* (London: Jonathan Cape, 1990), 197.

13. A letter of 1970 quoted in Beatson, *Eye in the Mandala,* 167.

14. "A Conversation with Patrick White," *Southerly: A Review of Australian Literature* 30 (1973): 136.

15. Ibid., 142.

16. For the remainder of this paper, page references to the novels will be included in parentheses in the text and will refer to the most easily available paperback edition of the series, that published by Penguin Books, Harmondsworth: *The Tree of Man,* 1961 (abbreviated TM), *Voss,* 1960 (V), *Riders in the Chariot,* 1964 (RC), *The Solid Mandala,* 1969 (SM), *The Vivisector,* 1973 (TV), *The Eye of the Storm,* 1975 (ES), *A Fringe of Leaves,* 1977 (FL).

17. Carolyn Bliss, *Patrick White's Fiction: The Paradox of Fortunate Failure* (London: Macmillan, 1986), 99, 103.

15. "What Can Be Known about God Is Plain to Them": A Meditation on Religious Unbelief

Stephen T. Davis

Gerald O'Collins is preeminently a theologian of the incarnation and resurrection of Jesus. As part of that role, he serves as a defender of and an apologist for the church's received tradition. Gerry does that, as we all know, with faithfulness, imagination, and power. But he also does it with a pastor's heart. He makes effective use of scripture in all his writings, and he is always alert to spiritual as well as purely intellectual considerations. And he recognizes clearly the limitations of apologetics as sheer argumentation. He knows that personal elements and subjective factors always enter into decisions as to what one is to believe.

What I hope to do in the present essay is apply some of Gerry's theological and apologetic methods to a problem I have long puzzled over: the problem of religious unbelief. I will make frequent reference to scripture, and while I want to recognize a role for arguments from natural theology in favor of religious and Christian belief, I will argue that other factors, like the work of the Holy Spirit, are crucial.

I

Let me then raise two questions that puzzle me. Both have to do with the phenomenon of religious unbelief. First, why do certain people who hear and understand the Christian message not accept it? This is a problem for me because (1) I think the Christian message is true; (2) I think it is in the interest of all persons to accept it; and (3) scripture seems to me to claim that, at least in some sense, all people know certain crucial aspects of the Christian message.

This last point constitutes my second puzzle. What did Paul mean in Rom. 1:19, where he says of unbelievers: "What can be known about God is plain to them because God has shown it to them"? Now what is it that we Christians think "can be known about God"? That's easy: We'll call it proposition 1:

1. God exists, and is the all-powerful,
   all-knowing, and loving creator of the heavens and the earth.

But in what sense, then, is this truth about God (as well as other things, of course) "plain" to nonbelievers? It surely seems that sincere atheists, agnostics, and members of nontheistic religions do not know proposition 1 at all. They don't even *believe* it. It would be odd, maybe even insulting, if I were to say to one of my atheist colleagues at the Claremont Colleges, "The existence of God is plain to you; indeed, you *know* that God exists." So my second puzzle is this: What can Paul possibly have meant?

One clue is that Paul seems to have thought of the problem of religious unbelief as a spiritual rather than an intellectual problem. He says (Rom 1:20–22):

> Ever since the creation of the world his eternal and divine nature, invisible though they are, have been understood and seen through the things he has made. So they are without excuse: for though they knew God, they did not honor him as God or give thanks to him, but they became futile in their thinking, and their senseless minds were darkened.

Let us say that an *intellectual problem* is one solved by learning, by the right application of human reason and experience. And let us say that a *spiritual problem* is one solved by being rightly related to God. Paul seems to have thought of religious unbelief as a matter of being wrongly related to God. To borrow Pascal's distinction, it is more a matter of the heart than of the mind.

We are trying to understand Paul's claim that "what can be known about God is plain to them." Such a claim, however, seems rather obviously false. Let us then see if we can figure out how it might nevertheless be true. Now it is a truism in philosophy that there are different senses of the word "know." Let us call all those uses of the expression "A knows p" that entail "A believes p" *strong senses* of "know." There are also *weak senses* of the word "know," that is, senses where knowing p does not entail believing p, or at least not consciously believing p. If I may speak personally, I am quite sure that before my conversion to Christianity years ago, I knew (in the weak sense) certain things about myself that I was then quite unwilling to believe. I was afraid they might be true, things about my own inherent pride, self-centeredness, and propensity for violence and lust. Sometimes in life we see what we want to see. Only after my conversion did I come to know, in the strong sense, these truths about myself.[1]

Is it then possible for the following three claims to be true for some person A and claim p:

2. A knows p (in the weak sense);
3. A does not know p (in the strong sense);

and

4. A *ought* to know p (in the strong sense); that is, A is culpable for not knowing p (in the strong sense)?

Yes, I think such a situation is quite possible. I once knew a young man who was, frankly, a malicious person. But his mother, whom I also knew, was unwilling to face the truth about him. I think she knew (in the weak sense) the truth about her son, but not in the strong sense. She always made excuses for him, overlooking his misdeeds, claiming that his behavior was just a phase that he would soon outgrow. Her unwillingness consciously to face the truth was, I think, at least somewhat culpable. In the weak sense, she knew that he was a bad person; but she did not (consciously) believe it; and she *should* have believed it.

This tension between knowing and not knowing is evident even in the Psalms. Psalm 19 begins as follows:

> The heavens are telling the glory of God;
> and the firmament proclaims his handiwork.
> Day to day pours forth speech,
> and night to night declares knowledge.

But then the Psalm seems to go in quite the opposite direction:

> There is no speech, nor are there words;
>   their voice is not heard.

And then it returns to the original affirmation:

> Yet their voice goes out through all the earth,
>   and their words to the end of the earth.

The psalmist seems to be saying that the heavens, God's handiwork, speak. Indeed, they speak constantly, day to day and night to night. What they speak about is the glory of God. The voice of the heavens goes out "through all the earth." This is an odd claim in and of itself. How can the stars tell anything? Yet, as we have seen, the next claim seems almost to contradict the first. "Their voice is not heard," the psalmist says; it is almost as if "there is no speech, nor are there words."

I read these lines as follows: the voice of the stars and of other created things declaring the glory of God is or should be clear to everyone. But if some people are unwilling to listen to that voice, they will hear no other voice. It will be for them as if there is no evidence of the glory of God at all.

The Bible has a metaphor for the phenomenon of culpable disbelief. The metaphor is "hardening of the heart." In other words, the truth is this:

1. God exists, and is the all-powerful, all-knowing, and loving
   creator of the heavens and the earth;
5. Everybody knows (in the weak sense) that (1) is true;

and

6. Those who do not know (1) in the strong sense are culpable
   for their ignorance.

Proposition 1 is a truth that unbelievers do not want to admit, so they refuse to accept it. They harden their hearts against it. Again, the problem is essentially spiritual rather than intellectual. It exists not in the state of the evidence but rather with us. We have a *defect* that prevents us from seeing the truth, from knowing (1) in the strong sense.

That defect is called *pride*. Those who accept the truth about God and know it (in the strong sense) must do several things that humans do not naturally want to do. First, they must believe what they cannot see or touch or prove. Second, they must humble themselves and admit that they owe their lives to the one who created them. Third, they must submit themselves to worshiping and obeying the commands of the one who created them. Pride works to prevent all three.

II

My claim, then, is that spiritual considerations prevent people from knowing (in the strong sense) certain truths that would otherwise be clear to them. Notice that visual metaphors naturally come into play here. The nonbeliever says of the existence and glory of God, "I just didn't see it." The believer says, "Your eyes need to be opened." Nonbelievers who convert and become believers frequently say things like, "It was as if blinders were removed from my eyes; I can now see what I didn't see."

Having taught virtually my entire academic career at entirely secular institutions, I think I have seen culpable disbelief in some of my religiously skeptical colleagues. Some of them, so far as I can tell, would be unwilling to accept

1. God exists, and is the all-powerful, all-knowing, and loving creator of the heavens and the earth,

even if it were as obvious as the noses in front of their faces. Indeed, I have a name for a certain atheological argument that nobody verbalizes but I think many people today live by. I call it the Lifestyle Argument Against the Existence of God. It is a simple argument, a two-step proof. It goes like this:

7. I am not living and don't want to live the kind of life that God would want me to live if God existed;
8. Therefore, God does not exist.

Of course what we have here is absurdly fallacious as an argument, but that does not prevent people from being influenced by it. There is no doubt that *the* most dogmatically anti-Christian folk in academia today are those intentionally following lifestyle choices that they know are not approved by Christianity.

Let me illustrate. I will describe a certain philosophy of life that I call "Meism." The essence of Meism is the notion that everything that I want in life is rightfully mine. Meism has a motto or, perhaps, mantra. It is the words, "I deserve it." This is what Meists always say when they think of something they want. If I want to be wealthy, then wealth is something I deserve. If I want to be physically attractive, then good looks are something I deserve. If I want to have complete freedom of choice, then power over other people and the ability to invent my own moral rules are something I deserve. If I want to have perfect relationships with others, especially with members of the opposite sex, then that too is something I deserve.

Meism is the dominant personal philosophy of our time. If I am a Meist, then I believe that I am the center of the universe. My only moral duties are to myself. I can be as self-indulgent as I want, because, after all, I deserve it. If other people prevent me from getting what I want, then I have the right to complain loudly, because, after all, they are standing in the way of my getting what is rightfully mine. I even have the right to elbow them aside if that is necessary to my achieving wealth or good looks or power over people or perfect relationships or whatever I want. I see Meism among some of my students and colleagues. The really dedicated Meists, knowing as they do that Meism and Christianity are incompatible, tend to be insistent anti-Christians. The deepest reason that they are nonbelievers is not intellectual but spiritual. Certain commitments that they have made render them incapable of seeing reality as it genuinely is. It is as if there were blinders over their eyes. They can't see things—like the presence of God in their lives—that they ought to see.

III

What is it that is ultimately real? What is the center, the core, the heart of the universe? If we could see reality as it genuinely is, what would we see?

Most atheists would say that what is ultimately real is atoms in motion; what is real is matter, in its various configurations. I know a person, a devout Vishnavite Hindu, who would insist that what is ultimately real is the karmic cycle of life, death, and rebirth. Some who embrace postmodernism hold, so far as I can tell, that there is no such thing as a unified whole that might be called "reality" and thus no unifying center of reality.

To Christians, at the center of reality is *a personal relationship*. At its deepest level, this claim points to the loving, open, and interpenetrating relationships among the trinitarian persons—the Father, the Son, and the Holy Spirit. But God created us human beings in God's image. One aspect of that image is that we too are essentially involved in a personal relationship. The Christian claim that a personal relationship stands at the heart of reality refers not just to the Trinity. It also means that we human beings were created for the sake of a relationship with God.

Well then, what is the nature of that relationship? It is a *covenant* between God and human beings. A covenant is simply a two-part agreement between persons: "I will do this if you will do that." The covenant at the heart of reality is tersely but sublimely summed up by the prophet Jeremiah: "I will be your God and you will be my people" (Jer 7:23). At the center of the universe is a loving, covenantal relationship between persons and a God who acts on its behalf. This is what unbelievers ought to see but cannot see.

The relationship between God and human beings was cosmically and morally severed with the entrance of sin and spiritual blindness into the universe. Personally, that relationship is broken whenever we separate ourselves from God by our pride, anger, lust, and self-centeredness. All of God's actions in salvation history are done for the sake of restoring human beings to the pristine splendor of that relationship. Christians believe that the relationship is fully restored through the action of God in the world and preeminently through God's actions in the world in Jesus Christ.

Is it possible to *see God*? Well, if God is ultimate reality, and if at the center of reality is a loving relationship between God and human beings, then it should be possible to see God, at least in some sense of the word "see." It ought to be clear.

The Bible has interesting thoughts about seeing God. In the first place, it is pointed out in several texts that seeing God, or at least seeing

God's face, is forbidden. There is, for example, the curious passage in Exodus 33 where Moses asks to see the glory of God. Eventually God does pass by, while Moses is hidden in a cleft of a rock, and he only gets to see God's back (whatever that means). But the key phrase in the text is Exod 33:20: "You cannot see my face; for no one shall see me and live."[2]

Perhaps humans cannot see God's face because of our sinfulness. I say this because the second point is that the scriptures also declare that people who are upright, holy, and pure in heart *do* get to see God. Psalm 11:7 says that "the upright shall behold his [the Lord's] face." The sixth beatitude says, "Blessed are the pure in heart, for they will see God" (Matt 5:8). And Heb 12:14 says: "Pursue peace with everyone, and the holiness without which no one will see the Lord."[3] But if our aim is to see God, to achieve what the medievals called "the beatific vision," these texts sound like bad news. Which of us is upright, or pure in heart, or holy?

But the hope of seeing God is still present in the scriptures. In Ps 27:7–8, the poet pleads for the sight of God:

> Hear, O Lord, when I cry aloud,
>   be gracious to me and answer me!
> "Come," my heart says, "seek his face!"
>   Your face, Lord, do I seek.
>   Do not hide your face from me.

And although there are thorny textual and lexical problems in this passage, the NRSV translates Job 19:25–27 as follows:

> For I know that my redeemer lives,
>   and that at the last he will stand upon the earth;
> and after my skin has been thus destroyed,
>   then in my flesh I shall see God,
> whom I shall see on my side,
>   and my eyes shall behold, and not another.

This hope that we will one day see God is surely eschatological. In 1 John 3:2, it says, "Beloved, we are God's children now; what we will be has not yet been revealed. What we do know is this: when he is revealed, we will be like him, for we will see him as he is." And in the text about the New Jerusalem in Revelation 22, it says: "But the throne of God and of the lamb will be in it [i.e., in the city], and his servants will worship him; they will see his face."

Now it is clear that I have been switching between two different senses of the expression "see God." The first is the sense in which believers do and nonbelievers do not, here and now, see God. This is clearly a metaphorical sense of the word "see." It means roughly that believers cannot avoid interpreting their experience, and indeed all of reality, in terms of the presence of God; and that nonbelievers do not do so. The second is the sense in which no one can now see God, not at least God's face, and that one day the blessed *will* see God. This, I think, is a literal sense of the word "see." Believing as I do in a general resurrection that is essentially bodily, I have no trouble with the notion that the blessed—the church triumphant—will one day literally see God.

IV

Precisely how do people come to believe in God or in the truth of the Christian message? This question is ambiguous; there are at least two ways in which it might be understood. First, it might be a question about the *origin* or initial cause of a belief. Suppose we ask a theist, "Why do you believe in God?" If the answer is something like, "I believe in God because as a child my parents taught me to believe in God," that would normally be taken to explain the origin or genesis of the belief. Second, sometimes we wonder about the *warrant* or evidence for or justification of a belief; that is, we wonder whether the belief is rational or can be intellectually justified. If the theist were to appeal, say, to some version of the cosmological argument for the existence of God, that would normally be taken as an attempt to provide warrant or justification for the belief.

We are asking how a person moves from the state of not seeing God, that is, being an unbeliever, to the state of seeing God. Suppose we are interested in the first question, the question of origin or initial cause. Then, in my opinion, the answer is this: People come to believe because of the illumination or inward testimony of the Holy Spirit. God changes their minds, turns on the lights, causes them to see things that they were not able to see before.

But what about natural theology? Is it ever the origin of any-body's belief? This is not an artificial question for me to ask, since one of my recent books is on the proofs for the existence of God.[4] Natural theology or apologetic arguments definitely have value in providing warrant for the Christian message, but for most believers natural the-ology has little to do with the origin of belief. There are exceptions, of course, but most Christians do not seem particularly interested in nat-ural theology. The origin of their belief lies elsewhere.

Notice that most Christians are *certain* that the Christian message is true, while most arguments in natural theology only produce, at best, more or less probability. And the force of any powerful argument can be resisted if one especially wants to do so; one need only find its weakest premise and call it into question. Arguments against that premise will not be hard to find, not if one is familiar with the litera-ture in the philosophy of religion anyway. Especially in situations where self-centeredness, pride, and the desire to resist any call from God are involved, it seems that objections can always be found and that accordingly apologetic arguments will produce few conversions.

As Paul says, "even if our gospel is veiled, it is veiled to those who are perishing. In their case the god of this world has blinded the minds of the unbelievers, to keep them from seeing the light of the gospel of the glory of Christ" (2 Cor 4:3–4). To people whose "sense-less minds were darkened" (Rom 1:21), even sound arguments in favor of the existence of God or the resurrection of Christ will seem like foolishness. Nor does it seem that the learned are more sensitive at detecting the religious truth than the unlearned. Otherwise, scholars would rank above ordinary believers in religious certainty and maybe even religiosity, and I see no reason to think that they do.

John Calvin argued as follows: "Credibility of doctrine is not established until we are persuaded beyond doubt that God is its Author."[5] Natural theology, as well as the testimony of the church, Calvin said, are both valuable, but do not protect us from "the instabil-ity of doubt" or from boggling "at the smallest quibbles." "The word of God will not find acceptance in men's hearts," he said, "before it is sealed by the inward testimony of the Holy Spirit."[6] This testimony pro-duces a certainty that each believer experiences; it is an illumination that opens the sinful heart to the message of the word of God and gives assurance of its truth. "Indeed," Calvin declared, "the Word of God is like the sun, shining upon all those to whom it is proclaimed, but with no effect among the blind. Now, all of us are blind by nature in this respect. Accordingly, it cannot penetrate into our minds unless the Spirit, as the inner teacher, through his illumination makes entry for it."[7]

What exactly is the "inward testimony of the Holy Spirit"? Let me define it as follows: it is *that influence of the Holy Spirit on the minds of believers that causes them to be certain that the Christian message, or some aspect of it, is true.* This is the origin of Christian certainty. The inward testimony is a species of persuasion, not of evidence. It is an illumination that opens eyes closed to the truth.

As we have seen, sin prevents people from recognizing truths that are uncomfortable to the ego, for example, that we owe our lives to God; that we don't deserve everything we desire; that we need a savior. Thus Paul says: "Those who are unspiritual do not receive the gifts of God's spirit, for they are foolishness to them, and they are unable to understand them because they are spiritually discerned" (1 Cor 2:14; see also 2:10). The Spirit's testimony does not supply new evidence of the truth of the Christian message; it illuminates or renders convincing evidence that is already there. It is not a question of propaganda or brainwashing or of making feeble evidence appear powerful. It is a question of removing blinders and helping us to grasp the epistemic situation correctly.

As we all know, Descartes was shocked and horrified when Gassendi argued that Descartes' *Cogito, ergo sum* was a deductive argument, a syllogism with a suppressed middle premise that said something like, *Omnia cogitantia sunt* ("Everything that thinks exists"). Descartes' reply was that the *cogito* was not an inference of any sort but rather a direct intuition of truth. I want to say the same thing about the inward testimony of the Holy Spirit. It is not a process of reasoning or weighing evidence but a direct intuition of truth, like the opening of blind eyes, the unplugging of deaf ears, the removal of a veil. Phenomenologically how does it work? We do not know. Bernard Ramm says that it is

> no audible voice; no sudden exclamation that "the Bible is the word of God"; no miracle removing us out of our normal routine of creaturely existence; no revelation with flashing lights and new ideas; no religious experience as such; no creation of some new or special organ of spiritual vision; but rather, it is the touch of the

Holy Spirit upon native and resident powers of the soul which had been rendered ineffectual through sin.[8]

Notice that the inward testimony is private or secret. The assurance that it provides cannot be communicated or proved. This is why nonbelievers typically take the Christian message to be sheer foolishness and the Bible a book like any other. Those of us with friends in departments of religious studies can speak authoritatively on this matter; we know people who have spent their professional careers teaching and writing about the Bible but who do not believe what it says. Since the inward testimony is essentially private, it is not directly communicable. Just because you claim that the Spirit has told *you* that p is true, that does not mean *I* must accept p. Of course, if you are a person whom I respect, especially in religious matters, your testimony will doubtless impress me and may even cause me to look at p in a new light. I may even become convinced that you are correct. But the point is that your testimony will not constitute for me the illumination of the Holy Spirit. It will not be normative for me. On any topic a mere appeal to the Spirit is insufficient to carry conviction; the Bible itself recognizes that many who are in error will try to validate their claims by appealing to the Spirit—thus the expressed need to "test the Spirits to see whether they are of God" (1 John 4:1; cf. 1 Cor 12:10).

One might object that the inward testimony is too subjective to warrant any religious beliefs at all. Muslims can claim what might be called Inward Testimony of Allah on behalf of the claim that the words of the Qur'an are from God; members of Christian Science can claim something similar for *Science and Health with Keys to the Scriptures.* But surely the mere fact that people disagree with one of my beliefs does not *by itself* cast doubt on that belief. More importantly, as I have stressed, the inward testimony of the Holy Spirit is not to be understood as an argument, and certainly not as an argument directed at those who doubt or deny the Christian message. The inward testimony constitutes the central reason why I (and presumably other Christians) accept proposition 1 and the other aspects of the Christian message. It is not meant as a vehicle for convincing others.

It is important to note that the inward testimony is not a source of new truth or revelation. It is not an "inner light" or mystical oracle or private vision that provides extrabiblical answers to theological questions.

It is a witness to the truth of scripture and of the Christian message. As Jesus said: "When the Advocate comes, whom I will send to you from the Father, the Spirit of Truth who comes from the Father, he will testify on my behalf" (John 15:26; cf. also 1 Cor 2:10). If this were not so—if the inward testimony provided new truths—the shape of the Christian gospel would be perennially dependent on private revelations and visions.[9]

In an article entitled "Is Faith Infused into Man by God?" Thomas Aquinas argued that the assent or belief aspect of faith is not adequately explained by external inducements such as being persuaded by someone or seeing a miracle.[10] Such influences obviously do not constitute sufficient explanation because some people are exposed to the same sermon or even see the same miracle yet do not believe. There must then be an internal cause of assent. The suggestion that our own free will is the cause was not acceptable to Aquinas because it smacked of Pelagianism. Thus, he concluded, the cause must be "some supernatural principle" that moves us inwardly by grace, and that (he says) is God.

Aquinas did not use any phrase like "the inward testimony of the Holy Spirit," but his central point was similar to Calvin's. A properly disposed heart (or, if you will, an illumined mind) is necessary to properly weigh the evidence. Those who have not been illumined by the Spirit are in an inferior epistemic position. They do not see everything that must be seen.

V

What about the question of warrant or justification for belief in the Christian message? Can the inward testimony provide it? In one sense, yes it can. The belief of a Christian that the Christian message is true does not need anything more than the inward testimony. It does not stand in need of public verification, for example, by arguments from natural theology, for it to be sensible, rational, defensible.

Who gets to decide which beliefs are warranted and which are not? Who gets to decide whether something essentially private like the inward testimony warrants certain Christian beliefs? Are atheists the privileged few who get to decide? Or people who reject the Christian message? Some people seem to think so; they seem to hold that acceptance of the Christian message is irrational or unwarranted until Christians can prove that message to the satisfaction of skeptics. But why should any Christian accept any such claim as that?

My argument, then, is this: If I accept the Christian message because of the inward testimony, and if that message has not been refuted or rendered improbable, then my acceptance of the Christian message is fully rational. Of course, if there exists evidence or a powerful argument *against* the truth of the Christian message—a disproof of (1), for example—that would be another matter. My belief would not then be warranted. But in my opinion no such evidence or argument exists.

But here is a point where natural theology can enter in. Many skeptics have strongly argued against the Christian message—against (1), among other items—and apologetic arguments can be used to respond to those objections. In order to answer critics outside the Christian community (or indeed, to convince anyone other than oneself), appeal to the inward testimony will not usually suffice. But rational arguments in favor of the truth of the Christian message can certainly be appealed to.

The reason that natural theology alone is rarely sufficient to produce a conversion is not hard to find. Suppose that some clever philosopher were to produce a proof of the existence of some being B, a proof no one is able to refute. That is, suppose the premises of the argument are clearly true, the argument is clearly formally valid, and it clearly commits no informal fallacy such as equivocation or question-begging. But now let's suppose that B is something that you have very good reason to believe does not exist, like, say, your thirteenth daughter. Your reaction to the proof probably would and indeed should be something like this: "Something is wrong here; the proof of B *must* be fallacious in some way that I did not see earlier; for example, one of its premises must be false after all." This, I think, is quite parallel to the attitude many atheists have toward theistic proofs—since they are firmly convinced that God does not exist, no piece of natural theology can possibly prove the existence of God.

Of course some arguments virtually everyone would accept—the Pythagorean theorem, for example. I have never heard of any rational person who both understood and rejected the claim that the square on the hypotenuse of a right triangle is equal to the sum of the squares on the sides. But it is hard to think of any arguments for substantive philosophical conclusions, let alone theological ones, that everybody would accept as successful arguments. Since rationality is person-relative, then as noted above no matter how logically impeccable a given piece of natural theology may be, a religious skeptic who wants to resist its conclusions can always find reason to do so.[11]

So natural theology is probably not best looked at as a vehicle for producing conversions. There are some things it can do, however. For some folk it can remove intellectual blockages that stand in the way of faith. For others it can cause them to consider the possibility of God more seriously than they had done previously. But that is about all. Natural theology presumably has other jobs in the Christian community that it does much better, for example, strengthening believers by replying to skeptical attacks on the faith. So to the extent that natural theologians hope to produce spiritual and not just intellectual results by their efforts, probably their best strategy is (1) to present arguments that are as powerful as possible; (2) to hope and pray that religious skeptics will come to believe; and (3) to leave the rest up to the mercy of God.

VI

We began with two questions: Why do some people not accept the Christian message? And what did Paul mean when he said of unbelievers, "What can be known about God is plain to them"? My answer to the first question is spiritual blindness. Sin has the pandemic effect of hardening the heart against the truth. People do not want to hear that they must live godly lives, that they have a moral defect called pride that has epistemological consequences, that they cannot save themselves, that they need to repent, that salvation is found only in Jesus Christ. If the heart is not right, both the mind and the eyes will be affected. People will not know what they should know. They will not see what ought to be plain.

My answer to the second question is that the truth about God, which I have summarized by

1. God exists, and is the all-powerful, all-knowing, and loving creator of the heavens and the earth,

is indeed "plain" to those not blinded by sin, those illuminated by the Holy Spirit. But what about unbelievers? Since, like all people, they are morally responsible for their sinful acts, they are also morally responsible for the epistemological consequences of their sinful acts. They morally *ought* to see that (1) is true. They ought to *know* (1) (and of course other truths) in the strong sense. What nonbelievers preeminently ought to see but cannot see is that we human beings are in relationship with God, a relationship that will culminate in the eschaton, when all believers will see God.

In the passion story in Mark's Gospel, a curious verse records an event that occurred immediately upon Jesus' death: "And the curtain of the Temple was torn in two, from top to bottom" (Mark 15:38). The curtain, of course, was the heavy laminated veil that separated the Holy of Holies from the Holy Place. The Holy of Holies was entered only by the high priest and only once a year, on Yom Kippur, to make atonement for the sins of Israel. Christian theology has always interpreted this verse as a signal from God (note that the tear in the curtain was from the top down) of the close of the Jewish sacrificial system. The final and perfect sacrifice for sin had just been made; no other sacrifice would ever be needed.

I have no wish to quarrel with that aspect of the rule of faith. I only wish to add that perhaps the evangelist was also saying something like this: before the passion of Jesus, God was hidden; no one was allowed to see God. God and humans could meet only once a year; at all other times, a curtain separated them. Since the curtain is now torn in two, we human beings can enter into God's presence. We have access to God. God no longer hides behind a curtain. We can now see God.[12]

Notes

Scriptural citations are given according to the New Revised Standard Version (NRSV).

1. This phenomenon of both believing and not believing a proposition can be variously described. Perhaps it is a matter of rejecting it consciously and believing it unconsciously. Perhaps it is a matter of wavering back and forth—believing it some of the time and rejecting it at other times. Perhaps it is a matter of believing with part of one's brain or even personality and rejecting it with another. However it is described, I am quite sure that the phenomenon occurs.

2. But the Pentateuch also insists that God and Moses spoke face to face; see Num 12:8; 14:14; and Deut 5:4; 34:10.

3. In Matt 18:10, Jesus declares, speaking of children, "in heaven their angels continually see the face of my father."

4. Stephen T. Davis, *God, Reason, and Theistic Proofs* (Edinburgh: University of Edinburgh Press, 1997).

5. John Calvin, *The Institutes of the Christian Religion* (Philadelphia: Westminster Press, 1960), I, vii, 4.

6. Ibid.

7. Ibid.

8. Bernard Ramm, *The Witness of the Spirit* (Grand Rapids: Eerdmans, 1959), 84.

9. Moreover, it goes without saying that the inward testimony is not a vehicle for solving scholarly problems, for example, about the biblical text, canon, authenticity, geography, archaeology, history, and so on.

10. Thomas Aquinas, *Summa Theologica* (New York: Benziger Brothers, 1947), 2-2, 6, 1.

11. This sort of thing is not true just of religious skeptics. If someone were to publish an apparently impeccable proof of the nonexistence of God in the next issue of the *Journal of Philosophy,* I'm sure I would try to find a rational way to reject one of its premises.

12. The present essay is meant in part as a proposal for bridging a gap that currently exists between two groups of Christian philosophers—those who embrace epistemological internalism and natural theology and those who embrace the epistemological externalism of Reformed Epistemology and eschew natural theology. My hope is to provide an important role for natural theology, and thus a way of speaking apologetically to nonbelievers, within an epistemological framework that is in sympathy with the aims and orientation of the Reformed Epistemologists.

IV

Resurrection and Christology

16. Jesus and Faith

Avery Dulles, S.J.

Gerald O'Collins has put his training in exegesis to excellent use in his many works in the field of Christology. Together with Daniel Kendall, he has been one of the strongest proponents of the thesis that Jesus had the gift of faith.[1] Opposed as it is to the teaching of Thomas Aquinas and many leading Catholic theologians up to our own day, this thesis calls for close examination. What is the testimony of scripture and tradition, and how does that testimony bear up under the light of contemporary Christian experience and rational scrutiny?

SCRIPTURAL FOUNDATIONS

In scripture the term "faith" belongs to the vocabulary of soteriology. It is the quality by which one becomes related in a saving way to God, who alone gives firmness and stability to our lives and projects. "If you will not believe, you shall not be established" (Isa 7:9).

In the Gospels faith figures prominently, but no texts clearly ascribe faith to Jesus. This absence is noteworthy, since there are many references to other virtues and sentiments of Jesus—for example, his love, his compassion, his sorrow, his fear, his anger, his trust in God, and his obedience to the Father. Why does Jesus never speak of his own faith, and why do the Gospels never speak of him as a believer? Jesus is portrayed rather as the catalyst of faith, the witness who awakens faith in others.[2] By testifying to what he knows, he elicits faith on the part of his hearers. Regularly in the Fourth Gospel, and occasionally in the Synoptics (e.g., Luke 10:18), Jesus' knowledge of divine things is described in terms of vision. Others are to put faith in his word and his teaching.

On the basis of the Gospels Romano Guardini, reaffirming the classical position, wrote concerning Jesus: "He himself does not 'believe.'...He stands not in the world of men who believe but in the world to which their belief stretches out. To be more precise: he makes faith possible."[3] Jean Galot, in an article published in 1982, carefully examined the relevant New Testament texts and concluded: "As Son he cannot believe but he makes men able to believe, leading them on the road to faith."[4]

This consensus, however, is no longer solid, if it can be said to survive at all. In addition to O'Collins and Kendall, a number of prominent Catholic exegetes and theologians, including Wilhelm Thüsing, James P. Mackey, and Jon Sobrino, maintain that Jesus did have faith, since he willed to become a wayfarer like ourselves.[5] Thanks to his faith, they say, Jesus can be a model for us in our struggle to believe.

Several passages from the Gospels have been interpreted as implying that Jesus had faith, notably his assertions that faith is needed to exorcize demons and to move mountains (Matt 17:19–20). But these interpretations are at best doubtful, since Jesus in these texts is talking not about his own miraculous power but about that of others.

The book of Acts and the Pauline epistles generally depict faith as a response to the apostolic preaching, the kerygma. Texts such as Acts 13:46 and Rom 10:17 indicate that to accept the kerygma is to embark on the way of salvation; to reject it is to condemn oneself. Jesus, quite evidently, does not have to accept the kerygma. For this reason, there is no question of his exercise of faith.

The New Testament authors regard the patriarchs and prophets as men of faith, but they understand such pre-Christian faith as directed to Christ as the Savior who is to come. The Christ in whom Christians explicitly believe, they hold, was implicitly believed in by the Israelites of old, as passages such as Luke 24:44; John 5:46; 8:55; and Heb 11:40 contend.

The Pauline expression *pistis Christou Iēsou* is variously interpreted.[6] Some understand the genitive as subjective, but they generally explain it as referring to the "faithfulness" of Jesus through which we receive our justification.[7] The majority of exegetes, it would seem, maintain with O'Collins and Kendall that the genitive is objective and means faith directed to Jesus.[8] Favoring a third interpretation, Hans Urs von Balthasar builds on the suggestion of Adolf Deissmann that we have here a "genitive of fellowship" or a "mystical genitive."[9] Without insisting on this new grammatical category, Balthasar holds that Paul's terminology has reference to Jesus as the "overflowing subject" who associates us with himself and enables us to participate in what he genuinely possesses.[10] All three interpretations of "the faith of Jesus" can be defended, but the third seems most consonant with Pauline soteriology, taken as a whole.

The strongest single text from the New Testament by which to support the thesis that Jesus had the virtue of faith would seem to be Heb 12:2, which describes him as the "author and perfecter" (*archēgon kai teleiōntēn*) of faith. This expression certainly includes the idea that Christ gives rise to our faith and brings it to completion; it seems to imply, in addition, that faith exists in him in an archetypal manner. As the exemplary source he would seem to have had either faith itself or something that includes everything positive in what we mean by faith. The question whether Jesus had faith in a formal and proper sense of the word is difficult to settle from scripture alone, but the theological tradition may perhaps bring further light.

SCHOLASTIC OPINIONS

In the Middle Ages the theology of faith undergoes a paradigmatic shift. Under the impact of Greek philosophy, faith comes to be viewed in epistemological terms. It is a mode of knowledge inferior to vision and demonstration but still superior to mere conjecture or opinion.

Peter Lombard sets the terms of the debate by his assertion:

> Christ, who possessed the gifts of heaven *(bona patriae),* indeed believed and hoped in his future resurrection on the third day, for which he also prayed to the Father; but he did not have the virtues of faith or hope because his knowledge of it was not obscure and reflected in a mirror but perfectly clear, because he knew the future as well as he knew the past…. He did not have the virtues of faith or hope, because he saw directly *(per speciem)* the things

that he believed in. (*Sententiarum Libri Quattuor,* bk. 3, dist. 26, ch. 4)

Thomas Aquinas proceeds from the premise that Christ from the first moment of his conception perfectly saw God's essence (*Summa theol.* III, q. 7, art. 3; III, q. 10, arts. 1–4). Knowing divine things by vision, he could not believe, for belief is a knowledge of divine things that are not seen. Thomas here puts the accent on the provisionality and obscurity of faith (as seeing "in a mirror dimly," 1 Cor 13:12) rather than on its positive aspect as the assurance of things hoped for (Heb 11:1).

Even if it were granted that Christ possessed the beatific vision, one could still argue against St. Thomas that he could have had faith. Some of the Scholastic theologians argued that because God was infinite, he could never be comprehensively known by any finite mind, even with the light of glory. Hence, as Matthew of Aquasparta put it, "it would not be inappropriate to say that the blessed believe something because they never know everything" (*Quest. disp. de fide,* q. 6, ad 3).[11]

Alexander of Hales in his early gloss on the *Sentences* holds that Jesus could not have had faith because his knowledge could not have been obscure.[12] But in his mature *Summa theologica* he gives a more nuanced opinion. Discussing the condition of Adam before the fall, he distinguishes three forms of cognition: without a mirror luminously, through a mirror luminously, and through a mirror obscurely. Adam, he says, knew divine mysteries in the second of these ways. He had what pertains to the perfection of faith—luminosity and certitude—but not what pertains to its imperfection, namely, obscurity. On the ground that virtues are to be defined in terms of their perfection, he concludes that Adam may be said to have had a *fides lucida,* like that of Christ.[13] In replying to an objection, Alexander adds that Adam knew not by external testimony but by interior hearing, which is a more perfect mode of faith.

Another Scholastic witness is Odo Rigaud, the Franciscan pupil of Alexander of Hales and close associate of Bonaventure. In discussing whether Adam before the fall had faith, he too reaches an affirmative verdict and argues from the fact that Christ had faith. To demonstrate this premise he holds that Christ had all the virtues according to what they contain of perfection. But faith is perfect to the extent that it includes knowledge *(cognitio)* and light *(lumen)*; it is imperfect to the extent that it is obscure *(aenigmatica)*. He concludes that Adam had either faith or something in place of faith.[14]

Bonaventure, in his commentary on the *Sentences,* agrees with Alexander and Odo that Adam in the state of innocence knew divine things only "through a mirror," as we do, but in his case the reflection was clear, not obscure. For such knowledge Bonaventure prefers not to use the term "faith" because, in common usage, it refers to obscure knowledge based on external testimony.[15] Regarding the question whether Christ had faith, Bonaventure shows some ambivalence. At one point he says that faith may be found in him insofar as it is a perfection, but not insofar as it bespeaks imperfection.[16] But later in the same work he rejects the idea that Christ had either faith or hope because these terms necessarily imply some imperfection.[17] Bonaventure's general principle is that in order to remedy the evil of ignorance as well as that of sin, he had to possess, in his human nature and here on earth, "all the treasures of wisdom and knowledge" (Col 2:3). Christ, as the fountainhead of all virtue, possesses every perfection more fully and completely than it is found elsewhere.[18]

As a final Scholastic witness we may turn to Nicholas of Cusa, who asserts that faith animated by charity is the most excellent of God's gifts and is the beginning of all knowledge and wisdom. He quotes from the Vulgate "Unless you believe, you shall not understand" (Isa 7:9). Faith in the highest degree, he says, cannot exist in a wayfarer who is not also a *comprehensor.* Christ, who is both *viator* and *comprehensor,* had *"fides maxima,"* which is the highest instance of faith and at the same time the minimal instance, since at that point faith ceases to be itself and passes over into indubitable certitude. We who are simple wayfarers should seek by faith to make ourselves "Christiform."[19]

These samples of Scholastic thinking may suffice to show that the shift from the soteriological to the epistemological concept of faith puts the question of Christ's faith in a new light. Faith is defined no longer in terms of the believer's relationship to Christ the Savior but with reference to God, the primal source of all truth and grace. In this perspective, which is theocentric rather than Christocentric, the Scholastics study Christ as a supremely graced wayfarer who, as incarnate Son, is more than a wayfarer.

While the New Testament teaches that Christ was like us in all things but sin (Heb 4:15), the medieval Scholastics hold that, to redeem us from ignorance, Christ had to have the fullness of wisdom and knowledge. On this ground they either deny that he had faith or they attribute to him a lucid faith based only on interior testimony. They analyze faith almost exclusively under its intellectual aspect, as a mode of cognition. They do not treat faith under the rubrics of trust, fidelity, and obedience.

The Scholastic thesis that Christ knew all things in the beatific vision has not persuaded most contemporary theologians, even those who, like Jean Galot, refuse to ascribe faith to Christ.[20] In his encounter with the risen Christ Peter exclaims, "You know all things" (John 21:17), yet according to the Gospels, Jesus in his earthly life explicitly denied knowing the hour of the end (Mark 13:32). He is said to have grown in wisdom (Luke 2:52). The Letter to the Hebrews speaks of him learning obedience by the things he suffered (Heb 5:8).

Nothing in scripture indicates that Christ continuously had the beatific vision. If he had been in a state of beatitude, it is hard to understand how he could have suffered as he did. Paul speaks of the *kenōsis* by which the Son of God took on the form of a servant (Phil 2:7). Such self-emptying would, it seems, include the willingness to share in the lot of those who learn. The reasons against ascribing the beatific vision to Christ in his earthly life have been succinctly marshaled by O'Collins and Kendall.[21]

CONTEMPORARY SPECULATION

In the twentieth century the theology of faith undergoes a new paradigmatic shift. The outlook becomes personalistic and existential. In contrast to the medieval view, the concern is not so much with knowledge as with a lived relationship. Faith is seen as a total personal act, having repercussions in the faculties of intellect, will, and affectivity. It involves belief, trust, and obedience. In terms of this "model" of faith, the question of Christ's faith presents itself in new form.

Among the theologians who have taken up this challenge, Hans Urs von Balthasar is outstanding. He speaks of "integral" faith, which involves not only believing that certain things are true but submitting one's whole existence to the God who is encountered. Faith in the sense of fidelity is first of all an attribute of God, and second an attribute of those who respond to God's gracious initiatives. Their "Amen" is simultaneously assent, trust, fidelity, and obedience, all of which are exhibited in a preeminent way by Christ as human. The human Christ opens himself totally to God, and by faith we enter into that relationship. Our faith is a participation in his.[22]

Balthasar also takes account of the patterns of redemptive history. Faith, for him, involves a covenantal relationship, which is intensified in the new covenant established by Christ. From God's side it involves the self-gift of the incarnate Son, and from the side of the redeemed it means an obedience that hands itself over totally to the Redeemer. It is an act of abandonment whereby the believer lets himself be conformed to Christ.[23]

Addressing the question of Christ's faith in this framework, Balthasar firmly rejects the position of liberal theologians, including Rudolf Bultmann, that Jesus was a pious Jew who had faith like any other.[24] In line with certain indications in the New Testament and with the Catholic dogmatic tradition, he holds that Christ from the dawn of his consciousness had an intuitive knowledge of himself as divine Son and of his own redemptive mission. In the case of Christ, person and mission perfectly coincide: he is his mission.[25]

Jesus had to implement his mission "step by step according to the Father's instructions (in the Holy Spirit)."[26] He did not decide how his mission was to unfold, especially in the final stages of his passion and death, in which he seems to have experienced anguish and turmoil. With respect to his fate, Jesus had to practice a kind of self-abandonment in trust and obedience that may be said to verify the notion of faith set forth in Heb 11:1: "Faith is the assurance of things hoped for, and the conviction [or "the proof"] of things not seen."[27]

The faith of Jesus, Balthasar contends, differs from ours insofar as we only receive our mission on the basis of coming to faith, whereas Jesus inalienably was his mission. His "faith" meant a trusting self-surrender and generous adherence to the Father's plan whereby he was to execute his mission.[28]

In his treatment of the faith of Jesus, Balthasar discusses primarily the way in which Jesus responded to God in living out his own mission. But on the basis of Balthasar's modest view of the scope of Jesus' intuitive knowledge, one could go further and speculate that

Jesus might have known the past history of Israel through faith in the Hebrew Scriptures and that he would have been assured of the coming resurrection of the dead and the blessedness of the life to come by faith rather than vision.[29]

CONCLUSION

Christology must always be on guard against the twin temptations of psychological Monophysitism and psychological Nestorianism. In earlier ages the former temptation was predominant. Many wrote as though Jesus could not be a believer because he knew all things in the beatific vision or because faith would be an imperfection repugnant to his divinity. Partly for this reason, they were disinclined to attribute faith to Jesus, except in some eminent or paradoxical sense. Today the Nestorian temptation is more prevalent. It is common to write of Jesus as though the divine personal subject had no influence on the functioning of his human faculties. Some authors confine themselves to a strictly anthropological approach, methodically bracketing out any reference to Christ's divinity. They take it as self-evident that Jesus had faith in the same sense that other believers do.

The psychology of Jesus is an unfathomable mystery but is not totally unknowable. On the basis of many passages in the Synoptic Gospels and especially in the Fourth Gospel, read in light of the church's dogmatic tradition, it seems safe to assert that Jesus had an immediate and indubitable consciousness of being the Son sent into the world as its redeemer.[30] This awareness should not be seen as excluding fear and anxiety about the future, nor should such apprehension be seen as inducing self-doubt or despair about his own identity and mission.

As a wayfarer on earth Jesus presumably learned through instruction from his parents and elders, through his familiarity with the Hebrew Scriptures, and through experience, suffering, and prayer. If this kind of spiritual and mental development be admitted, it seems altogether likely that Jesus could have come to know certain truths on the basis of the authority of God who revealed them, and thus have had faith in the cognitive sense. About his trust in the Father, his obedience, and his unswerving fidelity there can be no doubt.

Theologians who hesitate to ascribe faith to Jesus are often influenced, I suspect, by fear that it would compromise his divine authority and place him on a level with those whom he was sent to redeem. But faith, in its cognitive aspect, is not a mere human opinion; it is a firm adherence to the God who reveals. In the case of Jesus, faith perfectly corresponded to God's word, which he, as the beloved Son, received in incomparable fullness. His faith was unclouded by the effects of personal or original sin. In proclaiming what he knew by faith he could speak with an authority far greater than Moses and the prophets. Although he had an intimacy with God that far surpasses faith, this intimacy would not prevent him from having faith in revealed truths that he did not know intuitively.

These conclusions in no way conflict with the thesis that our faith is directed to Christ as Savior. Jesus does not possess Christian faith, but he is its exemplary source. Our entire pilgrimage of faith takes place "in Christ," the "author and perfecter" of faith. Although Jesus does not belong to the company of Christian believers, he preeminently exemplifies what we experience as faith. As some medieval Scholastics maintained, he had a uniquely "lucid" faith sharpened by his "interior hearing" of God's word.

Our conclusions confirm, and in some ways supplement, the contention of O'Collins and Kendall that Jesus' faith is analogously like ours. They also support, and give added precision to, my own previous statement: "Even though Jesus, as the incarnate Son, did not have faith in the same sense that other human beings do, he exemplifies in an eminent manner the obedience and trust that are constitutive of faith."[31]

Notes

Scripture citations are given according to the Revised Standard Version (RSV).

1. Gerald O'Collins, *Christology: A Biblical, Historical and Systematic Study of Jesus* (New York: Oxford University Press, 1995), 250–68. These pages reproduce the substance of the article co-authored by O'Collins and Daniel Kendall, "The Faith of Jesus," *Theological Studies* 53 (1992): 403–23.

2. Gerhard Ebeling, "The Witness of Faith," chapter 4 of his *The Nature of Faith* (Philadelphia: Fortress, 1961), 44–57. See also the chapter "Jesus and Faith" in his *Word and Faith* (Philadelphia: Fortress, 1963), 201–46, at 234–35.

3. Romano Guardini, *The Humanity of Christ* (New York: Pantheon, 1964), 85.

4. Jean Galot, "Gesù ha avuto la fede?" *Civiltà Cattolica* 133, no. 3 (September 1982): 460–72, at 472. In his *Who Is Christ?* (Chicago: Franciscan Herald, 1981) Galot concludes, after a nuanced discussion (pp. 379–82): "It is impossible to attribute faith to him in the strict sense of the word" (p. 382).

5. Wilhelm Thüsing, "New Testament Approaches to a Transcendental Christology," in Karl Rahner and Wilhelm Thüsing, *A New Christology* (New York: Seabury/Crossroad, 1980), 44–211, esp. 143–59; James P. Mackey, *Jesus the Man and the Myth* (New York: Paulist, 1979), 159–71; Jon Sobrino, *Christology at the Crossroads* (Maryknoll, N.Y.: Orbis Books, 1978), 79–145.

6. Within the Pauline corpus this and similar terms appear in Rom 3:22, 26; Gal 2:16, 20; 3:22; Eph 3:12; and Phil 3:9.

7. Richard B. Hays, *The Faith of Jesus Christ* (Chico, Calif.: Scholars Press, 1983), 140–42, 157–76. J. Louis Martyn, in the Anchor Bible Commentary on *Galatians* (AB 33A; New York: Doubleday, 1997), 263–75, interprets the "faith" of Jesus as his salvific action on our behalf. Thüsing declares that "the faith of Christ is essentially Christ's obedience to death as an orientation of his 'life for God' (Rom 6:10)" ("New Testament Approaches," 148).

8. O'Collins and Kendall, "The Faith of Jesus," 412 n. 30, citing J. Fitzmyer, F. F. Bruce, and H. Schlier in support of the objective genitive; cf. O'Collins, *Christology,* 258 n. 20. Joseph Fitzmyer, in his Anchor Bible Commentary on *Romans* (AB 33; New York: Doubleday, 1993), 345–46, adduces still other authorities (E. Käsemann, O. Kuss, and J. D. G. Dunn). "Does the vb *pisteuein*," he asks pointedly, "ever have Christ as the subject in the NT?" (p. 345).

9. Adolf Deissmann, *Paul: A Study in Social and Religious History* (Gloucester, Mass.: Peter Smith, 1972), 161–70. See Hans Urs von Balthasar, "Fides Christi," in his *Explorations in Theology, 2, The Spouse of the Word* (San Francisco: Ignatius, 1991), 43–79, at 57–58.

10. Balthasar, "Fides Christi," 55.

11. Matthew of Aquasparta, *Quest. disp. de fide,* 2nd ed. (Florence: Quaracchi, 1957), 156–57.

12. Alexander of Hales, *Glossa in Quattuor Libros Sententiarum Petri Lombardi,* Book III (Florence: Quaracchi, 1954), Dist. XIII (AE), p. 129; Dist. XIII (L), p. 134.

13. Alexander of Hales, *Summa theologica,* Lib. III, inq. 4, tract. 3, qu. 3, tit. 2, no. 512 (Quaracchi ed., vol. 2, pp. 752–53). It is also true that later, in *Summa theol.,* Lib. III, inq. 2, tract. 1, cap. 4, no. 694 (Quaracchi ed., vol. 4, pp. 1104–6) he asserts that because faith implies an imperfect knowledge of God, Christ could not have had it.

14. Jean Bouvy, "La nécessité de la grâce dans le *Commentaire des Sentences* d'Odon Rigaud," *Recherches de théologie ancienne de médiévale* 28 (1961): 59–96, at 91–92. This article reproduces the text of Odo's *Commentary on the Sentences,* Lib. II, Dist. 20, qu. 2, "Whether Man in His First State Had Faith."

15. Bonventure, *In II Sent.,* Dist. 23, art. 2, qu. 3; in *Opera omnia,* vol. 2 (Florence: Quaracchi, 1885), 544–45.

16. "Fides et spes,…ratione eius quod perfectionis est in eis, si quid est reperiri, habent esse in Christo" (*In III Sent.,* Dist. 13, art. 1, qu. 3, ad 1; in *Opera omnia,* vol. 3 [Florence: Quaracchi, 1887], 282b).

17. Bonaventure, *In III Sent.,* Dist. 36, qu. 1, ad 1; vol. 3, p. 793a. For the same reason Bonaventure holds that the blessed in heaven, having the light of glory, cannot have faith (*In III Sent.,* Dist. 31, art. 2, qu. 1; in *Opera omnia,* vol. 3, pp. 681–82).

18. Bonaventure, *Breviloquium,* Part IV, chap. 6; in *Opera omnia,* vol. 5 (Florence: Quaracchi, 1891), 246–47.

19. Nicholas of Cusa, *De docta ignorantia,* Lib. III, cap. 11 and 12 (Leipzig: Meiner, 1932), 151–59.

20. Jean Galot, *La conscience de Jésus* (Gembloux: Duculot, 1971), 132–52.

21. O'Collins and Kendall, "The Faith of Jesus," 407–8; O'Collins, *Christology,* 255–56.

22. Balthasar, "Fides Christi," 43–79.

23. Hans Urs von Balthasar, *The Glory of the Lord: A Theological Aesthetics 7. Theology: The New Covenant* (Edinburgh: T & T Clark, 1989), 303–7.

24. Balthasar, "Fides Christi," 60. Cf. Hans Urs von Balthasar, *Theo-Drama: Theological Dramatic Theory. 3. The Dramatis Personae: The Person in Christ* (San Francisco: Ignatius, 1992), 170 n. 11.

25. Balthasar, *Dramatis Personae,* 171.

26. Ibid., 170.

27. Ibid., 171.

28. Ibid.

29. O'Collins and Kendall, "The Faith of Jesus," 418–21; O'Collins, *Christology,* 264–66.

30. The biblical grounds for this statement are summarized by the International Theological Commission in its document "The Consciousness of Christ concerning Himself and His Mission" (1985), in *International Theological Commission: Texts and Documents (1969–1985)* (San Francisco: Ignatius, 1989), 305–16, esp. 307–11. O'Collins and Kendall reaffirm this position in "The Faith of Jesus," 418; see also O'Collins, *Christology,* 263.

31. Avery Dulles, *The Assurance of Things Hoped For: A Theology of Christian Faith* (New York: Oxford University Press, 1994), 280.

17. Blood and Defilement: Reflections on Jesus and the Symbolics of Sex

Janet Martin Soskice

THE PROBLEM

Does the so-called women's issue raise new questions for Christology today? Is there any doubt that a male savior can save women? Surely not. In a sense there is no problem—the Christian message of salvation is for all. Women quite rightly "have assumed they are included in the fully human that is Christ."[1] Christians have repeated the creedal "for us men and for our salvation" and understood, without even knowing the Latin, that it was *"homo"* not *"vir."* Jesus of Nazareth was, of course, male, but even to consider that Christ's humanity did not in some sense encompass that of female humanity would be to deny he was the savior of women—would be to deny he was truly savior of anyone at all. Such arguments are by no means new. Consider this one of Athanasius (I preserve the language of the translator): "And as the incorruptible Son of God was united to all men by his body similar to theirs, consequently he endued all men with incorruption by the promise concerning resurrection. And now no longer does the corruption involved in death hold sway over men because of the Word who dwelt among them through a body one with theirs."[2]

This classical christological argument becomes a nonsense if too much stress is put on the maleness of the body of the Incarnate Word. "A body similar to theirs" can only be a human body. Worse—serious christological dangers present themselves if we tie the signification of the Christ too closely to the masculinity of Jesus. To introduce, even accidentally, a two-tiered soteriology wherein men can fully signify

Christ and women can signify "very dear friends of God" would be theologically indefensible in terms of this Christology.

So there seems to be no problem, and yet there is a huge problem. It might be summarized in this way: "Man" means everyone, except when it doesn't mean "woman." One doesn't have to read far in the texts of historical theology to discover dual anthropologies. We may or may not give theological weight to the reading of Genesis that sees Adam and Eve as punished differently for the fall, but what do we make of the reading of 1 Corinthians 11:7–10 that suggests that women are perhaps not in the fullest sense in the image of God? John Chrysostom, for instance, says this:

> Then why is the man said to be in the "image of God" and the woman not? Because what Paul says about the "image" does not pertain to form. The "image" has rather to do with authority, and this only the man has; the woman has it no longer. For he is subjected to no one, while she is subjected to him; as God said, "Your inclination shall be for your husband and he shall rule over you" (Gen 3:16). *Therefore the man is in the "image of God" since he had no one above him, just as God has no superior but rules over everything. The woman however, is "the glory of man," since she is subjected to him.* (Discourse 2 on Genesis, my emphasis)[3]

The question as to whether Christ might have been born a woman was raised by medieval theologians. The conclusion—that it was most fitting that Christ be born a man—was never in doubt, yet the structures of argumentation are worth noting. Some, like Peter Lombard, argue from *complementarity* (one sex to counterbalance the other), so that while Christ *could* have been born a woman, it was "more appropriate that He was born of a woman and assumed a male body in order to show Christ's liberation of both sexes from sin."[4] Albert the Great, on the other hand, argued from *symmetry* (same sex amends for same): death, while introduced by a woman, was really propagated by a man (Adam) and so should be overcome by a man.[5] Bonaventure hazards the opinion that, since women are more sunk in wretchedness Christ might have come as a woman to indicate the extent of his charity. However, over and against this (and determinative of his conclusion), he argues that since Christ is fertile and the source of regeneration he should be male, for carnal generation comes from the male.

The belief that only males are truly generative appears in odd corners of theological history. It is invoked by both Anselm and Aquinas to explain why the persons of the (immanent) Trinity, while without sexual difference, are best styled as Father and Son and not as Mother and Daughter. But this belief is biological rather than doctrinal, for, according to the received biology of their time, the female is passive in generation and contributes only the matter to the growing embryo. Only the male bears the seed; only the male is truly creative and thus, so the argument goes, the First Person, as Unoriginate Origin, is best signified by masculine pronouns and as Father. To summarize this now counter-intuitive and biologically defeated chain of argument—women cannot fully signify God because only men can create new life.[6]

The *Summa Theologiae,* however, summarizes by far the most common argument why Christ should be born a man (admittedly in a section that may not be the work of Aquinas himself): "because the male excels the female sex, Christ assumed a man's nature." He adds: "So that people should not think little of the female sex, it was fitting that he should take flesh from a woman" (ST3a. 31, 4).

We find comments in a similar vein as recently as 1978. Here is the former Anglican Bishop of London, Graham Leonard:

> I believe that…Christ was incarnate as a male…not because of social conditioning, but because in the order of creation headship and authority is symbolically and fundamentally associated with maleness. For the same reason the highest vocation of any created being was given to a woman, Mary, as representative of mankind in our response to God because symbolically and fundamentally, the response of sacrificial giving is associated with femaleness.[7]

This puts gendered symbolism at the heart of Christology and of Christian ontology as well.

To recapitulate, the question of Christ's significance for women today seems at first sight easy to resolve, but on closer inspection reveals a network of symbolic associations that can far less obviously be reworked to suit modern sensibilities.[8] Thus, many feminist theologians agree with Rosemary Radford Ruether that the doctrine of Christ, while meant to be the most comprehensive statement of our hopes, a doctrine "that embraces the authentic humanity and fulfilled hopes of all persons," has nonetheless been the doctrine "most fully used to exclude women from full participation in the Christian Church."[9] The maleness of Jesus, *simpliciter,* is not the problem. Few, I think, share the curiously literalistic opinion that a male Christ cannot be a "role model" for women. (What, exactly, does it mean to say that Jesus is a role model for men?) Rather, as Elizabeth Johnson remarks, in Christology, story, symbol, and doctrine are so woven into a patriarchal worldview that it appears one can "unpick" only with great difficulty, if at all.

A number of attempts have been made to convey the New Testament message in other ways, ways that sideline the maleness of Jesus or avoid it entirely. Johnson herself develops a Jesus-Sophia Christology and complements it with accounts of Spirit-Sophia and Mother-Sophia. Rosemary Ruether and Elisabeth Schüssler Fiorenza seem to favor a Christology from below with Jesus as prophet and liberator on the side of the poor and marginalized, among whom most are women. Rita Nakashima Brock occludes the historical figure of Jesus almost entirely in focusing instead on the "Christa community."[10] Daphne Hampson, a self-defined "post-Christian feminist," does not think there is any Christology that is "good" for women. The nub of Christianity, she says, is "whether a Christology can be found of which it may be said that at least it is not incompatible with feminism" (and here she refers to a minimalist definition of feminism as *the proclaimed equality of men and women*).[11] In her opinion, it cannot.

Daphne Hampson's position, although I do not share it, seems to me honest and clear-eyed in a way many are not. It is certainly preferable to the "if your eye offends you pluck it out" strategies of some earlier feminist theology (i.e., if it offends women to call God "Father," then call God "Mother"), strategies that both ignore the symbolic complexity of religious language and show a certain naiveté about what is involved in real religious change.

The difficulty with many feminist retellings of the story of Jesus is that it leaves us with such thin fare. Anything sexist, hierarchical, and violent must go; so gone is talk of fathers, kings, lords, and blood. What we have left is often a genderless Good Figure who (or which) runs the risk of losing all historical particularity, or a jagged and moralizing prophet who loves the poor and about whose life great (but usually patriarchal) stories have been spun. It is paradoxical that feminist theologies, which so often stress particularity and embodiment, sometimes end up with a featureless and disembodied Christ.[12]

Classical Christology appears as one of those groundweeds whose root systems are so interconnected that uprooting any of it involves digging over the whole garden. Indeed we should pause to reflect on the remarkable agreement between so-called conservatives and post-Christian radicals on this matter, the former insisting that any flexibility in gender symbolism would amount to ontological violence, and the latter that, by virtue of its fixed and destructive gendered symbolism, Christianity is irredeemably sexist and can only be discarded.

THE ASSUMPTIONS

Yet it is precisely this issue of the symbolics of sex on which I wish to focus. A number of premises seem to be shared by the "antifeminist" position and the "post-Christian feminist" positions sketched above. The first is that religious symbols are static, both across historical theology and across the diversity of the biblical texts themselves; so, for instance, terms such as 'father' have one fixed cultural meaning. A second is that gender categories are constant across cultures and historical periods, and a third is that gender symbolisms are always tied in fixed ways to the biological sexes. All these assumptions are questionable.

A closer examination of the history of Christian theology discloses a happily diverse appropriation of sexed symbols, often used disruptively when speaking of God in order to free us from any idolatrous assumption that God is male or female. Gregory of Nyssa was happy to take verse 3:11 of the Song of Songs, "Daughters of Zion come and see King Solomon, wearing the diadem with which his mother crowned him on his wedding day" as referring to Christ (King Solomon) and God the Father (his mother). He explains, "No one can adequately grasp the terms pertaining to God. For example, 'mother' is mentioned in place of 'father.' Both terms mean the same, because the divine is neither male nor female. . . ."[13] Such a healthy flexibility in matters symbolic would go far in freeing the contemporary gridlock on Christ and gender, which often leaves Christians feeling that they must either deny the problem or discard the faith.

THE APPLICATION: BLOOD AND DEFILEMENT

How might this look in application? How can we discern the feminine in the story of Christ? I suggest that we might begin with the cross. Those familiar with feminist theology may find this odd. After all, feminist theologians have frequently singled out the atonement doctrine as a particular source of outrage, with penal theories of atonement and Jesus as sacrificial victim on the cross as most offensive of all.[14] The idea that God asks the death of his own Son has been compared more than once to child abuse. In short, the cross with its blood and death has not been much the focus of positive feminist reconstruction. But can any Christian ignore the cross? Is this really the place where, symbolically, we see only a brutal father demanding the life of a passive son?

In her book *In the Beginning Was Love,* Julia Kristeva gives an account of her understanding of the psychoanalytic task and uses overtly theological language to do so.[15] Noting Freud's insistence that the foundation of his cure is "Our God Logos," she describes psychoanalysis as about making word and flesh meet—making the word become flesh in a discourse of love directed to an "impossible other." These comments are developed by means of a discussion of the Apostles' Creed. Kristeva, writing as an analyst, not a theologian, notes that in the Genesis narratives God creates by separating. Separation is the mark of God's presence: the separation of light and dark, heavens and earth, sea and dry land, male and female. And this dividing and separating reach a climax in the Christian story with the crucifixion, the desertion of Christ on the cross, and the cry of dereliction. (To add my own theological gloss, this is the separation of God from God.) Yet it is because one is deserted, Kristeva suggests, that one may achieve ecstasy in completion and reunion with the father, who, she adds, is "himself a substitution for the mother."[16]

A striking feature of Kristeva's psychoanalytic/philosophical reading is the suggestion that the symbolic weight of this Christian narrative is to reestablish fusion with the Other, who is both maternal and paternal. ("So God created man in his own image, in the image of God he created him, male and female he created them.") The theologian is bound to reflect that the cross is, by tradition, simultaneously the place of death and of birth, of abjection and the emergence of new life. Death and birth come together—an obvious scriptural reflection born out by the Eastern liturgies—yet, because commonplace, often stale and neglected.

We need to recall those ancient and venerable traditions in which the blood and water that flowed from Christ's side on the cross were taken as emblematic of human birth. Medieval religious art was often explicit in its representation of the crucifixion as childbirth. We see the church (*ecclesia*) being pulled from Christ's wounded side as Eve was pulled from Adam's. More commonly we see the blood flowing from the side of Christ into chalices born by angels or flowing directly into the mouths of the faithful; this is, figuratively, the eucharistic blood on which believers feed, and by which feeding they become one with the body of Christ. While the iconography is familiar, we need to give weight to the overtly female nature of the imagery; the symbolic identification, that is, of the crucified Christ with the human female body, both in giving birth and in feeding. Caroline Walker Bynum has done much to bring this identification as it was made in medieval piety to our attention. The identification of women with the physicality of Christ was especially strong between the twelfth and fifteenth centuries. During this period in the West, women were thought by both men and women to be more physical creatures than men, and while frequently the basis for their disparagement, and even for misogyny, this greater physicality was also the way in which women were held to be closer to Christ, the physical side of God.[17]

The human body, or the concept of such, has a history. Ideas about the relationship of body and mind, of maleness and femaleness, conceptions of self and physical substance change. For instance, in the medieval period there was a sense in which everyone was thought to be male (since, following Aristotle, the female was a defective male) as well as female (since the soul is female to God). Sexual imagery, in its broadest sense, was both more pervasive and more fluid in Christian devotional writing than it has been in the modern period. A male mystic like Bernard of Clairvaux could understand himself in female images, as a bride to God and as a mother to his monks. F. Schleiermacher in the nineteenth century could wish he had been born a woman in order that he might know the world affectively (as he thought, according to romantic essentialism, women "naturally" did). Bernard in the twelfth century could affectively "be" female while not for a moment compromising his actual masculinity, for the gendered qualities associated with the two sexes were not rigidly attached to either.

The stylization of Jesus as mother in the medieval period has not only to do with psychological aspects of maternal nurturing, as modern treatments tend to be, but also with the physical side of what mothers do—bleed and feed. Bynum writes:

> As all medievalists are by now aware, the body of Christ was sometimes depicted as female in medieval devotional texts— partly, of course, because *ecclesia*, Christ's body, was a female personification, partly because the tender, nurturing aspect of God's care for souls was regularly described as motherly. Both male and female mystics called Jesus "mother" in his eucharistic feeding of Christians with liquid exuded from his breast and in his bleeding on the Cross which gave birth to our hope of eternal life.[18]

Some of these devotions seem repugnant to the modern mind. Catherine of Siena is sometimes represented nursing at Christ's breast, sometimes as feeding at his side, blood and milk interchangeable.[19] These assumptions "associated female and flesh with the body of God. Not only was Christ enfleshed with flesh from a woman; his own flesh did womanly things; it bled, it bleed food and it gave birth to new life."[20]

But this same nexus of imagery—blood death, birth, food, milk—is of greater antiquity than Bynum indicates. John Chrysostom draws on it in his *Third Baptismal Instruction,* once again in connection with John 19:34:

> But the symbols of baptism and mysteries (Eucharist) come from the side of Christ. It is from His side, therefore, that Christ formed His church, just as He formed Eve from the side of Adam....
> Have you seen how Christ unites to Himself his bride? Have you seen with what food He nurtures us all? Just as a woman nurtures her offspring with her own blood and milk, so also Christ continuously nurtures with His own blood those whom He has begotten.[21]

Here the bridegroom feeds his spouse with his own blood and milk— a good example of what Paul Ricoeur calls the "mutual contamination" of metaphors, where the text deliberately violates a simple reading in order to frustrate an overly literalistic reading.

We can indeed take this imagery of blood and birth right back to the New Testament itself, to John 19 and elsewhere in the Johannine writings. Teresa Okure, in an essay entitled "The Significance Today of Jesus' Commission to Mary Magdalene," draws our attention not so much to the fact of Christ's postresurrection commissioning a woman (often remarked), but rather to the specific nature of the commission (often overlooked). The Johannine Jesus says, "[G]o and tell my brothers and say to them, 'I am ascending to my Father and your Father, to my God and your God'" (Jn 20:17). This is the first time in John's Gospel that the disciples are told that the Father of Jesus is to be their Father too. At the Last Supper they are named as friends and not slaves, and now, with Mary's message, they are told "that they and Jesus now share the same parent...in God. They are in truth brothers and sisters of Jesus in God in much the same way as children related who share the same father and mother.... Only now does Jesus make his Father and God in the full sense the Father and God of his disciples."[22]

This revelation of the new family takes the reader back to the Prologue, where the believers are styled not only as children of God but as being born of God. It is such a birth Nicodemus is told he must have (Jn 3:1–21) to have eternal life.[23] This birth, Okure adds, has been "brought about by Jesus' passion, death and resurrection," and through his pierced side on the cross.

The commission to Mary Magdalene then tells primarily not of the resurrection but of the new family, the new kinship relations for the followers of Jesus. Jesus' words to Mary, "my God and your God," echo the words of Ruth to Naomi (Ruth 1:16), precisely at that juncture where the demands of patrilineage are put aside in favor of a family bound by faith.

Okure's conclusions are interesting in their own right and all the more so from an African New Testament scholar with a stated nearness to images of blood, kin, and birth, for she emphasizes that her own African understanding of such things make these Johannine associations resonant for her. The blood of kinship, she says, "is the blood of the ancestors and ancestresses who are always alive.... If this is true of human blood," she continues, "should it not be more so of the blood of

Christ which has given birth and life to us all as children of God, and which continues to nourish us daily through the eucharist?"[24]

The symbolics of blood and the cross, it would seem, are by no means restricted to punitive and penal readings. Indeed other readings, notably that of blood, birth, and kin, are not only present within historical theology but may well afford better ways into the New Testament texts whose kinship patterns are nearer to those of medieval Europe than of the modern West. Birth as well as death is a type of sacrificial giving. As far as my original plea for flexibility goes, it should be apparent that the symbolic orderings of Christianity are neither obvious nor unchanging. Similarly it is by no means clear that Christ is always and everywhere in the symbolic order a "male" figure. There is abundant sense in seeing Christ as our mother, and his blood as the source of new life—indeed by doing so we recover a proud heritage of patristic theology.[25]

So blood is the source of life. But is it not also the case that in the Bible female blood is a source of impurity and defilement? As the Jewish scholar Leonie Archer has pointed out, Levitical purity laws affected women particularly. Rulings on the impurities caused by female blood (whether of menstruation, childbirth, or irregular flows) were part of an "all-pervasive blood taboo" that covered foods and sacrifice and effected separations of the sexes.[26] Although both sexes were affected by the laws concerning bodily emissions, in both Levitical law and the common Judaism of Jesus' time women were a far greater source of contagion than men. Women were impure after childbirth, and the impurity lasted longer if the child was female. The birth of a male child resulted in forty days of childbirth impurity, a daughter resulted in eighty. Whereas contact with semen resulted in impurity for one day, menstruants "were impure for a week, and anyone who touched a menstruant, her bed or chair was impure for a day."[27] Through many Christian centuries, and still in some quarters, menstruation and irregular bleeding were seen as defiling and as grounds for exclusion from eucharistic reception. How can one compare, as we did in the previous section, the blood of Christ to the blood of women?

The obvious point in the New Testament at which to explore the symbolism of female blood is the story of the healing of the woman with the hemorrhage (Mark 5:21–43; Matt 9:18–34; Luke 8:40–56), yet when discussed, curiously little is made of the major theme of impurity and defilement that runs through it. Contemporary preachers (and many commentators) are far more likely to focus on the healing that takes place and on the woman's faith. Even when the issue of female impurity is raised, the tendency of the typical Western Christian (and here I include the typical Western Christian feminist) is resolutely Marcionite. Even those who otherwise go out of their way to reach out to Jewish brothers and sisters quickly respond to this story by saying that the Jewish law of purity was a nonsense and that Jesus, being wise, knew this to be so. Yet, even apart from the offense to Jews, so easy and brutal a resolution is not acceptable in terms of modern New Testament scholarship. Jesus did not dismiss the law.

The modern Christian reader then seems stuck between the Scylla of misogyny and the Charybdis of anti-Judaism. New Testament critics deploy a number of strategies. Elisabeth Schüssler Fiorenza largely skirts the issue of impurity by focusing on the woman's illness, isolation, and inferred poverty (she "had spent all that she had"). Gerd Theissen and many others focus almost entirely on the woman's faith, drawing attention to the fact that the story of the woman with the hemorrhage is the only miracle story apart from that of the Stilling the Storm in which all three Synoptics talk about faith. In the woman's "unspoken confidence...that Jesus can absorb her disease with being endangered himself," says Theissen, we see "a faith which incorporates and transcends even the ambivalent and illegitimate."[28] But if we are to consider these stories not as simple observer reportage but as theologically motivated,[29] we must admit the possibility that the precise nature of the woman's illness is *not irrelevant.* The Gospel writers have, after all, gone out of their way in all three Synoptics, to identify her ailment as irregular bleeding. If this were irrelevant to the story, it would be more seemly to say simply that she had been ill for twelve years.

Jesus, you will remember, is on his way to heal Jairus's daughter when the woman with the flow touches his robes. The Synoptic accounts differ in details, but in all three the woman is immediately cured. In Mark and Luke Jesus asks who has touched him, and the woman comes before him "in fear and trembling." Jesus says to her, "Daughter, your faith has made you well; go in peace, and be healed of your disease" (Mark 5:34). Jesus calls the woman "daughter" in all three accounts.

We can ask questions in more than one theological register about such a story. One can and should, for instance, ask some "historical Jesus" questions: Was Jesus, in terms of contemporary Judaism, potentially defiled by her touch? Did this affect only Temple purity and, if so, what might this suggest about attitudes to Temple purity, and so on? But for the purposes of christological reflection, we can see the Gospels, too, as already theological constructions, perhaps already christological constructions, with deliberate symbolic and associative links.

Interpretations that, like Theissen's, put virtually the whole emphasis on the woman's faith are reductive. His own displays a hermeneutical disposition to see faith as the crucial explanatory motif in the miracle stories. The suggestion that the woman has an "unspoken confidence" that Jesus can absorb her disease without endangering himself does not explain adequately why the woman came "in fear and trembling" (Mark and Luke) when confronted. She is represented as believing she would be healed if she touched Jesus' garment, but as uncertain of the wider consequences.

One explanation sometimes given for her fear is that, apart from behaving presumptuously, she fears she will have defiled the teacher in touching him.[30] Difficulties attend this reading. Is it an insight into the woman's presumed psychology? Would the crowd have known of her ailment? And so on. Added to this, Charlotte Fonrobert has argued that, in the masoretic text, a *zavah* (a woman with an irregular or extended blood flow) *does not* transfer impurity by touching someone.[31] These matters taken into consideration, it seems enough to say that the woman was in a state of impurity (which, if not culpable, is isolating) and also of disorder—unlike a normal flow, her blood was flowing to no purpose. Its flow precluded rather than foresaw the possibility of new life.

Theissen gives little weight to the placing of the story of the woman with the hemorrhage. But in all three Synoptics the story of the woman with the flow is contained within that of Jairus's daughter, not so obviously a story of faith. But what *more* might this placing suggest? Again, the commentaries are strangely silent. On the narrative level it seems that more than one feature links the two miracles. The woman has had the flow of blood for twelve years; the daughter of Jairus is twelve years old—the age at which Jewish girls were judged nubile. The woman with the flow is impure and infertile; Jesus risks defilement by entering a house that he is told contains a corpse and by touching the corpse/girl. The woman with the flow is made whole and (presumably) once again fertile by her healing and is called "daughter"; the daughter of Jairus is declared not dead but "sleeping" and rises to enter womanly life. Both stories have elements of defilement and "death," and of fecundity and new life.

Apart from the exhortation to faith, another shared feature of the Synoptic stories of the Stilling of the Storm is the questions the disciples ask: "Who then is this, that even the wind and the sea obey him?" The power to control the waves is, in the psalms, attributed to the Creator:

> Then they cried to the Lord in their trouble,
> and he brought them out of their distress;
> he made the storm be still,
> and the waves of the sea were hushed. (Ps 107:28–29)

In stilling the storm Jesus appears to participate in the creative power of God, as he does in the stories of the healing of the woman with the hemorrhage and of Jairus's daughter. In these, fertility, wholeness, and "peace" are restored, as befits one who is to fulfill the promises of Isaiah. In these stories Jesus displays a power over illness, infertility, and death emblematic of a new creation. To recapitulate, on this christological reading the story of the woman with the hemorrhage need have nothing to do with a dismissal by Jesus of Jewish purity laws. The woman has not necessarily transgressed in touching him, nor in milling with the crowd.[32] She is, however, isolated in her impurity and isolated in a different way by her infertility. It is possible then that the story does not dismiss purity laws or ignore them, but rather calls us back to the primal meaning of the Jewish laws surrounding blood and the flow of female blood. As Jewish women grow weary of pointing out, this "impurity" or "defilement" has nothing to do with sinfulness and a great deal to do with holiness—the holiness of birth and blood and life. The woman is in an excluded position by virtue of a bleeding that should betoken fertility but which in her case does not yield life.

Why might the Gospel writers wish to put these two female figures, the woman with the flow and Jairus's daughter, in symbolic alignment to Jesus? Early Christian legend and art identified the figure of the woman with the hemorrhage with the figure of St. Veronica, the historically shadowy figure whose cloth, on wiping the brow of Christ, was imprinted with the "true icon" (thus "veronica"). The blood of the flow is in this telling linked with the passion of Christ.[33] As the cloth of Christ's garment stopped the flow of the woman's blood, so Veronica's cloth stops the flow of Christ's blood. As the woman's flow of blood is stopped and her fertility restored (she is made fertile with faith), so Christ's flow of blood is turned from death to "new life." This ancient pairing of the woman with the flow with Veronica suggests an exegesis of the Synoptic story that is not concerned with "unclean female bodies," nor with dismissal of the Law.[34] Rather we are drawn back to the life-giving power of female blood—a power that the Jewish purity laws reflect and that this reading aligns with the blood shed on the cross. Once again, the blood of the cross is mapped on the symbolics of the feminine.

> The idiom of pollution lends itself to a complex algebra...[35]

> Blood, indicating the impure,...inherits the propensity for murder of which man must cleanse himself. But blood, as a vital element, also refers to women, fertility, and the assurance of fecundation. It thus becomes a fascinating semantic crossroads, the propitious place for abjection *where death* and *femininity, murder* and *procreation, cessation of life* and *vitality* all come together. "But flesh with the life thereof, which is the blood thereof, shall ye not eat" (Genesis 9:4).[36]

> Everyone who believes that Jesus is the Christ has been born of God, and everyone who loves the parent loves the child. By this we know that we love the children of God, when we love God and obey his commandments.... And his commandments are not burdensome, for whatever is born of God conquers the world.... Who is it that conquers the world but the one who believes that Jesus is the Son of God? This is the one who came by water and blood, Jesus Christ, not with the water only but with the water and the blood. (1 John 5:1–6)

The symbolism of the New Testament texts is constantly disruptive. Leviticus prohibits the eating of blood, yet the central Christian rite involves drinking blood. In Leviticus childbirth is defiling, yet John's Gospel describes God as giving birth to the chosen. In Levitical terms a corpse radiates impurity, especially for priests. In Christianity the central icon of holiness, of the Great High Priest, is a dead man on the cross.[37] The symbolism of blood is deep within the texts of Christianity and does not abandon its Jewish ancestry or dismiss it; it is rather inexplicable without it. Blood is holy; it is the life of the animal. And if one claims to be fed on the blood of God? Furthermore, the subversion of symbols, the turning, for instance, from shame and exclusion to glory, does not mark a departure from Jewish hermeneutics but is in continuity with it. In the New Testament, as in the Hebrew Scriptures, symbolic orders are constantly challenged, broken open, and renewed. It is this inversion of our human expectations that keeps us open to what God might newly, freely choose to do.

Notes

Scripture citations are given according to the Jerusalem Bible.

1. Ann Carr, *Transforming Grace: Christian Tradition and Women's Experience* (New York: HarperCollins, 1988), 16.

2. Athanasius, *De Incarnatione,* trans. Robert W. Thomson (Oxford: Oxford University Press, 1971), section 9. The Greek noun here is *anthrōpos.*

3. Cited in Elizabeth A. Clark, *Women in the Early Church* (Wilmington, Del.: Michael Glazier, 1983), 35.

4. Joan Gibson, "Could Christ Have Been Born a Woman?" in *Journal of Feminist Studies in Religion* 8, no. 1 (spring 1992): 69.

5. Ibid., 71–72. Gibson says that Albert, not Aquinas, was the first to introduce the Aristotelian argument that "a woman is a defective man, and...since Christ ought to represent perfection, not an imperfection of nature, He should be incarnate as a man."

6. I discuss this at greater length in "Trinity and the 'Feminine Other,'" *New Blackfriars* 75 (January 1994): 2–17.

7. Cited in Daphne Hampson, *Theology and Feminism* (Oxford: Blackwell, 1990), 66. See also the remarks on Hans Urs von Balthasar on p. 67. See also Manfred Hauke, *Women in the Priesthood? A Systematic Analysis in the Light of the Order of Creation* (San Francisco: Ignatius, 1988).

8. I have dealt elsewhere with the difficult question of whether the divine name of "Father" can be discarded in "Can a Feminist Call God 'Father'?" in *Women's Voices in Religion,* ed. Teresa Elwes (London: Collins/ Marshall Pickering, 1992), 15–29, 159–61.

9. Rosemary Radford Ruether, "The Liberation of Christology from Patriarchy," *New Blackfriars* 66 (July–August 1985): 324–35; 66 (November 1985): 503–4; 67 (February 1986): 92–93. See also Elizabeth Johnson, *She Who Is* (New York: Crossroad, 1993), 151; Carr, *Transforming Grace,* 178, and Hampson, *Theology and Feminism,* chapter 2. I note that, with the exception of Hampson, all these writers are Roman Catholics, which may reflect my reading list, but may also be of wider significance.

10. Rita Nakashima Brock, *Journeys by Heart: A Christology of Erotic Power* (New York: Crossroad, 1988).

11. Hampson, *Theology and Feminism,* 50.

12. This is especially true of Brock's work, which, despite its acutely physical title, supplants the physicality of Jesus entirely in its focus on the "Christa community."

13. Gregory of Nyssa, *Commentary on the Song of Songs,* cited in

Verna Harrison, "Male and Female in Cappadocian Theology," JTS 41, no. 2 (October 1990): 441. Admittedly Gregory also believes "male" and "female" to be a transitory (this-worldly) feature of human beings as well, unlike Augustine, who insists that the dead will be raised as women and men.

14. "Images of Jesus as sacrificial victim and of his sacrificial love and self-surrender on the cross, shown by Mary Daly and Judith Plaskow as destructive for women, are among the most difficult for feminist Christians" (Carr, *Transforming Grace,* 174).

15. Julia Kristeva, *In the Beginning Was Love: Psychoanalysis and Faith* (New York/Guilford: Columbia University Press, 1987).

16. Ibid., 32.

17. Caroline Walker Bynum, "The Female Body and Religious Practice in the Later Middle Ages," in *Fragmentation and Redemption* (New York: Zone Books, 1991), 181–238.

18. Ibid., 176.

19. We need recall that medieval biologists believed breast milk to be a transmuted form of the blood that nourished the fetus in the womb, which is not an unreasonable conjecture since in breast-feeding menstruation is suppressed (ibid., 182).

20. Ibid., 185.

21. John Chrysostom, *Baptismal Instructions,* ed. and trans. Paul Harkins, Ancient Christian Writers (New York: Paulist, 1963), 62. It is worth noting that Karl Rahner's successful doctoral thesis, after the rejection of *Geist in Welt,* was on the image of the birth of the church from the side of Christ in patristic thought.

22. Teresa Okure, "The Significance Today of Jesus' Commission to Mary Magdalene," *International Review of Mission* 81, no. 322 (April 1992): 182.

23. Ibid., 183.

24. Ibid., 186.

25. Graham Leonard may have a point in saying that "sacrificial giving is associated with femaleness." Where his remarks are theologically suspect is in their symbolic alignment of this "giving" with Mary/church *over and against Christ,* and in his failure to see as clearly as did the medievals that the primary Christian locus of this giving must be Christ. All good Marian theology rests on this. See n. 7 above.

26. Leonie Archer, "Bound by Blood: Circumcision and Menstrual Taboo," in *After Eve,* ed. Janet Martin Soskice (London: Marshall Pickering, 1990), 43.

27. E. P. Sanders, *Judaism* (London: SCM, 1992), 72. See also his *Jewish Law from Jesus to the Mishnah* (London: SCM, 1990), 142ff.

28. Gerd Theissen, *Miracle Stories of the Early Christian Tradition* (Edinburgh: T & T Clark, 1983), 134.

29. That is, minimally, to say that the Gospel writers have chosen to describe this particular incident and have done so for a reason. I do not wish to imply, in saying that the Gospels are literary constructions, that they are therefore literary fictions. A history of the Second World War can be a literary construction without being a fiction.

30. Elisabeth Schüssler Fiorenza notes "…this woman's predicament was not just incurable illness but also permanent uncleanness. She was not only unclean herself, but polluted everyone and everything with which she came into contact (Lev 15:19–31)." *In Memory of Her: A Feminist Theological Reconstruction of Christian Origins* (New York: Crossroad, 1983), 124. Another interpretation put forward is that Jesus' power heals her before any defilement takes place.

31. Charlotte Fonrobert, "The Woman with a Blood-flow (Mark 5:24–34) Revisited: Menstrual Laws and Jewish Culture in Christian Feminist Hermeneutics," in *Early Christian Interpretation of the Scriptures of Israel*, ed. Craig A. Evans and James A. Sanders, Journal for the Study of the New Testament Supplement Series 148 (Sheffield: Sheffield Academic Press, 1997), 130–31.

32. Fonrobert is critical of M. Selvidge on this point. I take Fonrobert to have made a good case for saying that the story is not concerned with an "abrogation of biblical traditions concerning menstruation and irregular discharges of blood" (p. 135), but believe she is on less solid ground in this article in suggesting that it is only important that the woman had a severe illness and that the nature of the illness is of no account. My suggestion is that the nature of the disorder is material to the narrative.

33. See Ewa Kurykuk, *Veronica and Her Cloth: History, Symbolism, and Structure of a "True" Image* (Oxford: Basil Blackwell, 1991), 7. See especially the introduction and chapters 5 and 6.

34. The idea that menstrual flow is in itself unclean in a repugnant (rather than ritual) sense Fonrobert sees as a distinctly Christian development and is, as she notes, ambiguously inconsistent. If in Christ the law has been abolished, then the law can no longer be the reason why Christian women are enjoined not to "approach the holy table" as they were in some traditions. Unlike the Jewish situation, that latter, distinctly Christian exclusion is, she suggests, the result of Western (and Greek) contempt for the body, especially the female body ("Women with a Blood-flow," 137).

35. Mary Douglas, *Purity and Danger* (New York: Praeger, 1966), 9.

36. Julia Kristeva, "The Semiotics of Biblical Abomination," in *Powers of Horror: An Essay on Abjection,* trans. Leon S. Roudiez (New York: Columbia University Press, 1982), 96.

37. See L. William Countryman, *Dirt, Greed and Sex* (Philadelphia: Fortress, 1988), and also a fascinating article by Timothy Radcliffe, O.P., "Christ in Hebrews: Cultic Irony," *New Blackfriars* 68 (November 1987), 494–504.

18. John Hick and the Historical Jesus

Paul R. Eddy

For years now, Father Gerald O'Collins has devoted significant energy to explicating and defending a historic orthodox understanding of Jesus Christ. In a recent article, "The Incarnation Under Fire," Father O'Collins responds to the work of John Hick, one of the most able and ardent contemporary critics of traditional incarnational Christology.[1] It is the purpose of this essay to complement Father O'Collins's engagement with Hick's work from a historic orthodox perspective. Specifically, I shall begin by briefly charting Hick's christological pilgrimage, from his early evangelical convictions through to his current pluralistic "inspiration" Christology. Finally, I will offer a summary discussion of some recent work in historical Jesus studies that call into question certain pillars of Hick's liberal "neo-Arian" pluralist Christology. It is my privilege to offer this essay in honor of Father Gerald O'Collins, S.J., a mentor and a friend.

JOHN HICK'S CHRISTOLOGICAL ODYSSEY

The British philosopher of religion John Hick is arguably the most influential exponent of the pluralist approach to religious diversity in the Western academic world today.[2] As a Christian theologian, he is at the forefront of contemporary efforts to re-vision and revise traditional Christian dogmas that would seem to conflict with a pluralist interpretation of human religious life. However, Hick has not always been a proponent of revisionist Christologies. In fact, for many years he was an ardent defender of a Chalcedonian form of Christology. Hick's christological pilgrimage is instructive on several counts, not least of which is the way it highlights the complex web of relationships between religio-philosophical presuppositions and theological conclusions.

Hick's christological pilgrimage can be traced from the early 1940s. At this point, following a profound conversion to an evangelical Christianity, Hick held to "Jesus as God the Son incarnate, born of a virgin, conscious of his divine nature, and performing miracles of divine power; redemption by his blood from sin and guilt; his bodily resurrection and ascension and future return in glory...."[3] Within a decade, he had moved to a decidedly "neo-orthodox" perspective. At this time, Hick still sees his theology as essentially tipped toward the "right."[4] With regard to Christology, Hick is still well within the range of a generally conservative perspective: "...the task of any Christology which intends to serve the historic faith of the ecumenical creeds is to illumine for modern man the conception of the deity of Christ—or, more cumbrously, of the substantival as distinguished from the adjectival divinity of Christ."[5] In fact, in a 1958 article, Hick analyzes D. M. Baillie's "paradox of grace" Christology and judges that this "adoptionist"-like Christology fails since it "does not perform the central Christological task of giving meaning to the dogma of the deity of Christ."[6]

At this same time, however, Hick recognized the problematic nature of the "static," substantival expression of the incarnation traditionally associated with Chalcedon and the *homoousion* formula. Thus, in 1959 he published an article in which he attempted to restate the dogma of the incarnation in a nonsubstantival—and yet dogmatically faithful—manner, using the dynamic category of *agapē*.[7] In Hick's words:

> The incarnation was, so to speak, a temporal cross-section of God's *Agape*.... We want to say of Jesus that he was "wholly God" in the sense that his *agape* was genuinely the *Agape* of God at work on earth, but not that he was "the whole of God" in the sense that the divine *Agape* was expressed without remainder in each or even in the sum of his actions.... Jesus' *agape* is not a representation of God's *agape*; it is that *Agape* operating in a finite mode; it is the eternal divine *Agape* made flesh, inhistorised.[8]

And so, by making use of the biblical notion of agapē, Hick proposes what he believes to be a more contemporarily relevant way of stating what has always been at the center of the Christian faith—the dogma of the incarnation of Jesus Christ.

The 1960s brought a distinct and self-conscious "liberal" turn in Hick's theology. Not surprisingly, various aspects of Hick's Christology underwent significant development at this time. For example, the traditional notion that Christ's death on the cross provides atonement and redemption is now classified as "myth."[9] Thus, the historic Christian understanding of the atonement as cosmically redemptive in an objective sense is exchanged for the view that the function of Jesus' death was primarily to manifest God's self-giving love.

In spite of his theological turn to the left, Hick continued to regard "the divinity of Christ," as expressed in his *agapē* Christology, as central to his theology.[10] In his 1966 essay "Christology at the Crossroads," Hick once again presents his *agapē* incarnational Christology. The majority of the article is given to arguing against a "neo-Arian"—or "degree"—and for a "neo-Chalcedonian" Christology. Yet, in the midst of an attempt to champion the historic understanding of the incarnation, the article ends on a christologically foreboding note: "But…if we make this Chalcedonian claim today we shall have to face the problem which it now brings with it in ever-increasing force: what does this claim imply concerning the other religions of the world? And do the facts of history permit us to believe what it implies?"[11]

At the heart of the problem raised by the Chalcedonian claim "lies the question of the uniqueness of Christ." It is in this sense, Hick writes, that "Christology stands…at the crossroads."[12]

The early 1970s brought Hick's move to a pluralist theology of religions. Initially, it was Hick's desire to somehow retain a place within the pluralist paradigm for both a literal incarnation and the (at least relative) uniqueness of Jesus.[13] However, Jesus' status as the literal incarnation of God's love did not long survive the new pluralist atmosphere. In his 1973 *God and the Universe of Faiths,* Hick develops his "incarnation as myth" thesis. Understood mythically, the Christian claim that Jesus is God (or, with Hick, God's *agapē*) incarnate

> cannot apply *literally* to Jesus. But as a poetic image—which is powerfully evocative even though it conveys no literal meaning—it expresses the religious significance of Jesus in a way that has proved effective for nearly two millennia. It thus fulfills its

function, which is to evoke an appropriate response of faith in Jesus…. The myth is thus an appropriate and valid expression of the experience [of one's having encountered God through Jesus].[14]

At this point, Hick offers three primary lines of argument that remain to this day at the core of his critique of a literal incarnation. First, drawing upon contemporary New Testament and historical Jesus studies, Hick argues that "almost certainly Jesus himself did not teach that he was God incarnate."[15] Second, Hick proposes that one can trace the genesis and development of the notion of the incarnation in the early church up through the fourth century, along with the purely human concerns that motivated it. Finally, Hick contends that the mythological nature of incarnational language is betrayed in the fact that every attempt to explain it on a philosophical level reveals it to be nothing short of logically incoherent (i.e., "a self-contradiction," on the same logical par as "the idea of a square circle") and thus literally meaningless.[16] Taken together, these three considerations provided the supporting arguments for Hick's rejection of a literal incarnation.

Hick continued to declare and develop his "incarnation as myth" thesis throughout the 1970s and into the early 1980s.[17] Over a period of three years during the mid-1970s, Hick met with six other scholars to discuss the path toward a reconstruction of the traditional understanding of the incarnation. The results of this collaborative venture, edited by Hick, were published in 1977 as the controversial work *The Myth of God Incarnate*. In this volume, Hick offers his own perspective in an essay entitled "Jesus and the World Religions." Here, Hick clearly expresses the problem posed by the incarnation: "Transposed into theological terms, the problem which has come to the surface in the encounter of Christianity with the other world religions is this: If Jesus was literally God incarnate, and if it is by his death alone that men can be saved, and by their response to him alone that they can appropriate that salvation, then the only doorway to eternal life is Christian faith."[18] The very suggestion that Christian faith might be the "only doorway to eternal life" is, of course, anathema to the pluralist paradigm—ergo, the incarnation must be relativized. By 1977, Hick's pluralist Christology was rounded out when he finally dropped the last sentimental vestiges of what had become merely the hollow shell of traditional "substantival" incarnation language and adopted the very "adjectival"/"degree" Christology he had rejected for so many years.

In a 1977 letter to the editors of the journal *Theology*, Hick writes: "Incarnation then becomes a matter of degree: God is incarnate in all men in so far as they are Spirit-filled, or Christ-like, or truly saintly."[19]

Throughout the 1980s, Hick worked diligently to develop and defend his pluralist hypothesis. During this decade he decisively proposed his well-known neo-Kantian solution to the perennial pluralist problem of conflicting religious conceptions of the divine.[20] The 1980s also brought further christological reflection from a pluralist perspective. Four points are worth noting. First, beginning in the very early 1980s, Hick began to consistently cite the work of Donald Baillie and Geoffrey Lampe as departure points for his own christological project.[21] Second, the conclusions of Baillie and Lampe serve to set the stage for Hick's own "inspiration" Christology.[22] For Hick, inspiration is simply another way of saying "grace."[23] He is clear on the "kind" versus "degree" question: "Incarnation in this sense has occurred and is occurring in many different ways and degrees in many different persons."[24] In his most critical departure from both Baillie and Lampe, Hick challenges their apparently a priori assumption that the Spirit's connection to Jesus was somehow fuller or more absolute than in anyone else. Third, Hick continued to develop his related critique of the traditional doctrines of the Trinity and the atonement.[25] Finally, Hick added a new line of argument to his critique of traditional Christology. Specifically, he made the charge that, throughout the eighteenth and nineteenth centuries, the type of "religious absolutism" represented by the traditional view had "sanctified violent aggression, exploitation, and intolerance" in the name of Christ.[26] Given the unfortunate role it had played in the expansion of Western imperialism, the traditional christological understanding of a unique and absolute Christ can no longer be justified in our contemporary world.

Throughout the 1990s, Hick devoted much of his time to delineating the implications for Christian theology that follow from his pluralist religious interpretation of religion. The essential core of Hick's "incarnation-as-myth" approach to understanding Jesus has undergone little real change since its genesis in the 1970s. This becomes evident as one compares his early pluralist Christology with his recent (1993) volume devoted to this topic, *The Metaphor of God Incarnate: Christology in a Pluralistic Age.*[27] Hick has described the "main conclusion" of this book as follows: "that the idea of divine incarnation in its standard

Christian form, in which both genuine humanity and genuine deity are insisted upon, has never been given a satisfactory literal sense; but that on the other hand it makes excellent metaphorical sense."[28]

Hick's critique of traditional Chalcedonian incarnational Christology remains largely unaltered. He continues to proffer four primary lines of counterargument. First, neither the teaching nor the apparent experience of the historical Jesus serves to authorize the claim of a literal incarnation.[29] Here, Hick claims to base his judgments upon the "modest but significant area of consensus" among New Testament scholars.[30] Among these consensus points, Hick includes: (1) a hard distinction between the Jesus of actual history and the Jesus presented in the New Testament documents (based on modern historical-critical methodology); (2) Jesus is most fundamentally understood as a first-century Jewish apocalyptic prophet; and (3) Jesus did not understand himself to be "God, or the Son of God incarnate," in fact, he would probably have regarded such a claim as "blasphemous."[31] In short, the history of the traditional incarnation doctrine is largely the history of how a first-century Jewish prophet was progressively "divinized" by his later devotees as certain titles (e.g., "son of God") began to be taken literally (in contrast to the original metaphorical intentions). This religious evolution of the Christ figure is understandable given the surrounding context of the Greco-Roman world, where concepts of "divinity" were quite elastic.[32]

Second, in retrospect, one can trace the historical process by which Jesus came to be thought of as "God," and can fully explain it in terms of human motives, both religious and even political (e.g., the Council of Nicaea). Through this process, "the metaphorical son of God" was transformed into "the metaphysical God the Son, second person of the Trinity."[33]

Third, according to Hick no rendition of the traditional model of "fully God and fully human," taken literally, has ever been shown to be *meaningful*; all attempts to do so err by privileging either the human or divine over the other. It is important to note that, now, Hick's charge against a literal understanding of the incarnation is no longer that it is necessarily logically self-contradictory. Rather, he simply argues that, to date, no attempt to render it "religiously acceptable"—and thus meaningful—has succeeded.[34] Fourth and finally, Hick continues to emphasize that "historically the traditional dogma has been used to justify great human evils."[35]

One will notice that Hick has substituted the term "metaphor" for "myth" in his recent christological proposal. This terminological change does not seem to signal any substantive modification of Hick's thesis. Rather, it appears that he is merely attempting to root his former notion of the incarnation as "myth" in more recent discussions that have focused on the metaphorical nature of language in general, and religious language in particular.[36] Whether or not Hick has been successful here is a matter of debate.[37]

JOHN HICK'S CHRISTOLOGY: THE (W)RIGHT JESUS?

Of Hick's four major arguments against the incarnation, two of them pose little real challenge to the traditional understanding of Jesus. As noted above, Hick himself has moved from charging the idea of a literal incarnation with "self-contradiction" to simply calling into question its "religious acceptability." While Hick may disagree, many scholars have concluded that some form of either a "two minds" or kenotic Christology can adequately answer the conceptual challenges that face a literal understanding of the incarnation.[38] And once this is recognized, one can go on to point out that great throngs of Christians—including philosophically sophisticated Christians—continue to find the idea of a literal incarnation religiously meaningful and significant.

With regard to the argument that the traditional notion of the incarnation fosters religious intolerance, arrogance, and even violence, it is worth noting that Hick himself will admit that there is no necessary connection between exclusive truth-claims and attitudes of religious arrogance and intolerance.[39] In fact, once the observation is made that religious arrogance and intolerance are matters not of truth-claim content, but rather attitudinal orientation, it becomes clear that one is just as likely to find an intolerant, arrogant pluralist as an exclusivist or inclusivist.[40]

It is Hick's last two-part argument—his claims regarding the historical Jesus and early Christianity—that poses the greatest challenge to the historic idea of incarnation. However, these types of arguments have been called into question by certain recent trends in historical

Jesus studies. In particular, the work of N. T. Wright—perhaps the most widely recognized Jesus scholar in the field today—offers an interpretation of the historical data that directly challenges Hick's assessment of the relationships between the historical Jesus, the early church, and traditional Christology. Space considerations prevent me from being able to offer a substantial defense of Wright's approach against opposing perspectives in this essay.[41] However, at the very least, Wright's conclusions present significant challenges to Hick's position, challenges that Hick—and others who hold similar views—will have to address. It is to a summary discussion of Wright's work on the historical Jesus that I will now turn.

There are new methodological winds blowing in the field of historical Jesus research today. Most notable, perhaps, is that represented by N. T. Wright's landmark two-volume study of Jesus.[42] Wright has provided a critique of various approaches in the field today as well as a revised methodology that offers promise. As Wright has noted, much of what goes on in the name of Jesus research today is "largely the projection of an undiscussed metaphysic."[43] In many quarters of the contemporary Quest, unstated and unargued religio-philosophical presuppositions—generally rooted in some variation of a deistic or naturalistic worldview—serve to bracket from serious consideration any historical methodology that deviates from the remains of a naive historical positivism whose day has come and gone.

Wright himself offers a concrete and well-developed alternative, complete with an explicit epistemology. Whether or not one agrees with every detail of his approach, he is to be recognized as one of a growing number of Jesus scholars today who are tracing out a new and fruitful methodological trajectory, one able to integrate serious historical investigation with a worldview that is not held captive to minimalism. This trajectory calls for a revised form-critical approach, one specifically *Jewish* in nature.[44] It is open to the role that "*informal* yet *controlled*" (i.e., a position between R. Bultmann and B. Gerhardsson) oral traditions played in the formation of the gospel tradition, and the implications this holds for questions of reliability.[45] It asks the question: Why not suppose that Jesus himself was at least as theologically creative as the standard form- and redaction-critical approaches assume the evangelists and early church were?[46] Thus, it recognizes that the multiple oral performances that would naturally have arisen during the course of Jesus' itinerant ministry are probably as important in explaining the variations within the tradition as are the creative energies of the early church.[47] Finally, it recognizes that only those models of Jesus that firmly situate him within the complex sociohistorical context of Second Temple Palestinian Judaism(s) have any claims to real historical plausibility.[48]

Wright's approach begins with and concentrates on large-scale historical hypotheses and their verification, as opposed to narrowly focused debates regarding isolated logia.[49] He recognizes that an analysis of a person's words, apart from the context of the symbolic acts and explanatory events in which they were originally embedded, is artificial and generally unfruitful.[50] He has largely exchanged the overly stringent and narrowly focused "authenticity criteria" of the New Quest for a broader set of tests designed to assess hypotheses as wholes, including comprehensiveness, simplicity, explanatory power, fit within historical constraints, and a refined "double criterion of similarity/dissimilarity" (i.e., both *dissimilar and similar* to Judaism and early Christianity).[51] With such moves, Wright's historiographical method is able to shift a good amount of the burden of proof to those who would approach the texts of the tradition with an a priori historical skepticism.[52] Thus, one of the important ramifications of this methodological trajectory is that it allows for a positive reassessment of the historical value of the canonical Gospels.[53] A growing number of Jesus scholars appear to view this newly developing methodological trajectory as both historically sane and refreshing.[54]

Working from this methodological basis, Wright comes to certain historical conclusions regarding Jesus that directly challenge Hick's thesis. Again, space considerations will allow for only a summary of his findings.[55] Wright first comes to a general conclusion with which Hick would agree: the primary paradigm that arises most naturally in the study of Jesus is that of "prophet." More specifically, Wright reads Jesus as a popular Jewish prophet who combined elements of both "oracular" (i.e., he spoke judgment to rebellious Israel) and "leadership" (i.e., he founded a liberation movement) types within the context of an itinerant ministry.[56] Finally, his message was characterized by an eschatological urgency. But unlike Hick (and those upon whom he depends), Wright's assessment of Jesus does not stop here. He goes on to make a historical case that

Jesus applied to himself the three central aspects of his own prophetic kingdom announcement: the return from exile, the defeat of evil, and the return of YHWH to Zion.... [H]e regarded himself as the one who summed up Israel's vocation and destiny in himself. He was the one in and through whom the real "return from exile" would come about, indeed, was already coming about. He was the Messiah.[57]

Thus, against Hick's thesis, Wright joins a growing group of Jesus scholars who offer historical evidence that Jesus demonstrated messianic aims and intentions.[58]

Finally, we come to Wright's most provocative conclusion regarding the historical Jesus. The final element of Wright's model comes to the fore as he identifies Jesus' treatment of an element of Jewish expectation regarding the kingdom of God—the long-anticipated return of Yahweh to Zion. Here Wright enters a field of discussion rarely traversed today in historical Jesus studies: "the christology of Jesus."[59] Wright clearly asserts that he is not asking the metaphysical question of whether or not Jesus *was* divine. Rather, he is exploring a historical question, one forced on us by the data, including the fact that Jesus was *worshiped* early on by his followers within a monotheistic Jewish context.[60] At this point, Wright explores the fertile terrain of Jewish prophetic "symbolic action," particularly as it relates to Jesus' final, fateful journey to Jerusalem. In the end, he concludes that "Jesus went to Jerusalem in order to embody the third and last element of the coming of the kingdom. He was not content to *announce* that YHWH was returning to Zion. He intended to enact, symbolize and personify that climactic event."[61] To summarize: Wright comes to the historical conclusion that Jesus of Nazareth was an eschatological prophet who, at the same time, understood himself to be both Israel's Messiah and, in some sense, the *very embodiment of Yahweh.*

Wright's model of Jesus, particularly the "Yahweh embodied" element, points toward the presence of the rudimentary elements of a "high" Christology historically rooted in Jesus' own self-consciousness. Wright himself has articulated the implications: "...those who have desired to explore and understand the incarnation itself have regularly missed what is arguably the most central, shocking and dramatic source material on the subject, which if taken seriously would ensure that the meaning of the word "god" be again and again rethought around the actual history of Jesus himself."[62]

If Wright's historical argument is on track, then the later christo-logical formulas of the orthodox creeds can be recognized as legitimate developments of a basic theological intuition whose generative impulse can be traced back to Jesus himself. For it is not a long stretch from Jesus as both Israel (i.e., as Messiah) and Yahweh embodied to Jesus as "fully God and fully human." At the same time, Wright's model would remind twentieth-century scholars that Jesus' own christo-logical self-consciousness was embedded within a distinctly Jewish mind-set, one that must be understood on its own historical and cul-tural grounds, lest decontextualized distortions rob it of its own pro-found and novel revelation. The implications of Wright's historical conclusions for Hick's Christology seem clear: if Wright is anything like correct, then the final foundation of Hick's critique of traditional Christology is severely undercut.[63]

Notes

1. Gerald O'Collins, "The Incarnation Under Fire," *Gregorianum* 76 (1995): 263–80.

2. Hick's pluralist hypothesis claims that "the great world faiths embody different perceptions and conceptions of, and correspondingly different responses to, the Real from within the major variant ways of being human; and that within each of them the transformation of human existence from self-centeredness to Reality-centeredness is taking place" (John Hick, *An Interpretation of Religion: Human Responses to the Transcendent* [New Haven: Yale University Press, 1989], 240).

3. Hick, *God Has Many Names* (Philadelphia: Westminster, 1982), 15.

4. Hick, *Faith and Knowledge: A Modern Introduction to the Problem of Religious Knowledge* (Ithaca, N.Y.: Cornell University Press, 1957), v.

5. Hick, "The Christology of D. M. Baillie," *Scottish Journal of Theology* 11 (1958): 4.

6. Ibid., 8, 11.

7. Hick, "A Non-Substance Christology?" *Colgate-Rochester Divinity School Bulletin* (1959): 41–54; edited and reprinted as Hick, "Christology at the Crossroads," in *Prospect for Theology: Essays in Honour of H. H. Farmer,* ed. F. G. Healey (London: Nisbet, 1966), 139–66.

8. Hick, "Non-Substance Christology?" 50.

9. Hick, *Evil and the God of Love* (London: Macmillan, 1966; reprint, London: Collins-Fontana, 1968), 283–84; here Hick speaks of "the great creation-fall-redemption myth."

10. Hick, *Christianity at the Centre* (New York: Herder & Herder, 1970), 16; see esp. pp. 31–40, "Christology at the Crossroads."

11. Hick, "Christology at the Crossroads," 166.

12. Ibid., 139.

13. Hick, "The Reconstruction of Christian Belief for Today and Tomorrow" [part 2], *Theology* 73 (1970): 404.

14. Hick, *God and the Universe of Faiths,* 2d ed. (London: Collins-Fontana, 1977), 172 (emphasis in text).

15. Ibid., 169.

16. Ibid., 169–70. On the "self-contradiction," see John Hick, "Letter to the Editors: Incarnation," *Theology* 80 (1977): 204; idem, "Jesus and the World Religions," in his *The Myth of God Incarnate* (Philadelphia: Westminster, 1977), 178.

17. See, e.g., Hick, *The Center of Christianity,* 2d ed. (London: SCM, 1977), 26–32; idem, "Christology in an Age of Religious Pluralism," *Journal*

of Theology for Southern Africa 35 (1981): 4–9; idem, "Pluralism and the Reality of the Transcendent," *Christian Century* 98 (January 21, 1981): 48.

18. Hick, "Jesus and the World Religions," 180.

19. Hick, "Letter to the Editors: Incarnation," 205.

20. For an exposition and critique of Hick's neo-Kantian pluralist apologetic, see Paul R. Eddy, "Religious Pluralism and the Divine: Another Look at John Hick's Neo-Kantian Proposal," *Religious Studies* 30 (1994): 467–78.

21. See, e.g., the published results of two conference papers presented by Hick in 1980 and 1981, respectively: "Christology in an Age of Religious Pluralism," 9; Hick, "A Recent Development within Christian Monotheism," in *The Concept of Monotheism in Islam and Christianity*, ed. Hans Koechler (Vienna: Braumueller, 1982), 65–70. The two works cited by Hick are Baillie's *God Was in Christ* (New York: Scribner's, 1948) and Lampe's *God as Spirit* (New York: Oxford University Press, 1977).

22. See Hick, "The Non-Absoluteness of Christianity," in *The Myth of Christian Uniqueness: Towards a Pluralistic Theology of Religions,* ed. John Hick and Paul Knitter (Maryknoll, N.Y.: Orbis Books, 1987), esp. 31–34; Hick, "An Inspiration Christology for a Religiously Plural World," in *Encountering Jesus: A Debate on Christology,* ed. Stephen Davis (Atlanta: John Knox, 1988), 5–22.

23. Hick, *The Metaphor of God Incarnate: Christology in a Pluralistic Age* (Louisville, Ky.: Westminster/John Knox, 1993), 111; "Non-Absoluteness of Christianity," 32.

24. Hick, "Non-Absoluteness of Christianity," 32.

25. Ibid., 33. Both of these moves closely parallel those of Lampe in *God as Spirit.* See also Hick, "Trinity and Incarnation in the Light of Religious Pluralism," in *Three Faiths—One God: A Jewish, Christian, Muslim Encounter,* ed. John Hick and Edmund Meltzer (Albany: SUNY Press, 1989), 197–210; Hick, "Rethinking Christian Doctrine in the Light of Religious Pluralism," in *Christianity and the Wider Ecumenism,* ed. Peter Phan (New York: Paragon, 1990), 89–102.

26. Hick, "Non-Absoluteness of Christianity," 17–18; see pp. 17–20.

27. See also the less comprehensive, though more recent, clarification and defense of his pluralistic Christology in Hick, *A Christian Theology of Religions: The Rainbow of Faiths* (Louisville, Ky.: Westminster/John Knox, 1995), 82–103.

28. Hick, *Metaphor of God Incarnate,* 12.

29. See ibid., chapters 2 and 3. Hick's understanding of the historical Jesus is indebted to the work of E. P. Sanders and Paula Fredriksen. This locates Hick within a definite school of thought within the contemporary

Jesus Quest. With these two scholars, he emphasizes the Jewishness of Jesus and the importance of Jesus as an apocalyptic prophet (ibid., 15–22). Hick goes on to acknowledge that his portrait of Jesus "falls within the tradition of 'liberal' interpretation established by Schleiermacher, Strauss, Harnack and others," wherein the fundamental importance of Jesus is traced to "his strong and continuous awareness of God as *abba,* 'father'" (p. 18).

30. Hick, *Metaphor of God Incarnate,* 15.

31. Ibid., 27; on these points, see chapter 2.

32. Ibid., 40–42.

33. See ibid., 44–45; for this line of argument, see chapter 4.

34. Ibid., 4; see also p. 104.

35. Ibid., ix; see chapter 8 for Hick's discussion of this point.

36. Hick can be found using the phrase "Incarnation as Metaphor" as far back as 1980; see "Christology in an Age of Religious Pluralism," 8. Hick makes the myth-metaphor connection clear: "myth," the essential definition of which has not changed for Hick since the 1970s, is further described as a "much extended metaphor" (*Metaphor of God Incarnate,* 105).

37. Both Chester Gillis and Gerard Loughlin have argued that Hick is working with an outmoded and seriously flawed theory of metaphorical language. See Gillis, *A Question of Final Belief: John Hick's Pluralistic Theology of Salvation* (London: Macmillan, 1989), 164–70; Loughlin, "Squares and Circles: John Hick and the Doctrine of the Incarnation," in *Problems in the Philosophy of Religion: Critical Studies of the Work of John Hick,* ed. Harold Hewitt (New York: St. Martin's, 1991), 189–93.

38. E.g., see Thomas V. Morris, *The Logic of God Incarnate* (Ithaca, N.Y.: Cornell University Press, 1986); Stephen Davis, "Jesus Christ: Savior or Guru?," in *Encountering Jesus: A Debate on Christology,* ed. S. Davis (Atlanta: Knox, 1988), 39–59.

39. E.g., Hick, *Christian Theology of Religions,* 87, 100, 134.

40. This is simply a general, matter-of-fact statement. I want to be clear here that the personal dealings I have had with Professor Hick would never lead me to conclude that he is an example of such a pluralist.

41. For an appreciative critical assessment of Wright's general proposals, see Paul R. Eddy, "The (W)Right Jesus: Eschatological Prophet, Israel's Messiah, Yahweh Embodied," in *Jesus and the Restoration of Israel: A Critical Assessment of N. T. Wright's 'Jesus and the Victory of God',* ed. Carey C. Newman (Downers Grove, Ill.: InterVarsity, 1999).

42. N. T. Wright, *The New Testament and the People of God* (Minneapolis: Fortress, 1992); idem, *Jesus and the Victory of God* (Minneapolis: Fortress, 1996); henceforth these two works will be cited as NTPG and JVG respectively.

43. NTPG, 31. This has been true from the beginning; see Henk J. de Jonge, "The Loss of Faith in the Historicity of the Gospels: H. S. Reimarus (ca. 1750)," in *John and the Synoptics,* ed. A. Denaux (Leuven: Leuven University Press, 1992), 409–21.

44. NTPG, 418–35; JVG, 86–88, 372–83.

45. JVG, 133–37; emphasis in text. Here Wright follows Kenneth Bailey's remarkably balanced approach to this issue; see Bailey, "Informal Controlled Oral Tradition and the Synoptic Gospels," *Asia Journal of Theology* 5 (1991): 34–54.

46. JVG, 478–79.

47. JVG, 170–71; 632–33.

48. Hick's dependence on the work of E. P. Sanders et al. leads him to share this perspective.

49. NTPG, 98–109; JVG, 86–91.

50. JVG, 79, 131–37, 171, 543, 554.

51. JVG, 338. See also NTPG, 98–109; JVG, 131–32, 367, 489, 522, 540–43, 597, 613.

52. As opposed to the Jesus Seminar, which claims that one of the "seven pillars of scholarly wisdom" is that the burden of proof lies with those who argue for the authenticity of a biblical text (Robert W. Funk, Roy W. Hoover, and the Jesus Seminar in *The Five Gospels: The Search for the Authentic Words of Jesus* [San Francisco: HarperSanFrancisco, 1993], 4–5). Judging from the manner in which he makes authenticity decisions, Wright would disagree (e.g., JVG, 303–4, 348–49, 512–19, 521–28, 648–50).

53. JVG, 89. Wright confines himself almost exclusively to the data of the Synoptic Gospels.

54. E.g., see the various appreciative essays in *Jesus and the Restoration of Israel.* More broadly, see *Crisis in Christology: Essays in Quest of Resolution,* ed. William Farmer (Livonia, Mich.: Dove, 1995). Note also the methodological approach of Ben Witherington, who investigates Jesus' revealed intentions through an examination of his relationships; see Witherington, *The Christology of Jesus* (Minneapolis: Fortress, 1990).

55. See endnotes for references to the relevant supporting sections of Wright's works.

56. JVG, 152–54; 162–86.

57. JVG, 477, 517.

58. Others include Markus Bockmuehl, *This Jesus: Martyr, Lord, Messiah* (Edinburgh: T & T Clark, 1994); Marinus de Jonge, *Jesus, the Servant-Messiah* (New Haven: Yale University Press, 1991); Witherington, *Christology of Jesus.* Hick, on the other hand, cites and apparently follows Wolfhart Pannenberg's conclusions to the contrary; see Hick, "Conclusion,"

in *Four Views on Salvation in a Pluralistic World,* ed. Dennis L. Okholm and Timothy R. Phillips (Grand Rapids: Zondervan, 1996), 84.

59. JVG, 612.

60. Ibid.

61. Ibid., 615 (emphasis in text).

62. Ibid., 661.

63. I am appreciative to the members of the Bethel Theology Discussion Group (PDs) for helpful comments on an earlier draft.

19. Universality of the Word and Particularity of Jesus Christ

Jacques Dupuis, S.J.

In my book *Toward a Christian Theology of Religious Pluralism* I suggested as a model for a theology of religious pluralism that of a trinitarian and pneumatic Christology.[1] It seemed that such a model, while clearly preserving the constitutive value of Jesus Christ for the salvation of all humankind, would help recognize the salvific significance of the paths to salvation proposed by other religious traditions to their followers. This model can take things beyond what Gerald O'Collins has written in "Saving Revelation for all Peoples" and in "Universal Redeemer."[2]

The solution I proposed to solve the apparent dilemma between the two affirmations consists in uniting three complementary and convergent ways in which, within the one divine plan for humankind, salvation reaches persons in the concrete circumstances of their lives. The three elements are: (1) the lasting actuality and universal efficacy of the event of Jesus Christ, notwithstanding the historical particularity of the event; (2) the universal operative presence of the Word of God, whose action is not restricted by the human existence assumed by him in the mystery of the incarnation; and (3) the equally universal action of the Spirit of God, which is neither limited nor exhausted by its outpouring through the risen and glorified Christ.[3]

Without repeating what has been said in my book, it seems useful to offer further explanations and to meet possible difficulties. Here I will not touch on the pneumatological aspect, but will limit myself to the problem of how to combine in an adequate manner the action of the Word of God and the efficacy of the Christ-event.

Questions may be asked that have to do either directly with the relation between the Word of God and the man Jesus Christ, or with the relation between the pre-paschal Jesus and the Paschal Christ. These questions, though not new, become more acute in the context of the theology of religions; they take on here new dimensions and become more searching. Who is the Savior? Jesus Christ or the Word of God? Since the event of Jesus Christ is historically limited and particular, how can it have an efficacy that goes beyond the limits imposed on it by time and space? Should we play down the salvific meaning of the historical event in favor of the universal action of the Word of God, which knows no such limits? One would then conclude that it is indeed the Word of God who saves, while the meaning of the Jesus Christ event consists in testifying to the salvific action of the Word. Or, else, while one preserves a salvific efficacy of the risen Jesus for Christians who have recognized in him the sacrament of their salvation, this efficacy would seem limited to those who have believed in him. One would then come to the conclusion that, while Christians are saved through Jesus Christ, the members of the other religious traditions reach salvation through the universal action of the Word of God. But does affirming this not postulate two parallel economies of salvation and thereby destroy the organic unity of the saving plan of God for humankind?

In my latest book, while giving an overview of current positions in the debate on the theology of religions, I alluded to, among other things, a paradigm that seems to be developing in recent years and that I called "Logocentrism." This paradigm would tend to separate the action of the Word of God from the Jesus Christ event in two different ways: either the proper action of the Word is considered to be representing an economy of salvation distinct from that which takes place in Jesus Christ and parallel to it; or, while the economy of salvation remains one, salvific action comes to be attributed no longer to the Word as humanly incarnate and active, but to the Word itself, independently from his human existence, whatever significance might continue to be assigned to this human existence in the order of salvation.[4]

Against such tendencies to unduly separate the universal action of the Word from the salvific efficacy of the Jesus Christ event it must be shown that, on the one hand, the two aspects are distinct, notwithstanding the personal identity of the historical Jesus with the Word or the Son of God; and, on the other hand, that they remain nonetheless united, within the unique divine plan for humankind, in such a way that they can never be separated and seen as representing two distinct economies of salvation.

The essay consists of two parts. In the first part, I will show through some concrete recent examples that a certain danger may exist of seeming to establish an undue separation between the saving Word of God and Jesus Christ. The second part will explain that, though never being separated, the action of the Word remains nevertheless distinct from that of the human being of Jesus Christ, even in his risen and glorified state. It needs therefore to be shown how the action of the Word of God and the efficacy of the Christ-event are combined as two inseparable aspects in the unique economy of salvation willed by God for humankind. This will allow us to see that, while the Jesus Christ event is truly "constitutive" of universal salvation, the other paths, in which the Word of God is operative, exercise a salvific role for their followers in the order of salvation, within the same divine plan.

THE WORD OF GOD AND JESUS CHRIST CANNOT BE SEPARATED

It seems useful to start here from a passage in the encyclical *Redemptoris Missio* (1990), on the nonseparability, according to Christian faith, between the Word of God and Jesus Christ. The personal identity of Jesus Christ with the Word of God must be firmly maintained, as also that between Jesus and the Christ. This personal identity with the Son of God confers on the human existence of Jesus a unique singularity and endows it with universal saving significance. The text must be quoted in its integrity.

> Christ is the one mediator between God and humankind...(1 Tim 2:5–7; cf. Heb 4:14–16). No one, therefore, can enter into communion with God except through Christ, by the working of the Holy Spirit. Christ's one, universal mediation, far from being an obstacle on the journey towards God, is the way established by God himself.... Although participated forms of mediation of different kinds and degrees are not excluded, they acquire meaning and value *only* from Christ's own mediation, and they cannot be understood as parallel or complementary to his (n. 5).

To introduce any sort of separation [*separationem*] between the Word and Jesus Christ is contrary to the Christian faith. Saint John clearly states that the Word, who "was in the beginning with God," is the very one who "became flesh" (Jn 1:2, 14). Jesus is the Incarnate Word—a single and indivisible person. One cannot separate [*separare*] Jesus from the Christ or speak of a "Jesus of history" who would differ from the "Christ of faith." The Church acknowledges and confesses Jesus as "The Christ, the Son of the living God" (Mt 16:16): Christ is none other than Jesus of Nazareth; he is the Word of God made man for the salvation of all.... It is precisely this uniqueness of Christ which gives him an absolute and universal significance, whereby, while belonging to history, he remains history's centre and goal....

Thus, although it is legitimate and helpful to consider the various aspects of the mystery of Christ, we must never lose sight of its unity. In the process of discovering and appreciating the manifold gifts—especially the spiritual treasures—that God has bestowed on every people, we cannot separate [*seiungere*] those gifts from Jesus Christ, who is at the centre of God's plan of salvation...(n. 6).[5]

The key word here is the "nonseparation" between the Word of God and Jesus Christ, on the one hand, and between the Jesus of history and the Christ of faith, on the other. The personal identity between the one and the other must always be preserved in virtue of the assumption of Jesus' human being by the divine person of the Word through the mystery of the "hypostatic union." It follows that the salvific efficacy of the Word and the salvific significance of the historical event of Jesus Christ cannot be separated in such a way as to attribute salvific work exclusively to the Word, independently from and to the prejudice of the humanity of Jesus.

The encyclical does not refer to any concrete instance where a tendency to establish an undue separation between a saving efficacy of the Word and that of Jesus Christ would be found; and it is not my intention to consider who might be implied here. It may, however, be useful to reflect on some concrete ways in which one could seem to suggest an undue "separation" between the Word and Jesus. This would enable us to show more clearly the enduring distinction-in-unity that endures between the action of the Word and the historical event of Jesus Christ, within the one, multifaceted divine plan of salvation for all humankind. This in turn will allow us to draw consequences with regard to the plurality of paths through which God's saving action reaches to people in various religious traditions.

Carlo Molari is right, I think, to "affirm the transcendence of the Word of God in respect of its historical expression, that is, to recognize a 'surplus' of the Word in relation to Christ."[6] But, in the process, he seems to reduce the significance of the historical event Jesus Christ, failing to consider the "transhistorical" or "metahistorical" state of Jesus' glorified humanity. This needs to be substantiated at some length.

Molari notes that the "surplus" of the Word is clearly implied by the kenosis or self-emptying (see Phil 2:7), which constitutes the inevitable reverse side of the incarnation. This "surplus" is implied also in the dogma of the hypostatic union, as expressed by the definition of Chalcedon. Molari writes:

> The kenosis is the historical reverse side of the divine surplus in relation to the humanity of Jesus. In this perspective, to affirm the definitive and normative character of Christ does not mean to affirm that all that is contained in the divine Word has already become completely known to men or exhausted by the Christ event; it means to hold that the Word that resounded in Jesus, is the unique and eternal Word, which however keeps its transcendence since the union is *without confusion and without change,* as the Council of Chalcedon establishes.[7]

While intending to maintain—rightly—the salvific transcendence of the Word in relation to the historical action of Jesus Christ, Molari seems to reduce the salvific significance of the historical event, and notably the universal saving power of Christ's glorified humanity. Here is how another Italian theologian interprets his thought:

> The Word begins to act in creation and is at work in all the events through which God leads men to encounter his mystery. The revealing and salvific Word of God is, therefore, one, but there are many historical mediators of salvation. Jesus is one of these and Christians welcome the Word in reference to him. However, he is but the "human sacrament of God." For the centrality of Jesus Christ is substituted that of the Word which reveals itself in Jesus.... In the last analysis, the person of Jesus is not the principle of universal salvation; Jesus is only the one who has lived in

a radical way the universal values which reflect the eternal Word of God.[8]

This judgment is perhaps unduly severe. Molari is not wrong—as the second part of my essay will argue—in insisting that, the union notwithstanding, a distinction must be maintained between the Word and its expression in Jesus. He stresses that point in another paper, without apparently implying a separation. He writes as follows:

> Jesus has been the paradigm of [the] law of salvific history, but he has not exhausted the possible expressions of the eternal Word.... The opinions which affirm a separation (such as is excluded by *Redemptoris Missio,* n. 6) are certainly inadequate in Christian perspective. But it remains equally true that according to the doctrine of the faith the Word has a field of action much vaster than that realized in Jesus. That is why the Prologue of the Gospel of John, before speaking of the incarnation, describes the various ways of presence of the creating and enlightening Word of God in human history. It is in this sense that very soon in Christianity the seeds of the Word were seen present in the diverse cultures.[9]

However, Molari has again returned to the argument more recently in the "Introduction" he wrote for the Italian edition of two controversial volumes on the problem of the uniqueness of Christianity and of the pluralistic theology of religions.[10] He insists here—rightly again—that the historical event of Jesus Christ is particular in space and time and therefore historically limited. But from this he deduces, with less plausibility, that the event cannot therefore have an efficacy that transcends temporal and spatial limits. He fails to recognize that, due to the real transformation it has undergone through the mystery of his resurrection and glorification, the human being of Jesus has become "transhistorical" or "metahistorical," and can thus exercise an efficacy that goes beyond the normal limits of time and space. This oversight allows Molari to argue that, while the efficacy of the Word knows no limits, the Jesus Christ event never overcomes its own historical conditioning.

Molari asks therefore:

> When it is said: "There is salvation in no one else"..., the problem consists in deciding to what does the Name refer, which is being

invoked and in which the salvific power resides. Does it refer to the symbolic name (Jesus), or to the ineffable divine Name of God who reveals himself in Jesus, and, therefore, to the inexpressible power of the eternal Word which resonates in Jesus?"[11]

He answers that, in whatever divine manifestation, it is always the Word of God that carries revelation and salvation. The case of Jesus is no exception. The titles of "Only begotten" or "Son" can be applied to him insofar as he is "constituted Messiah because of his faithfulness to the will of the Father and the revelation which God has realized in him."[12]

Against the "inclusivists," whom he accuses of wrongly identifying the Christ and the Word, Molari affirms that "according to Christian tradition the salvific action in history is attributed to the eternal Word and to the Spirit of God, in view of the faith professed about Jesus dead and risen. When we recognize Jesus as Lord, we proclaim an action of the eternal Word, which revealed himself in Jesus, and of the Holy Spirit, which he communicates to those who are his, but always exclusively as glorified creature of God."[13]

What I miss here is an affirmation of the unique sonship of God possessed and lived by Jesus Christ, even in his human being, and consequently, the affirmation of a unique and universal salvific value of his human life and of the Paschal Mystery of his death and resurrection. Briefly, while Molari rightly affirms a multiple revelation and manifestation of God through his Word, he ignores the unique significance that accrues to the Christ-event, because of the very Word of God being incarnate in the human being of Jesus Christ.

Another case I would like to examine is that of Aloysius Pieris. One may ask whether in his recent works Pieris postulates an undue separation between the saving Word of God and Jesus the Christ. According to him it is the Word of God who saves in any event and in all circumstances, not, properly speaking, the Word-of-God-made-flesh, that is, Jesus Christ.[14] He writes: "He who reveals, who saves and transforms is the Word himself."[15] "The Christ" is a title; a title does not save. Jesus is [only?] "he in whom Christians recognize the Word, as seen, heard and touched by human senses."[16] The singularity of Jesus the man consists in that "Jesus is the contradiction between Mammon and Yahweh…, the defense pact between the oppressed and Yahweh."[17] He reveals and embodies the contradiction that exists between God and the poor who are oppressed at the hands of the rich. Jesus thus seals God's covenant with the poor. Such "singularity" is accessible to members of other religious traditions, while the "onto-logical oneness" of the Word incarnate is not. In every event, the Word as such is he who saves; Jesus Christ is he in whom the Word is recognized by Christians. Pieris thus writes:

> The belief that Jesus of Nazareth is *the* enfleshed historical man-ifestation of this word-medium-path turns Christian theology into a Christology. Such naming, however, is not a condition for sal-vation demanded by the Word which, being universal, operates even among those who do not recognize it by that name. It is the word-medium-path that saves, not the name one gives it. Naming which belongs to theology cannot be universal.[18]

In a well-documented and cautious evaluation of the entire work of A. Pieris, Philip Gibbs wrote the following:

> If, as Pieris claims, salvation is through the Word, is he referring to the Word incarnate? There are several possibilities. Salvation could be through the universal Word which is not incarnate. Or it could be incarnate in various ways which leaves open the possi-bility of giving a name other than Christ to the saving reality. Or the Word could be present in other religious traditions but ordered to the plenary revelation that would take place in Christ. Recent Roman magisterium follows the latter option. Pieris also supports the latter option in his early work, but recently appears to favour one or both of the first two options.[19]

The position of Pieris raises several questions. To begin with: What does it mean to say that "the Christ" is just a title and that a title does not save? If we go back to the early kerygma, it stands out clearly that the title "Christ" is given to the Jesus of history by the apostolic church in view of his resurrection at the hands of God his Father. He has become the Christ by being raised from the dead, as Peter's speech on Pentecost day according to the Acts of the Apostles makes clear: "Let all the house of Israel therefore know assuredly that God has made him both Lord and Christ, this Jesus whom you crucified" (Acts 2:36). Lordship and saving power are thus attributed to Jesus himself in his risen state in view of the real transformation that his human existence has undergone by being raised by God; it is not assigned exclusively to the Word of God independently of Jesus' human existence. By stating that only the Word of God as such saves, does not Pieris overlook the salvific significance of the historical event of Jesus Christ? Does he not, that is, separate the Word of God, which is saving in himself, from the historical Jesus, in whom Christians come to know and meet this saving Word, without, however, that event being in itself universally salvific? To assign saving action only to the Word as such—does that do full justice to the New Testament witness? And does the affirmation of a universal saving action of the Word of God as such necessarily play down a certain universal saving significance of the historical event Jesus Christ? This Logocentric model fails to combine the saving power of both the Word as such and the Word as made human in Jesus Christ. It seems to posit a dichotomy between Logocentrism and Christocentrism, which are construed as mutually exclusive paradigms. What needs, on the contrary, to be shown is how, far from excluding each other, the saving action of the Word as such and of the Word made human in Jesus can be and need to be combined, if we wish to account for a plurality of paths designed by God for human salvation. To show this is the burden of the second part of this essay.

THE WORD OF GOD AND JESUS CHRIST: DISTINCTION AND UNITY

As the headings for the two parts of this paper show, everything depends on the kind of relationship that is recognized between the Word of God as such or in itself and the same Word in his human existence in Jesus Christ: Are both to be so separated from each other that saving action belongs only to the Word as such, even while it may come to be known through Jesus Christ? Or are they, on the contrary, so united in their mutual distinction that universal saving action needs to be assigned to both, within the overall divine plan for humankind in which they are mutually interrelated? What needs to be shown is that between the universal operative presence of the Word of God and the unique saving significance of the historical event of Jesus Christ, there is no contradiction or opposition, but interrelatedness and complementarity. Both aspects are combined and harmonized together in the saving plan of God. It will be argued that the action of the Word as such reaches beyond the limits of time and space and, therefore, its saving power cannot be reduced by being simply identified with the historical event of Jesus Christ. But it is equally true that the personal insertion of the Word of God into the history of humankind through the mystery of the incarnation confers upon the historical event of Jesus Christ, in the unfolding of the history of salvation, a unique value and significance that make it "constitutive" of universal human salvation.

The Universal Action of the Word

In my book I wrote:

> The New Testament affirmation of Christ the man's uniqueness as "the way" (Jn 14:6), the "only mediator" (1 Tim 2:5), the "one name" (Acts 4:12) in whom human beings must find salvation does not cancel out faith in the *Logos asarkos* of which the Johannine Prologue speaks, through whom all people may be saved and in whom all ways may converge. He who was "the true light that enlightens every human being by coming into the world" (Jn 1:9) is the same who was to "become flesh" (Jn 1:14) in the "fulness of time" (Gal 4:4) in Jesus Christ.[20]

To avoid all possible ambiguity, let me say immediately that, when I speak of a universal action of the *Logos asarkos* that continues beyond the risen state of Jesus' humanity, no reference is made to a *Logos* "nonincarnate," other than the one who has become human in Jesus Christ. What is being affirmed is that the action of the *Logos as such*, after the incarnation, or even after the resurrection and glorification of Jesus, is not circumscribed or limited by Jesus' humanity. The incarnation of the Word, once it has taken place in history, endures forever; but the action of the *Logos as such* is not confined to this enduring humanity, even in its glorified risen state. The Prologue of the Gospel of John can be so interpreted as to account for a universal saving action not only of the *Logos* before the incarnation *(Logos asarkos)* but also of the *Logos as such,* after the incarnation and the resurrection. To show this, it is necessary to turn to the exegesis of the Prologue, especially of John 1:9.

According to Xavier Léon-Dufour, John's Prologue until v. 14 (notwithstanding the incidental clause of vv. 6–9) envisages the action of the *Logos* as such through human history since the beginning, and not Jesus Christ,[21] as some exegetes hold either for the entire Prologue or at least from v. 6 onward.[22] For Léon-Dufour, the *Logos* has been operative from the beginning of creation (vv. 2–5), as principle of life and light, establishing a personal relationship between God and human beings: "coming into the world," as did the Wisdom of God in Ben Sira 24, he is the source of light for all people, and to those who received him he gave "power to become children of God" (vv. 9, 12). Léon-Dufour writes about the synergy that takes place between God and human beings in welcoming the Word: "That enlightening action, insofar as it is welcomed, produces divine sonship. And this is so, even before the *Logos* takes a human face, that is independently from any explicit allegiance to Jesus Christ." He adds:

> The "coming" of the *Logos* has already been spoken of in 1:10f: he "was in the world" and "he came to his own home." If it is true that the *Logos* is God communicating himself, this communication has begun not with the Incarnation but since creation, and it has continued through the whole history of revelation. However, the incarnation of the *Logos* marks a radical change in the mode of the communication.

The change consists in the fact that "henceforth [revelation] happens through the language and the existence of a man among others: this phenomenon of concentration in a man will make it possible for the revelation of God to be formulated directly in an intelligible way, and for all people to have access to a definitive communication with God." Léon-Dufour goes on, however, to insist that, notwithstanding the novelty introduced by the incarnation, "this new stage does not supersede the previous one. The Logos continues to express himself thanks to creation of which he is the author and the witness given to the light: many can receive him and become children of God. Henceforth, however, revelation is also and mostly concentrated in him who will be designated by his name: Jesus Christ (1:17).[23]

This point of view is shared by some other recent exegetes. According to J. Dupont, John uses the term *Logos* purposely to stress the universal activity of him who "was with God" "in the beginning." He writes:

Through the use of this term *[Logos]*, the apostle did not intend to say what Christ is in himself, but to show that his action on the world has not begun with his earthly life: this action is at the very source of the world, at the origin of all things. It is with the Word of God *ad extra,* with the creative Word which God addresses to the world, that John identifies Christ. He does so, not to tell us who the person of Jesus is, but to make us see whereto his action on the universe extends.[24]

That the Word's universal action in the world endures even today is put into even greater relief by D. Mollat. Here is what he writes about v. 9 of the Prologue:

Ergo in hoc v. explicite revelatur hic *adventus* Verbi in mundum, qui in vv. 4 et 5 implicite affirmabatur.... Haec lux vera dicitur "illuminare omnem hominem." Praesens "illuminat"...significat quod hoc est eius proprium munus et constans operatio. Illa oper- atio intelligenda est in sensu supernaturalis illius illuminationis quae in v. 4 declarata est, scl. illuminationis salvificae qua homo docetur et liberatur et transfiguratur et sanctificatur et etiam judi- catur. Ad omnem hominem sese extendere dicitur huius verae lucis illuminativa virtus. Nullus invenitur homo, qui ea non attin- gatur seu ad quem non perveniat. Ergo cuiusvis hominis person- alis relatio ad Verbum affirmatur.[25]

One understands then how Yves Raguin, in a recent book, can account for the possibility of salvation for all human beings who have not known the Word as incarnate, either before or after the incarnation, by appealing to the knowledge they have had of the nonincarnate Word, that is, of the Word as such. He affirms their knowledge of the Word as such with explicit reference to John 1:9. He writes:

Those who will not have known the Father through the Incarnate Word will be able to know him through his non-incarnate-Word. Thus, all human beings can know the Word of God, even without knowing him in his incarnation.... We read in the Prologue of the Gospel of John that the Word of God is the life of all things and that this life becomes the light of human beings. Now, every human being can make in himself this experience of life become light and thus enter, through union with the Word, in the intimacy of the Father. This is how the greatest part of humankind can enter into relationship with God, source of all life and of all love, through the mediation of the Word, without having encountered Jesus and without having known him.[26]

Another recent author writes in the same vein, with explicit reference to Léon-Dufour's reading of John 1:9: "By not identifying straightaway the *Logos* with Jesus-the-Christ, it is easy to conceive a broad revealing action of the *Logos* throughout the history of salvation, not only before, but also after the incarnation."[27]

It would then seem permissible to speak of an action of the Word of God not only before the incarnation but also after the incarnation, extending beyond the saving action of Jesus' humanity, even in its risen and glorified state, provided such continued action be not separated from the event in which there takes place the insuperable "concentration" of the redemptive self-revelation of God in accordance with the one divine plan for the universal salvation of humankind. We shall have to show hereafter how this continued enlightening and life-giving action of the Word as such is "correlated" with the "concentration" of divine salvation in the Word as incarnate in Jesus Christ and to the lasting actuality of the historical event through his risen state. The incarnation marks, as I wrote, "the unsurpassed—and unsurpassable—depth of God's self-communication to human beings, the supreme mode of immanence of his being-with-them," indeed the "key of interpretation" of the entire process of God's self-involvement with human beings throughout the whole of history.[28]

What has thus far been affirmed on biblical grounds can—though perhaps paradoxically for some people—be confirmed by having recourse to the christological dogma as enunciated by the Chalcedonian definition. In *Redemptoris Missio,* as we saw above, John Paul II noted: "To introduce any sort of separation between the Word and Jesus Christ is contrary to the faith.... Jesus is the Incarnate Word, an indivisible person" (no. 6). This is the faith, as expressed in the classical christological dogma, but it represents but one aspect of that faith. The christological dogma is made up of two complementary aspects that need to be combined and held together. While the two natures, the divine and the human, are united in Jesus Christ—in the words of Chalcedon—"without division or separation," they are so also "without confusion or change."[29] This means that, while being "hypostatically united," the natures remain nonetheless "distinct." It is in fact this abiding distinction that the monophysite heresy threatened by absorbing the authentic human nature of Christ into the divine. The danger of monophysitism exists even today and does so under two different forms. The well-known form holds a certain absorption of the human nature into the divine, often connected with a loose transfer of the divine attributes to Jesus as man, based on a wrong interpretation of the *communicatio idiomatum*. But less attention is paid to another form—which could be called "inverted monophysitism"—that supposes a certain absorption of the divine nature by the human, by which the divine nature is reduced to the measure of the human. In this case, while the human nature of Jesus is united to the divine Word, the divine attributes of the person of the Word are lost, or at least narrowed in some way to the dimensions of the human. I am alluding to the "kenotic theories" which flourished in the last century but which strangely seem to threaten us even today. The Chalcedonian dogma tells us clearly, however, that the divine nature remains as distinct and entire in the union of both, as does the human, and that, therefore, one cannot speak of a lessening of divinity that would reduce it to the dimension of the human, any more than of an absorption of humanity by the divine. The language used by Chalcedon to express the union in distinction of the two natures has been taken up by the Council of Constantinople III at the level of wills and "operations."[30] Those too, while not being separated, remain nevertheless mutually distinct. This means that, while the human action of Jesus is truly the action of the Word, the divine action of the Word remains nevertheless distinct from his human action.

One may recall here the famous text of St. Leo the Great in his *Tomus ad Flavianum,* partly picked up again by the Council of Constantinople III, where Leo wrote: "God suffers no change because of his condescension, nor is man consumed by such dignity. For each of the two natures performs the functions proper to it in communion with the other: the Word does what pertains to the Word and the flesh what pertains to the flesh.... And as the Word does not lose the glory which is his in equality with the Father, so the flesh does not abandon the nature of our race...." To which the Council of Constantinople III adds the following explanations: "For we do not in any way admit one natural action of God and the creature, so as neither to raise to the divine essence what is created nor lower the sublime divine nature to the level proper to creatures. . . ."[31]

That, while becoming man, "the Word does not lose the glory which is his in equality with the Father" must mean that he keeps exercising, in union with the Father, the actions that belong to him by reason of the divine nature: the mediation in creation (cf. John 1:3), the universal enlightening action with regard to human beings (cf. John 1:9), even the communication to them of the power to become children of God (cf. John 1:12), of which the Prologue of John spoke. It is in this sense that I wrote: "The Christ-event, however inclusively present, does not exhaust the power of the Word of God, who became flesh in Jesus Christ."[32]

It seems, therefore, to follow from the Chalcedonian dogma itself, that the divine action of the Word cannot, by its very nature, be reduced to the mode in which the Word expresses itself through his human action in Jesus. The divine action of the Word is not "circumscribed" by, "exhausted" by, or "reduced" to its expression through human nature. Classical christological dogma seems then to confirm the enduring existence of an action of the Word of God as such, beyond any conditioning by the human nature of the Word-as-incarnate, even in its glorified state. The saving action of the risen Christ does not exhaust the "enlightening" and the "life-giving" power of the Word of God, of which the Prologue of John spoke.

New and unexpected as this may sound to some people, it does nothing more than state that, while becoming man, the Word of God remains God anyway; or, even, that God remains God, his becoming man notwithstanding. And if the Word remains God, he too continues to act as God, beyond and over above his own human action. The human action of the risen Christ does not "exhaust" the saving divine power of the Word. One must speak of a "surplus" of the Word as such in relation to the Word-as-incarnate—in the sense, that is, that the divine nature transcends the human, hypostatically united with the divine person. The person is one, the divine Word, in the enduring distinction of the natures and the actions; but the action of both natures remains distinct, the unity of person notwithstanding. The action of the Word as such "exceeds" that of the Word incarnate in his glorified humanity. This, as will be shown more clearly below, allows for a positive view of other religious traditions as conveyers of a divine action of the Word of God and as channels of divine salvation.

The Jesus Christ Event: Universal and Particular

The personal identity of Jesus Christ with the Word of God must be clearly affirmed. Jesus Christ is no other person than the Word of God made man in history. No separation can be supposed, which would contradict this personal identity. This belongs to the essential meaning of the "hypostatic union." That union exists and perdures through the two distinct states, kenotic and glorified, of Jesus' human existence. In both situations the same humanity of the Word of God incarnate is involved. This humanity begins to exist in time with the mystery of the incarnation and is subject to time and space conditioning, but it endures beyond death in its glorified and risen state, in which it has become "transhistorical" or "metahistorical," and as such has overcome normal conditioning by time and space. This real transformation of the human being of Jesus through his resurrection confers upon his human existence, and in particular upon the paschal event of his death and resurrection, universal salvific value. Through it the Christ-event, constitutive of human salvation, is inclusively present and remains actual throughout time and space.

The unique significance of the event of Jesus Christ, as "constitutive" of universal salvation—of which the Christian tradition speaks—must be clearly established on its true theological foundation. I have suggested elsewhere that, in the last analysis, it depends on his personal identity as the Son of God. I wrote:

> No other consideration seems to provide such an adequate theological foundation. The "Gospel" values which Jesus upholds, the Reign of God which he announces, the human project or "program" which he puts forward, his option for the poor and the marginalized, his denouncing of injustice, his message of universal love: all these, no doubt, contribute to the difference and specificity of Jesus' personality; none of them, however, would be decisive for making him and recognizing him as "constitutively unique."[33]

Through the mystery of the incarnation the Word of God has inserted himself, once and for all, personally in human reality and in the history of the world. In him God has established with the entire human race a bond of union that can never be broken. As the Constitution *Gaudium et Spes* affirms: "By his incarnation, the Son of God has in a certain manner united himself with every human being" (no. 22). The incarnation represents the deepest and most immanent possible manner of God's personal involvement with humankind in history. The entire Christ-event, from incarnation to resurrection and glorification, seals on a lasting basis a decisive covenant established by God with humankind. The event remains throughout history the sacrament of that covenant. In this sense, the Jesus Christ event occupies a unique, irreplaceable place in the history of salvation. It is truly "constitutive" of the mystery of salvation for all humankind.

It remains, however, true that the historical event of Jesus Christ is necessarily particular and circumscribed by the limits imposed on it by time and space. The human story of Jesus belongs to a precise point in space and in time. The mystery of the resurrection itself is an event inscribed punctually in human history, even though it introduces the human being of Jesus into a metahistorical condition. And, while it is true that in and through the glorified state of the risen One, the historical event of salvation becomes present and remains actual for all times and places, it is equally true, as has been explained above, that that event does not exhaust—and cannot exhaust—the revealing and saving power of the Word of God. While no separation can be established between the human being of Jesus and the person of the Word of God, they cannot be identified, for the two natures remain distinct in their very personal union.

In this sense it is legitimate to ask whether the way of speaking of some early fathers of the church was altogether justified when they affirmed that in the incarnation "the Word in its entirety" *(totum Verbi)* had been revealed. Justin Martyr—to give one example—wrote that, while outside the incarnation the Word has been communicated "partially" *(kata merous)*, in Jesus Christ "the Word in his entirety has been manifested for us" *(2 Apol.* 8.1). He added: "It is one thing to possess a seed *(sperma),* and a likeness proportioned to one's capacity, and quite another to possess the reality itself, both the partaking and the imitation of which are the result of the grace which comes from him"

(*2 Apol.* 13.6).[34] I have argued that the *Logos,* the "seeds" of which *(spermata tou Logou)* are found according to St. Justin and St. Irenaeus outside Christianity, is none other than the *Logos* of the Prologue of John.[35] It is he who is universally communicated by God to human beings, even though his self-disclosure in the human flesh of Jesus has a density all its own. Against the opinion, often expressed, according to which the *Logos* of the early fathers would merely refer to "human reason" present in every human being through nature, it has been pointedly remarked: "The distinction [between the two ways of disclosure of the Word, outside and in the incarnation] cannot be assimilated or identified with that of later theology between the natural order and the supernatural; it only marks a difference of clarity, of certitude, of fulness."[36] Both in Jesus Christ and outside of him, it is the same Word of God who is revealed and manifested.

Undoubtedly the Word has been manifested in Jesus Christ in the most deeply human way that may ever be conceived, and hence in the way best adapted to our human nature. But, paradoxically, this most human way of self-manifestation involves in itself and by its very nature its own limitations and imperfections. The Word of God reaches beyond whatever the human being of Jesus, assumed by him personally, is capable of manifesting and revealing. Jesus Christ is, therefore, in his humanity the universal sacrament of the mystery of salvation offered by God to the whole of humankind through his Word (and his Spirit). But the God who saves through him remains beyond the human being of Jesus, even in his glorified state, his personal identity with the Word notwithstanding. Jesus Christ risen and glorified does not substitute for the Father, nor does his glorified human existence take the place of the Word himself, never fully revealed through any historical manifestation.

We arrive thus at the affirmation of a diversity and a multiplicity of divine manifestations by the Word of God throughout human history. Not all those manifestations take place at the same depth or have the same value or significance. All of them are, however, "Logophanies," in the sense of being self-disclosures of God through his Word. In this sense the ancient fathers of the church could see the theophanies of the First Testament as manifestations of God through his Word, that is, "Logophanies." For Irenaeus the entire economy of salvation was made up of various divine manifestations through the

Word; yet it remained true that the incarnation of the Word of God in Jesus Christ—which he had been "rehearsing" through his previous involvements in human history—involved "something entirely new" (*omnem novitatem attulit seipsum afferens*) (*Adv. Haer.* 4.34.1),[37] because it marked the personal coming in the flesh of the Word of God.

This means that God's salvific action, which operates always within the framework of a unique design, is one, and at the same time has diverse facets. It never abstracts from the Christ-event, in which it finds its highest historical density. Yet the action of the Word of God is not bound by his becoming man historically in Jesus Christ; nor is the action of the Spirit of God in history limited to its outpouring upon the world by the risen and glorified Christ. The mediation of the salvific grace of God to humankind takes on different dimensions which must be acknowledged, combined, and integrated. Claude Geffré writes pointedly:

> Jesus is the icon of the living God in a unique manner, and we need not wait for another "Mediator." But this does not lead to identifying the historical contingent aspect of Jesus with the "Christic" or divine aspect. The very law of God's incarnation through the mediation of history leads [us] to think that Jesus does not put an end to the story of God's manifestations…. In conformity with the traditional view of the Fathers of the Church, it is, therefore, possible to see the economy of the Son incarnate as the sacrament of a broader economy, that, namely, of the eternal Word of God which coincides with the religious history of humankind.[38]

The Christ-event, even while it is inclusively present and actual in all times and places through the glorified humanity of Jesus, does not exhaust the power of the Word of God who became flesh in Jesus Christ. The action of the Word reaches beyond the limits imposed on the operative presence of the humanity of Jesus, even in its glorified state, just as the person of the Word exceeds the human nature of Jesus Christ, the hypostatic union notwithstanding. One can understand then how elements "of truth and grace" (*Ad Gentes* 9) can be found in the other religious traditions of the world and how these serve, for their followers, as "paths" or "ways" to salvation. It is the Word of God who went sowing his seeds in the religious traditions. Nor must these seeds

be understood as representing merely human "stepping stones" awaiting a divine self-manifestation to take place in an indeterminate future.
They form an actual divine self-manifestation and self-gift, however
incomplete it may be.

The unbound "enlightening" power of the divine Word—which
was "the true light that enlightens every human being by coming into
the world" (John 1:9)—has been universally at work before its manifestation in the flesh and remains at work throughout the history of salvation, even after the Jesus Christ event and beyond the confines of
Christianity. As the first apologists had already seen, individual persons
could in fact be "en-light-ened" by the Word, who is the one source of
divine light. It was not only individual persons—Socrates, Buddha and
others—who received divine truth from the Word; but human designs
and endeavors—Greek "philosophy" as well as Asiatic wisdom—could
be the channels through which the divine light reached persons.[39]

The religious traditions, in which the memory has been preserved
of experiences with divine truth made by the seers and prophets of various peoples, contain elements "of truth and of grace" (*Ad Gentes* 9),
which the Word has sown in them, and through which his enlightening
power remains operative. The Word of God continues even today to
sow his seeds in the hearts of people and in their religious traditions.
Revealed truth and salvific grace are present in them through his
action.

It is important to preserve the unity of the divine plan for the salvation of humankind, which embraces the whole of human history. The
becoming-man of the Word of God in Jesus Christ, his human life,
death, and resurrection, are the culminating point of the historical
process of divine self-communication, the hinge sustaining the entire
process, its hermeneutical key. The reason for this is that the "human-
ization" of the Word marks the unsurpassed—and unsurpassable—
depth of God's self-communication to human beings; the supreme
modality of his being-with-them.[40]

But the centrality of the incarnational dimension of the salvific
economy of God must not be allowed to overshadow the permanent
presence and action of the Word of God. The enlightening and salvific
power of the Word is not circumscribed by the particularity of the historical event. It transcends all barriers of space and time. The historical
event Jesus Christ, which is constitutive of salvation, and the universal

action of the Word of God do not, for that matter, represent two different and parallel economies of salvation; they are, on the contrary, complementary and inseparable aspects in the one, but diversified, divine plan for all humankind.

CONCLUSION

My intention has been to show that a trinitarian model of Christology can help us see how the two affirmations can be combined: on the one hand, the event Jesus Christ is constitutive of salvation for the whole humanity; and, on the other hand, the "paths" proposed by the other religious traditions have authentic saving value for their followers. One can thus in some way discover the meaning, within the framework of a unique divine plan for humankind, of the religious pluralism in which we are living.

Far from competing with each other, the different paths proposed by the different religious traditions, compose, together with Christianity, the entirety of the divine plan of salvation for humankind. One must, however, always remember that it is not in fact the religious traditions that save people, but God himself through his Word and his Spirit. The diverse "paths" are conducive to salvation because they have been traced by God himself in his search for people; and, even though not all have the same meaning or represent the same depth of divine involvement with people, all converge in the one plan designed by God eternally. The hidden manifestation of the Word of God through the seers of other religions and through the traditions that have found their origin in them, as well as the historical coming of the Word in the flesh in Jesus Christ to which the Christian community witnesses, combine together in the overall ensemble of a unique divine plan.

The task of a Christian theology of religious pluralism is to discover the breadth and the depth of the divine plan for humankind, which reflects in history the immensity of the divine mystery. Without pretending ever to fathom the divine plan which issues from the divine life itself, we must welcome with thankfulness its bounty and munificence—perhaps never imagined before—as it gushes forth from God's infinite love. As scripture says: "God is greater than our hearts" (1 John 3:20).

Notes

1. J. Dupuis, *Toward a Christian Theology of Religious Pluralism* (Maryknoll, N.Y.: Orbis Books, 1997).

2. G. O'Collins, *Retrieving Fundamental Theology* (Mahwah, N.J.: Paulist, 1993), 79–86; idem, *Christology* (Oxford: Oxford University Press, 1995), 296–305.

3. J. Dupuis, *Toward a Christian Theology of Religious Pluralism,* 203–390.

4. Ibid., 195–97.

5. Text in AAS 83 (1991): 254–55.

6. See Carlo Molari, "Assolutezza e universalità del cristianesimo come problema teologico," *Credere oggi* 9, no. 6 (1989): 17–35, esp. 27.

7. Ibid., 27.

8. G. Canobbio, "Gesù Cristo nella recente teologia delle religioni," in *Cristianesimo e religioni in dialogo* (Brescia: Morcelliana, 1994), 86–88.

9. C. Molari, "Riconoscere il Dio di tutti i popoli," in *La svolta planetaria di Dio,* ed. C. Cantoni (Rome: Borla, 1992), 283–307, esp. 301.

10. See *L'unicità cristiana: Un mito?,* ed. J. Hick and P. F. Knitter (Assisi: Cittadella, 1994) (introduction by C. Molari, pp. 11–48); and *La teologia pluralista delle religioni: Un mito?,* ed. G. D'Costa (Assisi: Cittadella, 1994) (introduction by C. Molari, pp. 11–37).

11. C. Molari, "Introduzione," in *L'unicità cristiana: Un mito?,* ed. Hick and Knitter, 35–36.

12. Ibid., 44.

13. Molari, "Introduzione," in *La teologia pluralista delle religioni: Un mito?,* ed. G. D'Costa, 27.

14. I am referring to the following: A. Pieris, "An Asian Paradigm: Interreligious Dialogue and Theology of Religions," *The Month* 26 (1993): 129–34; idem, "Universality of Christianity," *Vidyajyoti* 57 (1993): 591–95; idem, "The Problem of Universality and Inculturation with Regard to Patterns of Theological Thinking," *Concilium* no. 6 (1994): 70–79; idem, "Inculturation in Asia: A Theological Reflection on an Experience," in *Jahrbuch für interkulturelle Kommunikation* (Frankfurt a. M.: Missionswissenschaftliches Institut Missio e. V., 1994), 59–71.

15. Pieris, "Inculturation in Asia," 60.

16. Ibid.

17. Pieris, "Universality of Christianity," 595.

18. Pieris, "The Problem of Universality," 72.

19. P. Gibbs, *The Word in the World: Divine Revelation in the Theology*

of Jean-Marc Ela, Aloysius Pieris and Gustavo Gutiérrez (Rome: Editrice Pontificia Università Gregoriana, 1996), 219–20.

20. Dupuis, *Toward a Christian Theology of Religious Pluralism,* 288.

21. X. Léon-Dufour, *Lecture de l'Evangile selon Jean,* I (Paris: Seuil, 1988), 62–144.

22. See, e.g., R. E. Brown, *The Gospel according to John,* 2 vols., AB 29, 29A (Garden City, N.Y.: Doubleday, 1966, 1970).

23. Léon-Dufour, *Lecture,* 109, 112, 124.

24. J. Dupont, *Essais sur la Christologie de Saint Jean* (Bruges: Saint-André, 1951), 48.

25. D. Mollat, *Introductio in Exegesim Scriptorum Sancti Joannis* (Rome: Pontificia Università Gregoriana, 1961), 21–24.

26. Y. Raguin, *Un message de salut pour tous* (Paris: Vie chrétienne, n.d.), 31.

27. B. Senécal, *Jésus le Christ à la rencontre de Gautama le Bouddha: Identité chrétienne et Bouddhisme* (Paris: Cerf, 1998), 213.

28. J. Dupuis, *Toward a Christian Theology of Religious Pluralism,* 320–21.

29. J. Neuner and J. Dupuis, eds., *The Christian Faith: In the Doctrinal Documents of the Catholic Church* (Staten Island: Alba House, 1996), n. 615.

30. Ibid., nn. 635–37.

31. Ibid., nn. 612, 636.

32. Ibid., 319.

33. Ibid., 297.

34. Ibid., 58–59.

35. Ibid., 53–83.

36. G. Bof, "La dottrina dei 'semi del Verbo': origine e sviluppi," *Credere oggi* 9, no. 6 (1989): 54.

37. Dupuis, *Toward a Christian Theology of Religious Pluralism,* 60–66.

38. C. Geffré, "La singularité du Christianisme à l'âge du pluralisme religieux," in *Penser la foi: Recherches en théologie aujourd'hui: Mélanges offerts à Joseph Moingt,* ed. J. Doré and C. Theobald (Paris: Cerf-Assas, 1993), 365–66.

39. Dupuis, *Toward a Christian Theology of Religious Pluralism,* 53–83.

40. See J. Dupuis, *Jesus Christ at the Encounter of World Religions,* trans. R. Barr (Maryknoll, N.Y.: Orbis, 1991), 99–104; idem, *Who Do You Say I Am?* (Maryknoll, N.Y.: Orbis Books, 1994), 144–50.

20. The Person of Christ

John O'Donnell, S.J.

> Chalcedon proved to be more a beginning than an end. The notion of "person" was to undergo a long development which would seriously affect what we might mean when we speak of Christ's person.
>
> *Gerald O'Collins*[1]

> Karl Rahner's now classical observation about Chalcedon being more a beginning than an end, if it holds true about anything, bears on the notion of person.
>
> *Gerald O'Collins*[2]

The Contemporary Problematic

It is common in pastoral experience to find that ordinary folk refer to Jesus as a human person. One sometimes hears this said casually in homilies at mass. Recently, in teaching a synthetic seminar in systematic theology, I was surprised that a good number of students made this assertion in the final exam. When questioned on the teaching of the Council of Chalcedon, they knew that the council had defined Jesus as a divine person. Nonetheless many simply referred to Jesus in passing as a human person.

Why is this so? A first answer might be that from the perspective of turn-of-the-millennium Western culture the most obvious point about Jesus is his humanity. Those wanting to assert Jesus's full humanity often draw the conclusion that Jesus is a human person. Roger Haight, in his book *Jesus, Symbol of God,* makes the point explicit: "Given historical consciousness and the christological problematic today, people spontaneously accept Jesus as a human person . . . (as long as the divine and human natures) are not conceived in a static and abstract way, one can say that Jesus was one human person with an integral human nature in whom not less than God, and thus a divine nature is at work."[3]

Another reason is the assumption, either implicitly or at times explicitly stated, that if Jesus were the eternal divine person of the Son, this affirmation would compromise his full humanity. An eternal subject contradicts the full reality of the humanity of Jesus. John Macquarrie expresses this opinion: "As I said when we were considering the teaching of John, I believe it can be read in such a way that while it undoubtedly affirms that the Logos has existed 'from the beginning' this does not imply a personal pre-existence of Jesus Christ." He goes on to draw the conclusion that, while some New Testament writers "also believed that this pre-existent hypostasis dwelt in the human Jesus, they did not teach that Jesus himself was pre-existent. If they had, that would have been a denial of his true humanity and a lapse into mythology."[4]

Another reason is the assumption in modern thinking that "person" means center of consciousness and freedom. This concept of person has prevailed since the Enlightenment and is the one that we have inherited from German idealistic philosophy. Given the emphasis in contemporary thought on Jesus' humanity, many thinkers naturally assume that Jesus had a human consciousness and was the center of free self-determination. Given the modern concept of person, they draw the conclusion that Jesus was and is a human person.

The Tradition of Faith

Before examining more closely how we should speak about Jesus' personhood today, let us pause for a moment to recall the teaching of church tradition. Gerald O'Collins notes that the Council of Chalcedon named the "'one person and subsistence' as the principle of unity between Christ's two natures."[5] Strictly speaking, Chalcedon doesn't identify this one hypostasis with the eternal divine Logos, but the council certainly implies this, especially when "it moved straight from affirming the oneness of person to talk of one and the same Son and only-begotten God the Word, Lord Jesus Christ."[6] In case there was any doubt, however, the Second Council of Constantinople (A.D. 553) anathematizes anyone who "does not confess that our Lord Jesus Christ who was crucified in the flesh is true God,...the Lord of glory and one of the Holy Trinity" (DS 432). In making this affirmation the council is using the doctrine of the *communicatio idiomatum,* which means that properties of one nature can be predicated of the person even when the person is being named with reference to the other nature, for example, "the Son of God died." In O'Collins's words, "Despite the duality of natures, there is only one subject of attribution—the divine person of the Son of God who can act through his divine nature as well as through his human nature."[7]

SYSTEMATIC REFLECTION

Let us now reflect systematically upon these affirmations of faith, seeking the intelligibility of what we believe as Christians. Jean Galot, a colleague of Gerald O'Collins, wrote a number of incisive reflections on the personhood of Christ, beginning with an article in *Gregorianum* in 1974 entitled "Valeur de la notion de personne dans l'expression du mystère du Christ." Later he incorporated these insights into his larger christological essay *Who Is Christ? A Theology of the Incarnation* (Rome: Gregorian University Press, 1980).

Galot argues that the fundamental affirmation of Chalcedon is that Jesus Christ is the eternal person of the Logos. The eternal hypostasis of the Logos is the subject of all Jesus' human acts. Chalcedon's ground-breaking insight is to distinguish person and nature. The person identifies who Jesus is. It answers the question: Who is it? Nature rather answers the question: What is it? Galot refers to the scholastic distinction between *principium quod* and *principium quo.* The *principium quod* is the principle which acts, that is, the divine subject. The *principium quo* is the principle by which the subject acts, namely, the human nature. Jesus is the divine Logos who acts by his human nature.

Galot also notes that in the Western tradition insights into the meaning of personhood derive from Christology and trinitarian theology. The councils of the church emphasize that personhood in Christology and in Trinity has to do with subsistence. The person exists in himself. The person possesses a reality of his own. But person also indicates relationship. This is especially true in trinitarian theology. The Cappadocian fathers were the first to suggest that the persons of the Trinity are relationships. St. Thomas in the *Summa Theologica* defines the persons of the Trinity as subsistent relations (see *Summa Theologica,* 1, 29, 4).

This insight is important for Christology. Jesus in his whole being is relationship. He comes from the Father and he returns to the Father. In the Trinity his whole being is a being from. He is begotten from the Father. The hypostatic nature of his relationship to the Father in the Trinity grounds his relationship to God the Father on earth. His being grounds his mission. In biblical terms Jesus is pure obedience to the Father, pure openness to mission, pure availability to the Father's plan of salvation. The Fourth Gospel especially accents this aspect of Jesus' identity. In John 4, Jesus says "My food is to do the will of him who sent me" (John 4:34). Later in John 8 Jesus says "I always do what is pleasing to him" (John 8:28). So Jesus is pure relationality. As Hans Urs von Balthasar puts it, whether the Son is in the bosom of the Father or walking the paths of his earthly pilgrimage, the reality of his being and identity is the same: to live from the Father.[8] But, as Joseph Ratzinger has shown, this ontological relation of Jesus to the Father is what grounds his relationship to us. His whole life is mission and self-gift. His whole being on earth is to be "for us." But he is able to be this for us, precisely because he is for the Father. His being as "for the Father" grounds his availability "for us."[9]

How would Galot handle the question of Jesus' consciousness and freedom? As he says in his *Gregorianum* article cited above, the key insight of Chalcedon is to distinguish person and *esprit. Esprit* involves self-consciousness. *Esprit* involves knowledge of self and others. *Esprit* involves autonomy, self-determination—in other words freedom. But *esprit* is the realm of nature, not of person. So, Galot concludes, Jesus of course possesses self-consciousness. And he argues that Jesus Christ becomes conscious of himself in a human way. He becomes conscious of his divine identity in a human process of self-discovery. And of course Jesus possesses human freedom. He must do so for he has a complete human nature. Being a divine subject in no way contradicts his human freedom. This would only be the case if we thought of the human and divine as being in competition with one another. The opposite is the case. The divine always frees the human to be itself. The relationship between divine and human freedom is always that of a direct proportion: the greater the dependence on the divinity, the greater the human autonomy.

Let us now turn to the reflections of Gerald O'Collins on the personhood of Christ. First, we note that O'Collins takes as his starting point the Chalcedonian definition that Jesus Christ is a divine person. There is no human subject of identity in Jesus Christ. He writes: "Jesus Christ was (and is) then a man, a human being and human individual, *but not* a human person."[10] He continues in the same vein as the reflections of Galot above:

> The hypostatic union means that the human reality of Jesus belongs to the Son of God in a personal and absolute way, but not that this humanity is in any way diminished through the absence of human personhood. Full humanity is not necessarily identified with or dependent upon the presence of human personhood. Human characteristics and 'perfections' come at the level of nature and of a given individual's qualities as a human being. At that level personhood as such contributes nothing.[11]

O'Collins lists five characteristics of the person in contemporary thought. Persons are (a) distinct and individual beings, who (b) enjoy rationality and freedom, (c) exist and act in relationship with other persons, (d) experience their self-identity in such a relational existence, and (e) have an inalienable dignity.[12]

Applying these characteristics to Jesus and taking into account the Chalcedonian definition, O'Collins gives the following interpretation of Jesus Christ:

> Jesus Christ was (and is) (a) a distinct and individual being, who (c) existed and acted in relationship with others and (d) experienced his self-identity in such a relational existence—above all, in and through his unique relationship to the One he called "Abba." As *divine* person he had no independent centre of consciousness and freedom, but participated with the Father and the Spirit in one intellect and will. Yet through his humanity (b) Jesus Christ enjoyed his own rationality and freedom. Lastly, his existence as Son of God (e) gave his person an absolutely sovereign dignity.[13]

Like Galot, O'Collins is at pains to refute the contemporary equation of personhood with consciousness. He argues that some simple commonsense reflections reveal that we cannot equate the two. For example, a person who is sleeping is still a person even if he or she is not conscious. The same applies to a person in a coma. Another example would be that of a human fetus. Nevertheless, O'Collins acknowledges that our sense of identity does depend on our awareness of ourselves. He writes: "Through my awareness of my one self, I know myself to be this 'I'. In brief, self-identification depends on self-consciousness."[14]

What then are we to say in the case of Christ? His "I" is not that of a human subject. O'Collins admits that even if there is no human personhood in Christ, we have in Christ a fully human consciousness and therefore the conditions for a human psychological center of reference, a human "I" or ego. He explains:

> In all other cases one "I" corresponds to and expresses one self or subject. Here, however, the human ego of Jesus is not such an autonomous subject. The ego of his human consciousness is also the Word of God as humanly conscious and self-conscious, that is, as operating in and through *this* human awareness. God the Son takes as his own this human self-consciousness, self-identity, and center of reference.[15]

O'Collins further defends the doctrine of the preexistence of Christ against such critics as Macquarrie cited above. He is led to do this because he finds it in the biblical witness but also because it is part of the church's belief. O'Collins notes the phrase of the First Council of Constantinople: "begotten from the Father before the ages" (DS 150). O'Collins admits that the term "preexistence" can be confusing. It could be read to imply a "before" and "after" of his personal, divine existence. Thus, it would be better to speak simply of his eternal personhood. He writes: "Pre-existence means rather that Christ personally belongs to an order of being other than the created, temporal one. His personal, divine existence transcends temporal (and spatial) categories; it might be better expressed as trans-existence, meta-existence, or, quite simply, eternal existence."[16]

How does Jesus become aware of his eternal personhood? This is a speculative question, and the church has never given an official explanation. O'Collins suggests an approach based on the human experience of God. As human beings we experience ourselves and our world as finite. But in being conscious of the finite we at the same time intuit the Eternal and Infinite. The Infinite is co-present to us in our experience of the finite. O'Collins suggests that "in knowing what was finite and temporal through his human consciousness, Jesus co-experienced the Infinite and Eternal as One to whom he stood in the intimate, personal relationship of Son to Father. This co-experience of the Infinite differed from ours, inasmuch as it essentially involved the sense of a unique personal relationship to the God whom Jesus named as 'Abba.'"[17] Thus O'Collins comes back, as does Galot and indeed many systematic theologians, to Jesus' human experience of a unique relationship with God, which was expressed in his prayer experience to his Abba God, in his unique sense of being sent, and in his pervasive sense of obedience to his filial relationship and mission.

A final point might be worth mentioning. O'Collins, along with number of contemporary theologians, distinguishes person and personality. Person denotes the subject of identity, in the case of Jesus, the divine "I" of the Logos. Personality rather belongs to nature and indicates those human traits, characteristics, and habits that give concrete contour to the individual. I may be described as introverted, sociable, humorous, moody. I may be a person who has a highly developed right brain rather than left brain. I can be highly intuitive in my perceptions of persons and situations. I may have a poetic temperament. I have perhaps cultivated the habit of intellectual discipline and a clear writing style. All these traits and characteristics by which I express myself and by which the other comes to an appreciation of me are part of the makeup of my personality. Nothing prevents us from affirming that Jesus had a human personality. His divine identity did not exclude a particular, distinctive assemblage of traits and habits that made up his human personality. Indeed, his human historical existence entailed an assemblage of individual traits and habits that in the concrete made him the uniquely striking personality he was. But ascribing to him human personality is different from affirming that he was and is a human person. In summary, although Christian tradition denies him human personhood, it is equally stringent in affirming that Jesus was fully human. Being a divine person takes nothing away from the fullness of his humanity.

LIGHT ON HUMAN PERSONHOOD

We have seen that only Jesus of Nazareth is the unique person of the eternal Logos made flesh. Nonetheless, as Joseph Ratzinger points out, it would be a mistake to so emphasize Jesus' uniqueness, that we fail to reflect on how his unique personhood sheds light on the mystery of the personhood of every human being.[18] Walter Kasper, in his reflections on the personhood of Christ, notes that on the one hand personhood indicates that which is incommunicable but on the other hand it is the nature of persons to be open. Personhood is ex-sistence, stepping out of self toward the world, toward others and toward God. Kasper writes:

> A human being experiences himself on the one hand as a unique and incommunicable I, as this one here, an absolutely unique being who is responsible for himself and in his own charge. On the other hand, he finds himself in a world around him and in the society of his fellow men; he is not closed in on himself, he is a being that is already determined by reality and that opens out on all reality; he is mind, spirit, by his very nature, essentially of a kind to be *quodammodo omnia.*[19]

In Ratzinger's penetrating article, he makes a similar point. He explains that it is precisely the nature of human persons to be with the other. Relationality is at the heart of human personhood. Human persons are open to the other; they are self-transcendence. But when we examine in depth the meaning of this self-transcendence, we see that the openness of human persons is unrestricted. No limits can be placed on their self-transcendence. Ultimately we must define human persons in their openness to God.[20]

Self-transcendence, then, is the key to understanding the relationship between Christ's personhood and ours. Christ is the eternal subsistent hypostasis of the Logos. But, as the Word, his whole being is from the Father. He is the eternally begotten Son. His very being then is defined in terms of the living out of this relationship with the Father. As we saw above, relationship defines his being both in the Trinity and in the time of his living out of his mission on earth. But in this way Christ sheds light on our personhood. We too can only be ourselves by living out fully our self-transcendence, by placing ourselves continually in relationship to God, by living out in our lives Christ's filial relationship with his Abba God. In his original study in Christology, Wolfhart Pannenberg thinks in a similar way, arguing that Jesus is the fulfillment of human personality. He notes that Chalcedon has an anthropological presupposition, namely, the openness of the human being to God. That is why the divinity and humanity of Jesus are not in conflict. That is why the affirmation that Jesus is the divine person of the Son does not detract from Jesus' humanity. Pannenberg writes that, through the event of the incarnation, "it becomes apparent that all human existence is designed to be personalized by its dependence upon God, to be integrated into a person through its relation to God the Father in such a way that men are constituted as persons by the Fatherly God in confrontation with him."[21] Jesus is Son in his filial dependence on the Father, and we human beings fulfill our self-transcendence when we acknowledge our dependence on God through the Son.

CONCLUSION

Where have our reflections led us? We have seen that the Catholic tradition of faith seeking understanding has led to the affirmation that Jesus is the eternal person of the Son. Jesus is not a human person.

However, systematic reflection shows that this affirmation does not conflict with the constant tradition of the church that Jesus is fully human. As Ratzinger has shown, step by step in the patristic period, the church fought tenaciously to uphold the full humanity of Jesus.[22]

As Gerald O'Collins has insisted, a key to understanding this truth is the distinction between person and nature. Person answers the question, Who is Jesus? Nature answers the question, What is Jesus? Jesus is the divine person of the Word. But Jesus has a fully integral human nature. Hence Jesus possesses a human self-consciousness. Jesus has his own human autonomy. Jesus grows in knowledge and wisdom.

The acknowledgment of Jesus' divine personhood does not take anything away from Jesus' human personality. In his openness to the Father, Jesus fulfills and illumines the meaning of human personality. As Jean Galot explains, the person of the Word vivifies and personalizes Christ's human nature, and this so completely that Galot can affirm, "No human nature was ever so profoundly personified as the human nature of Jesus."[23]

As Gerald O'Collins so often insists, it is necessary to make the appropriate distinctions. A key one is to distinguish person from self-consciousness. They are not the same. But once we make these necessary distinctions we have every reason to be bold in proclaiming Jesus' divine identity and personhood without the least fear of compromising his full humanity.

Notes

Scripture citations are given according to the Revised Standard Version (RSV).

1. Gerald O'Collins, *Interpreting Jesus* (London: Geoffrey Chapman and Mahwah: Paulist Press, 1983), 180.

2. Gerald O'Collins, *Christology* (New York: Oxford University Press, 1995), 235.

3. Roger Haight, *Jesus, Symbol of God* (Maryknoll, N.Y.: Orbis Books, 1999), 461.

4. John Macquarrie, *Jesus Christ in Modern Thought* (London: SCM, 1990), 389–90. O'Collins discusses Macquarrie's objections to prexistence in his *Christology*, 242–43.

5. O'Collins, *Interpreting Jesus*, 180.

6. Ibid., 182.

7. Ibid., 183.

8. See Hans Urs von Balthasar, *The Christian State of Life* (San Francisco: Ignatius, 1983). Balthasar writes: "For whether the Son is in the bosom of the Father or treading the paths of earth, there can be no doubt that the 'where' that determines his state of life is the mission, the work, the will of the Father. In this 'where', the Son can always be found, for he is himself the epitome of the paternal mission" (p. 188).

9. See Joseph Ratzinger, *Introduction to Christianity* (San Francisco: Ignatius, 1990). Ratzinger writes: "To John, 'Son' means being-from-another; thus with this word he defines the being of this man as being from another and for others, as a being that is completely open on both sides, knows no reserved area of the mere 'I.' When it thus becomes clear that the being of Jesus as Christ is completely open being, a being 'from' and 'towards,' that nowhere clings to itself and nowhere stands on its own, then it is also clear at the same time that this being is pure relation (not substantiality) and, as pure relation, pure unity" (p. 134).

10. O'Collins, *Interpreting Jesus*, 182.

11. Ibid., 182.

12. Ibid., 181.

13. Ibid., 183.

14. O'Collins, *Christology*, 236.

15. Ibid., 247.

16. Ibid., 238.

17. Ibid., 248.

18. See Joseph Ratzinger, "Zum Personverständnis in der Theologie," in *Dogma und Verkundigung* (Munich: Erich Wewel Verlag, 1973), 205–23.

19. Walter Kasper, *Jesus the Christ* (London: Burns & Oates, 1976), 345.

20. The Jesuit philosopher W. Norris Clarke has echoed precisely the points made by Kasper and Ratzinger in his small volume *Person and Being* (Milwaukee: Marquette University Press, 1993). Clarke finds three indispensable elements in the meaning of the human person. First, the human person exists in himself or herself. Personhood means self-possession. In other words, personhood is characterized by interiority. Second, persons are by their very being self-communicative or relational. "To be a person is to *be with...*, to be a sharer, a receiver, a lover" (p. 112). Finally, personhood means self-transcendence, or that decentering by which the person opens himself or herself up to the love of God.

21. Wolfhart Pannenberg, *Jesus—God and Man* (Philadelphia: Westminster Press, 1968), 345.

22. See Ratzinger, "Zum Personverständnis," esp. 215ff.

23. Jean Galot, *Who Is Christ? A Theology of the Incarnation* (Rome: Gregorian University Press, 1980), 302, 285.

21. Why Some Still Doubt
That Jesus' Body Was Raised

Paul Gwynne, O.M.I.

The resurrection of Jesus is not only one of the most central articles of the Christian faith but also a rich and multifaceted belief. One of
its more controversial dimensions concerns the fate of Jesus' body. The
traditional understanding holds that Jesus' corpse did not remain in the
grave but was raised up and transformed in some glorious manner. The
historical underside of this assertion is the gospel claim that his tomb
was found open and empty soon after his death. However, this way of
envisaging Jesus' resurrection has been questioned in modern theological reflection, especially with the rise of the historical-critical method
of biblical exegesis. This has generated an ongoing debate between
those who argue, on one hand, for a historical empty tomb with its
implication that Jesus' body was involved in his resurrection, and those,
on the other hand, who claim that this tradition is legendary and that his
corpse suffered the same fate as ours, namely, corruption in the earth.

Jesus' resurrection has been a major theme in the writings of
Gerald O'Collins over the years. Few authors in English have spent as
much ink on the subject as he. His publications include six books and
many articles dedicated to the topic as well as significant sections of
his various christological works. In 1996 he was one of the organizers
of an international symposium on the resurrection of Jesus in
Dunwoodie, New York.[1] It is clear from these writings and the tenor of
the symposium that O'Collins is a committed defender of the historicity of the empty tomb tradition and the theological coherence of the
belief that Jesus' corpse was raised. The symposium is significant
because it contrasts with the 1995 Jesus Seminar, which focused on

Christ's resurrection.[2] In that meeting, among other things, the vast majority of participants agreed that belief in Jesus' resurrection does not depend on the fate of his corpse and that his body probably decayed in an unknown grave.

The subject matter of this article, written in honor of Gerald O'Collins's dedication to theological research and education, is the most recent chapter in the debate over Jesus' corpse. The two seminars mentioned serve as symbols of the division of opinion that continues to characterize the scholarly community. The bulk of the discussion on both sides has been directed at the question of the historical reliability of the burial and tomb traditions found at the end of the canonical Gospels. This, in itself, is a fascinating and complex network of arguments that would require another article to be dealt with adequately. Our main concern in this article, however, is to delve beneath this first level of exegesis and history to a deeper stratum of philosophical and theological principles.

Before we seek those subterranean principles at work in the debate, however, we should take a quick look at the main arguments concerning the historicity of the empty tomb over the last ten years or so. Authors such as John Dominic Crossan and John Shelby Spong appeal to the usual Roman practice, which was either to leave the body of the crucified to be devoured by wild animals or throw the corpse into a common grave for executed criminals. This general historical fact, coupled with a reference in Acts 13:29 to Jesus being buried by his enemies, leads them to assert that the Gospel burial and empty tomb traditions are the result of Christian midrash and have no historical basis.[3] Others such as Barnabas Lindars, Gerd Lüdemann, and Thorwald Lorenzen rely more on the lack of any explicit mention of the empty tomb in the Pauline corpus to ground their hypothesis that the stories are legendary. They add a particular interpretation of 1 Corinthians 15, which suggests that, for Paul, our resurrection does not require any involvement of our corpse. It is argued that the "new" body is best understood as being numerically different from the earthly body. This is the case for the general resurrection of humankind, and they see no reason why Jesus' case should be any different.[4] Another approach, represented by Gerald Bostock, admits that the tomb was found empty soon after Jesus' death but sees theft by the Jewish authorities as the best explanation.[5]

Needless to say, there are also scholars who are confident that the burial and tomb traditions contain a solid historical kernel. Writers such as Gerald O'Collins, William Lane Craig, Stephen Davis, and Pheme Perkins marshal evidence that not only offers effective counterarguments to the above proposals but also provides significant positive arguments in favor of a historical empty tomb.[6] All in all, there is not a great deal on either side that is new, which is probably not surprising, as theological debates often move along at a modest pace with original elements appearing only occasionally. Moreover, one thing stands out—those who seek a decisive, unequivocal verdict on the historical evidence will probably be disappointed because there is a significant element of ambiguity. This is mainly due to the paucity of information available and the mix of historical and religious meanings that define the Gospel narratives themselves. The assessment of this author is that the weight of evidence still lies in favor of a historical empty tomb. Given this evidence as well as the stories of the appearances, it is not unreasonable for faith to conclude that the tomb was empty because Jesus' resurrection involved his corpse. However, an honest scholar would have to admit to a considerable difference of opinion in the academic community. The historical debate will undoubtedly continue.

It has been apparent for some time that this particular debate, not unlike other debates that concern a mix of history and theology, is influenced by elements pertaining to the latter as well as the former. In other words, the frustrating lack of clear historical evidence allows for significant shaping of authors' opinions by other concerns. These concerns are not the specific details of biblical exegesis or sociocultural studies of the New Testament world, but lie at another level altogether. They concern the deeper philosophical and theological presuppositions that every author brings to the issue. These are an unavoidable part of the scholar's intellectual baggage and affect their conclusions regarding the empty tomb, regardless of whether they eventually opt for its historicity or not. The impression is that these often hidden presuppositions ultimately determine an author's stance on the matter rather than a so-called impartial reading of the historical-exegetical arguments.

A number of such presuppositions can be identified in the writings of both sides and comprise important philosophical-theological questions in themselves. Some years ago, I suggested at least six such issues: the goodness of the material world; the meaning of human bodiliness before and after death; the basis of personal identity and continuity; the uniqueness of Jesus vis-à-vis his solidarity with human experience; the relationship between faith and historical-exegetical method; the problem for the scientific mind of occasional divine intervention in the world.[7] The last ten years of literature on the empty tomb have not required a drastic revision of the list, except that some have emerged as more crucial, or at least more discussed, than others.

The principle of the inherent goodness of the material world, a cornerstone of the Judeo-Christian tradition, naturally lends itself to support an empty tomb. Jesus' body is raised up by God as a sign that, even in the new world of Easter, the material dimension of reality is not to be simply discarded but transformed. Yet it has not figured greatly in the recent debate. Peter Jensen and J. Barclay mention this point in passing, but neither author dwells on it much.[8] In an attempt to develop Karl Rahner's thoughts on how the risen Christ can be the "heart of the world," Denis Edwards reiterates the point that this material world cannot simply be the temporary stage on which the human drama is played out or merely the launching pad for the human spirit. He does not use the empty tomb in his arguments, however, perhaps because even Rahner himself was unclear about the actual fate of Jesus' corpse. In Rahner's words, the vessel that was the Lord's body was "shattered," and Christ was "poured out" over the cosmos to become its very center. In a sense, the universe becomes the body of the risen Christ who, in Edwards's thinking, acts as the inner drive for the evolutionary movement.[9] Similar cosmic-ecological concerns lead Janet Martin Soskice not only to endorse a historical empty tomb but to take it beyond the "etiolated orthodoxy" of Christian apologetics, where it serves merely as proof of Jesus' survival beyond death, to "full-blooded resurrection faith." By this she means a real concern for this present, temporal, material world, which has inherent value and will be transformed at the eschaton.[10]

Discussion of human bodiliness and personal continuity beyond death appear from time to time in the literature. Unlike the goodness of matter, however, a more nuanced understanding of the body, both during this life and in the next, tends to undermine a historical empty tomb. Science has revealed our physical bodies as complex biochemi-

cal organisms constantly interacting with the environment and in a per-
petual state of flux. The material constituting my body today is not the
same stuff that constituted it thirty years ago or will constitute it thirty
years hence. With such an understanding, it is difficult to obtain a
sense of continuity that is strictly physical. What endures seem to be
the patterns and structures, themselves evolving over time, rather than
the actual atoms that comprise these at any particular moment. If this
is true, then storing bones or corpses to ensure that the "same" person
will be raised on the last day may be deeply sacred from a religious
point of view, but appears misguided from a biological perspective.
The empty tomb tradition and its implication that Jesus' corpse is literally transformed into his new risen body seems terribly at odds with
this broader understanding. As Marie-Emile Boismard states, the significance of the notion of "resurrection" is that it protects the wholeness of the human person as an embodied creature, even beyond death.
An immortal, disembodied soul is an "amputation" of the person. But
the danger of the notion is that it conjures up images of corpses rising
from graves when these corpses are really no longer human but "an
amass of cells in the process of decomposition and returning to the
cycle of the azote."[11]

Yet this more subtle understanding of the human "body" does not
really explain the degree of skepticism regarding the historicity of the
empty tomb and its theological implications concerning Jesus' corpse
that typifies authors such as Spong, Crossan, Lüdemann, Lorenzen,
Lindars, and Bostock. We get closer to the real issues when we consider the next presupposition, namely, the objection that an empty
tomb would mean that Jesus' experience of death is fundamentally different from our own, as his corpse did not decay while ours surely will.
This argument was prominent in the conversation between Geoffrey
Lampe and Donald MacKinnon in the late 1960s. It appears again in a
number of the scholars mentioned above. For example, it is clearly a
defining principle for Lüdemann who writes:

> In denying that the tomb was empty I have deliberately spoken,
> provocatively, of the "full tomb." I have done so to hammer home
> that Jesus was truly human and really died a brutal death.... In
> other words, the factual statement that Jesus' body decayed is the
> starting point for all further concern with the questions surround-
> ing his "resurrection." Whoever avoids that conclusion by evasive

theological reflections will rightly become the target of David Friedrich Strauss' ominous statement that the history of the resurrection of Jesus can be described as the greatest hoax of world history.[12]

In the same manner, Bostock quotes Lampe when he argues that if Jesus' corpse does not decay like ours then "he remains our Lord but ceases to be our brother." This asymmetry imperils our salvation at the critical point of our existence.[13] The objection should be taken seriously, but it is not without reply. It can be argued that the difference between the fate of Jesus' corpse and that of our corpses is a minor one and does not in any serious way undermine the fundamental solidarity that the doctrine of the incarnation upholds. In fact, there are many aspects of ordinary human existence that Jesus did not experience firsthand: for example, feminine gender, blood siblings, marriage, parenthood, old age, and so on. The particularity of each person allows for such differences without compromising the fact that we are all part of the human story. Moreover, according to the same doctrine of the incarnation, Jesus is different from all other human persons in that he is a divine person in a human nature. The principle of his solidarity with us must be balanced by the principle of his unique identity and role.

It seems to me that the real obstacle for many of these authors is the question of divine intervention and the scientific background that renders such a concept so difficult to accommodate. Although the appearances of the risen Lord also constitute highly unusual phenomena from the point of view of science, the disappearance or transformation of Jesus' corpse is the most external, physical dimension of his resurrection. Whereas psychology is involved in the question of the disciples "seeing" the Lord, physics is involved in the case of the empty tomb. And it seems that many theologians are deeply uncomfortable with divine activity affecting the laws of physics. For some, God is allowed to act on people's minds but not in the external world of objects, where science explains processes with great accuracy and claims of exceptional phenomena are treated with the greatest suspicion. Moreover, this prejudice against physical miracles has deeply infiltrated certain instances of historical-critical exegesis even though the investigators claim to be thoroughly "objective and scientific." Although not often overtly acknowledged, several of the authors discussed above who have serious doubts about the historicity of the empty tomb have confessed to this fundamental assumption. In the case of Crossan, Paul Rhodes Eddy notes his admission that he did not think that "anyone, anywhere, at any time brings dead people back to life." Thus Eddy is quite correct in concluding that such an a priori metaphysical assumption will have a direct impact upon his presumably a posteriori conclusions regarding the historical evidence for the gospel tradition's claims of resurrection.[14]

In a similar fashion, Lüdemann complains that many exegetes have long abandoned any historical basis to Jesus' nature miracles, his virginal conception, and his ascension into heaven, but cannot bring themselves to dispense with an empty tomb. As far as he is concerned, statements about Jesus' resurrection have "lost their literal meaning with the revolution in the scientific picture of the world." His aim is to present a hypothesis concerning the resurrection of Jesus that "causes the least offence and solves the most difficulties"—presumably for the scientific minds that cannot accept that such an event could have happened. In particular, one of the reasons for his "scientific" rejection of Jesus' resurrection from the grave is his contention that we can no longer accept a literal ascension into heaven or return on the clouds with angels. Quoting an article by Emanuel Hirsch in 1963, Lüdemann argues that the empty tomb must be jettisoned along with these other two ideas because they involve a "single necessary consequence in which no member can be altered without everything breaking into pieces." Lüdemann admits that this seems to reduce Christianity to a science-friendly minimum in comparison to former times, but this does not perturb him since "it does no harm from now on for Christians to live by the little that they really believe, not by the much that they take pains to believe. That is a great liberation, which already bears within it the germ of the new."[15] Apart from the highly contentious claim that Jesus' resurrection from the grave must be treated in the same way as his supposed physical ascension into the clouds, Lüdemann simply, and unjustifiably, presumes that believers who accept the scientific explanation of the physical world cannot simultaneously accept the possibility of miraculous divine action within that world, as in the case of Jesus' resurrection from the tomb. The verdict has really been handed down before the case has even been heard. Like certain other scholars down through the decades, he presupposes that resurrection is impossible and then sets out to show from exegesis that this is the case.

Spong is no different when he argues at the end of his work that the traditional understanding of Jesus' resurrection is the stuff of magic. Such a belief might be sustained in a "pre-modern" age of faith, but such "sleight of hand" can never survive in the contemporary world, where miracle and the supernatural are both suspect. To assert an empty tomb in an age of science is to doom Easter faith to a "death of irrelevance." Determined to avoid any possible clash with science, Spong is happy to speak of "ultimate moments" and of a Jesus who is "with God" in some mysterious manner, but he dismisses as idle all theological reflection on Jesus' fate and general eschatology. "Those books on life after death that I read in my earlier life will remain in a row on a shelf in my library. I will not open them again. . . . That is not my business. My business is to live now, to love now, and to be now."[16] While Spong's stress on the importance of present reality is admirable and justified, its direct competition with matters beyond the grave is highly artificial. There is no reason why theology cannot deal with both. In fact, it would surely be an abrogation of duty if the Christian theologian were not to reflect on the mystery of death and beyond. Spong's language is passionate but imbalanced. Moreover, Spong simply presumes that scientifically minded people in this "modern" age cannot cope with such a notion as Jesus' resurrection from the grave. As one author puts it, such a ban on special divine activity within the world leaves us "with a God who cannot save because he has no control over nature and history."[17]

Without intending to belabor the point, Lindars and Bostock also display the same fundamental presupposition concerning God's action in the physical world, which leads them to reject the involvement of Jesus' corpse in his resurrection. Although not as forthright in his condemnation of worldviews that allow for miracles, Lindars wants to place Jesus' resurrection into "another perspective," as the question of whether a miracle was involved in the resurrection is really a "red herring." For Lindars, it is better to think of miracles in attenuated terms such as triumph over evil and personal salvation. The Gospel miracle stories are intended to convey a deeper significance in relation to universal well-being. To take them literally is to succumb to the rationalisation process whereby people express "abstract truths" in "concrete forms."[18] Meanwhile, Bostock begins his article by frankly stating the problems an empty tomb raises in terms of divine action. If we admit that God acted on the physical world in the case of Jesus' corpse, then we have a God who could intervene at other points in history—especially in situations where evil dominates and the innocent suffer—but chooses not to. This leads to a deity that appears "arbitrary, unjust and at odds with a rational universe." An empty tomb raises more problems than it solves, for it undermines the principle of the incarnation—that "God works within the constraints of his own creation. He does not break or bend the normal laws of life to his own advantage as would seem to be the case with the 'empty tomb.' He does not smash the workings of human history with a sledgehammer, but transforms them from within."[19]

In his paper at the 1996 Seminar, Alan Padgett targeted precisely this aspect of the historical-critical method used by some of our authors. The a priori ruling out of events claimed to have been caused by the action of God is in grave danger of reducing theology to a mere social-scientific explanation. In the end, this is "just a piece of Enlightenment bias." Padgett pleads that we "take off the mask of pure objectivity and speak to each other face to face."[20] Fellow philosophers of religion Richard Swinburne and William Alston agree that the real issues of the empty tomb debate are these underlying presuppositions in the various stances of the authors, especially the question of divine activity in the world. In Swinburne's words, the "background evidence" plays a key role in determining a scholar's attitude to the empty tomb. This background evidence is first shaped by the general biological fact that dead bodies do not normally rise from the grave, but it is further qualified by the question of the possibility of occasional special divine action.

> There is a significant balance of detailed historical evidence in favour of the resurrection, but it is not strong enough to equal the very strong force of the background evidence—if the latter is construed only as evidence of what are the laws of nature. But in my view that is not the right way to construe the background evidence. My belief is that there is a lot of evidence for the existence of God—a being essentially omnipotent, omniscient and perfectly free.... The laws of nature depend for their operation from moment to moment on God, who, in virtue of his omnipotence, can suspend them as and when he chooses.[21]

Likewise, Alston feels that the historical evidence leans toward an understanding of Jesus' resurrection that involves his corpse being raised. The resistance of so many scholars to this evidence raises the question of hidden presuppositions, especially a sense of awkwardness with forms of the miraculous they consider crude, sensational, melodramatic, blatant or simply "gauche."[22]

The same applies, of course, to defenders of a historical empty tomb. They also must admit their own presuppositions, especially the crucial issue of divine activity. Thus, Sarah Coakley is correct in criticizing Wolfhart Pannenberg's valiant effort to prove the historicity of Jesus' resurrection from a "purely" historical viewpoint with significant emphasis on the empty tomb. Pannenberg's arguments are built against a background that is already theistic and allows for divine intervention at certain crucial points in history.[23] Francis Schüssler Fiorenza also recognizes this as the key issue in the entire debate when he writes:

> I am aware that certain background assumptions about God's action in history might lead me to give one account, another Christian a different account, and an atheist a still different account. Consequently, I can offer my historical account as to how the events fit together in order to justify my conviction that God raised Jesus. Yet, at the same time, I am aware that others with different background assumptions will weigh the evidence and various warrants differently, and may not be convinced. Consequently, I do not think that fundamental theology can demonstrate even with probability that God raised Jesus. It can offer—and argue—its historical narrative as a probable and possible narrative to those who accept, as I do, that God can act in history.[24]

Given the intricacies and ambiguities of the historical evidence, it has been apparent for a long time that deeper philosophical and theological presuppositions exercise considerable influence on the minds of the protagonists. Arguably, it is here that the real battle must be fought. Admittedly these issues should not dictate what actually happened in those first few days after Jesus' death. But they certainly determine what authors think was possible or impossible historically. Moreover, moving to this deeper level means leaving behind the details of exegesis and history and taking up the broader questions that are raised. It is not my intention to begin that task here—only to point to where other, properly philosophical and theological, debates impinge on the historical question of Jesus' tomb. O'Collins is not the only scholar to have noted this, but he did state it succinctly when he wrote many years ago: "I suspect...that the real problems with the empty tomb are theological, not historical."[25]

Notes

1. The papers delivered at this symposium are published in *The Resurrection: An Interdisciplinary Symposium on the Resurrection of Jesus,* ed. S. Davis, D. Kendall, and G. O'Collins (Oxford: Oxford University Press, 1997).

2. The papers and voting results from this seminar are published in *Forum* 10, nos. 3–4 (1994).

3. See John Dominic Crossan, *Jesus: A Revolutionary Biography* (San Francisco: Harper, 1994), 123–58; John Shelby Spong, *Resurrection: Myth or Reality?* (San Francisco: HarperCollins, 1994), 221–29.

4. See Barnabas Lindars, "The Resurrection and the Empty Tomb" in *The Resurrection of Jesus Christ,* ed. Paul Avis (Darton, Longman & Todd, 1993), 116–35; Gerd Lüdemann, *What Really Happened to Jesus?* (London: SCM, 1995), 131–37; idem, "The Resurrection of Jesus: The Greatest Hoax in History," *Forum* 10:3–4 (1994): 161–75; idem, *The Resurrection of Jesus: Experience, History, Theology* (London: SCM, 1994), 21–32, 180–84; Thorwald Lorenzen, *Resurrection and Discipleship* (Maryknoll, N.Y.: Orbis Books, 1995), 116–26, 167–81.

5. See Gerald Bostock, "Do We Need an Empty Tomb?" *Expository Times* 105 (1993–94): 201–5.

6. See Gerald O'Collins, "The Resurrection: The State of the Questions" in *Resurrection,* ed. Davis et al., 13–17; William Lane Craig, "The Empty Tomb of Jesus" in *In Defense of Miracles,* ed. R. Douglas Geivett and Gary Habermas (Downers Grove, Ill.: InterVarsity Press, 1997), 247–61; idem, "John Dominic Crossan and the Resurrection" in *Resurrection,* ed. David et al., 249–71; Stephen Davis, *Risen Indeed: Making Sense of the Resurrection* (Grand Rapids: Eerdmans, 1993), 62–84; Pheme Perkins, "The Resurrection of Jesus of Nazareth" in *Studying the Historical Jesus: Evaluations of the State of Current Research,* ed. B. Chilton and C. Evans (New York: E. J. Brill, 1994), 423–42.

7. See Paul Gwynne, "Theological Issues Behind the Empty Tomb Debate," *Australasian Catholic Record* 71 (1994): 45–60.

8. See Paul Barnett, Peter Jensen, and David Peterson, *Resurrection: Truth and Reality* (Sydney: Aquila, 1994), 41–42; J. Barclay, "The Resurrection in Contemporary New Testament Scholarship" in *Resurrection Reconsidered,* ed. Gavin D'Costa (Oxford: Oneworld, 1996), 23.

9. See Denis Edwards, "The Relationship between the Risen Christ and the Material Universe," *Pacifica* 4 (1991): 1–14.

10. See Janet Martin Soskice, "Resurrection and the New Jerusalem," in *Resurrection,* ed. Davis et al., 48–49, 56–58.

11. See Marie-Emile Boismard, *Faut-il encore parler de "résurrection"?* (Paris: Cerf, 1995), 157–62.

12. Lüdemann, "Resurrection," 168.

13. Bostock, "Do We Need," 204.

14. See Paul Rhodes Eddy, "Response," in *Resurrection*, ed. Davis et al., 283–84.

15. See Lüdemann, "Resurrection," 162–65, 168; Lüdemann, *What Really Happened*, 135–37; Lüdemann, *Resurrection*, 180–81.

16. See Spong, *Resurrection*, 290–93.

17. Barnett, Jensen, and Peterson, *Resurrection*, 9.

18. Lindars, "Resurrection," 118–19.

19. See Bostock, "Do We Need," 201, 205.

20. See Alan Padgett, "Advice for Religious Historians: On the Myth of a Purely Historical Jesus," in *Resurrection*, ed. Davis et al., 304, 307.

21. Richard Swinburne, "Evidence for the Resurrection," in *Resurrection*, ed. Davis et al., 202.

22. William Alston, "Biblical Criticism and the Resurrection," in *Resurrection*, ed. Davis et al., 182, 183.

23. Sarah Coakley, "Is the Resurrection a Historical Event?" in *Resurrection of Jesus Christ*, ed. Avis, 110–11.

24. Francis Schüssler Fiorenza, "The Resurrection of Jesus and Roman Catholic Fundamental Theology," in *Resurrection*, ed. Davis et al., 247.

25. Gerald O'Collins, *The Easter Jesus* (London: Darton, Longman & Todd, 1973), 91. See also Craig, "Empty Tomb," 258–59; Boismard, *Faut-il encore*, 159.

Contributors

Carmen Aparicio is a Professor at the Gregorian University, Rome, Italy.

Brendan Byrne, S.J., is a Professor of Scripture at the United Faculty of Theology, Parkville, Victoria, Australia.

Stephen T. Davis is Professor of Philosophy of Religion at Claremont McKenna University, Claremont, California.

Avery Dulles, S.J., is the Lawrence J. McGinley Professor of Religion and Society at Fordham University, Bronx, New York.

James D. G. Dunn is the Lightfoot Professor of Divinity at the University of Durham, Durham, England.

Jacques Dupuis, S.J., is Professor Emeritus at the Gregorian University, Rome, Italy.

Paul R. Eddy is Professor of Biblical and Theological Studies at Bethel College, St. Paul, Minnesota.

John Fuellenbach, S.V.D., is Professor of Theology at the Gregorian University, Rome, Italy.

Michael Paul Gallagher, S.J., is Professor of Theology at the Gregorian University, Rome, Italy.

Paul Gwynne, O.M.I., is Professor of Theology at St. Mary's Seminary, Mulgrave, Victoria, Australia.

Michael Heher is Pastor of St. Irenaeus Church, Cyprus, California.

William Henn, O.F.M. Cap., is Professor of Theology at the Gregorian University, Rome, Italy.

Daniel Kendall, S.J., is Professor of Theology at the University of San Francisco, San Francisco, California.

Nicholas King, S.J., is Professor of Theology at St. John Vianney Seminary in Pretoria, South Africa.

Dominic Maruca, S.J., is a Spiritual Director and Professor of Spirituality at St. Mary's Seminary and University, Baltimore, Maryland.

Karl H. Neufeld, S.J., is Professor of Theology at the University of Innsbruck, Innsbruck, Austria.

John O'Donnell, S.J., is Professor of Theology at the Gregorian University, Rome, Italy.

Donna Orsuto is Director of the Lay Centre at Foyer Unitas Institute, Rome, Italy.

William Reiser, S.J., is Professor of Theology at Holy Cross College, Worcester, Massachusetts.

Janet Martin Soskice is University Lecturer in the Faculty of Divinity, University of Cambridge, and a Fellow of Jesus College, Cambridge, England.

Francis A. Sullivan, S.J., is Professor Emeritus from the Gregorian University, Rome, and currently teaches theology at Boston College, Boston, Massachusetts.

Jared Wicks, S.J., is Professor of Theology at the Gregorian University, Rome, Italy.

Bibliography of Gerald O'Collins, S.J.

1953

*"Bede Tsang," *Madonna* 57:312–13.

1955

*"Blessed Robert Southwell," *Madonna* 59:44–46.
*"Geoffrey Chaucer," *Madonna* 59:283–85.

1956

*"Hilaire Belloc," *Madonna* 60:12–14, 25.
*"How Greek Are Our Olympic Games?" *Twentieth Century* 10:360–71.

1958

*"The Miracle of Lourdes," *Sacred Heart Messenger* (February): 87–90.
*"The Story of Lourdes," *Sacred Heart Messenger* (February): 99–106.

1960

*"Patrick McMahon Glynn: A Migrant of 1880," *Twentieth Century* 15:25–34.

1962

*"An Amendment to a Preamble: The Recognition of God in the Australian
    Constitution," *Twentieth Century* 17:126–32.

1965

*Patrick McMahon Glynn (Melbourne: Melbourne University Press).
"Anti-Semitism in the Gospel," *Theological Studies* 26:663–66.

1966

"Revelation as History, *Heythrop Journal* 7:394–406.
"Divine Revelation, *Month* 221:332–36.

*Published in Australia

Book Reviews	*In*

T. F. Torrance, *Theology in Reconstruction*   *Heythrop Journal* 7:344–45.
(London: SCM Press, 1965).

1967

"Reality as Language: Ernst Fuchs's Theology of Revelation," *Theological Studies* 28:76–93.
"Is the Resurrection an 'Historical Event?" *Heythrop Journal* 8:381–87. Spanish translation: "Es la Resurrección de Cristo un suceso 'histórico'?" *Selecciones de Teologia* 26 (1968): 179–80.
"The Christology of Wolfhart Pannenberg," *Religious Studies* 3:369–76.

Book Reviews	*In*
John McIntyre, *The Shape of Christology* (London: SCM Press, 1966).	*Heythrop Journal* 8:87–89.
Dietrich Bonhoeffer, *Christology* (London: Collins, 1966).	*Heythrop Journal* 8:89.
Karl Rahner, *Theological Investigations,* vol. 5, *Later Writings* (London: Darton, Longman & Todd, 1966).	*Heythrop Journal* 8:210–11.
Karl Rahner and Joseph Ratzinger, *Revelation and Tradition* (London: Burns & Oates; Freiburg: Herder, 1966).	*Heythrop Journal* 8:456.
Charles W. Kegley, ed., *The Theology of Rudolf Bultmann* (London: SCM Press, 1966).	*Heythrop Journal* 8:211–12.
Schubert M. Ogden, *The Reality of God* (London: SCM Press, 1967).	*Heythrop Journal* 8:425–27.
W. D. Davies, *The Sermon on the Mount* (Cambridge: Cambridge University Press, 1966).	*Heythrop Journal* 8:456.

1968

Theology and Revelation, Theology Today, 2 (Cork: Mercier Press). Italian translation: *Theologia della rivalzione* (Catania: Ed. Paoline, 1969). French translation: *La Révélation* (Sherbrooke: Editions Paulines, 1970). Also in Korean.
"Spes Quaerens Intellectum," *Interpretation* 22:36–52; "Hope Seeking Understanding," *Theology Digest* 16:155–59.
"The Principle and Theology of Hope," *Scottish Journal of Theology* 21:129–44.

"The Theology of Hope," *The Way* 8:260–69.
"The Promise of Easter," *The Tablet,* April 13, p. 360.

Book Reviews   In

Dietrich Ritschl, *Memory and Hope*   *Interpretation* 22:483–87.
   (New York: Macmillan, 1967).
T. Patrick Burke, ed., *The Word in History*   *Heythrop Journal* 9:89–90.
   (New York: Sheed & Ward, 1966).
James M. Robinson and John B. Cobb, eds.,   *Heythrop Journal* 9:206–7.
   New Frontiers in Theology, vol. 3,
   Theology as History (New York:
   Harper & Row, 1967).
C. F. D. Moule, ed., *The Significance of*   *Heythrop Journal* 9:453–55.
   the Message of the Resurrection for
   Faith in Jesus Christ (London:
   SCM Press, 1968).

1969

Man and His New Hopes (New York: Herder & Herder). Spanish translation:
   El hombre y sus nuevas esperanzas (Santander: Ed. Sal Terrae, 1970).
"Christology from Below," *Interpretation* 23:228–32.
"On Richard P. McBrien's 'Do We Need the Church?'" *Heythrop Journal*
   10:416–19.

Book Reviews   In

Wolfhart Pannenberg, *Jesus—God*   *Interpretation* 23:228–32.
   and Man (Philadelphia:
   Westminster Press, 1968).

1970

"Thomas Aquinas and Christ's Resurrection," *Theological Studies* 31:512–22.
"Tübingen Revised," America 122:275–76.

Book Reviews   In

Wolfhart Pannenberg, ed., *Revelation*   *Heythrop Journal* 11:439–41.
   as History (London/Sydney:
   Sheed & Ward, 1969).
Gustaf Wingren, *An Exodus Theology:*   *Interpretation* 24:407–8.
   Einar Billing and the Development
   of Modern Swedish Theology
   (Philadelphia: Fortress Press, 1969).

1971

Foundations of Theology (Chicago: Loyola University Press).
"Power Made Perfect in Weakness: 2 Cor 12:9–10," *Catholic Biblical Quarterly*
    33:528–37; also in *Focus on Jesus* (1996), 185–95.
"La esperanza cristiana y las utopias del futuro," *Razon y Fe* 887 (Diciembre):
    465–72.
"Watching Our Language," *America* 24:207–8.
"Jesus and Our Search for Security," *America* 124:237–38.
"Christianity and Change," *America* 124:264.
"Christians and the Old Testament," *America* 124:291–92.
"No More Cross?" *America* 124:320.
"The Empty Tomb: Does It Matter?" *America* 124:345.
"The Greening of Christianity," *America* 124:410.
    All the above articles from *America* are also found in *Faith Under Fire* (1974).

Book Reviews   *In*

Harvey K. McArthur, ed., *In Search*   *Heythrop Journal* 12:206–7.
    of the Historical Jesus
    (London: SPCK, 1970).
Richard Batey, ed., *New Testament Issues*
    (London: SCM Press, 1970).
Willi Marxsen, *The Resurrection of*   *Heythrop Journal* 12:207–11;
    Jesus of Nazareth   also in *What Are They Saying*
    (London: SCM Press, 1970).   *About the Resurrection?*
                                               (1978), 106–15.
Wolfhart Pannenberg, *Basic Questions*   *Heythrop Journal* 12:438–39.
    in Theology (London:
    SCM Press, 1970).
C. F. Evans, *Resurrection and the*   *Heythrop Journal* 12:439–40.
    New Testament
    (London: SCM Press, 1970).
C. H. Dodd, *The Founder of Christianity*   *Heythrop Journal* 12:460.
    (London: Collins, 1970).

1972

"Jesus Known or Unknown," *America* 126:238–39. Also in *Faith is a Journey,* ed.
    W. Guatta (Melbourne: Dove Communications, 1972), 19–21; and *Faith.
"Paul or Jesus?" *America* 126:263.
"Christian Laughter," *America* 126:294.
"The Miracles of Jesus," *America* 126:321–22.
"The Pope and Easter," *America* 126:359–62.
    All the above articles from *America* are also in *Faith Under Fire* (1974).

Book Reviews	**In**
Ernst Käsemann, *Pauline Perspectives* (London: SCM Press, 1971).	*Heythrop Journal* 13:335–36.
Walter H. Capps, *Time Invades the Cathedral* (Philadelphia: Fortress Press, 1972).	*Interpretation* 26:474–76.

1973

The Resurrection of Jesus Christ (Valley Forge, Pa.: Judson Press). In England as *The Easter Jesus* (London: Darton, Longman & Todd). Italian translation: *Il Gesù Pasquale* (Assisi: Cittadella Editrice, 1975).

"Karl Barth on Christ's Resurrection," *Scottish Journal of Theology* 26:85–99.

"St. Paul and the Language of Reconciliation," **Colloquium* 6:3–8 (with T. Michael McNulty); also in *Focus on Jesus* (1996), 196–203.

"The Theology of Development," **Social Survey* 22:201–7, 216; also in *Faith Under Fire* (1974), 55–66.

"The Christmas Jesus," *The Tablet,* December 29, pp. 1220–21.

"Letter From Melbourne," *America* 128:222–23.

"Coming of Age in New Guinea," *America* 128:576–78.

"An Argument for Women Priests," *America* 129:122–23.

Book Reviews	**In**
Julien Harvey et al., *Résurrection: Espérance Humaine et Don de Dieu* (Paris/Tournai: Desclée, 1971).	*Theological Studies* 34:340–41.
Klaus Koch, *The Rediscovery of Apocalyptic* (London: SCM Press, 1972).	*Heythrop Journal* 14:206–7.
D. H. van Daalen, *The Real Resurrection* (London: Collins, 1972).	*Heythrop Journal* 14:365–66.
Arend Th. van Lieuwen, *Critique of Heaven* (New York: Charles Scribner's Sons, 1972).	*Interpretation* 27:246–47.

1974

*Faith Under Fire (Melbourne: Polding Press).

The Theology of Secularity (Dublin/Cork: Mercier Press).

*Patrick McMahon Glynn: Letters to His Family (1874–1927) (Melbourne: Polding Press).

"Past versus Present," *The Way* 14:83–91.

"The Ordination of Women," *The Tablet,* February 23, pp. 175–76; March 2, pp. 213–15; also as "The Argument from Rome," in *Women Priests? Yes-*

Now! ed. Harold Wilson (Nutfield, Surrey: Denholm House Press, 1975), 37–50.
"A Light in Africa," *The Tablet,* August 24, pp. 813–14.
"Out of Suffering Comes Joy in the Gospel," *New Spectator,* August 8, pp. 4–5.
"Pembroke Theologians," *Pembroke College Society Annual Gazette* 48:13–14.
"Some Theologians and Easter," *America* 130:286–87.
"Slings and Arrows at Cambridge," *Commonweal* 99 (January 25): 406–7.

Book Reviews	*In*
Rolf Schäfer, *Der Evangelische Glaube* (Tübingen: J. C. B. Mohr [Paul Siebeck], 1973).	*Heythrop Journal* 15:248–49.
Ewert H. Cousins, ed., *Hope and the Future of Man* (London: Teilhard Center, 1973).	*Heythrop Journal* 15:247–48.
Wolfhart Pannenberg, *The Apostles Creed in the Light of Today's Questions* (Philadelphia: Westminster Press, 1972).	*Interpretation* 28:224–27.

1975

Has Dogma a Future? (London: Darton, Longman & Todd). In the United States as *The Case Against Dogma* (New York: Paulist Press).
"Third World Theology," *Doctrine and Life* 25:14–18.
"Faith and Order in Ghana," *Theological Studies* 36:130–44.
"Come nasce la fede nella risurrezione?" *Rassegna di Teologia* 16:409–19.
"'Fede e Ordine' nel Ghana," *Unitas* 30:33–38.
"Jesus the Martyr," *New Blackfriars* 56:373–75; also in *The Calvary Christ* (1977), 1–15.
"Living Theology," *The Tablet,* March 8, pp. 222–23.
"The Hidden Years," *The Tablet,* December 27, pp. 1236–37; also in *The People's Christmas* (1984), 42–52.
"The Imagination of Jesus," *America* 133:437–38; also in *What Are They Saying About Jesus?* (1977), 63–74.

Book Reviews	*In*
John Bowker, *The Sense of God* (Oxford: Oxford University Press, 1973).	*Gregorianum* 58:187–88.
Paul Winter, *On the Trial of Jesus* (Berlin: Walter de Gruyter, 1974).	*Gregorianum* 56:383–84.
John Robinson, *The Human Face of God* (London: SCM Press, 1973).	*Gregorianum* 56:384–85.

Walter Kasper, *Jesus der Christus*
(Mainz: Matthias-Grünewald-
Verlag, 1974).

Gregorianum 56:385–86.

Xavier Léon-Dufour, *Resurrection and
the Message of Easter* (London:
Geoffrey Chapman, 1974).

Gregorianum 56:584–85.

Charles Kannengiesser, *Foi en la
Résurrection, Résurrection
de la Foi* (Paris: Beauchesne, 1974).

Heythrop Journal 16:242.

1976

"Jesus Between Poetry and Philosophy," *New Blackfriars* 57:160–66; also in
Focus on Jesus (1996), 53–62.
"Christ the Tiger (Luke 24:13–35): A Sermon for Easter Sunday," *Clergy Review*
61:147–48; also in *The Second Journey* (1978), 73–83.
"The Religious and 'The Second Journey,'" *Review for Religious* 35:386–93.
"Jesus in Current Theology, I: Beyond Chalcedon," *The Way* 16:291–308; also
in *What Are They Saying About Jesus?* (1977), 1–33.
"A Neglected Source for the Theology of Revelation," *Gregorianum* 57:757–68;
also in *Fundamental Theology* (1981), 107–13.
"Christ and China," *New Blackfriars* 57:548–56.
"Meditations Mar 28–April 3," in *The Upper Room Disciplines* (Nashville: The
Upper Room, 1976), 100–106.
"The Death of Jesus," *The Tablet,* April 10, p. 382.
"The Crucifixion," *Doctrine and Life* 26:247–63.
"Eucharistic Congress," *The Tablet,* August 14, pp. 783–84. German translation:
"Eindrücke von Philadelphia," *Orientierung,* September 15, pp. 187–88.

Book Reviews   In

Wilfrid J. Harrington, *Christ and Life*
(Dublin: Gill & Macmillan, 1975).

Doctrine and Life 26:350–51.

Dermot A. Lane, *The Reality of Jesus*
(Dublin: Veritas Publications, 1975).

Morna Hooker and Colin Hickling, eds.,
*What About the New Testament?
Essays in Honour of Christopher
Evans* (London: SCM Press, 1975).

Heythrop Journal 17:341–43.

Jürgen Moltmann, *The Experiment Hope*
(London: SCM Press, 1975).

Heythrop Journal 17:463–64.

Harvey Cox, *The Seduction of the Spirit*
(London: Wildwood House, 1974).

Heythrop Journal 17:468–69.

Dermot A. Lane, *The Reality of Jesus*
(Dublin: Veritas Publications, 1975).

Heythrop Journal 17:484.

Hans Schwarz, *The Search for God*   *Gregorianum* 57:773.
(Minneapolis: Augsburg Publishing
House, 1975).
David Tracy, *Blessed Rage for Order:*   *Gregorianum* 57:778–81.
The New Pluralism in Theology
(New York: Seabury Press, 1975).
Michael Schmaus, *La Fede della Chiesa,*   *Gregorianum* 57:166–67.
vol. 1, La Rivelazione e la Teologia
(Turin: Marietti, 1975).

1977

The Calvary Christ (London: SCM Press).
What Are They Saying About Jesus? (New York: Paulist Press). Second edition,
New York/Ramsey, N.J.: Paulist Press, 1983.
"Jesus in Current Theology, II: Salvation and Commitment," *The Way* 17:51–64;
also in *What Are They Saying About Jesus?* 35–62.
"Jesus in Current Theology, III: Christ's Resurrection and Our Imagination,"
The Way 17:135–44; also in *What Are They Saying About the
Resurrection?* (1978), 68–86.
"The Second Journey," *Catholic Mind* 75:30–37; also in *The Way* 17:267–77.
"Christ and China II," *New Blackfriars* 58:30–38; also in *The New China: A
Catholic Response,* ed. Michael Chu (New York: Paulist Press, 1977),
124–45. (This book also appeared as *Esperienza cinese e fede cristiana*
[Bologna: EMI, 1976].)
"Verso una teologia della croce," *Rassegna di Teologia* 18:345–59; also in *The
Cross Today* (1978), 30–47.
"Hans-Georg Gadamer and Hans Küng: A Reflection," *Gregorianum* 58:561–66.
"Theology and Experience," *Irish Theological Quarterly* 44:279–90; also in
Fundamental Theology (1981), 32–48.

Book Reviews   *In*

Joseph F. Kelly, ed., *Perspectives on*   *Gregorianum* 58:201.
Scripture and Tradition
(Notre Dame: Fides Publishers, 1976).
Peter Baelz, *The Forgotten Dream*   *Gregorianum* 58:357–58.
(London/Oxford: Mowbrays, 1976).
Rechtfertigung: Festschrift für Ernst   *Gregorianum* 58:573–74.
Käsemann zum 70. Geburtstag
(Tübingen: J. C. B. Mohr
[Paul Siebeck]; Göttingen:
Vandenhoeck & Ruprecht, 1976).
Marianne H. Micks and Charles C.   *Heythrop Journal* 18:365–66.
Price, eds., *Towards a New Theology
of Ordination: Essays on the*

Ordination of Women (Alexandria, Va.:
Virginia Theological Seminary, 1976).

Gerhard Heinz, *Das Problem der*   *Heythrop Journal* 18:366.
Kirchenentstehung in der deutschen
protestantischen Theologie des 20.
Jahrhunderts (Mainz: Mattias-
Grünewald);

Frans Mussner, *Theologie der Freiheit nach*
Paulus (Freiburg: Herder, 1976).

Norman Perrin, *The Resurrection*   *Heythrop Journal* 18:466–67.
Narratives (London:
SCM Press, 1977);

Klaus Kienzler, *Logik der Auferstehung*
(Freiburg: Herder, 1976).

Hans Küng, *On Being a Christian*   *The Ampleforth Journal* 82
(London: Collins, 1977).   (Summer): 58.

Bernard Orchard, *Matthew, Mark & Luke*   *The Month* (September): 319.
(Manchester: Koinonia Press, 1976).

Walter Kasper, *Jesus the Christ*   *The Virginia Seminary Journal*
(New York: Paulist Press, 1976).   (November): 32–33.

1978

A Month with Jesus (Denville, N.J.: Dimension Books).

What Are They Saying About the Resurrection? (New York: Paulist Press).

The Second Journey (New York: Paulist Press). Italian translation: *Il Secondo Viaggio* (Milan: Ancora, 1987). Excerpt: "The Second Journey," *The Tablet,* September 16, pp. 889–90.

The Cross Today: An Evaluation of Current Theological Reflection on the Cross of Christ, with R. Faricy and M. Flick (New York: Paulist Press; Dublin: Villa Books; Rome/Sydney: Dwyer).

"Fare teologia cristiana," *Rassegna di Teologia* 19:161–72; also in *Fundamental Theology* (1981), 5–21.

"Jesus's Concept of His Own Death," *The Way* 18:212–23.

"Christianity for Losers: A Sermon for the Thirty-third Sunday of the Year (Proverbs 31:10–31; Matthew 25:14–30)," *Clergy Review* 63:417–18; also in *Experiencing Jesus* (1994), 64.

"Criteria for Discerning Christian Traditions," *Science et Esprit* 30, no. 3:295–302; also in *Fundamental Theology,* 208–24; and *Problemi e Prospettive di Teologie Fondamentale* (1980), 397–411.

"Rome Letter," *The Tablet,* September 2, p. 838.

"Rome Letter," *The Tablet,* September 9, p. 876.

"The Easter Witness: A New View of the Petrine Ministry," *The Tablet,* March 25/April 1, pp. 297–98.

Book Reviews	**In**
Thomas J. Norris, *Newman and His Theological Method: A Guide for the Theologian Today* (Leiden: E. J. Brill, 1977).	*Gregorianum* 59:210.
Raymond E. Brown, *The Birth of the Messiah: A Commentary on the Infancy Narratives in Matthew and Luke* (London: Geoffrey Chapman, 1977).	*Gregorianum* 59:756–57.
David Tracy, ed., with Hans Küng and Johann B. Metz, *Toward Vatican III: The Work That Needs to be Done* (Dublin: Gill & Macmillan, 1978).	*Gregorianum* 59:760–61.
Theodore Jennings, Jr., *Introduction to Theology: An Invitation to Reflection Upon the Christian Mythos* (London: SPCK, 1977);	*Heythrop Journal* 19:222–23.
Anders Jeffner, *Kriterien Christlicher Glaubenslehre* (Uppsala: Almqvist & Wiksell International, 1976).	

1979

The Second Journey: Spiritual Awareness and the Mid-life Crisis, new edition (Dublin: Villa Books).

"The Second Journey: Interview by D. O'Grady," *St. Anthony Messenger* 86:18–24.

"Filosofia e teologia," *Rassegna di Teologia* 20:155–60.

"Philosophy and Theology," *Irish Theological Quarterly* 46:170–76; also in *Fundamental Theology* (1981), 24–31.

"Whatever You Bind," *The Way* 19:13–24.

"He Has Risen," *The Tablet,* April 14/21, p. 364; also in *Zealandia* (New Zealand).

"Letter from India," *The Tablet,* November 17, pp. 1117–18.

"Integrating the Second Journey into Spiritual Life," *Sursum Corda,* 15:505–14.

Book Reviews	**In**
Henry Wansbrough, *Risen From the Dead* (Slough: St. Paul Publications, 1978).	*Heythrop Journal* 20:192–94.
Frederick E. Crowe, *Theology of the Christian World: A Study in History*	*Gregorianum* 60:590.

(New York/Ramsey, N.J./Toronto:
Paulist Press, 1978).

Raymond E. Brown, *An Adult Christ at*   *Gregorianum* 60:622.
Christmas: Essays on the Three
Biblical Stories (Collegeville, Minn.:
Liturgical Press, 1977).

William E. Reiser, *What Are They*   *Gregorianum* 60:757–58.
Saying About Dogma? (New York/
Ramsey, N.J.: Paulist Press, 1978).

1980

Problemi e Prospettive di Teologia Fondamentale (Brescia: Queriniana), with
    R. Latourelle. English translation: *Problems and Perspectives of*
    Fundamental Theology (New York/Ramsey, N.J.: Paulist Press, 1982).
    French translation: *Problèmes et perspectives de théologie fondamentale*
    (Tournai: Desclée; Montreal: Bellarmin, 1982). Spanish translation:
    Problemas y perspectivas de teologia fundamental (Salamanca: Ed.
    Sigueme, 1982). German translation: *Probleme und Aspekte der*
    Fundamental Theologie (Leipzig: St. Benno- Verlag, 1985). Portuguese
    translation: *Problemas e Perspectivas de Teologia Fundamental* (São
    Paulo: Edições Loyola, 1993).

The Easter Jesus, new edition (London: Darton, Longman & Todd).

"The Second Journey," *Studies in Formative Spirituality* 1:345–56.

"The Living Spirit," *The Tablet,* January 5, p. 23; also in *Zealandia* (New
    Zealand).

"The Shroud of Turin," *The Way* 20:140–47; also in *Interpreting Jesus* (1983),
    99–105.

"The Prodigal Son (Luke 15:11–32): A Sermon for the Fourth Sunday in Lent,"
    Clergy Review 65/3:99–100; also in *Experiencing Jesus* (1994), 72–76.

"Una lettura attuale delle 'Regole per sentire con la Chiesa,'" in *Sentire con la*
    Chiesa, by M. Fois et al. (Rome: Centrum Ignatianum Spiritualitatis,
    1980), 97–112.

"Doing Christian Theology," in *Imagination and the Future,* ed. J. A. Henley
    (Melbourne: Hawthorne Press, 1980), 8–22; also in *Fundamental*
    Theology (1981), 5–21.

"A Glimpse of Japan," *The Tablet,* October 4, p. 967.

"The Second Journey," *Studies in Formative Spirituality* 1, no. 3:345–56.

"Christmas for the People," *The Tablet,* December 20/27, p. 1252; also in
    Catholic Truth Society (London) D 555, pp. 3–13; and in *The People's*
    Christmas (1984), 11–16.

Book Reviews	**In**
Franco Ardusso et al., eds., *Dizionario Teologico Interdisciplinare,* 3 vols. + supp. (Turin: Marietti, 1977).	*Journal of Religion* 60, no. 1:90–91.
Edward Schillebeeckx, *Jesus: An Experiment in Christology* (New York: Seabury Press, 1979).	*Gregorianum* 61:372–76.
Frans Jozef van Beeck, *Christ Proclaimed: Christology as Rhetoric* (New York/Ramsey, N.J./Toronto: Paulist Press, 1979).	*Gregorianum* 61:580–81.
Peter L. Berger, *The Heretical Imperative: Contemporary Possibilities of Religious Affirmation* (Garden City, N.Y.: Doubleday, Anchor, 1979).	*Gregorianum* 61:582.
D. S. Russell, *Apocalyptic Ancient and Modern* (London: SCM Press, 1978).	*Heythrop Journal* 21:116.
Don Cupitt, *Jesus and the Gospel of God* (Guilford/London: Lutterworth Press, 1979).	*Heythrop Journal* 21:1909–93.
Charles B. Ketcham, *A Theology of Encounter* (University Park/London: Pennsylvania State University Press, 1978).	*Heythrop Journal* 21:234.
New York International Bible Society, sponsor, *Holy Bible: New International Version* (London: Hodder & Stoughton, 1979).	*Heythrop Journal* 21:327–38.

1981

Fundamental Theology (New York/Ramsey, N.J.: Paulist Press, 1981). Also in Korean. Italian translation: *Teologia Fondamentale* (Brescia: Queriniana, 1982). Portuguese translation: *Teologia Fundamental* (São Paulo: Edições Loyola, 1991).

"Peter as Easter Witness," *Heythrop Journal* 22:1–18.

"What Are They Saying About Jesus Now?" *The Furrow* 32:203–11; also in *Focus on Jesus* (1996), 1–16.

"Cosa si dice di Gesù Cristo?" *Rassegna di Teologia* 22:173–79.

"Saint Mark and the Mystery of God," *Sisters Today* 52:287–90.

"Christ Today," *The Way* 21:3–13; also in *Focus on Jesus* (1996), 17–29.

"Cribs at Christmas," *America* 145:396; also in *Catholic Truth Society* (London) D555, pp. 1–2; *The Tablet,* December 19/26, p. 1256.

"The Trinity: 3x1=1," *U.S. Catholic* 46:6–10.

Book Reviews	In
Gerhard Ebeling, *Dogmatik des christlichen Glaubens* (Tübingen: J. C. B. Mohr [Paul Siebeck], 1979).	*Heythrop Journal* 22:223–24.
Jürgen Moltmann, *The Future of Creation* (London: SCM Press, 1979).	*Heythrop Journal* 22:225–26.
Renford Bambrough, *Moral Scepticism and Moral Knowledge* (London: Routledge & Kegan Paul, 1979).	*Heythrop Journal* 22:233.
Johann Baptist Metz, *Faith in History and Society* (London: Burns & Oates, 1980).	*Heythrop Journal* 22:432–33.
Johann Baptist Metz, *Glaube in Geschichte und Gesellschaft: Studien zu einer praktischen Fundamental Theologie* (Mainz: Matthias-Grünewald-Verlag, 1977); *Faith in History and Society: Toward a Practical Fundamental Theology* (New York: Seabury Press, 1980); *La foi dans l'histoire et dans la société: Essai de théologie fundamentale pratique* (Paris: Les Éditions du Cerf, 1979).	*Gregorianum* 62:194–96.
Stephen Sykes and Derek Holmes, eds., *New Studies in Theology* (London: Duckworth, 1980).	*Gregorianum* 62:338.

1982

"What Peter Does for the Church," *Catholic Truth Society* (London), D 539.
"Il Ministero Petrino," *Rassegna di Teologia* 23:469–82.
"Our Peace and Reconciliation," *The Way* 22:112–21; also in *Focus on Jesus* (1996), 84–94.
"A Child is Born," *The Tablet,* December 25/January 1, pp. 1294–95; also in *Advocate, Catholic Weekly,* and *Southern Cross.*
"Letters to the Pope," *America* 146:337.
"A Play, a Bishop and a Book," *America* 146:280.
"A Woman for all Seasons," *America* 147:212–23.

Book Reviews	In
Jürgen Moltmann, *Trinität und Reich Gottes: Zur Gotteslehre* (Munich: Chr. Kaiser, 1980). *The Trinity and*	*Gregorianum* 63:158–60.

the Kingdom of God: The Doctrine
of God (London: SCM Press, 1981).

A. E. Harvey, ed., *God Incarnate: Story*   *Gregorianum* 63:582–83.
and Belief (London: SPCK, 1981).

B. T. France and David Wenham,   *Gregorianum* 63:583–84.
*Gospel Perspectives: Studies of
History and Tradition in the Four
Gospels,* 2 vols. (Sheffield:
JSOT Press, 1980).

Rowan Williams, *Resurrection: Interpreting*   *Gregorianum* 63:747–48.
the Easter Gospel (London: Darton,
Longman & Todd, 1982).

Paul Johnson, *Pope John Paul II and the*   *America* 147:156–57.
Catholic Restoration (New York:
St. Martin's Press, 1981);

Frank Pakenham (Lord) Longford,
*Pope John Paul II: An Authorized
Biography* (London: Morrow, 1982).

Anthony Harvey, *Jesus and the Constraints*   *America* 147:194–95.
of History (Philadelphia:
Westminster Press, 1982).

Otto Weber, *Foundations of Dogmatics*   *America* 147:258.
(Grand Rapids: Eerdmans, 1981).

Rosemary Haughton, *The Catholic Thing*   *Heythrop Journal* 23:234.
(Dublin: Villa Books, 1980).

David McKenzie, *Wolfhart Pannenberg*   *Heythrop Journal* 23:467.
and Religious Philosophy
(Lanham, Md.: University Press
of America, 1980).

Salvatore Fisichella, *Hans Urs von*   *Civiltà Cattolica* 3158:199.
Balthasar (Roma: Città Nuova, 1981).

1983

Interpreting Jesus (London: Geoffrey Chapman; Ramsey, N.J.: Paulist Press).
Spanish translation: *Para interpretar a Jesús* (Madrid: Ed. Paulinas,
1986). Italian translation: *Gesù Oggi* (Cinisello Balsamo: Edizione
Paoline, 1993).

Finding Jesus: Living Through Lent with John's Gospel (New York: Paulist
Press).

"Cristo, nostra pasqua e nostro futuro," in *Problemi e Prospettive di Spiritualità,*
ed. T. Goffi and B. Secondin (Brescia: Queriniana, 1984), 197–206.
Spanish translation: "Cristo, nuestra pascua y nuestro futuro," in
Problemas y perspectivas de espiritualidad (Salamanca: Sigueme, 1986),
210–20.

"Anathema," "Articles of Faith," "Assent," "Decretals," "Deposit of Faith,"
"Dogma," "Dogmatic Theology," "Fundamental Theology,"
"Magisterium," "Prolepsis," "Venial Sin," in *A New Dictionary of
Christian Theology,* ed. Alan Richardson and John Bowden (London:
SCM Press). In the United States as *The Westminster Dictionary of
Christian Theology* (Philadelphia: Westminster Press, 1983).

"Christmas for the People," *Catholic Truth Society* (London) D 555.

"A Consumer's Guide to the Message of Life," *Advocate, Southern Cross*
(South Africa), *Catholic Weekly, Zealandia* (New Zealand).

"Three Wise Men," *The Tablet,* December 24–31, p. 1252; also as "Christmas
1945," in *America* and in *Catholic Weekly, Zealandia* (New Zealand),
Advocate, Southern Cross (South Africa) 34.

"Reconciliation, According to Paul," in *Sowing the Word,* ed. P. Rogers (Dublin:
Dominican Publications, 1983), 205–12.

"Jesus the Questioner," *America* 148:134.

"Further Questions," *America* 148:153.

"Encountering Jesus," *America* 148:173.

"Further Encounters," *America* 148:194.

"The Sick, the Sinful," *America* 148:213.

"Meeting the Risen Lord," *America* 148:237.

> These six articles from *America* are also in *Finding Jesus.*

"Journey, Second," in *A Dictionary of Christian Spirituality*, ed. G. W.
Wakefield (London: SCM Press, 1983), 235–36.

"Interpreting Jesus Today," *America* 149:165–68.

"Christmas 1945," *America* 149:415; also in *The People's Christmas* (1984),
17–21.

Book Reviews	**In**
Alister Hardy, *The Spiritual Nature of Man: A Study of Contemporary Religious Experience* (Oxford: Clarendon Press, 1979).	*Gregorianum* 64:157–58.
James M. Robinson, *The Problem of History in Mark and Other Marcan Stories* (Philadelphia: Fortress Press, 1982).	*Gregorianum* 64:336–37.
Helmut Pfeiffer, *Gott offenbart sich: Das Reifen und Entstehen des Offenbarungsverständnisses in ersten and zweiten vatikanischer Konzil* (Frankfurt am Main/Bern: Peter Lang, 1982).	*Gregorianum* 64:577–78.

Bernard Lauret and François Refoulé,   *Gregorianum* 64:578–79.
Initiation à la pratique de la théologie
(Paris: Les Éditions du Cerf, 1982).
Peter C. Hodgson and Robert H. King, eds.,   *Gregorianum* 64:728–29.
*Christian Theology: An Introduction
to Its Traditions and Tasks*
(Philadelphia: Fortress Press, 1982).
Helmut Pfeiffer and Klaus Rohmann, eds.,   *Gregorianum* 64:729.
Theologie-Grund und Grenzen
(Paderborn/Munich/Vienna/Zurich:
Ferdinand Schöningh, 1982).
Raymond E. Brown, *The Critical Meaning*   *Heythrop Journal* 24:313.
of the Bible (New York/Ramsey, N.J.:
Paulist Press, 1981).
E. C. Hoskyns and Noel Davey,   *Heythrop Journal* 24:313.
*Crucifixion—Resurrection: The
Pattern of the Theology and
Ethics of the New Testament*
(London: SPCK, 1981).
William M. Thompson, *Jesus Lord and*   *Heythrop Journal* 24:72–73.
*Savior: A Theopathic Christology
and Soteriology* (Leominster:
Fowler Wright, 1981).
William A. van Roo, *Basics of a*   *Civiltà Cattolica* 3198:547–48.
Roman Catholic Theology
(Rome: Analecta Gregoriana, 1982).

1984

The People's Christmas (New York/Ramsey, N.J.: Paulist Press).
"Christ's Resurrection as Mystery of Love," *Heythrop Journal* 25:39–50; also in
A Companion to the Bible, ed. M. Ward (New York: Alba House, 1985),
335–51; Jesus Risen (1987), 188–200.
"The Founder of Christianity," *Studia Missionalia* 33:385–402; also in *Focus on
Jesus* (1996), 67–83.
"Luminous Appearances of the Risen Christ," *Catholic Biblical Quarterly*
46:247–54; also in *Jesus Risen* (1987), 210–16.
"Jesus the Communicator," *America* 150:260–61; also in *Focus on Jesus* (1996),
63–66.
"Sistine Resurrection," *Commonweal* 111:228–29.
"Sharers in the Mystery," *The Tablet,* April 21/28, p. 382; also in *Zealandia*
(New Zealand), *Catholic Weekly,* *Advocate, Southern Cross* (South
Africa), *Catholic Digest.*
"Easter: A Wake-up Call for a Rise-and-shine Faith," *U.S. Catholic* 49/4 (April):
6–11.

"Christology Today," *Australasian Catholic Record* 61/2:151–57.
"Murray and Ottaviani," *America* 151:287–88.
"Jesus and the Scholars," *The Tablet,* October 13, pp. 1002–3.
"Trust in the Resurrection," *The Tablet,* October 20, pp. 1028–29.
"On First Seeing Bethlehem," *The Tablet,* December 22/29, pp. 1292–93; also in
　　*Advocate, *Catholic Weekly, Southern Cross* (South Africa).
"Vedere e credere: due cose diverse," in *La Storia di Gesù* (Milan: Rizzoli) #78,
　　p. 1833.
"La mediazione della testimonianza apostolica," in *La Storia di Gesù* (Milan:
　　Rizzoli) #78, pp. 1856- 57.

Book Reviews	**In**
Hans Küng, *Eternal Life? Life after Death as a Medical, Philosophical and Theological Problem* (Garden City, N.Y.: Doubleday, 1984).	*The Tablet,* May 5, pp. 427–28.
Avery Dulles, *Models of Revelation* (Garden City, N.Y.: Doubleday, 1983).	*Gregorianum* 65:181.
Raymond E. Brown and John P. Meier, *Antioch and Rome: New Testament Cradles of Catholic Christianity* (London: Geoffrey Chapman, 1983).	*Gregorianum* 65:181–82.
Jacques Le Goff, *La Nascità del Purgatorio* (Turin: Giulio Einaudi editore, 1982).	*Gregorianum* 65:518–19.
Aylward Shorter, *Revelation and Its Interpretation* (London: Geoffrey Chapman, 1983).	*Gregorianum* 65:519–20.
William J. Abraham, *Divine Revelation and the Limits of Historical Criticism* (Oxford: Oxford University Press, 1982).	*Heythrop Journal* 25:496–97.
Rowan Williams, *Resurrection* (London: Darton, Longman & Todd, 1982).	*Heythrop Journal* 25:121.

1985

"At the Origins of 'Dei Verbum,'" *Heythrop Journal* 26:5–13.
"Easter Witness and Peter's Ministry," *Heythrop Journal* 26:177–78.
"The Resurrection of Jesus," *Catholic Truth Society* (London) D 561.
"La resurrezione, mistero d'amore," in *Amore, morte, resurrezione*
　　(Collevalenza, Perugia: Edizioni "L'amore Misercordioso," 1985),
　　139–47.
"The Second Journey: An Epilogue," *Australasian Catholic Record* 62
　　(January): 9–16.

"Her Father," *Madonna* (November): 9–11.

"Thy Resurrection of Jesus: Four Contemporary Challenges," *Catholic Theological Review* 6:5–10.

"His Bride," *Catholic Digest*, 49 (July): 138–39; also in *Jesus Today* (1986), 15–17.

"The Empty Tomb," *The Tablet*, April 6/13, pp. 355–56; also in *Catholic Weekly*, *Advocate*.

"In Praise of Mannix," *The Tablet*, June 8, pp. 604–5.

"Ratzinger's Sad Book," *The Tablet*, July 13, pp. 723–24.

"The Resurrection of Jesus: Some Current Questions," *America* 153:422–25; also in *Focus on Jesus* (1986). 102–10; also in *Civiltà Cattolica* 3331 (1989): 31–35.

"A Bloody Christmas," *Catholic Weekly* (for Christmas).

"The Living and the Dead," *Southern Cross* (South Africa) (for Christmas).

Book Reviews	**In**
Vesilin Kesich, *The First Day of the New Creation: The Resurrection and the Christian Faith* (Crestwood, N.Y.: St. Vladimir's Seminary Press, 1982);	*Heythrop Journal* 26:58.
Pinchas Lapide, *The Resurrection of Jesus: A Jewish Perspective* (London: SPCK, 1983);	
John Wenham, *Easter Enigma* (Exeter: Paternoster Press, 1984).	
J. Duncan M. Derrett, *The Anastasis: The Resurrection of Jesus as an Historical Event* (Shipston-on-Stour: P. Drinkwater, 1982).	*Heythrop Journal* 26:58–60.
Francis Schüssler Fiorenza, *Foundational Theology: Jesus and the Church* (New York: Crossroad, 1984).	*Heythrop Journal* 26:201.
Pheme Perkins, *Resurrection: New Testament Witness and Contemporary Reflection* (London: Geoffrey Chapman, 1984).	*Gregorianum* 66:756; and *The Tablet*, July 13, p. 731.
Nikola Bizaca, *Rivelazione e teologia in Gottlieb Söhngen* (Rome: Città Nuova, 1985).	*Civiltà Cattolica* 3238:404–5.

1986

Jesus Today: Christology in an Australian Context (New York: Paulist Press; Melbourne: Dove Communications).

"Saying 'Yes' to the Cross," *St. Anthony Messenger* 93/10:37–40; also as "Christ's Cross...Your Cross," *Catholic Truth Society* (London) D 576.

"On Consulting the Faithful," *The Furrow* 37:279–84; also in *Civiltà Cattolica* 3319 (1988): 40–45.

"Believing in the Risen Christ," in *Gottes Zukunft: Zukunft der Welt, Festschrift for Jürgen Moltmann's 60th birthday* (Munich: Chr. Kaiser, 1986), 68–77; also in Jesus Risen (1987), 128–47.

"The Faith of an Unbeliever," *The Tablet,* March 29, p. 338.

"Beyond David Jenkins," *The Tablet,* August 9, pp. 830–31.

"Face the Truth About the Earthly Jesus," *Southern Cross* (South Africa) (Christmas issue); also in **Catholic Weekly* and **Advocate.*

"Pope John Paul—Theologian of the post-Vatican II Church," *Catholic Weekly,* November 9, p. 26.

Book Reviews / In

Avery Dulles, *Models of Revelation* (Dublin: Gill & Macmillan, 1983); Benedict Englezakis, *New and Old in God's Revelation* (Cambridge: James Clarke, 1982); Paul Helm, *Divine Revelation: The Basic Issues* (London: Marshall, Morgan & Scott, 1982); Aylward Shorter, *Revelation and Its Interpretation* (London: Geoffrey Chapman, 1983).

Heythrop Journal 27:181–83.

1987

Jesus Risen: An Historical, Fundamental and Systematic Examination of Christ's Resurrection (New York/Mahwah, N.J.: Paulist Press; London: Darton, Longman & Todd). Spanish translation: *Jesús resucitado* (Barcelona: Herder, 1988). Italian translation: *Gesù risorto* (Brescia: Queriniana, 1989).

"Jesus," in *The Encyclopedia of Religion,* vol. 8, ed. Mircea Eliade (New York: Macmillan, 1987), 15–28.

"The Appearances of the Risen Christ," *America* 156:317–20; also in *Thanatology: A Liberal Arts Approach,* ed. M. A. Morgan and J. D. Morgan (London, Ontario: King's College, 1988), 259–63.

"Belo Horizonte," **Madonna* (March): 28–29.

"The Blood of Christ," *The Tablet,* April 18/25, pp. 419–20; also in the Easter editions of *Southern Cross* (South Africa) and **Catholic Weekly.*

"La risurrezione di Cristo," *Rassegna di Teologia* 28:118–26; also as "The Resurrection of Christ," in *The New Dictionary of Theology,* ed. J. A. Komonchak et al. (Wilmington, Del.: Glazier), 880–84.

"Christ our Savior is Born," *The Tablet,* December 19/26, pp. 1384; also in
*Advocate, *Catholic Weekly, Southern Cross (South Africa).
"Interpreting Christmas," *America* 156:470–71; also in *Focus on Jesus* (1996),
47–49.
"Rivelazione: passato e presente," in *Vaticano II: Bilancio e Prospettive,* ed.
René Latourelle (Assisi: Citadella), 125–35. French translation: *Vaticano
II: Bilan et Perspectives* (Montréal: Bellarmin; Paris: Les Éditions du
Cerf, 1988), 141–52. English translation: *Vatican II: Assessment and
Perspectives* (New York/Mahwah, N.J.: Paulist Press, 1988), 125–37.
Spanish translation: *Vaticano II: Balance y perspectivas* (Salamanca:
Sigueme, 1989), 95–116.
"Mary Magdalene as Major Witness to Jesus' Resurrection," *Theological Studies*
48:631–46, written with D. Kendall; also in *Interpreting the Resurrection*
(1988), 22–38.

Book Reviews	**In**
P. Carnley, *The Structure of Resurrection Belief* (Oxford: Clarendon Press, 1987).	*The Tablet,* September 12, p. 975; also in **Pacifica* 1:227–29; *Theological Studies* 50 (1988): 178–89; "Resurrection Belief: A Note on a Recent Book," *Gregorianum* 70 (1989): 341–44.

1988

*Interpreting the Resurrection: Examining the Major Problems in the Stories of
Jesus' Resurrection* (New York/Mahwah, N.J.: Paulist Press).
"Did Jesus Eat the Fish (Luke 24:42–43)?," *Gregorianum* 69:65–76; also in
Interpreting the Resurrection, 39–52.
"The Meaning of Easter," *The Tablet,* April 2/9, pp. 386–87.
"University of Nations," *America* 158:486–68.
"St. Patrick," *The Furrow* 39:474–76.
"The Fearful Silence of Three Women (Mark 16:8c)," *Gregorianum*
69:489–503; also in *Interpreting the Resurrection,* 53–67.
"Why Do We Need to Be Saved and Who Saves Us? A Catholic Perspective,"
Face to Face 14:15–20; also in *Focus on Jesus* (1996) pp. 176–84.
"Problemi e prospettive di teologia fondamentale: Inventario critico," in *Gesù
Rivelatore,* ed. Rino Fisichella, (Casale Monferrato: Piemme), 46–52.
"Fundamental Theology: An Agenda for the 1990s," **Pacifica* 1:290–97.
"Emmanuel," *America* 159:510–11; also in *Focus on Jesus* (1996), 50–52.
"Our Faith in Jesus," *The Tablet,* December 24/31, p. 1478; also in the
Christmas editions of the **Advocate* and the **Catholic Weekly.*

Book Reviews	*In*
R. E. Brown, *Biblical Exegesis and Church Doctrine* (London: Geoffrey Chapman, 1986).	*Gregorianum* 69:147–48.
W. Pannenberg, *Antropologia in prospettiva teologica* (Brescia: Queriniana, 1987).	*Civiltà Cattolica* 3315–3316:305–6.

1989

Friends in Faith: Living the Creed Day by Day (New York/Mahwah, N.J.: Paulist Press). Italian translation: *Amici nella Fede* (Milan: Paoline). Portuguese translation: *Amigos na Fé* (São Paulo: Paulinas, 1997).

"He descended to the dead," *The Tablet*, March 25, pp. 340–41.

"Alcuni problemi attuali sulla risurrezione di Gesù," *Civiltà Cattolica* 3331:31–38.

"Christ's Resurrection and Ascension," *America* 160:262–65; also in *Focus on Jesus* (1996), 149–52.

"A Season for all Ages," *The Tablet*, December 23/30, pp. 1504–5; also in *Catholic Weekly*.

"Christ, Pre-existence of," *New Catholic Encyclopedia*, 18:92–93.

Book Reviews	*In*
R. Thiemann, *Revelation and Theology* (South Bend, Ind.: Notre Dame University Press, 1985).	*Heythrop Journal* 30:73–74.
P. Carnley, *The Structure of Resurrection Belief* (Oxford: Clarendon, 1987).	*Theological Studies* 50:178–79.
M. Kelsey, *Resurrection, Release from Oppression* (New York: Paulist Press, 1985).	*Heythrop Journal* 30:118–19.
T. V. Morris, *The Logic of God Incarnate* (Ithaca, N.Y.: Cornell University Press, 1986).	*Heythrop Journal* 30:449–50.
I. Broer and J. Werbick, eds., *Der Herr ist wahrhaft auferstanden (Lk 24, 34): Biblische und systematische Beiträge zur Entstehung des Osterglaubens* (Stuttgart: Katholisches Bibelwerk, 1988).	*Gregorianum* 70:567–68.

1990

"Catholic Theology (1965–90)," *America* 162:86–87, 104–5; also in *Bróteria* 130:3–9.

"I Believe in God, the Father Almighty," *The Furrow* 41:203–11.

"The Empty Tomb," *The Tablet,* April 14/21, pp. 479–80.

"Newman's Seven Notes: The Case of the Resurrection," in *Newman after a Hundred Years,* ed. I. Ker and A. G. Hill (Oxford: Clarendon Press, 1990), 337–52; also in *Focus on Jesus* (1996), 135–48.

"God's Body Language," *The Tablet,* December 22/29, p. 1632.

Five lectures in *Cuestiones Actuales de Cristologia y Ecologia,* ed. Secretariado del Episcopado Colombiano (Bogotá, 1990), 51–61, 77–85, 111–37.

"Amore," "Christiani Anonimi," "Esperienza," and "Mistero pasquale: Risurrezione," in *Dizionario di teologia fondamentale,* ed. R. Latourelle and R. Fisichella (Assisi: Cittadella Editrice, 1990), 17–20, 231, 403–6, 800–810.

1991

Believing (New York/Mahwah, N.J.: Paulist Press; London: Harper Collins), with Mary Venturini.

A Concise Dictionary of Theology (New York/Mahwah, N.J.: Paulist Press; London: Harper Collins), with Edward G. Farrugia. Italian translation: *Dizionario sintetico di teologia* (Vatican City: Libreria Editrice (Vaticana, 1995). This dictionary has also appeared in Indonesian, Polish, and Ukrainian.

Luca-Atti: L'interpretazione a servizio della Scrittura (Assisi: Cittadella), edited with G. Marconi.

"Luca sulla fine delle apparizioni pasquali," in *Luca-Atti,* 234–42.

Luke and Acts (Mahwah, N.J.: Paulist Press, 1993), edited with G. Marconi.

"'Dei Verbum' and Biblical Scholarship," *Scripture Bulletin* 21:2–7.

"Risen in Reality," *The Tablet,* March 30/April 6, p. 388.

"Words to Watch," *The Tablet,* May 25, p. 638.

"Chalking up a Good Year," *The Tablet,* December 21/28, p. 1575.

"St Ignatius Loyola on Christ's Resurrection," *America* 164:346, 359–62; also in *Focus on Jesus* (1996), 128–34.

Book Reviews	*In*
R. E. Brown, *Responses to 101 Questions on the Bible* (London: Geoffrey Chapman, 1990).	*The Tablet,* February 2, p. 137.
K. Grayson, *Dying, We Live* (Oxford: Oxford University Press, 1990).	*Commonweal* 118:201–2.

J. S. Spong, *Rescuing the Bible from Fundamentalism* (London: Harper Collins, 1991).

The Tablet, August 31, p. 1058.

L. J. O'Donovan and T. H. Sanks, eds., *Faith Witness: Foundations of Theology for Today's Church* (London: Geoffrey Chapman, 1989).

Heythrop Journal 32:557–58.

A. J. Conyers, God, *Hope and History: Jürgen Moltmann and the Christian Concept of History* (Macon, Ga.: Mercer University Press, 1988).

Heythrop Journal 32:455–56.

1992

"The Uniqueness of the Easter Appearances," *Catholic Biblical Quarterly* 54:287–307, written with Daniel Kendall; also in *Focus on Jesus* (1996), 111–27. Hungarian translation: "A Húsvéti Megjelenések EgyedülállóVoltávól," *Mérleg* 94/1:18–42.

"Crucifixion," in *Anchor Bible Dictionary,* 1:1207–10.

"Salvation," in *Anchor Bible Dictionary,* 5:907–14.

"Selling Jesus," *The Tablet,* September 26, pp. 1184–86.

"An Easter Healing of Memories," *America* 166:322–23; also in *Experiencing Jesus* (1994), 110–19.

"The Truth Revealed," *The Tablet,* April 18/25, p. 501.

"The Faith of Jesus," *Theological Studies* 53:402–23, written with Daniel Kendall; also in *Focus on Jesus* (1996); also in *Christology* (1995), 250–68.

"The Pope's Theology," *The Tablet,* June 27, p. 801.

"All Loves Excelling," *The Tablet,* December 19/26, p. 1606.

"Some Major Challenges for Christology," *Melita Theologica* 43:67–76.

Book Reviews
In

J. Barton, *What is the Bible?* (London: SPCK, 1991).

The Tablet, June 13, pp. 749–50.

S. Mitchell, *The Gospel According to Jesus* (London: Rider Books, 1992);

The Tablet, May 9, p. 584.

J. D. Crossan, *The Historical Jesus* (Edinburgh: T & T Clark, 1992);

J. L. Houlden, *Jesus: A Question of Identity* (London: SPCK, 1992).

1993

The Resurrection of Jesus Christ: Some Contemporary Issues (Milwaukee: Marquette University Press).

Retrieving Fundamental Theology (New York/Mahwah, N.J.: Paulist Press; London: Geoffrey Chapman). Italian translation: *Il Recupero della teologia fondamentale: i tri stili della teologia contemporanea* (Vatican City: Libreria Editrice Vaticana, 1996).

"Christ's Resurrection and the Aorist Passive of *egeirō*," *Gregorianum* 74:725–35, written with Daniel Kendall.

"Good News and Old Nonsense," *The Tablet,* April 10/17, p. 469.

"Theology According to the Second Vatican Council," in *Penser la foi: Recherches en théologie aujourd'hui: Mélanges offerts à Joseph Moingt* (Paris: Les Éditions du Cerf, 1993), 727–36; also in *Retrieving Fundamental Theology,* 19–27.

"A Gospel for the Unemployed," *The Tablet,* September 18, p. 1182.

"Holy Madness," *The Tablet,* December 25, p. 1696.

"Resurrection" in *The Blackwell Encyclopedia of Modern Thought,* ed. A. E. McGrath (Oxford: Blackwell), 553–57.

Book Reviews

	In
N. T. Wright, *Who was Jesus?* (London: SPCK, 1992).	*The Tablet,* February 20, p. 245.
T. Burns, *The Use of Memory* (London: Sheed & Ward, 1993).	*Commonweal* 120 (May 21), pp. 20–21.
W. Pannenberg, *Metaphysics and the Idea of God* (Edinburgh: T & T Clark, 1990).	*Heythrop Journal* 34:226–27.
H. Küng, *Credo: The Apostles' Creed Explained for Today* (London: SCM Press, 1993).	*The Tablet,* June 5, pp. 722–23.
J. V. Taylor, *The Christlike God* (London: SCM Press), 1992;	*The Tablet,* August 17, p. 1045.
K.-J. Kuschel, *Born Before All Time: The Dispute over Christ's Origin* (London: SCM Press, 1992).	
D. N. Freedman, ed., *The Anchor Bible Dictionary* (Garden City: N.Y.: Doubleday, 1992).	*Gregorianum* 74:563–65.

1994

Experiencing Jesus (London: SPCK: New York/Mahwah, N.J.: Paulist Press). Italian translation: *Con Gesù* (Vatican City: Libreria Editrice Vaticana, 1996).

Introduction in *Call and Response,* ed. Frances Makower (London: Hodder & Stoughton), 5–8.

"On Not Neglecting Hatred," *Scottish Journal of Theology* 47:511–18, written with Daniel Kendall.

"Augustine on the Resurrection," in *Saint Augustine the Bishop,* ed. F. LeMoine and C. Kleinhanz. (New York/London: Garland), 65–75.

"In the End, Love," in *Faith and the Future,* ed. John Galvin (New York/Mahwah, N.J.: Paulist Press), 25–42. Italian translation: "Alla fine... l'amore," *Rassegna di teologia* 35 (1994): 645–42.

"On Reissuing Venturini," *Gregorianum* 75:241–65, written with Daniel Kendall; also in *Focus on Jesus* (1996), 153–75.

"Did Joseph of Arimathea Exist?" *Biblica* 75:235–421, written with Daniel Kendall; also in *Focus on Jesus* (1996), 95–101.

"In the End, Heaven," *The Tablet,* March 26, pp. 385–86.

"Revelation Now," *The Tablet,* May 21, p. 616.

"Surprised by Christmas," *The Tablet,* December 24/31, p. 1643.

"What They are Saying About Jesus Now," *America* 171/5 (August 27/September 3): 10–14; also in *Focus on Jesus* (1996), 1–16.

"University of the Nations," *Informationes Theologiae Europae,* 3:261–65.

Book Reviews	*In*
John D. Crossan, *The Historical Jesus* (Edinburgh: T & T Clark, 1991).	*Heythrop Journal* 35:66–67.
Richard Swinburne, *Revelation: From Metaphor to Analogy* (Oxford: Clarendon Press, 1991).	*Heythrop Journal* 35:84–85.
Hans Hübner, *Biblische Theologie des Neuen Testaments* (Göttingen: Vandenhoeck & Ruprecht, 1993).	*Gregorianum* 75:163–64.
David Power, *The Eucharistic Mystery* (Dublin: Gill & Macmillan, 1992).	*Pacifica* 7:104–5.
Paul Avis, ed., *The Resurrection of Jesus Christ* (London: Darton, Longman & Todd, 1993).	*The Tablet,* April 16, pp. 466–67.
John Spong, *Resurrection: Myth or Reality?* (London: HarperCollins, 1994).	*The Tablet,* April 30, pp. 529–30.
Robert Funk, Roy Hoover, and the Jesus Seminar, *The Five Gospels: The Search for the Authentic Words of Jesus* (London: Macmillan 1993).	*The Tablet,* September 17, pp. 1170.
Richard McBrien, *Catholicism* (London: Geoffrey Chapman, 1994).	*The Tablet,* October 15, pp. 1312–13.

Stephen Davis, *Risen Indeed:*
Making Sense of the Resurrection
(London: SPCK, 1994).

Reviewed with the books of Avis
and Spong (above) in
Theology 97:462–65.

1995

Christology: A Biblical, Historical, and Systematic Study of Jesus (Oxford/New
York: Oxford University Press). Italian translation: *Cristologia, Biblioteca
di teologia contemporanea 90* (Brescia: Queriniana).
Second Journey (Leominister: Gracewing), third edition with foreword by Terry
Waite; first edition 1978.
"Easter's Immediacy," *The Furrow* 46:251–52.
"Filling Our Senses," *America* 173/20 (December 16/23): 21.
"The Incarnation Under Fire," *Gregorianum* 76:263–80; also in *Focus on Jesus*
(1996), 30–46.
"Lord of the Heart," *The Tablet*, April 15/22, pp. 482–83.
"Making the Word Come Alive," *Priests and People* 9:150–53.
"Atonement, Doctrine of," "Chalcedon, Council of," "Redemption,"
"Revelation," "Theologian," and "Theology" in R. P. McBrien,
Encyclopedia of Catholicism (San Francisco: HarperCollins), 110–11,
294–95, 1089–91, 1112–14, 1249, 1250–51.

Book Reviews

In

R. E. Brown, *The Death of the Messiah,*
2 vols. (Garden City, N.Y.:
Doubleday, 1994).

Gregorianum 76:388.

P. Gardiner, *Mary MacKillop:*
An Extraordinary Australian
(Harrisburg, Pa.: Morehouse
Publishing, 1994).

America 173/5 (August 26): 28.

D. Tracy, *On Naming the Present:*
God, Hermeneutics and the Church
(London: SCM Press, 1995).

The Tablet, November 4, p. 1413.

F. J. van Beeck, *God Encountered*
(Collegeville, Minn.:
Liturgical Press, 1993).

America 172/6 (February 25):
22–24.

1996

Focus on Jesus: Essays in Christology and Soteriology (Leominster;
Gracewing), with Daniel Kendall; a revised version of twenty-one articles
published between 1971 and 1995.
The Christian Faith, collaborated with J. Dupuis et al. on the sixth revised and
enlarged edition (Bangalore: Theological Publications in India); also published by HarperCollins (London) and Alba House (New York); O'Collins

was responsible, among other things, for the revising and enlarging of chapters 3 and 6.

"Did Apostolic Continuity Ever Start? Origins of Apostolic Continuity in the New Testament," *Louvain Studies* 21:138–52; also appeared as "Origins of Apostolic Continuity in the New Testament," in *Ecclesia Tertii Millennii Advenientis,* ed. E. Chica et al. (Casale Monferrato: Piemme, 1997), 830–41; also in *The Bible for Theology* (1997), 101–16; also translated into Croatian.

"Fraintendimenti e concezioni inadequate sull'incarnazione," *Servizio della Parola* 28, no. 283:8–12.

"Knowing the Christmas Story," *America* 175/19 (December 14/21): 10–11.

"Love Conquers All," *The Furrow* 47:223–25.

"The Mission Christology of General Congregation 34," *Review of Ignatian Spirituality* 27:39–44.

"Overcoming Christological Differences," *Heythrop Journal* 37:382–90, with Daniel Kendall.

"The Resurrection Summit," *Church* 12, no. 3:21–22.

"Resurrection that Challenges the Norm," *The Tablet,* April 27, p. 548.

"Your Theology Library," *The Furrow* 47:563–66.

Book Reviews

	In
Dan Cohn-Sherbok and Christopher Lewis, eds., *Beyond Death: Theological and Philosophical Reflections on Life after Death* (London: Macmillan, 1995).	*The Tablet,* April 6/13, pp. 485–86.
Ingolf Dalferth, *Der auferweckte Gekreuzigte: Zur Grammatik der Christologie* (Tübingen: J. C. B. Mohr [Paul Siebeck], 1994).	*Gregorianum* 77:164–65.
Gavin D'Costa, ed., *Resurrection Reconsidered* (Oxford: Oneworld, 1996).	*The Tablet,* September 28, pp. 1264–65.
Hans Hübner, *Biblische Theologie des Neuen Testaments,* vol. 3 (Göttingen: Vandenhoeck & Ruprecht, 1995).	*Gregorianum* 77:576–77.
Gerd Luedemann, *The Resurrection of Jesus* (Minneapolis: Fortress, 1994).	*Gregorianum* 77:357–59; *Theological Studies* 57:341–43.
Wolfgang Beinert and Francis Schüssler Fiorenza, *Handbook of Catholic Theology* (New York: Crossroad, 1995).	*America* 175/18 (December 7): 29.

1997

Editor, with Stephen Davis and Daniel Kendall, *The Resurrection* (Oxford/New York: Oxford University Press).
"The Resurrection: The State of the Question," in *The Resurrection*, 5–28.
"No Greater Love," *The Tablet,* March 29/April 5, p. 421.
"In Praise of Cathedrals," *America* 177/16 (November 22): 12–15.
"Christmas at the Railway Station, *America* 177/20 (December 20/27): 8–9.
"Images of Jesus and Modern Theology," in S. E. Porter et al., eds., *Images of Christ Ancient and Modern* (Sheffield: Sheffield Academic Press), 128–43.
"Jesus," *Church* 13:7–9.
"Images of Jesus: Reappropriating Titular Christology," *Theology Digest* 44:303–18.

Book Reviews	**In**
Hans Hübner, *Biblische Theologie als Hermeneutik: Gesammelte Aufsätze,* ed. A. and M. Labahn (Göttingen: Vandenhoeck & Ruprecht, 1995).	*Gregorianum* 78:160.
Hans Hübner, *Vetus Testamentum in Novo,* Band 2, *Corpus Paulinum* (Göttingen: Vandenhoeck & Ruprecht, 1997).	*Gregorianum* 78:777–78.
Thorwald Lorenzen, *Resurrection and Discipleship* (Maryknoll, N.Y.: Orbis Books, 1995).	*Gregorianum* 78:383–84.

1998

All Things New (Mahwah, N.J.: Paulist Press).
"Jesus Christ the Liberator: In the Context of Human Progress," *Studia Missionalia* 47:21–35.
"Peter's Good News at Easter," *The Tablet,* April 11/18, p. 464.
"Grappling with the Trinity," *The Tablet,* May 9, p. 606.
"Obituary: Frank Doria Pamphilj," *The Tablet,* October 10, pp. 1344–45.

Book Reviews	**In**
Jacques Dupuis, *Towards a Christian Theology of Religious Pluralism* (Maryknoll, N.Y.: Orbis Books, 1997).	*The Tablet,* January 24, pp. 110–11.
Stanley M. Burgess, *The Holy Spirit. Medieval Roman Catholic and Reformation Traditions* (Peabody, Mass.: Hendrickson), 1997.	*Gregorianum* 79:766–67.

1999

Following the Way: Jesus Our Spiritual Director (London: HarperCollins).
The Tripersonal God (Mahwah, N.J.: Paulist Press).
Editor, with Stephen Davis and Daniel Kendall, S.J., *The Trinity* (Oxford/New York: Oxford University Press).
"The Holy Trinity: The State of the Questions," in *The Trinity,* 1–25.
"God's Clown: An Advent Reflection," *Church* (Winter): 9–10.
"My Millennium Resolution," *The Tablet,* December 25/January 1, p. 1741.
"Resurrection and New Creation," *Dialog* 38:15–19.
"The Risen Jesus: Analogies and Presence" in S. E. Porter et al., eds., *Resurrection* (Sheffield: Sheffield Academic Press), 195–217.

2000

(with Edward Farrugia) *A Concise Dictionary of Theology,* revised and updated (Mahwah, N.J.: Paulist Press).
"Between the Lines of the Easter Story," *The Tablet,* April 22/29, pp. 551–52.
"The Resurrection of Jesus: The Debate Continued," *Gregorianum* 81, 589–98.

Index of Names